THE FREE WORLD COLOSSUS

DAVID HOROWITZ

The Free World Colossus

A Critique of American Foreign Policy
in the Cold War

HILL AND WANG · NEW YORK

TO MY PARENTS

Contents

PREFACE   *Page* 11

PART ONE   FROM ALLY TO BELLIGERENT: 1945–9   23

              Chronology   25

              Introduction   27

              1. *Frictions and the Creation of the UN*   31

              2. *The Old Relations and the New*   42

              3. *The Dissolution of the Coalition*   53

              4. *Interlude: Greece*   65

              5. *The Cold War Begins*   69

              6. *Retrospect*   86

PART TWO   LEADER OF THE FREE WORLD: 1950–63   97

              7. *Containing Conspiracy*   99

              8. *Containment into Liberation: Korea*   114

              9. *Viet Nam*   141

              10. *Guatemala*   163

              11. *Iran–Greece–Turkey*   187

              12. *Cuba*   198

              13. *The US and the World Revolution*   213

PART THREE UNDER THE SWORD OF DAMOCLES: 1945–63   239

              I. Containment and Liberation   241

              14. *The Division of Europe*   243

              15. *The Atomic Bomb*   263

              16. *East Europe: 1949–56*   280

              II. Agonizing Reappraisals   293

              17. *Lippmann, Kennan and Sputnik*   295

              18. *Dogmas and Disengagement*   305

III. The Eisenhower Years   323

   19. *The Failure to Make Peace*   325

   20. *The Summit Collapse*   334

   21. *Nuclear Strategies and the Missile Gap*   342

IV. The Kennedy Years   353

   22. *Creating Situations of Strength*   355

   23. *Tipping the Balance of Power*   368

   24. *Showdown: The Cuban Crisis*   382

V. Detente and After   399

   25. *Nuclear Armistice*   401

   26. *The Unity of America's Cold War Program*   411

BIBLIOGRAPHY   435

INDEX   441

Preface

Perhaps the major American casualty of the cold war has been the idea of history. This wound in the American intellect has, for the most part, gone unnoticed; yet to neglect it is to chance the cancer of cynicism. For the idea of history is the secular conscience of the West, the moral and intellectual impulse which enables us to face up to the implications of Auden's classic lines about the decay of Hongkong in the late thirties.

> We cannot postulate a General Will;
> For what we are, we have ourselves to blame.

History is the record of man's efforts to transform the real into the ideal. It is therefore a mirror in which man can look himself in the eye. Thus the idea of history is nothing less than the notion of honesty which provokes us to measure our performance.

WILLIAM APPLEMAN WILLIAMS

EVERY WAR generates myths that serve to justify and perpetuate it, and the cold war has been no exception. In both camps, public consciousness has long been dominated by historical legends which invest the central actions of its own side with unassailable righteousness, and identify its own cause with the cause of all mankind.

Naturally, the myths of one camp tend to appear in more accurate light only when viewed by members of the other; viewed from their own side, they staunchly retain the appearance of truth. In such a situation, historians of the two camps become the bearers of a possible enlightenment from 'within', which is of more than mere academic significance. For these myths have been employed to justify repression in the name of freedom and to perpetuate conflicts in the name of peace. Moreover, unless the myths of two decades of cold war can be replaced with premises more firmly rooted in reality, it seems likely that the opportunities offered by the US – USSR *détente* will be squandered, and the prospects for peace will grow dim.

It is historians who, in differing degrees, have access to a record

which they may use to undermine these fictions and to prepare a
ground on which real justice and genuine settlements may be built.
It is in the West, moreover, that such records are most available, and
in the West that such reappraisal should have most immediate effect.
That such an effort is not only possible, here, but necessary, is
perhaps best illustrated by the American posture at the time of the
Cuban confrontation in 1962.

On October 23, 1962, Adlai Stevenson addressed the UN Security
Council in a moment of great international peril. The United States
had just instituted a naval blockade against the Republic of Cuba in
an attempt to secure the withdrawal of Soviet missiles from the
island. In taking this action, the US had by-passed the UN and
ignored the fundamental principle of the UN Charter which enjoins
members to settle disputes by peaceful negotiation.

Stevenson's speech was, therefore, an attempt to explain and
justify the course of action taken by the United States. To do this,
he reviewed the history of the cold war, endeavouring to show that
the Russians had dedicated themselves to the destruction of the
world order envisioned by the UN Charter – and thus to contend
that they could not always be dealt with within the framework of the
Charter:

> The record is clear: treaties, agreements, pledges and the morals
> of international relations were never an obstacle to the Soviet
> Union under Stalin. ... No one can question that Chairman
> Khrushchev has altered many things in the Soviet Union. ... But
> there is one thing he has not altered – and that is the basic drive
> to abolish the world of the Charter, to destroy the hope of a
> pluralistic world order. ...
> ... the world has not yet seen ... changes in Soviet foreign
> policy.
> It is this which has shadowed the world since the end of the
> Second World War – which has dimmed our hopes of peace and
> progress, which has forced those nations determined to defend
> their freedom to take measures in their own self-defense. In this
> effort, the leadership has inevitably fallen in large degree on the
> United States.

Thus in Stevenson's view, the Soviet Union is held unilaterally responsible for the 'dimmed hopes of peace and progress' since World War II. The US itself is seen in an opposite light:

> Our response to the remorseless Soviet expansionism has taken many forms.
> We have sought loyally to support the United Nations, to be faithful to the world of the Charter, and to build an operating system that acts, and does not talk, for peace.
> We have never refused to negotiate. We have sat at conference after conference seeking peaceful solutions to menacing conflicts.

To be sure, Stevenson's statement can be regarded as merely another example of the rhetoric which has become traditional in political affairs or as the summing up by a very competent attorney on behalf of his client. Yet, delivered before the court of international opinion at a moment when the world teetered on the brink of nuclear holocaust, his words were invested with a more significant and far-reaching meaning: they formed the case on which the US Government justified its action in risking the future of civilization and, as such, they embodied the quintessence of the American cold war cause.

There is little doubt that most US political leaders and a majority of Americans subscribe to Stevenson's version of the issues in the cold war and how the conflict developed. This public consensus, in turn, serves as a limiting factor on the evolution of American policy – and on America's ability to pursue the opportunities for peace which the present *détente* offers.

The necessity for undertaking this study of US policy during the cold war, may be suggested, therefore, by a brief examination of Stevenson's main defense of the US action in the Cuban crisis – his contention that America had never refused to negotiate its differences with an obstreperous, and obstructionist Soviet Union. For this position is hardly tenable in the face of historical fact.

It should first be noted that it was President Truman and not Marshal Stalin who, in November 1945, unilaterally terminated the meetings of the Big Three and thus initiated a ten-year period when there was no meeting between US and Soviet heads of State. It was, moreover, US Secretary of State Dean Acheson who, in 1950, vetoed the proposal for a top-level conference between Truman and

Stalin which had been advanced by Churchill and others at a time when the Soviet dictator had indicated his willingness to participate. More crucial by far than these particular incidents (and they can easily be multiplied[1]) was the fundamental premise on which US foreign policy in the critical cold war years – 1947 and after – was based:

At the root of [the State Department's[2]] philosophy about Russian–American relations and underlying all the ideas of the Truman Doctrine there is a disbelief in the possibility of a settlement of the issues raised by this [cold] war. . . . [The State Department] has reached the conclusion that all we can do is 'to contain' Russia until Russia changes, ceases to be our rival, and becomes our partner.

This conclusion is, it seems to me, quite unwarranted. The history of diplomacy is the history of relations among rival powers which did not enjoy political intimacy and did not respond to appeals to common purposes. Nevertheless, there have been settlements . . . to think that rival and unfriendly powers cannot be brought to a settlement is to forget what diplomacy is about.[3]

When the Democrats were succeeded by Republicans in 1952, foreign policy came under the direction of John Foster Dulles, a man whose aversion to negotiated settlements is notorious enough not to require chapter and verse documentation at this point.

Thus, not only was Ambassador Stevenson deeply in error in his characterization of a fundamental US attitude in the cold war, but more importantly, the unilateral action which the US took in the Cuban crisis was typical, not extraordinary, among US cold war

---

[1] 'Two-party talks between this country and Russia have long been an objective of Kremlin policy, and their avoidance has long been one of our objectives.' – The Alsops, New York *Herald Tribune*, December 12, 1949, cited in D. F. Fleming, *The Cold War and Its Origins*, 2 vols., 1961.

[2] This passage is taken from Walter Lippmann's critique of George Kennan's ' "X" philosophy;' but as Lippmann also indicates in this critique, Mr X was the Director of the Policy Planning Staff of the State Department and the publication of his article 'was an event, announcing that the Department of State had made up its mind, . . . to disclose . . . the estimates, the calculations and the conclusions on which the Department was basing its plans' – cf. discussion p. 249 below.

[3] Walter Lippmann, *The Cold War*, 1947.

actions. Indeed, had US commitments really been to the world of the Charter, as Stevenson asserted, then the two years preceding the missile crisis would not have seen the US impose an embargo on Cuba, refuse to negotiate outstanding differences, finance and promote sabotage raids and engineer a full-scale exile invasion of the island. All of these acts were in fundamental violation of the UN Charter and, whatever may be adjudged of Soviet moves, it cannot be claimed that Cuba had acted in any similar fashion against the United States.

This failure in America's self-appraisal is not limited to the areas of negotiated settlement and international law, nor is it restricted to statements by American advocates before the UN. In 1960, while campaigning for the Presidency, the late John F. Kennedy declared, 'The cause of all mankind, is the cause of America. . . . We are responsible for the maintenance of freedom all around the world.'

A year later, the distinguished British historian Arnold Toynbee gave a series of lectures in the United States in which he radically challenged this view:

'. . . America is today the leader of a world-wide anti-revolutionary movement in defence of vested interests. She now stands for what Rome stood for. Rome consistently supported the rich against the poor in all foreign communities that fell under her sway; and, since the poor, so far, have always and everywhere been far more numerous than the rich, Rome's policy made for inequality, for injustice, and for the least happiness of the greatest number. America's decision to adopt Rome's role has been deliberate, if I have gauged it right.'[1]

Between the assessments of Kennedy and Toynbee, there is a gap which most Americans, perhaps most Westerners, will find difficult to bridge. Where it is not simply due to a dearth of information, this gap has been created by the mythical conceptions which underlie American thinking on the cold war. By an examination of the fictional basis of Western, cold war mythology, it is the hope of this essay to lay the foundations for a more accurate understanding of the US role during the cold war decades.

[1] Arnold Toynbee, *America and the World Revolution*, 1961.

The conflicting world views of Kennedy and Toynbee provide the proper starting point for such a project, because they raise in essential form a problem whose existence, if not importance, is already generally acknowledged by Western observers. This problem is the apparent disparity between the US cold war program in Western Europe and the US role in the underdeveloped world (including Greece, Portugal and Spain). For whereas in Western Europe the US was able to identify itself with the reconstruction and defense of democratic societies, in the underdeveloped world, with few exceptions, it threw its enormous weight behind ruthless dictatorships resistant to even minimal social progress and change.[1]

The contradiction posed by these facts has generally been explained away by reference to the 'backwardness' of the underdeveloped regions; this 'backwardness', it is claimed, is the real source of the reactionary dictatorial régimes which have developed and flourished under US tutelage in these areas. Apart from the questionable assumptions and attitudes of such a thesis, it is apparent that an indigenous 'backwardness' cannot be made to explain away those US activities in many of the underdeveloped countries which validate Toynbee's thesis.

In South Viet Nam, for example, US responsibility for the creation of the repressive Ngo Dinh Diem régime in 1954, was both overt and absolute. Ngo Dinh Diem was not a dictator with whom the US was saddled, but one whom the US Government chose, and whose brutal consolidation of power against democratic opposition groups the US not only sanctioned but made possible by its support.[2] As the correspondent for the conservative London *Economist* and *Sunday Times* wrote in 1957 when Diem's isolation from the Vietnamese population was already causing repercussions:

> ... Diem's problem is that he is not a leader who has been

[1] As of 1960 when Kennedy made his statement about US responsibility for maintaining freedom around the world, US aid and support was probably the decisive factor in the maintenance of dictatorial régimes in Spain, Greece, Turkey, Thailand, Formosa, South Viet Nam, South Korea and Pakistan. The US was an important contributor to other dictatorships and police states in Iran, Saudi Arabia, Lebanon, Morocco, South Africa, Nicaragua, Paraguay and Haiti. In addition, the US exercised its own military dictatorship over Okinawa and the associated islands, fifteen years after Hiroshima and eight after the Japanese peace.

[2] cf. discussion of Viet Nam below.

merely *helped* by the West; he has been *created* by the West. The emperor, Bao Dai, appointed him, but that was only a formal act. It was Bidault and Dulles who chose him and put him in his position. The objectionable word 'puppet', so often used by both sides in the propaganda war, is in his case literally true; . . . The fact that he has acted against Western advice on several occasions does not contradict this. [Emphasis in original.][1]

An even more significant example, perhaps, is Guatemala. For in Guatemala, it was not indigenous 'backwardness' that ended ten years of uninterrupted democratic rule, but a US engineered *coup*. In the eleven years since the *coup*, the Guatemalan army has exercised effective rule in the country first through a dictatorship, then a rigged election and, after the spring of 1963, a military *junta*, all three recognized and supported with substantial economic and military aid by the United States.

The foregoing serves to indicate the task of the present study, which is to review the major US actions in the cold war (from the death of Roosevelt to the death of Kennedy), and to pose some of the larger questions raised by this record. In particular it seeks to show that the two examples cited above are not isolated incidents but are part of a consistent pattern of US policy in the underdeveloped areas. Further, this pattern can be related to US policies in Europe (especially US resistance to a negotiated settlement) and, despite surface contradictions, shown to be fundamentally consistent with them.

Part I, therefore, contains an account of the formative period of the cold war in Europe, substantially different from orthodox accounts, and examines the adequacy of the consensus view which sees US policy as primarily a response to the thrust of remorseless Soviet expansion. Part II traces the principal global actions of the US cold war program from Korea to Cuba, showing in the process the validity of Toynbee's thesis and underscoring the failure of US policy to conform to its generally supposed intentions. Finally, Part III reviews the major background to these events and to the present phase of the cold war, namely the evolution of US approaches to the Soviet Union and to the problem of divided Europe in the post-

[1] David Hotham in *Viet-Nam: The First Five Years*, ed. R. Lindholm, 1959.

war world. Only on the basis of this analysis is it possible to integrate the findings of the three parts of this study and to establish the underlying unity of US foreign policy in the cold war.

The analyses in Part III take into account a factor which has not before been adequately dealt with in its role as a policy determinant, although it has had a decisive effect on the dynamics of the cold war. This is the Atomic Bomb and the nuclear weapons which have succeeded it. Indeed, the very development of these weapons, the radical change in their capabilities and increase in their numbers, have exerted a profound influence over post-World War II political developments. The writer who first recognized and analyzed the full weight of this factor was P. M. S. Blackett, holder of the Order for Merit (US) for his contributions to allied defense in World War II, and winner of the Nobel Prize for Physics, who published a classic study in 1948 titled *Military and Political Consequences of Atomic Weapons*[1] and has since made several notable contributions in this crucial field.

Technological advances since 1948 have continued to result in new military capabilities, new strategies and changed political situations. Most significant among these advances was the launching of Sputnik in 1957. This dramatically confirmed the Soviet Union's capabilities in the field of Intercontinental Ballistic Missiles, and with it the fact that the United States had itself become clearly vulnerable for the first time.

Hitherto, no attempt has been made to integrate the insights provided by studies of these strategic developments with the diplomatic history of the cold war, an integration that Blackett himself has urged. The far-reaching importance of such an integration can be appreciated from the analyses of containment (1947), disengagement (1957) and the Cuban Crisis (1962) which appear in Part III. Regardless of whether these analyses appear correct, it will be evident that no critical turn of world events can be fully understood without insight into the existing nuclear equation.

Inevitably, the following account of the cold war's development will seem one-sided to many. No doubt, it will appear to some that I have merely reversed the crucial terms of the orthodoxy whose critique I have undertaken, that in attempting to correct a version of

[1] Published in the US as *Fear, War and the Bomb*.

events in which American cold war policy appears as essentially and primarily a response to Soviet strategies, I have proceeded to the other extreme, and have ascribed to American leaders the same monopoly of initiative and Freedom of maneuver which Western commentators usually ascribe to the rulers in the Kremlin.

Needless to say, while such simplistic notions about the complex dynamics of international events may provide the framework for political tracts and government white papers, they have no place in serious historical studies, whose intention is to understand conflicts, and not merely to prosecute a particular side of them. In so far as the historical constructions of the present work may be misconstrued to suggest support for such erroneous theses, therefore, it is important to consider at least the most obvious source of potential confusion.

This lies in the fact that the focus of the present study is on *American* foreign policy in the cold war and the very organization of the material, therefore, tends to stress the dynamic aspect of American policies. However, even had I tempted to present a full account of Soviet foreign policy in the period, with more attention paid to *its* dynamic aspects, I do not believe that the essential features of the analysis would have been altered. For the point which I have tried to establish beyond all others, and which has been virtually ignored in previous cold war studies, is that the early post-war power situation was such as to give the United States a near monopoly on the *strategic* decisions which would affect the basic structure of international relations in the post-war period.[1] Conversely, the Kremlin rulers, *whatever their long-range intentions*, were bound by the same imbalance of power to make moves of primarily *tactical* significance.

This is not to say that Soviet actions had no significant effect on the evolution of the cold war. Nor is it to say that US leaders had unlimited flexibility in their choice of strategic policies. Major policies once adopted often set in motion forces of their own. Thus the Truman Administration was compelled to reverse its China policy in 1950 as a result of pressures generated in the political atmosphere which had been created by its earlier European strategy (cf. Chapter VII).

[1] During the entire course of the cold war, for example, the US has been the sole power economically capable of financing a UN administered international development agency, which would free developing nations from the pressures,

What I have tried to demonstrate is that the structure of the cold war (as a 'cold war') was established by a series of policy decisions taken in Washington in 1945–7, which received 'classic' formulation in the Truman Doctrine. To say this, is to say that if, for example, Lippmann's strategic policy recommendations had been adopted by Washington as an alternative to containment, it is certain (within the limits of all such hypotheses) that Europe would not be divided today. Moreover, at the time when the key strategic decisions which became embodied in the Truman Doctrine were taken, Soviet expansionary pressures could only have been a pretext, not a cause of the policy (as is evidenced in the very fact that Lippmann could put forward an alternative policy). Finally, because of its weak power position, the Soviet Union – whatever its long-range intentions – could not of its own accord have risked provoking as reactions, the very moves which this US policy prescribed.[1] It is in this sense that I speak of the strategic options available to US policy-makers and denied their Kremlin counterparts.

A full account of the cold war (which the present study does not pretend to offer) would, of course, have more to say about tactical dynamics than is said here. The influence of Soviet tactics on European politics, for example, is a subject of major importance not only for the light it sheds on the way in which the cold war evolved, but for what it may indicate about future developments. I have kept my discussion of these aspects to a basic minimum, only to prevent the present volume from expanding to inordinate length. I have felt justified in pursuing this course because of the priority which strategy normally takes over tactics and because the immense preponderance of American power during the cold war years (and particularly the early ones) has made its strategic decisions even more binding on the world community than would otherwise have been the case.

---

[1] For evidence of Stalin's consciousness of Soviet weakness and his consequent caution, see p. 84n. below.

---

exerted by politically administered aid, to enter one of the existing power blocs. The absence of such an agency has been a fact of immense significance in determining the structure of international relations in the post-war period, indeed, in making inevitable the cold war's penetration of the 'third world'. The point is, that the existing distribution of economic power in the world, has given the United States and the United States alone, the strategic option to create or block such an agency. US opposition to the UN special fund (SUNFED) represents a strategic decision of major significance, denied to other powers.

In the pages that follow, my indebtedness to many writers and scholars on whose research and interpretations I have drawn, will be obvious. I feel called upon to acknowledge here, however, the special debt I owe to D. F. Fleming, whose painstaking reconstruction of the cold war, published as *The Cold War and Its Origins*, was indispensable to designing the present study.

Acknowledgements

THIS study was undertaken at the request of the Swedish Liberal organization Verdandi in Uppsala. The research and writing were done independently of any institutions, however, and my debts, consequently, are personal and of a kind that cannot be adequately expressed. I wish, however, to note here my gratitude to Ralph Miliband and D. F. Fleming who gave me valuable criticisms and helped me with the manuscript, and to Christian Bay and Sven Hamrell, without whose kindness it would never have been conceived in the first place, let alone written.

London, March 1965   D.H.

PART ONE

From Ally to Belligerent: 1945-49

... it was the United States and Great Britain who *first* shook the mailed fist, who *first* abrogated the collective decisions. ...

ELLIOT ROOSEVELT, 1946

The image of a Stalinist Russia poised and yearning to attack the West, and deterred only by our possession of atomic weapons, was largely a creation of the Western imagination, against which some of us who were familiar with Russian matters tried in vain, over the course of years, to make our voices heard.

GEORGE KENNAN, 1956

Chronology

OF EARLY COLD WAR EVENTS

February 4–11, 1945	The Yalta Conference.
April 12, 1945	The death of Roosevelt.
April 23, 1945	White House Meeting.
April 25, 1945	UN Conference opens in San Francisco.
May 8, 1945	V-E Day.
May 25, 1945	Harry Hopkins arrives in Moscow.
July 5, 1945	Polish Government recognized by Western powers.
July 16, 1945	Successful Atomic Test at Alamogordo, New Mexico.
July 17, 1945	Potsdam Conference opens.
August 6, 1945	Hiroshima.
August 8, 1945	Russia declares war on Japan.
August 9, 1945	Nagasaki.
August 14, 1945	Japan surrenders.
August 18, 1945	Byrnes attacks rigging of elections in Bulgaria.
September 1945	Council of Foreign Ministers Meeting in London.
December 1945	Council of Foreign Ministers Meeting in Moscow.
March 5, 1946	Churchill's Iron Curtain Speech in Fulton, Missouri.
May 1946	Russia leaves Iran after pressure from UN.
October 1946	Peace treaties for Nazi satellites agreed upon.
March 10, 1947	Moscow Conference.
March 12, 1947	Truman Doctrine Speech.
March–August, 1947	Communists smash ruling party in Hungary.
June 5, 1947	Marshall Plan announced.
August 2, 1947	Marshall Plan rejected by Russia.

October 5, 1947	Formation of Cominform.
February 25, 1948	Czech *coup*.
June 1948	Cominform expels Yugoslavia.
June 1948–May 1949	Berlin Blockade.
March–August 1949	Formation of Nato.

Introduction

ANY ATTEMPT to clarify the immediate origins of the cold war must begin with the fact that at this time the United States and the Soviet Union, together with Great Britain, were working partners in a wartime alliance, and that within this alliance, the US played a mediating role between the other two powers. The existence of this working alliance is a fact of central importance in understanding subsequent events, for it shows that the US and the USSR not only could, but actually did cooperate in a dangerous and difficult enterprise, at a time, moreover, when Stalin was firmly in control of Soviet foreign policy. Although welded, it is true, by the necessity of the hour, this cooperation was maintained during a time of great national peril for the powers involved, amidst events affecting the whole future of Europe. In the circumstances, it should not be surprising that the alliance was subject to significant tensions and strains.

Only a month before Roosevelt died, the worst of these conflicts, the famous 'Bern incident' seemed to threaten the very existence of the alliance. When the Russians learned that Field-Marshal Alexander was to meet General Kesselring, in Bern, Switzerland, to discuss the terms of German surrender in Italy, the Soviet leaders became convinced that the Allies intended to make a separate peace which would permit German manpower to be shifted to the Eastern front. Roosevelt was deeply offended by Stalin's charges and by the fact that the dictator maintained the truth of his contentions in the face of the President's denial. Finally, a strongly worded message from Roosevelt assuring Stalin that the whole 'incident' was the work of the Nazis was accepted. Stalin wrote that he had never doubted Roosevelt's honesty and dependability, and on April 11, the day before he died, Roosevelt thanked Stalin and said:

There must not, in any event, be mutual mistrust, and minor misunderstandings of this character should not arise in the future. . . .

27

Thus a working relation with the Russians was possible as late as April 1945, despite ingrained suspicions and the existence of areas in which considerable conflicts of national interest could arise. What then produced the collapse of this coalition? Ambassador Stevenson's October 1962 review of events provides an answer to this question which is straightforward and simple.

According to Stevenson, the conflict began 'even before the nations gathered at San Francisco [for the UN Conference in April 1945]. As soon as the defeat of the Nazis appeared certain, the Soviet Union began to abandon the policy of wartime cooperation to which it had turned for self-protection . . . the historical record is clear. As soon as the Soviet Government saw no further military need for the wartime coalition, it set out on its expansionist adventures. . . . [This] forced those nations determined to defend their freedom to take measures in their own self-defense'.

The difficulty in maintaining the thesis that immediate unambiguous and 'remorseless' expansion by the Soviet Union, even prior to the armistice, was solely responsible for what followed, is that it fails to account for certain key facts, and that it depends on certain assumptions which are untenable. The thesis fails to explain, for example, the fact that it took the Russians four years (from 1945 to 1949) to effect a remorseless expansion *behind their own military lines*.

Similarly, the thesis overlooks the contrast between Russian conduct in Hungary, where a free election was allowed to take place in 1945, and in Bulgaria and Rumania, where the Red Army installed Communist régimes almost at once. In point of fact, Soviet machinations in these latter two countries were carried out under the terms of an agreement between Churchill and Stalin, made in October 1944.[1] While Stalin was given what amounted to a free hand in Bulgaria and Rumania by the accord, Churchill was given a free hand in Greece, which he used to forcibly suppress the anti-Fascist resistance movement and to establish his own preferred regime, a rightist monarchy. The fact that Stalin kept his side of the agreement is of key significance, since Churchill could in no event have affected matters in Bulgaria or Rumania, whereas Stalin's refusal to provide aid to the Greek Communist and leftist forces in their battle with the British, was of critical, even decisive importance.

[1] cf. discussion of this agreement p. 58f. below.

In addition to their inability to deal with these intractable events, orthodox theses about the cold war's origins generally rest on another shaky assumption, namely, the unilateral demobilization of the US military machine. In theory, this demobilization resulted in a vacuum, which the Soviets could not have failed to exploit.[1]

> ... our commitment, then as now, was to the world of the Charter − ... In the service of this commitment. ... we dismantled the mightiest military force we had ever assembled. Armies were disbanded wholesale. ... Within two years after the end of the war, our defense spending had fallen by nearly $70 billion. Our armed forces were slashed. ... History has not seen, I believe, a more complete and comprehensive demonstration of a great nation's hope for peace and amity. (STEVENSON.)

The difficulty in accepting this version of events comes from two sources. In the first place, America's demobilization was not unique, but was parallelled by the demobilization of the Soviet armies:

> Contrary to what is often believed in the West, the USSR made a very big reduction of the armed forces after the war, in fact, reducing them to 25 per cent of the 1945 figure, compared with the US reduction to 13 per cent.
> Considering that the USSR had long and potentially hostile frontiers, in Europe, the Midde and the Far East, whereas the USA had atomic bombs and no potentially hostile frontiers bordering the USA itself, the 1948 total Soviet manpower figures of 2·9 million would hardly seem excessive from a purely military standpoint, when compared with the American 1·5 million.[2]

In the second place, US military capability is not adequately measured in terms of land forces, since the United States is primarily an air and sea power. The fact that during the first year of

[1] This thesis is advanced by W. W. Rostow in *The US in the World Arena*, 1960.
[2] P. M. S. Blackett, *Studies of War*, New York, 1962, p. 242, cf. Edgar O'Ballance, *The Red Army*, 1964 p. 189. Great Britain had at this time 0·75 million men under arms.

peace, the United States took steps to establish bases in the Pacific (by 1949 there were 400 U S bases around the perimeter of the Soviet Union), the fact that it tested the atomic bomb *before* the first control proposals were discussed and the fact that it continued its production of B-29's and planned production of B-36's all point to an intention different from that of unilateral disarmament.[1]

These observations suggest that there are many questions which orthodox attitudes towards the early post-war period leave unanswered, and that an examination of U S policy, particularly with regard to the dissolution of the wartime coalition is a prerequisite for understanding what happened later. With the above considerations in mind, we now turn to the task of examining the immediate post Yalta period and the actions which rapidly led to the outbreak of 'cold war'.

[1] cf. the discussion of the Wallace memorandum p. 62f. below.

CHAPTER I

Frictions and the Creation of the UN

ROOSEVELT died on April 12, 1945. His last words on the question of relations with the Soviet Union, sent but an hour before his death to Winston Churchill, were measured and confident:

> I would minimize the general Soviet problem as much as possible because these problems, in one form or another, seem to arise every day, and most of them straighten out, as in the case of the Bern meeting.
> We must be firm, however, and our course thus far is correct.[1]

Since Roosevelt had been a prime mover of the wartime coalition and had guided it through its worst as well as its best days, his words carry a special weight and serve as a logical starting point for a study of its deterioration and eventual collapse. For within two weeks of this message, it became clear that the Russian policy of the new Administration was predicated on a very different set of assumptions. When President Truman made his debut in American–Soviet diplomacy in his famous first confrontation with Foreign Minister Molotov on April 23 at the White House, a striking new emphasis was apparent – one which seemed far removed from any attempt to 'minimize the general Soviet problem'.

When the Foreign Minister arrived at the White House, Truman 'lost no time in making very plain to Molotov our displeasure at the Soviet failure to carry through the agreement made at Yalta about the character of a new Polish Government'. Truman's 'blunt language [was] unadorned by the polite verbiage of diplomacy'.[2] Columnist Drew Pearson later wrote that Molotov had 'heard Missouri mule-driver's language', and Charles Bohlen, a seasoned

[1] Feis, *Churchill, Roosevelt, Stalin*, 1957, p. 596.
[2] Leahy, *I Was There*, 1950, pp. 351–2.

diplomat who served as interpreter for the meeting, reported that 'he had never heard a top official get such a scolding'.[1]

'I have never been talked to like that in my life,' Molotov said at the end of the meeting.

'Carry out your agreements,' Truman answered, 'and you won't get talked to like that.'[2]

Thus Harry Truman, 'from the eminence of eleven days in power' had laid down the law to the Russians.[3]

The episode is all the more remarkable because Stalin had sent Molotov to the US for the founding conference of the UN 'to give some immediate assurance to the American people to indicate his desire to continue on a cooperative basis with this country' despite Roosevelt's death. Indeed, Stalin's reluctance to send Molotov had been overcome by the urgent pleading of W. A. Harriman, American Ambassador to the USSR, that this would be the most meaningful gesture to the American people.[4]

How this sudden shift in US policy came about has been recorded, in its essentials, by President Truman's principal military and diplomatic advisors who participated in the White House conference which preceded the Truman–Molotov meeting. The conference began with Secretary of State Stettinius informing the group[5] that while discussions with Molotov had begun favorably, the Russians had now gone back on their agreement at Yalta with President Roosevelt on the Polish question; they continued to insist on a United Nations seat for the Lublin Government which they had recognized as the government of Poland. 'In his [Stettinius's] view this was directly contrary to the Yalta understanding that Russia would join Great Britain and the United States in sponsoring and encouraging an entirely free and democratic election in Poland. He said that completely reliable State Department information was to the effect that the Lublin Government *did not in any way represent the Polish people* – that any free election would be certain to compel

---

[1] Fleming, op. cit., p. 270.
[2] Truman, *Memoirs*, I, p. 82.
[3] Fleming, op. cit.
[4] Sherwood, *Roosevelt and Hopkins*, 1948, p. 883.
[5] Others present were Secretary of War Stimson, Navy Secretary Forrestal, Admiral King, General Marshall, Fleet Admiral Leahy, Major-General John R. Deane, Assistant Secretary of State James Dunn, Ambassador to Russia Harriman and Charles Bohlen.

inclusion in the government of people like Premier Mikolajczyk and others of the Polish Government in exile.'[1] [Emphasis in original.]

The central question, thus, was the approach to be taken with Molotov on the Polish question. At the heart of the issue was whether the Russians were clearly and deliberately breaking the Yalta Agreement. The Russians, it will be remembered, had actual military control in Poland. They had agreed to the formation of the government of liberated Poland under certain guiding principles. If the Russians kept these agreements, it would be a strong sign of good faith on their part because, in the absence of Western power in the area, the West had no means of compelling them to do so. If the Russians sought to circumvent the agreements, a strong Western objection would serve the interests of future as well as present cooperation.

On the other hand, if the Russians were keeping the agreements *as they understood them,* and the West went out of its way to accuse the Soviets of bad faith, this would have a severely divisive effect on relations between the two countries. It would be tantamount to an attempt by one of the parties to impose its will on the other. As Molotov actually put it to Truman when they met and the charge of bad faith was made: 'The three governments [at Yalta] had dealt as equal parties, and there had been no case where one or two of the three had attempted to impose their will on another and . . . as a basis of cooperation this was the only one acceptable to the Soviet Government.'[2]

At the White House briefing, it was Secretary of War Stimson who asked how the Russians actually understood the agreement. Stimson had been a cabinet member in four administrations since 1911, either as Secretary of War, or as Secretary of State, and was beyond doubt the most experienced statesman in the room. Pointing out that the Russian conception of freedom, democracy and independent voting was quite different from the American or British, Stimson said, 'he hoped we would go slowly and avoid any open break. He said that the Russians had carried out their military engagements quite faithfully and was sorry to see this one incident project a breach between the two countries'. Stimson also said, 'he

---

[1] *The Forrestal Diaries*, ed. by Walter Millis, 1951, pp. 48–51.
[2] Truman, *Memoirs,* I, p. 81. This is Truman's recollection of Molotov's statement.

thought that the Russians perhaps were being more realistic than we were in regard to their own security'.[1]

The question of security had, of course, been paramount for the Russians as they did not hesitate to make known. 'Twice in the last thirty years our enemies, the Germans, have passed through this corridor.' Stalin had said at Yalta. 'It is in Russia's interest that Poland should be strong and powerful, in a position to shut the door of this corridor by her own force.'[2] The Russians, therefore, had stipulated that the new Polish Government must be 'friendly' to the Soviet Union.[3]

Fleet Admiral William D. Leahy, Chief of Staff to the Commander-in-Chief, was also asked his views at the White House conference. One of Truman's main advisors after the death of Roosevelt, Leahy subsequently became known as 'one of the principal architects of the "tough policy" toward Russia'.[4] Yet, Leahy 'thought the agreements were susceptible to two interpretations' and expressed hope that 'the matter [at hand] could be put to the Russians in such a way as not to close the door to accommodation'.[5] This outlook was consistent with Leahy's original reaction to the agreement when it was signed at Yalta. Then, he had complained to the President that it was 'so elastic that the Russians can stretch it all the way from Yalta to Washington without ever technically breaking it'. 'I know, Bill – I know it,' was Roosevelt's reply.[6]

But this was indeed the crucial point. If the Russians were not technically breaking the agreement, if there was a strong possibility that they were acting in good faith (i.e. towards the coalition, not

[1] Forrestal, ibid. The quotes are from Bohlen's notes.

[2] James F. Byrnes, *Speaking Frankly*, New York, 1947, pp. 31–2.

[3] Of course one such stipulation could be stretched to empty the term 'free elections' of all meaning. At best the agreement was, as it has been called, a compromise between the impossible and the inevitable. With regard to the question of security, however, it is important to remember that the 1939 Polish Government (from whom the London Poles stemmed) had been openly 'unfriendly' to the Russians and had refused them permission to set their troops on Polish soil to repulse the expected Nazi invasion.

[4] Frank Gervasi, 'Watchdog in the White House', *Colliers*, October 9, 1955.

[5] Forrestal, op. cit.

[6] Leahy, op. cit., pp. 315–16; also, cf. C. Marzani, *We Can Be Friends* (Origins of the Cold War), 1952. While some of the theses of this book are untenable, it remains a provocative work and offers many useful insights on the subject of early post-war US–Soviet relations to which the present account is considerably indebted.

necessarily towards the Poles), then too tough a line would not only be futile (since the power in the area was theirs) but dangerous as well. It is not surprising, therefore, that the third of the most distinguished advisors present, General George C. Marshall, was 'even more cautious' than Leahy or Stimson, and 'was inclined to agree that it would be a serious matter to risk a break'.

Advocating the firm stand which was to be taken, were Major General Deane, head of the Military Mission to Russia, Ambassador Harriman (whose dispatches in the weeks before the conference had consistently urged the necessity of taking a 'tough' line with the Russians) and Navy Secretary Forrestal, who said 'he had felt that for some time the Russians had considered that we would not object if they took over all of Eastern Europe into their power. He said it was his profound conviction that if the Russians were to be rigid in their attitude we had better have a showdown with them now, than later'.

Truman minced no words in registering his feeling that 'our agreements with the Soviet Union so far had been a one-way street and that he could not continue; it was now or never. He intended to go on with the plans for San Francisco and if the Russians did not wish to join us, they could go to hell'.[1]

It was characteristic of the new President to formulate his opinions bluntly, and this very bluntness makes them easier to evaluate. In this case, the historical record provides no support for the estimate upon which Truman decided to face the Russians with the choice of joining him or going to hell. The record shows that the Yalta Agreements were not a one-way street, simply allied concessions to Soviet demands. In the words of Stettinius, who accompanied Roosevelt to Yalta, 'the Soviet Union made more concessions to the United States and Great Britain than were made to the Soviet Union. . . .'[2] Moreover, all the agreements reached were, in a sense, Soviet concessions: '*As a result of the military situation, it was not a question of what Great Britain and the United States would permit Russia to do in Poland, but what the two countries could persuade the Soviet Union to accept. . . .*'[3] [Emphasis in original.]

This view was shared by Winston Churchill, certainly second to

[1] Forrestal, op. cit.
[2] Edward Stettinius, *Roosevelt and the Russians*, 1949, p. 6.
[3] ibid., p. 301.

no statesman in his antipathy for the Soviet régime, whose post-war influence in East Europe he had feared and tried to frustrate by strategies throughout World War II. On February 27, 1945, two months before the White House conference, Churchill had reported to the House of Commons:

> The impression I brought back from the Crimea, and from all my other contacts, is that Marshal Stalin and the Soviet leaders wish to live in honorable friendship and equity with the Western democracies. I feel also that their word is their bond. I know of no government which stands to its obligations, even in its own despite, more solidly than the Russian Soviet Government. I decline absolutely to embark here on a discussion about Russian good faith. It is quite evident that these matters touch the whole future of the world. Sombre indeed would be the fortunes of mankind if some awful schism arose between the Western democracies and the Russian Soviet Union, if all the future world organizations were rent asunder, and if new cataclysms of inconceivable violence destroyed all that is left of the treasures and liberties of mankind.[1]

Against the cautionary views of the officials most experienced in American–Soviet relations, the decision at the White House conference was to talk 'tough' to Molotov on the Polish issue. The same posture was also to be carried into the initial discussions within the newly created United Nations Organization at the founding meeting in San Francisco just getting underway. The lines of the 'awful schism', which Churchill feared, were rapidly being drawn.

Truman's approach to the Soviet Foreign Minister was warmly supported by one of the most important members of the United States delegation to the San Francisco Conference, Senator Arthur H. Vandenberg. On January 10, 1945, Vandenberg had made an extraordinary speech to the Congress,[2] which catapulted him over-

---

[1] Cited in Fleming, op. cit., p. 207.

[2] Most observers took the speech to be evidence of Vandenberg's conversion from isolationism. A more reflective view of D. F. Fleming characterizes it as 'first and foremost, a demand for "justice" for Poland'. Vandenberg himself has said that it was inspired by his 'deep conviction that it was time to anticipate what ultimately became the "Moscow menace"' – cf. *The Private Papers of Senator Vandenberg*, 1953, p. 130. For a penetrating analysis of Vandenberg's outlook at this time, cf. Fleming, op. cit., pp. 273, et. seq.

night from his position in the minority right wing of the Republican Party to that of spokesman and legislative leader for America's post-war bi-partisan foreign policy.

Vandenberg's reaction on being told of the Truman–Molotov interview was recorded in his diary:

> *Tuesday, April 24, 1945 (San Francisco)*
> Stettinius reached here from Washington this morning . . .
> . . . He immediately met our delegation and gave us a *thrilling* message. The new President [Truman] has declined to even wink at a surrender to Stalin on his demand for representation for the Lublin Poles. He has just sent a blunt message to Stalin including a general demand for Frisco cooperation. Stettinius said Eden could scarcely believe his eyes when he saw a copy – and cheered loudly. Stettinius added that he explained to Molotov that future Russian aid from America depends entirely upon the temper and mood and the conscience of the American people – and that Frisco is his last chance to *prove* that he deserves this aid. This is the best news in months. F.D.R.'s appeasement of Russia is over. . . . Stettinius does not know what the result will be. . . . But the crisis will come when Stalin's answer arrives. Russia may withdraw. If it does the conference *will proceed without Russia*. Now we are getting somewhere! [Emphasis is the Senator's.][1]

Thus Truman's delegate to the San Francisco Conference was not at all dismayed by the prospect that the Russians might withdraw from the United Nations altogether. Neither Vandenberg nor the President seemed to comprehend what lay behind Churchill's forebodings in his House of Commons' speech only two months earlier.

By this time, Vandenberg had already become a key figure in shaping United States foreign policy.[2] Further insight into his outlook is afforded by a diary entry of March 7, 1945. On that date, a month before the death of Roosevelt and a month and a half before the Molotov interview, Vandenberg had written:

---

[1] Vandenberg, op. cit., pp. 175–6.
[2] It was Vandenberg who commanded the support of the isolationist opposition for all of the important Truman cold war legislation. His role in framing and passing the Marshall Plan was so important, that Marshall wanted it called the Marshall–Vandenberg Plan.

> I could get no greater personal satisfaction out of anything more
> than from joining – aye, in leading – a public denunciation of
> Yalta. . . . But . . . I am forced from the circumstances to believe
> that we cannot get results by trying to totally combat decisions
> which are supported by our own American Administration and
> by the British Parliament. . . . We must find some other way. . . .
> I must primarily work . . . through the Frisco Conference and
> not in a public campaign of denunciation.[1]

Here, then, was Vandenberg formulating his purpose in going to
San Francisco. And what was that purpose? To undo the Yalta
decisions – that is, precisely the decisions which Truman six weeks
later was to accuse the Russians of violating! And the news that
Truman had given Molotov a drubbing for allegedly violating those
decisions, Vandenberg found thrilling!

When Vandenberg reached San Fancisco, he lost no time in trying to make provision for modifying the Yalta Agreement at some
future time to accord more closely with his idea of justice. He proposed no less than eight amendments to the Dumbarton Oaks draft.
Amendment No. 7 provided that if the Security Council finds
situations involving injustice, 'it shall recommend appropriate
measures which may include revision of treaties and of prior international decisions. . . .'

Molotov accepted all the British and American amendments with
a 'friendly attitude' except this Vandenberg proposal. 'He thought
that such recommendations would give the Germans a chance to
propagandize everlastingly for revision of the settlements in their
favor, as they had done after World War I.'[2]

Despite these underlying tensions, a cordial and cooperative
atmosphere prevailed during much of the first United Nations
session and considerable headway was made. The United States and
the Soviet Union clashed seriously, however, when Washington
ordered the United States delegation to push through the admission
of Argentina.[3]

---

[1] Among other things, Vandenberg considered the Curzon Line 'indefensible'
as the eastern boundary for Poland. Vandenberg, op. cit.

[2] Fleming, op. cit., p. 277.

[3] cf. Arthur Krock, the New York *Times*, November 21, 1946, cited in
Fleming p. 280.

At Yalta, Roosevelt had promised Stalin twice that he would not support the admission of Argentina to the United Nations.[1] According to Cordell Hull, Roosevelt's Secretary of State, Argentina had become 'the refuge and headquarters in this hemisphere of the Fascist movement' and was obviously aiming at 'Argentine hegemony of South America'.[2]

When the question of Argentina's admission was brought up, Molotov quoted castigation of the Argentina régime by Roosevelt and Hull, and said:

> Up to now all invitations to this Conference have been approved unanimously by the four sponsoring governments which hold an equal position here. . . . The Soviet delegation suggests that the question of inviting Argentina to the conference be postponed for a few days for further study. This is the only request made by the Soviet delegation.

Secretary of State Stettinius spoke against this request and it was voted down 28–7, then 31–4 and afterwards Argentina was admitted.[3]

Hull was also a member of the United States delegation but was too ill to attend the meetings. From his sickroom, he telephoned Stettinius that 'irreparable harm had been done' by the vote, and 'if the American delegation were not careful we should get Russia into such a state of mind that she might decide that the United Nations organization was not going to furnish adequate security to her in the future'.[4]

Hull's reaction was shared by other observers. The New York *Herald Tribune* found that the United States had 'built a steamroller' in the United Nations and Walter Lippmann warned that we 'had adopted a line of conduct which, if it becomes our regular line, will have the most disastrous consequences'. In a later article Lippmann referred to this action as 'riding roughshod through a world conference with a bloc of twenty votes [the Latin American countries]'; he regretted that the United States had lost 'its central position as mediator' particularly since Anglo-Soviet difficulties

[1] Cordell Hull, *Memoirs*, 1948, p. 1408.
[2] ibid., pp. 1405, 1419.
[3] Fleming, op. cit., p. 279.
[4] Cordell Hull, op. cit., p. 1722.

extended in 'a wide arc through the Balkans to the Middle East and Persia'.[1]

It was plainly evident that, with the Latin American governments in tow, the United States could always muster an anti-Soviet majority. If she sought consistently to do so, the organization would lose its value as an agency of compromise and international co-operation and could very well turn into a public pillory of the Soviet Union. Soviet fears in this regard had their roots in Russia's having been the only nation expelled from the League of Nations (for her attack on Finland), and at the urging, it will be remembered, of Argentina. The League, of course, had taken no similarly vigorous steps over the previous interventions by Fascist Italy and Germany in Ethiopia and Spain.

Against this background, Hull warned prophetically that if Russia could not find security in the United Nations, 'she might decide that, while giving lip service to the organization and keeping up her membership and paying her dues, she ought at the same time to go back home and establish outposts, bases and warm water harbors in many areas and add buffer territory and otherwise prepare her own outward defenses just as fully as if the United Nations were not in existence'.[2]

Despite the Argentine issue, the San Francisco conference succeeded in launching the United Nations. The conservative columnist, Arthur Krock, commented that Molotov could report to Stalin that Russia had conducted itself at the Conference 'as a great power and a generally cooperative one on the task in hand'. James Reston documented this appraisal in the New York *Times* of June 12: 'The conference record shows, the delegates note, ten concessions by Russia which have contributed greatly to the liberalizing of the Dumbarton Oaks proposals.'

Significantly, however, for the development of American popular thinking on the cold war, large portions of the United States press, had printed quite another version of the conference. 'The delegates here are conscious of reports that the Soviet Union has come here and demanded what they wanted and got what they demanded,' Reston added, 'and there is a general feeling that these reports

---

[1] New York *Herald Tribune*, May 2 and 15, 1945, cited in Fleming, p. 281.
[2] Hull, op. cit., p. 1722.

do not give an accurate impression of what has happened.'[1]

The United States and Soviet delegations left San Francisco dead-locked on only one important issue, besides the seating of the Poles. Not inexplicably, in light of the handling of the Argentine admission, the Russians had insisted that the veto power be extended to include discussion of a complaint brought against a permanent member of the Security Council. This would end the possibility of turning the United Nations into a pillory of the Soviet Union, but it would also severely curtail the power and effectiveness of the organization.

'When Secretary Stettinius explained over the telephone Russia's attitude on the veto by permanent members of the Security Council.' wrote Cordell Hull later, 'I said I felt that the Russian position would definitely narrow the base of the United Nations organization and that we must continue, with great patience – I emphasized that last phrase – to press the Russians to modify their attitude.'[2]

---

[1] New York *Times*, May 2, 1945 (Krock) – Reston and Krock cited in Fleming, op. cit., pp. 285–7.

[2] Hull, op. cit., p. 1723.

CHAPTER II

The Old Relations and the New

The inability of the wartime allies to reach agreement on the veto question or the seating of the Lublin Poles, had cast something of a pall over the San Francisco Conference. As the chief delegates headed home, it appeared quite possible that the Conference itself might be 'going on the rocks'.

> Harriman and Bohlen were on an airplane flying eastward . . .
> with a sense of despair in their hearts. They asked each other
> whether there was any conceivable way of saving the situation.
> . . . Bohlen suggested the possibility that President Truman might
> send Hopkins to Moscow. Harriman was enthusiastic about the
> suggestion. . . .[1]

There was an element of cynicism, unconscious perhaps, in the decision to send Harry Hopkins, already a 'seriously ill' man, to parley with Stalin. Hopkins himself was surprised when Truman agreed to the suggestion that he undertake the mission, for Hopkins had been the key man in implementing Roosevelt's approach to the Soviet Union, an approach that had already fallen into disrepute.

Harriman took care to emphasize to Stalin, at the actual meeting, that Hopkins 'had not only been very close to President Roosevelt but personally was one of the leading proponents of the policy of cooperation with the Soviet Union'.[2] At that moment, of course, Harriman was himself one of the chief advocates of the view that it was impossible to continue along the present lines of cooperation with the Soviets, and that the Roosevelt–Hopkins approach would have to be modified until 'our entire attitude toward them became characterized by much greater firmness'.[3]

[1] Sherwood, *Roosevelt and Hopkins*, p. 885.
[2] ibid., p. 892.
[3] Forrestal, op. cit., pp. 39–41.

In gauging the difference between the approaches advocated by Harriman and Hopkins, no incident is more instructive than the famous stoppage of Lend–Lease Aid on May 8, 1945, just three weeks before Hopkins' talks with Stalin. The stoppage of aid (not only to the Russians, but to all the Allies) was so abrupt that ships were even turned around and brought back to port for unloading.[1]

At the Moscow meeting with Hopkins, Stalin did not question the *right* of the United States to curtail Lend–Lease shipments, but stressed his feeling that an agreement between the two governments had been ended 'in a scornful and abrupt manner. He said that if proper warning had been given to the Soviet Government, there would have been no feeling of the kind he had spoken of; that this warning was important to them since their economy was based on plans'.[2]

Hopkins' answer to Stalin is crucial to an understanding of the profound change that was taking place in American foreign policy as Roosevelt, Hopkins and Hull departed from the scene:

Mr Hopkins replied that what disturbed him most about the Marshal's statement was the revelation that he believed that the United States would use Lend–Lease as a means of showing our displeasure with the Soviet Union. He wished to assure the Marshal that however unfortunate an impression this question had caused in the mind of the Soviet Government he must believe that there was no attempt or desire on the part of the United States to use it as a pressure weapon. *He said the United States is a strong power and does not go in for those methods.*[3] [Emphasis added.]

One can only wonder what Ambassador Harriman thought as he listened to this plea and to Stalin's reply that 'he believed Mr Hopkins and was fully satisfied with his statement in regard to Lend–Lease'. For Harriman had been the most persistent spokesman for the position that precisely this kind of pressure tactic *must* be used against the Soviet Union in order to compel the Russians to

[1] Truman later claimed that he had not read the order and that if he had, he would not have signed it. – *Memoirs*, I, pp. 221–2.
[2] Sherwood, op. cit.
[3] Sherwood, ibid.

cooperate. He had, in fact, called for the selection of 'one or two
cases' where Soviet actions had been 'intolerable' and urged
'effective reprisals' in order to make the Soviets realize that they
'cannot continue their present attitude except at great cost to
themselves'.[1]

Now the Russo-American wartime alliance was not an exception-
ally smooth one, and had been characterized by moments when one
side thought the other's actions 'intolerable' before. Nevertheless,
Roosevelt and Hopkins had been able to maintain the working
partnership on the basis of trust and mutual advantage, ironing out
differences when they arose. In gauging Harriman's judgement of
what he must have considered a series of new incidents, that is *new
in kind*, so that they required a radical revision[2] of policy, it is
instructive to consider an important concrete case.

Harriman was at the White House conference on April 23rd at
which it was decided that the Russians should be firmly faced with
their failure to live up to their commitments on the Polish question.
He was not only the Ambassador to Russia at the time, but had been
at Teheran and Yalta as well, and this increased the weight that his
judgement carried. According to Truman's account, Harriman con-
ceded Stimson's point that Russia had kept its 'big' agreements on
military matters. But he sought to controvert Stimson's conclusion
(viz. that the Russians were still reliable partners, deserving, as
equals, the benefit of the doubt) by observing that the 'big' agreements

> were decisions the USSR had already reached by itself, *but on
> other military matters it was impossible to say that they had lived up
> to their commitments. For example, over a year ago they had agreed
> to start on preparations for collaboration in the Far Eastern*

---

[1] 'On April 4, Harriman was cabling that "we now have ample proof that the
Soviet Government views *all* matters from the standpoint of their own selfish
interests. . . . On April 6, Harriman was cabling again, in general advocating a
"tough" policy with Russia as the one possible way of maintaining a soundly
friendly relationship with her. . . .' – Forrestal, op. cit., pp. 39–41, 47, 49, 57.
cf. Marzani, op. cit.

[2] Since the United States was incomparably stronger than the USSR, a policy
of 'effective reprisals' against the Russians and '*quid pro quo*' dealings with them
involved treating them no longer as equals, that is, no longer as members of the
wartime alliance. It also signified that the United States no longer considered
Russia a basically friendly power.

war, but none of these had been carried out.[1] [Emphasis added.]

Even a person unfamiliar with the facts about the Far Eastern War would have cause for surprise that Harriman should use Russia's delay in preparing its entry as the ground on which to base his general conclusion, that they were only reliable partners in decisions which they had already arrived at themselves (which is to say that they were never really 'partners' at all). For a parallel case, with the roles of the United States and the USSR reversed, had already occurred.

On July 8, 1941, Litvinov had raised the demand for a second front. On May 29, 1942, Molotov came to Washington and was 'assured' that the United States was preparing for a second front and expected to open it in 1942.[2] The opening of the second front was a far more critical matter to the Russians in the year before the victory at Stalingrad, than the entry of Russian forces into the Japanese War in 1945 was to the United States (although the American leadership was deeply concerned to secure Russia's participation). Yet, the second front was not opened until June 6, 1944, or more than a year and a half later than it was promised, and after the Russians at great cost, had achieved their main objectives of repulsing Hitler's invasion and removing the threat of their own defeat.

·Despite this history, Harriman was willing to cite the apparent Soviet posture on the Far Eastern War as conclusive evidence that on military questions which did not directly concern their self-interest 'it was impossible to say that they had lived up to their commitments' and thus to infer that on matters of the peace they would also prove unreliable. It was not only Harriman's historical view that was shortsighted, however: events subsequent to the April White House conference served, dramatically, to expose the emptiness of his estimate as well.

The Soviet commitment to enter the Pacific War had been made in formal terms at Yalta (hence its significance for the White House conference). Stalin had first estimated that it would require six months to move his armies from Germany to Manchuria. 'At Yalta, after reflection, he shortened that period to three months and made

[1] Truman, *Memoirs*, I, p. 79.
[2] Fleming, op. cit., pp. 149–50.

it a pledge.'[1] Germany was defeated on May 8, 1945 (two weeks after the White House conference). On August 8, three months to the day, as pledged, the Russians declared war on Japan.[2]

Thus, precisely that portion of the Yalta Agreement which Harriman seized upon as evidence that the Russians were not keeping their commitments was fulfilled by them *to the letter*. Yet, as Ambassador to Russia, Harriman was the principal White House advisor in estimating Russian intentions. During the weeks directly prior to the April conference, in a series of cables (which the influential Forrestal incorporated verbatim into his diary) Harriman asserted without qualification that 'our experience has incontrovertibly proved that it is not possible to bank general goodwill in Moscow' and that in future dealings with the Russians we must act 'always on a *quid pro quo* basis'.[3]

In light of this, it is all the more disconcerting that Harriman should have been enthusiastic about sending the ailing Harry Hopkins to Moscow. For Hopkins was sent with absolutely nothing to offer the Russians, unless it were 'goodwill'. Harriman was well aware of this and despite his assertion that it had been 'incontrovertibly proved' that goodwill could not be banked in Moscow, he took pains to make sure that Stalin would not miss the attempt that, in fact, was being made to do this.[4]

Hopkins began his talks with Stalin, predictably enough, by holding out the one thing he had to offer in return for the concessions which he was going to ask the Russians to make. Without the support of American public opinion, Hopkins told Stalin, it would be difficult for the new President to continue Roosevelt's policy of 'working with the Soviet Union'. Public opinion in the United States, Hopkins said, had been adversely affected by recent developments, in particular, by the Allies 'inability to carry into effect the Yalta Agreement on Poland'. In order to retain the reservoir of goodwill, built up by the Russians' 'brilliant achievements' in the war, it would be necessary to show progress on this question.

---

[1] Fleming, op. cit., p. 196; Snell, *The Meaning of Yalta*, 1956, p. 35.
[2] Fleming, p. 302.
[3] Forrestal, op. cit., pp. 39-41.
[4] Harriman even reported the success of this attempt to the White House: 'Harry's visit had already dispelled the growing suspicion felt by Stalin and Molotov.' – ibid., p. 68. The actual wording is John J. McCloy's.

In his reply, Stalin showed that he was wary of the British and the French, particularly the intentions of the former regarding attempts to create an anti-Soviet Poland. What he feared from the United States itself, at this point, was not hostility, but something far closer to the realities then at hand. It was the impression of Soviet Government officials, he said, 'that the American attitude towards the Soviet Union had perceptibly cooled once it became obvious that Germany was defeated, and that *it was as though the Americans were saying that the Russians were no longer needed.*'[1] [Emphasis added.]

This, of course, is precisely what the American leaders *were* saying, viz. that they intended to go on with their plans 'and if the Russians did not wish to join us they could go to hell'.

Despite the fact that Hopkins was not able to offer concretely the goodwill of the American leadership, but only that of American public opinion (for which the dictator predictably showed disdain),[2] Stalin did show a willingness to gamble, or more likely, to strengthen the hand of those members of the American Government who might share Hopkins' views. By making two important concessions, he also demonstrated that he was interested in preserving the alliance and Russo-American cooperation, at a time when the decisive section of the American leadership (including the President) were contending that he was not.[3] As a result of the Hopkins talks, Stalin yielded on the two points which the United States considered most crucial and most pressing: the composition of the Polish Government and the United Nations veto.

The Yalta accord had specifically provided that Poles from abroad be included in the reconstituted Polish régime. During the San Francisco Conference, the Russians had become increasingly difficult on this point and insisted on vetoing all candidates from among the London Poles, on the grounds that they were 'unfriendly'. It was at this juncture that the decision was taken to send Hopkins to Moscow to see if he could break the deadlock.

Actually, this question of broadening the Lublin Government had

---

[1] Sherwood, p. 893. Stalin cited American actions that had led the Russians to conclude this, including stoppage of Lend–Lease and Argentina's admission to the United Nations. cf. Marzani, op. cit.

[2] 'Marshal Stalin said [in reply to Hopkins] he would not attempt to use Soviet public opinion as a screen.' – ibid.

[3] The nature of the Polish concession makes it unlikely that this was merely a 'tactical maneuver'.

also been brought up at the White House conference, although the decision reached referred mainly to the issue of whether the original formation of the government (i.e. using the Lublin Poles as a basis) was in accord with the Yalta agreements. Secretary of War Stimson raised the question of Soviet motives. He noted that the Soviets had kept their word in the big military matters and had often done better than they had promised. 'On that account he felt that it was import-ant to find out what motives they had in connection with these border countries and what their ideas of independence and democ-racy were in areas they regarded as vital to the Soviet Union.'[1]

In other words, the question was to what extent the Soviets wished to exert influence over the policies of liberated Poland. Would they limit their aims to seeking a pro-Soviet foreign policy for the new régime, or would they seek total domination of the country?

Ambassador Harriman was at no loss for an answer to this question. Indeed, as Truman reports, it was Harriman's belief that 'the real issue was whether we were to be a party to a program of Soviet domination of Poland'. Furthermore, Harriman said 'ob-viously we were faced with the possibility of a break with the Russians, but he felt that, properly handled, it might still be avoided'.[2]

The analysis via which Harriman arrived at this conclusion is also reported by Truman:

> Ambassador Harriman, in replying to Mr Stimson's question about issues and motives, said he felt that when Stalin and Molotov had returned to Moscow after Yalta they had learned more of the situation in Poland, and had realized how shaky the provisional [Lublin] government was. On that account they had come to realize that the introduction of any genuine Polish leader such as Mikolajczyk would probably mean the elimination of the Soviet hand-picked crop of leaders. It was his belief, therefore, that the real issue . . . etc.

Harriman's analysis is interesting from more than one point of

---

[1] Truman, *Memoirs*, I, p. 79.
[2] ibid., p. 78. Note that this is April 23, *1945*, when the Ambassador to Russia is speaking of a break that '*might*' still be avoided'.

view. In the first place it shows the consistency of his thinking. The Soviets had made an agreement at Yalta which they felt would not interfere with, and might even facilitate their eventual domination of Poland. Now they had realized that this was not the case. They could not broaden the government without fatally injuring their plans for domination. Self-interest, 'the principle of power politics in its crudest and most primitive form'[1] dictated to the Russians that they must break the Yalta Agreement and at all cost prevent leaders like Mikolajczyk (former premier of the London Poles) from entering the new Polish Government. The Soviet motives were so clear, moreover, that although it meant risking a break,[2] they had to be called firmly to account.

In the second place, the analysis shows again the erroneous grounds on which Harriman based his viewpoint.[3] For at Moscow (a month later) when Hopkins put the question of Poland 'as clearly and forcibly as he knew how', saying that 'it had become a symbol of our ability to work out problems with the Soviet Union', the *first* concrete proposal suggested by Stalin was the admission of four ministers from democratic groups other than that of the present provisional government. 'He added that Mikolajczyk had been suggested and he thought he was acceptable and that the question was now, who else. He inquired of Mr Hopkins whether possibly Professor Lange [of the University of Chicago] might be willing to join the government.'

Both Lange and Mikolajczyk were willing, and a list of candidates was soon agreed upon. On June 21 the new government was formed with Mikolajczyk as one of the vice-premiers, and on July 5 Britain and America gave it their recognition. In this way Harriman was again proven crucially wrong, even to the letter of his prediction. Yet Harriman's report to Truman after the meeting contained no modification of his position; nor did Stalin's amicability prevent Harriman's viewpoint – already widely held by other members

[1] In a dispatch of May 14, 1945, Harriman cabled that Soviet conduct was, and would be, based on 'the principle of power politics in its crudest and most primitive form' – Forrestal, op. cit.

[2] Even on this point Harriman was wrong. For the issue was most improperly handled, but the Russians made no diplomatic move of reprisal.

[3] Harriman, it should be noted, was a member of the three-man commission (Molotov and Sir A. Clark Kerr were the others) specifically designated by the Yalta Agreement, to preside over the formation of the new Polish Government.

of the government – from gaining predominance in Washington.

The second concession made by Stalin (involving the United Nations veto) also serves to illuminate the important difference in the attitudes shaping United States policy towards the Soviet Union before and after Roosevelt's death.

On June 2, Secretary of State Stettinius sent a 'top secret' message to Hopkins in Moscow, telling him that the United States delegation (with the President's approval) had come to the conclusion that the Soviet position on the veto, if accepted, 'would make a farce out of the whole proposed world organization'. 'Please tell him [Stalin],' the message urged, 'in no uncertain words that this country could not possibly join an organization based on so unreasonable an interpretation. . . .'[1]

This ultimatum never reached Stalin. When, on June 6, Hopkins took up the veto question, he did not mention the contents of the communication except to say that he had received 'an urgent message' from President Truman, instructing him to discuss the veto with Stalin and 'to indicate the seriousness of this matter'. That was all Hopkins said about the contents of Stettinius' message. He then went on to say to Stalin 'that the United States thought the Yalta formula as agreed on safeguarded the freedom of discussion [which the veto in question would hinder]'. Hopkins 'hoped the Marshal would see eye to eye with us and the other sponsoring powers and France who were agreed on this question'. At this point, Molotov entered the discussion to defend the Soviet position, but Stalin cut him off. Then 'Marshal Stalin . . . stated that he had no objection to a simple majority being applied in discussions relating to pacific settlement'. The veto crisis was over.

The news arrived in San Francisco the next day, June 7, and that night, without having received any specific report on the actual contents of the Hopkins–Stalin exchange, Vandenberg wrote in his diary,

> *America wins!* The 'Veto' crisis broke today – and it broke *our* way. . . . It is a complete and total surrender. No attempt at any weasel-worded compromise. Just a straight-out acceptance of unhindered hearing and discussion . . . [Emphasis in original.]

[1] Vandenberg, op. cit., pp. 204–6.

> *I think everyone is convinced that the blunt, unconditional*
> *message which Stettinius sent to Moscow turned the trick.* I hope
> some of our people have learned a lesson. Many of them were
> beginning to weaken under the 'war of nerves'.[1] [Emphasis
> added.]

Thus, even Russian concessions served to confirm the proponents
of the tough line in their new approach. Harriman went so far as to
interpret the productive Stalin–Hopkins talks as further evidence of
the Soviets' new uncooperative line. In the words of President
Truman:

> The Russian dictator, Harriman later reported, showed that he
> did not fully understand the basis of the difficulties. He *took the*
> *offensive* in complaining 'about our misdeeds' and *aggressively*
> indicated that if we did not wish to deal on a friendly basis with
> the Soviet Union, she was strong enough to look after herself.[2]
> [Emphasis added.]

In the public record of the Stalin–Hopkins talks, the only remark
by Stalin which can be bent into this mold was that already quoted
in regard to Lend–Lease Aid. There, in what was quite clearly an
attempt to help Hopkins out of an embarrassing position, the dictator recognized the right of the United States to stop aid if it
wished to, and suggested that the Russians would not have been so
hurt by the stoppage if they had been warned in advance.

It would have been most surprising if Stalin had, in fact, 'aggres-
sively' indicated that the Russians were ready to go-it-alone, if
necessary. The United States was the one major power with a
totally intact industrial plant. The Russians made no secret of the
enormous losses they had suffered in the war.[3] If either of the two

---

[1] Vandenberg, ibid., p. 208.
[2] Truman, *Memoirs*, I, pp. 262–3.
[3] According to an official statement of the Extraordinary State Committee
(USSR), between 15 and 20 million Soviet citizens had been killed. The Germans had destroyed completely or partially 15 large cities, 1,710 towns and
70,000 villages. They burned or demolished 6 million buildings and deprived
25 million people of shelter. They demolished 31,850 industrial enterprises,
65,000 kilometers of railway track, 4,100 railway stations, 36,000 postal, telegraph and telephone offices, 56,000 miles of main highway, 90,000 bridges and

parties would have been unadversely affected, from a purely national standpoint, by going-it-alone, then it was the United States. And indeed, the only remarks in the talks which did resemble the formula recalled by Harriman were those in which Stalin expressed his fears that United States leaders were, in effect, saying that if the Soviets did not wish to go along with United States plans, they could go to hell.

Hopkins himself had a more perceptive and, unfortunately, a more prophetic comment to make on these and related events, that is, on the change that had taken place in the United States approach to the Soviet Union. Shortly before his death, some six months after the Moscow talks, he warned: '*Our Russian policy must not be dictated by people who have already made up their minds there is no possibility of working with the Russians and that our interests are bound to conflict and ultimately lead to war. From my point of view, this is an untenable position and can but lead to disaster.*'[1]

[1] Sherwood, op. cit., p. 923.

10,000 power stations. They ruined 1,135 coal-mines and 3,000 oil wells, carried off to Germany 14,000 steam boilers, 1,400 turbines and 11,300 electric generators. They sacked 98,000 collective farms and 2,890 machine and tractor stations and slaughtered or carried off 7 million horses, 17 million cattle, 20 million hogs, 27 million sheep and goats, 110 million poultry. They looted and destroyed 40,000 hospitals and medical centres, 84,000 schools and colleges and 43,000 public libraries with 110 million volumes. They destroyed 44,000 theatres, 427 museums and 2,800 churches. – cited in Fleming, op. cit., p. 923.

CHAPTER III

The Dissolution of the Coalition

AFTER the Stalin–Hopkins talks, preparations were made for the final wartime meeting of the 'Big Three' to discuss, among other things, the occupation of Germany. It was the first, and last, face-to-face encounter between Stalin and Truman.

In the period before the talks, Truman made a series of changes in his cabinet. Of ten members of the Roosevelt cabinet, six either resigned or were replaced between June 30 and the opening of the Potsdam Conference on July 18.[1] Of the six Truman appointees (including such right-wing Democrats as Tom Clark and Fred Vinson), four were from states west of the Mississippi, creating, as Truman himself described it, 'an unprecedented situation' from the point of view of regional representation in the cabinet. The region which Truman chose to give such overwhelming representation was, of course, that section of the country which was most isolationist and nationalist.

Of the two remaining cabinet changes, one was the replacing of Henry Morgenthau, Jr, Secretary of the Treasury. Morgenthau's famous plan for de-industrializing Germany had received support the previous September from Churchill and Roosevelt, but opposition in Britain and America had caused the projected scheme to be abandoned. Stalin, himself, was under the impression that the Western Allies had pronounced against dismemberment.[2] The replacement of Morgenthau was probably indicative of the new

[1] Of the remaining four, two had left by the end of 1945 and the last two by the end of 1946. 'Of the 125 most important government appointments made by President Truman in the first two post-war years,' wrote Howard K. Smith, '49 were bankers, financiers, and industrialists, 31 were military men, and 17 lawyers, mostly with Big Business connections. The effective locus of government seemed to shift from Washington to some place equidistant between Wal Street and West Point.' – Howard K. Smith, *The State of Europe*, 1949, p. 83 cf. also p. 95.

[2] Kenneth Ingram, *History of the Cold War*, London, 1955, pp. 20–21.

mood in Washington regarding Russian reparations claims (which were to be discussed at Potsdam) and their request for a multi-billion dollar loan, rather than opposition to the already abandoned program.[1]

Truman's final cabinet change was his appointment of James F. Byrnes, a South Carolina Dixiecrat, to the post of Secretary of State, replacing Stettinius. 'I felt it my duty,' Truman wrote afterwards, 'to choose without too much delay a Secretary of State with proper qualifications to succeed, if necessary to the presidency. At this time, I regarded Byrnes as the man best qualified.'[2]

As the Potsdam Conference got under way, Truman promptly put forward two proposals which had been drawn up by the American delegations. The first was to establish the Council of Foreign Ministers, and this was accepted with such speed, that the Americans were put into a state of high hopes as they 'went to lunch'.[3] The second American proposal is perhaps best described by Byrnes himself: 'Our paper stated flatly that the obligations assumed in the Yalta Declaration had not been carried out,' and proposed 'joint action in reorganizing the governments of Bulgaria and Rumania to permit participation of all democratic groups.'

The Russian response to this paper, delivered by Molotov, was an attack on British intervention in Greece. The British denied the Soviet assertions and claimed that there had been free elections. Molotov countered with British and American press reports that 'there were greater excesses in Greece than in either Rumania or Bulgaria'.[4]

Thus began the process of claim and counter-claim, charge and counter-charge which characterized so much of the relations between the former allies in the ensuing period. While a number of accords were reached at Potsdam, including the establishment of a Council of Foreign Ministers and a formula for the occupation of Germany, these were overshadowed by the changed spirit within the

---

[1] On the eve of Yalta, Morgenthau wrote: 'I am convinced that if we were to come forward now and present to the Russians a concrete plan to aid them in the reconstruction period it would contribute a great deal towards ironing out many of the difficulties we have been having with respect to their problems and their policies.' – cited in Wm. A. Williams, *American–Russian Relations*, 1952, p. 274.

[2] Truman, op. cit., p. 23.

[3] Byrnes, *Speaking Frankly*, 1947, p. 21.

[4] ibid., p. 73.

coalition. Sumner Welles, Roosevelt's Under-Secretary of State went so far as to pin-point the source of the change. With the death of Roosevelt, he wrote, 'the direction of American policy passed into other hands. The dire change this brought about in Soviet-American relations was apparent to every objective observer present at the meeting at Potsdam'.[1]

But Potsdam as a symbol of the deterioration of Soviet-American relations was soon eclipsed by events at the other end of the globe: the bombings of Hiroshima and Nagasaki.

On August 9, the day the second Atomic Bomb was dropped on Japan, President Truman explained that these bombs were used 'to shorten the agony of war, in order to save the lives of thousands and thousands of young Americans'. The justification for his statement seemed to lie in the fact Japan would not surrender. It had cost 70,000 lives to take Iwo Jima and Okinawa the previous spring. Any invasion of the home islands would cost hundreds of thousands of lives.

But no land invasion of these islands had been planned to take place before November 1, 1945![2] The United States knew, moreover, that the Japanese Government was suing for peace, through its Moscow Ambassador, a month before the bomb was actually dropped.[3] Even earlier, on May 28, Harry Hopkins had cabled to Truman:

> By August 8 the Soviet Army will be properly deployed on the Manchurian positions [i.e. for entry into the war] . . .
> Japan is doomed and the Japanese know it.

[1] Sumner Welles, *Where Are We Heading?*, 1946, pp. 375–9. Not surprisingly the Potsdam accords were short-lived. Nor was it only the Russians who failed to honor them: 'Potsdam today is to a large extent a dead letter in the Western Zones of Germany.' – Barbara Ward, *The West at Bay*, 1948, p. 28.

[2] see Secretary of War Stimson's article in *Harpers*, February 1947, also in Stimson and Bundy *On Active Service*, 1947, p. 365.

[3] cf. *Forrestal Diaries* entry dated July 13: 'The first real evidence of a Japanese desire to get out of the war came today through intercepted messages from Togo . . . to Sato, Jap Ambassador to Moscow, instructing the latter to see Molotov if possible before his departure for the Big Three meeting . . . to lay before him the Emperor's strong desire to secure a termination of the war. . . . Togo said further that the unconditional surrender terms of the Allies was about the only thing in the way of termination . . .' According to US Strategic Bombing Survey No. 4, 'certainly prior to December 31, 1945, Japan would have surrendered, even if the atomic bombs had not been dropped, even if Russia had not entered the war, and even if no invasion had been planned or contemplated'.

Peace feelers are being put out by certain elements in Japan and *we should therefore consider together our joint attitude* [i.e. Soviet and American] *and act in concert about the surrender of Japan.* Stalin expressed the fear that the Japanese will try to split the allies.[1] [Emphasis added.]

Hopkins' advice to act in concert about the surrender of Japan, as would be normal for allies, went unheeded. Stalin's fear that the Allies would be split proved correct, though it was not a Japanese initiative that served as cause.

According to Hopkins' cable, Stalin had a proposal for dealing with the Japanese. He thought it was necessary to achieve the effects of unconditional surrender, namely, elimination of the emperor and the warlords, so that they could not start a war of revenge. He did not think, however, that the Japanese would submit to unconditional surrender. Therefore, if the Japanese sought surrender on modified terms, he thought the Allies should accept these modified terms and then impose their will through the occupying forces. Truman, however, was not interested in Stalin's proposal.

On July 26, just thirteen days before the Russians were scheduled to enter the war and three months before any invasions jeopardizing American lives were planned, Great Britain, China and the United States issued an ultimatum to the Japanese calling on them to surrender unconditionally or face 'prompt and utter destruction'. No hint was offered that a new and previously inconceivable weapon was to be used against them.

'The declaration was immediately released for publication,' writes Byrnes, 'and a copy was sent by special messenger to Mr Molotov.' Molotov phoned later in the evening and asked that the declaration 'be held up two or three days'. When he was told it already had been released, he seemed disturbed. The next day, Byrnes explained to Molotov that the Soviet Union had not been informed of the ultimatum to the Japanese to surrender, because 'we did not want to embarrass the Soviet Union by presenting it with a declaration affecting a country with which it was not yet at war'. (The fact that the United States had concluded an agreement with the Russians at Yalta to enter the war, and that the Russians

---

[1] Sherwood, op. cit.

had indicated they would do so thirteen days hence, apparently made no difference.) Molotov replied 'simply' that the Allies 'should have consulted him'.[1]

On July 29, Molotov called again and said that Stalin had instructed him to discuss (with Truman and Byrnes) 'the immediate cause of the Soviet Union's entry into the war'. 'The request,' wrote Byrnes later, 'presented a problem to us.' 'The Soviet Union,' Byrnes explained, 'had a non-aggression pact with the Japanese. . . . We did not believe that the United States Government should be placed in the position of asking another government to violate its agreement without good and sufficient reason. . . . The President was disturbed.'[2]

This intense concern for the niceties of international law seems scarcely credible in view of the Administration's willingness to atomize the 400,000 civilian inhabitants of Hiroshima and Nagasaki at a moment when their government was suing for peace. A more palpable explanation of the dismay felt by Truman and Byrnes was candidly expressed by the latter when he wrote, 'As for myself, I must frankly admit that in view of what we knew of Soviet actions in Eastern Germany and the violations of the Yalta Agreements in Poland, Rumania and Bulgaria, I would have been satisfied had the Russians determined not to enter the war.'[3]

This admission is borne out by the historical record. On July 28, the day before Molotov's phone call, Forrestal noted in his diary a conversation with Byrnes: 'Byrnes said he was *most anxious* to get the Japanese affair over with before the Russians get in, with particular reference to Dairen and Port Arthur. Once in there, he felt, it would not be easy to get them out. . . .' [Emphasis added.] Looking backward this may well seem like the realistic and prescient view of a hard-headed statesman seeking to thwart the designs of Russian imperialism. Of no small consequence, in making such an assessment, however, is the fact that Russia had been *guaranteed rights* to be in Dairen and Port Arthur, by mutual agreement at Yalta. Dairen was to be internationalized as a commercial port (the

---

[1] Byrnes, op. cit., p. 207. Stalin, it should be noted, had informed Truman of the Japanese attempts to get the Russians to intervene in their behalf and help mediate a peace.

[2] Byrnes, pp. 207–8.

[3] ibid., p. 208.

Russians being guaranteed access) and Port Arthur was to be leased to the Russians as a naval base. Actually this did not even amount to a restoration of the rights Russia had already had in these ports, and had lost in the Russo-Japanese War of 1905.[1]

Thus, instead of wishing to keep Russia out of the Japanese War because the Russians had violated the Yalta Agreements, Byrnes wanted to keep them out so the United States might ignore the agreements – or at least circumvent them.

In retrospect, the desire to keep the Russians out would seem to have been the primary reason for the use of the Atomic Bombs.[2] Only this can explain the haste with which they were dropped (without waiting to see the effect of Russian entry on the war) and the lack of any reasonable time space or a second ultimatum between them. Indeed, the second bomb was dropped on August 9, the day that Russian troops entered Manchuria. On August 10, the Japanese offered to surrender on modified, not unconditional terms. After a reply by the Allies on August 11, they did so on August 14.

On August 18, in the perceptible wake of the Atomic Bomb, Byrnes publicly charged that the Bulgarian elections were not being conducted democratically. As a result, the elections were postponed. Byrnes' statement, according to one historian of Russian affairs, marked the beginning of 'the tragic impasse in Soviet-American relations'.[3]

The significance of Byrnes' attack lies in the fact that while the Russians were definitely breaking the Yalta Agreements by rigging the elections in Bulgaria, they were doing so under the terms of an agreement with the West that had already cost them a great deal, politically, to maintain. This was the already mentioned secret Churchill–Stalin agreement on the Balkans made in Moscow in October 1944. According to Churchill's own account, he proposed a 'ninety per cent predominance in Rumania' for Russia, the same for Britain in Greece, and 50–50 in Yugoslavia. Then he added a proposed split in the five Balkan countries, Hungary 50-50, Bulgaria 75 per cent control for Russia and 25 per cent to the others.[4]

[1] Snell, *The Meaning of Yalta*, pp. 129, et seq.
[2] This is Blackett's conclusion in *Military and Political Consequences of Atomic Weapons.*
[3] Frederick L. Schuman, 'The Devil and Jimmy Byrnes', *Soviet Russia Today*, 1948, p. 7.
[4] Churchill, *The Second World War*, Vol. VI, 1953, pp. 227–8.

On March 8, 1945, Churchill cabled Roosevelt (who disapproved of the agreement) that 'Stalin adhered very strictly to this understanding'.[1] What Churchill meant was that Stalin had stood by while the British forces broke the back of the Greek anti-fascist (but also anti-monarchist and Communist-dominated) resistance movement, EAM-ELAS, and restored the rightist monarchy in Greece. For his patience, Stalin was allowed to install his own favored element in the axis satellites, Rumania and Bulgaria. In Hungary, by way of contrast, Stalin allowed a free election in autumn 1945,[2] which he lost. In Yugoslavia, he actually tried to induce Tito to bring King Peter back and restore the monarchy.[3]

Byrnes' protest on the handling of the Bulgarian elections thus could only be seen by the Russians as an attempt to convict them in the eyes of world opinion of having broken their solemn publicly made agreements. They could counter with statements about Greece, but any international debate with the West, on the subject of free elections, was one that they were eventually bound to lose. The deeper significance of Byrnes' statement was that it indicated to the Russians that the West was no longer interested in working with them, and was even ready to use overt pressure against them. This was the effective end of the coalition.

It is instructive to consider the reasons why the American leadership should have chosen this period (July 26–August 18) to end the coalition. In terms of Yalta, which is usually cited as a pretext, this was probably the high tide of Russian good faith, from a Western point of view. The Russians had just completed the arduous task of shifting their troops from Germany to Manchuria to open the 'second front', which at Yalta had been a matter of prime urgency for the Americans. In Poland, they had broadened the government allowing Mikolajczyk and other Poles from abroad to assume cabinet posts, and the West had duly recognized the régime.

If no Russian action at this time warranted a break, the only explanation can be that the United States no longer needed the Russians for the undertaking of any joint enterprise. The factor which had induced this change between April 23 (when the prospect of a break disturbed Marshall and Stimson because of the effect it

---

[1] Byrnes, op. cit., p. 53.

[2] Hugh Seton-Watson, *The East European Revolution*, 1950, p. 193.

[3] The Alsops, June 24, July 23, 1951, cited in Fleming, p. 199.

would have on the Japanese War) and July 26, when the ultimatum was issued without consulting the Russians, could only have been the first successful Atomic Bomb test at Alamogordo, on the day before the Potsdam Conference opened. The extent of this change in attitude can be gleaned from Churchill's statement at the time: 'We were in the presence of a new factor in human affairs,' he said, referring to the Bomb. 'We possessed powers which were irresistible . . . our outlook on the future was transformed.'[1]

On September 11, the Council of Foreign Ministers met in London and 'failed to agree on anything'. In the words of Sumner Welles, Secretary of State Byrnes 'adopted a position of intransigence'. His tough line was supported by another member of the delegation, John Foster Dulles, who had been invited at the suggestion of Senator Vandenberg.[2] The result was, as Welles put it, 'one of the most disastrous international conferences of modern times'.[3] After the failure of the London Council Truman announced that there would be no more Big Three meetings.

The foreign ministers, however, were still supposed to meet every three months. When Byrnes proposed a second meeting, the Russians accepted, and in December he went to Moscow. Aided by three private talks with Stalin, he arrived at substantial agreements on a number of important questions, and thus proved that even non-friendly powers could negotiate. The agreements reached concerned, among other things, the liberalization of the régimes in Bulgaria and

---

[1] New York *Times*, August 17, 1945, cited in Fleming, p. 310. After the completion of this manuscript, new evidence, confirming the above interpretation of events, was provided by Byrnes in the course of a television documentary, *The Decision to Drop The Bomb*, shown on January 5, 1965, according to *Reuters*: '. . . Mr James Byrnes, the then Secretary of State, said President Truman was in a quandary about how much to tell Stalin after America's first successful atomic bomb test. . . . Mr Byrnes said he and the President decided to withold details of the bomb from Stalin because they did not want to encourage the Russians to join the war against Japan. In dealing with the Soviet ally at this time, Mr Byrnes was also considering whether to collaborate with the Russians in the early stages of nuclear development "or whether we should try to out-distance them in the race", according to Mr Gordon Arneson, who was the recording secretary of the committee which handled top-secret bomb decisions. "He decided against collaboration." '

[2] Byrnes, op. cit., p. 234.

[3] Welles, op. cit., pp. 67, 380.

Rumania (the Russians accepted the United States proposal on this without changes)[1] and draft treaties for the German satellites. These were ratified without substantial change by the twenty-one nation peace conference which ended the following October.

When Byrnes returned to the United States, however, he discovered that a portion of the press had termed the Moscow agreements 'appeasement'. Moreover, the President was angry. So was Senator Vandenberg, who was afraid that Byrnes had agreed to give away atomic energy secrets without guarantees of inspection and control. Truman's ire eventually cost Byrnes his job. In a memorandum to Byrnes, the President complained that Byrnes had not kept him adequately informed during the discussions, and had not protested Russian actions in Iran.[2] Then he wrote:

> There isn't a doubt in my mind that Russia intends an invasion of Turkey and the seizure of the Black Sea Straits to the Mediterranean. Unless Russia is faced with an iron fist and strong language, another war is in the making. Only one language do they understand – 'how many divisions have you?'
>
> I do not think we should play compromise any longer. We should refuse to recognize Rumania and Bulgaria until they comply with our requirements; we should let our position on Iran be known in no uncertain terms and we should continue to insist on the internationalization of the Kiel Canal, the Rhine–Danube waterway and the Black Sea Straits and we should maintain complete control of Japan and the Pacific. . . .
>
> . . . we should insist on the return of our ships from Russia and force a settlement of the Lend–Lease debt of Russia.
>
> I'm tired of babying the Soviets.[3]

Truman's memorandum to Byrnes was not merely a rebuke to his Secretary of State, but in the President's own words, 'the point of departure of United States policy'.[1]

[1] Byrnes, pp. 110, et seq.
[2] cf. Discussion on Iran, pp. 89–90 below.
[3] Truman, p. 552. Truman's use of the word 'babying' with regard to the Soviets may be better understood when set next to his statement in July 1941, as the Nazi armies moved into Russia: 'If we see that Germany is winning the war we ought to help Russia, and if Russia is winning we ought to help Germany, and in that way let them kill as many as possible . . .' – New York *Times*, July 24, 1941.

The memorandum was dated January 5, 1946. A month and a half later, an 8,000-word dispatch was received from the American Embassy in Moscow. The dispatch which had been written by a scholar-diplomat, provided a perfect rationalization for the 'get-tough' policy which had already been adopted. The diplomat, George Frost Kennan, was brought to Washington.[1]

Kennan's dispatch had struck a particularly sympathetic chord in Navy Secretary Forrestal. 'It was exactly the kind of job for which Forrestal had looked vainly elsewhere in the government,' writes Walter Millis, editor of the Forrestal diaries, and its conclusions on how to deal with the Soviets, 'accorded very closely with those Forrestal had already been developing'. The nature of Forrestal's conclusions is indicated in the note to the preceding diary entry by editor Millis: 'It is clear that from this time on he felt increasingly that policy could not be founded on the assumption that a peaceful solution of the Russian problem would be possible.'[2]

'To any thoughtful mind,' writes Millis, '[Kennan's] analysis must, if accepted, have ended all hope of establishing conventional or "normal" international relations with this dark dictatorship, hag-ridden by the ghosts of the Russian past; it rendered foolish the ideas – which were to flourish popularly for long after – of settling everything by concessions, by a meeting of the "heads of state" or by some similar form of reasonable give-and-take around a peaceful conference table.'[3]

Thus, Kennan supplied the rationalization and the rhetoric for the policy of 'containing' Soviet power; but by the time he had arrived in Washington, the program was well under way. By February 28, 1946, Navy Secretary Forrestal was asking the Secretary of State for permission to send a naval task force to the Mediterranean 'to buttress Turkish resistance to the seeping advance of Soviet power'.[4] By July, the American build-up was such that Secretary of Commerce Henry A. Wallace could write in a private memorandum to the President:

How do American actions since V-J Day appear to other nations? I mean by actions the concrete things like $13 billion for the

[1] ibid.
[2] Forrestal, op. cit., pp. 135–9.   [3] ibid., p. 135.
[4] Forrestal, p. 141 (the words are Millis's).

War and Navy Departments, the Bikini tests of the atomic bomb and continued production of bombs, the plan to arm Latin America with our weapons, production of B-29's and planned production of B-36's and the effort to secure air bases spread over half the globe from which the other half of the globe can be bombed. I cannot but feel that these actions must make it look to the rest of the world as if we were only paying lip service to peace at the conference table.

These facts rather make it appear either (1) that we are preparing ourselves to win the war which we regard as inevitable or (2) that we are trying to build up a predominance of force to intimidate the rest of mankind. How would it look to us if Russia had the atomic bomb and we did not, if Russia had 10,000 mile bombers and air bases within 1,000 miles of our coastlines, and we did not? . . .[1]

When Wallace raised these questions publicly, the following September, Truman asked for his resignation. Later Truman wrote that while Wallace had urged that American foreign policy be modified in order to allay any reasonable Russian grounds for fear or suspicion, Wallace 'had no specific proposals how this might be accomplished without surrendering to them on every count'.[2]

But in a memorandum to the President, four months previously, Wallace had made a specific proposal that did not seem to involve surrender. First, Wallace noted a primary source of the difficulties experienced with the Soviets. 'We know,' he wrote, 'that much of recent Soviet behaviour which has caused us concern has been the result of their dire economic needs and of their disturbed sense of security. The events of the past few months have thrown the Soviets back to their pre-1939 fears of "capitalist encirclement" and to their erroneous belief that the Western World, including the USA, is invariably and unanimously hostile.'

In light of this situation. Wallace proposed the following:

I think we can disabuse the Soviet mind and strengthen the faith of the Soviets in our sincere devotion to the cause of peace by proving to them that we want to trade with them and to cement our economic

---

[1] Submitted July 23, 1946; cited in Fleming, pp. 420–21.
[2] Truman, op. cit.

relations with them. To do this, it is necessary to talk with them in an understanding way, with full realization of their difficulties and yet with emphasis on the lack of realism in many of their assumptions and conclusions which stand in the way of peaceful world co-operation.[1] [Emphasis added.]

Truman's reaction to the initiative is best expressed in his own words: 'I ignored this letter of Wallace's.'[2]

'I had expressed my policy to Bedell Smith [new Ambassador to Russia],' continued Truman, 'and had suggested the approach he should take to the Kremlin.' Truman's approach, of course, had been outlined by him in the memorandum to Byrnes two months earlier ('Unless Russia is faced with an iron fist and strong language – another war is in the making. . . . I do not think we should play compromise any longer.') Though this policy had been more or less in practice since April 23, 1945, and consistently so since August 18, it had only been presented to the public nine days prior to the Wallace memorandum, that is, on March 5, 1946, at Fulton, Missouri. There Truman listened while Winston Churchill intoned his famous words ('From Stettin in the Baltic to Trieste in the Adriatic an iron curtain has descended across the Continent,') and called for an alliance of English-speaking peoples who, with their combined resources and their naval and airforce bases 'all over the world', could provide 'an overwhelming assurance of security' to the peoples on their side of the curtain. Russian actions since the war had so little prepared the public for this view that there was an uproar against it on both sides of the Atlantic. In America this reaction was so great, that Truman had to deny, falsely, that he had known the contents of Sir Winston's speech.[3]

[1] Truman, ibid.
[2] ibid.
[3] cf. Fleming, pp. 348–57.

CHAPTER IV

Interlude: Greece

IN order to understand the events of the year 1947, which proved to be the decisive turning point of the post-war period, it is necessary to view them against the background of the civil war in Greece. For it was this civil war which provided Truman with the occasion to declare that the world was divided between alternative ways of life and to proclaim an ideological crusade against the un-American way.

When World War II ended in Greece in 1944, the EAM, one of two resistance movements, was in control of nearly the whole country.[1] Among the leaders of EAM were many liberals and social democrats, but the Communists were clearly dominant. Had the issue of Greek sovereignty been left to be contested between this force and the returning Greek Army (controlled by monarchist officers), the outcome would have been an EAM victory. Thus, at the end of 1944, when civil war broke out, the army was at once surrounded and immobilized by the ELAS (military forces of the EAM).[2]

But EAM was not allowed to reap its victory. For aligned against them were not merely the discredited monarchists, but also the British forces. 'The decisive factor in the ensuing struggle for power was the British Army, which entered the country as the Germans left.'[3] Reinforced by two divisions from North Africa, the British mounted an all-out offensive using tanks and planes. On February 12, 1945, the beaten Greeks surrendered and yielded up their arms.

---

[1] Its membership at this time has been estimated at 1½–2 million Greeks. cf. Wm. H. McNeil, *The Greek Dilemma*, 1947.

[2] Smith, op. cit., pp. 232–4.

[3] ibid., cf. also Hugh Seton-Watson, *The Pattern of Communist Revolution*, 1960. 'This was a defeat for the Greek Communists, and it was not due to factors within Greece, but to British intervention: without British action Greece would have had the same régime as Yugoslavia.' p. 217.

One would prefer [writes Howard K. Smith] to be generous to the British and say that they attempted to bolster what middle-way and democratic forces there were in order to create compromise and a basis for democracy. Unfortunately, there seems little evidence to support this, and one is forced to conclude that the British were determined to break EAM and install in power the discredited monarchy and its blindly vengeful rightist supporters.[1]

In the panic of the fighting, Premier Papandreou opened the ranks of the National Guard. 'The whole force of the Nazi "security battalions" enlisted . . .' A British military commission placed monarchist officers in control of the Greek Army which it was to help rebuild, while a British commission assigned to reform the Greek police failed to do so with the result that 'largely it remained the police force that had served the Nazis'. Then, with the left subdued, the British sent troops through the country, followed by the pro-Nazi National Guard to 'pacify' it.[2]

. . . Thousands of young men fled to the mountains; others fled into Yugoslavia for protection. Revulsion abroad to the right-wing excesses was such that Prime Minister Attlee felt constrained to issue a public protest. . . .

With the country thus pacified, elections were held on March 31, 1946, against the objections of Premier Sophoulis, and in the face of a boycott by the left. The monarchists won, and seven months later a referendum restored King George to the throne, making the renewal of civil war 'inevitable'.[3]

The ground on which this civil war gained a footing was the incredible social and economic misery of the Greek people and the failure of the fascist and monarchist rulers to take steps to alleviate it:

One could excuse some of the violence of the Greek right [comments Smith] and the connivance at it by the British had its purpose been to protect against Communist sabotage some

[1] Smith, loc. cit.
[2] ibid., pp. 234–5.
[3] ibid., p. 235.

plan or project for rebuilding and actually pacifying the nation. But the new government, led by the monarchist Tsaldaris, apparently had no plans for reconstruction whatsoever.

In the first three post-war years the British poured $760 million worth of supplies into Greece, but 'no stone was laid atop another to repair the dreadful damage of war'. While '75 per cent of all Greek children were suffering from malnutrition', the governments fostered by the British placed 'all tax burdens on the poor' and one government by selling Greece's gold reserves to private buyers at the rate of 500,000 gold sovereigns a month depleted Greek capital by huge amounts. 'UNRRA reckoned that more wealth was leaving the country at the time than UNRRA was bringing in to save the Greek people from starvation.'[1]

'Half the Tsaldaris Government's expenditures was on army and police, only six per cent on reconstruction.'[2] Typical of this government's methods was its treatment of the labor unions:

> ... At the end of the war, union elections were held throughout Greece under the watchful eyes of British trade-union leaders. Leftists, with the Communists in the lead, swept the board. On assuming power, the royalist government removed the whole elected administration and set up an executive for the Greek Confederation of Labor with sixteen hand-picked rightists dominating five leftists and with Fotios Makris, a union official of the wartime quisling government, as chief. The five leftists rejected their appointments. With its organization crippled, labor's position was miserable. . . . There are few modern parallels for government this bad.[3]

This was the Greece Truman described to Congress in his 'Doctrine' speech in March 1947 as one of the 'free peoples' that it 'must be the policy of the United States to support'. 'Greece and Turkey,' he later wrote, 'were still free countries' at this time, 'being challenged by Communist threats both from within and without.[4]

---

[1] ibid., pp. 227–8.   [2] ibid., p. 236.   [3] ibid., p. 236.
[4] Foreign aid for the rebels was, of course, 'an uncontested fact'. Both Yugoslavia and Bulgaria were offering them supplies and the safety of their territory 'whenever pinched by a Greek Government offensive'. This was considerably

These free peoples were now engaged in a valiant struggle to preserve their liberties and their independence.'[1]

With this background in view, it becomes possible to assess the critical events of 1946-7 which surrounded the promulgation of the Truman Doctrine and the formation of two hostile world camps.

[1] Truman, *Memoirs*, II, p. 101.

less aid, however, than that given by the British to the rightists. Moreover, the rebels had widespread popular support. When the Greek Communist Vafiades (later purged as a 'Titoist') launched his rebellion in the autumn of 1946, *Time* estimated his forces at 2,500. By 1948, though the Greek Government claimed to have killed or captured many times that number, the E L A S was estimated to have 25,000 troops or ten times the original number. – Smith, pp. 236-7.

CHAPTER V

The Cold War Begins

AFTER the dissolution of the wartime alliance, there remained only one possible bulwark against the imminence of a dangerous 'world split'; that bulwark was the nascent United Nations. The destructions of the war had left an extraordinary imbalance in the world's industrial power structure. Three-quarters of the world's invested capital and two-thirds of its industrial capacity were concentrated inside one country, the United States; the rest was shared over the other 95 per cent of the earth's inhabited surface. 'One nation had acquired a near monopoly on [the] all-important factor for sustaining life.'[1] It was the United States, therefore, that was faced with the decision which it alone could make: whether to use its industrial capacity to promote international reconstruction through an international agency, thus laying the groundwork for a stable world order – or whether to use its capacity as an instrument of power-politics, that is, to establish an American hegemony over the existing international power structure, to reconstruct one power center at the expense of others and in that way to promote American political and economic ends. This decision had already been taken by 1946.[2]

The United Nations Relief and Rehabilitation Administration had been set up in 1943 to provide aid in food and goods to populations which might otherwise have starved. It was financed by the United States and administered through the United Nations. Fiorello La Guardia, former New Deal mayor of New York who administered

[1] Smith, op. cit., p. 92.
[2] It had been advocated by Harriman in his April 1945 cables: 'I thus regretfully come to the conclusion that we should be guided ... by the policy of taking care of our Western Allies and other areas under our responsibility first, allocating to Russia what may be left.' By 1946, Russia was not to receive anything; Washington maintained 'steady opposition to Soviet reparation demands, while at the same time ignoring Moscow's specific request for a major loan'. – Wm. A. Williams, *American–Russian Relations*, 1952, p. 278.

the program, told the United Nations General Assembly in 1946 that unless relief of this kind continued, there would be widespread starvation. He proposed to set up a Food Fund to carry on the work of UNRRA (which had been scheduled for completion by 1947 – though its work proved to be far from done) and this was warmly supported by the other representatives, except the American and British delegations.

To the dismay of the Assembly, the British and Americans recommended instead that individual governments and international organizations give assistance to those countries which they saw fit to help. America and Britain turned down every amended proposal which was suggested and announced that they would refuse to accept any majority vote on the subject that did not meet their point of view. In other words, any further relief was to be given under conditions of strict political discrimination.[1]

La Guardia was horrified. 'Does the Government of the United States,' he exclaimed, 'intend to adopt a policy which will make innocent men and women suffer because of the political situation which makes their Government unacceptable to the United States ? . . . Each rich nation will choose the recipient and make its own conditions. That's plain, ordinary, old-time power politics that has produced war after war.'[2]

The UNRRA case illustrates how ready the new United States leadership was to abandon far-sighted wartime policies. Had the new Administration, in fact, continued to pursue the Roosevelt course of treating nations as equals,[3] of seeking to create and strengthen truly international agencies, they might have had a more credible case in

[1] Ingram, op. cit., pp. 56–7.
[2] Ingram, ibid. It should be noted that some of UNRRA's work was carried on by agencies like UNICEF, which were truly international and thrived. The United States generously gave $15 million to UNICEF. It is just this persistence of some aspects of the Roosevelt program that has misled historical commentators and prevented them from seeing that the main lines had been altered. Moreover, 'It is a highly important key to the Cold War that with UNRRA – that is, aid with no strings tied, internationally administered – American observers were for the first time allowed free run inside Soviet Russia.' – Smith, op. cit., p. 94.
[3] Not even England escaped America's 'neo-imperialism'. In 1946 the United States offered England a loan whose discriminatory terms brought her 'to her knees'. Robert Boothby, a Tory MP, complained at the time: 'Comparable terms have never hitherto been imposed on a country that has not been defeated in war. . . .' – Smith, op. cit., p. 88.

disclaiming, as they did,[1] all responsibility for the failure to lay the foundations for international order in the post-war world. But this UNRRA case proved to be only the beginning of a consistent United States pattern of by-passing international agencies and orienting key global programs from the standpoint of its own narrow national interest.[2]

The Soviet veto has long been held up as the force that single-handedly rendered the United Nations ineffective in these years, but this is not borne out by the record. Of forty uses of the veto by the Russians through 1949, twenty-two were on membership applications, an aftermath of the Argentine affair and the decision of the United States to marshal bloc majorities instead of working towards compromise in terms of existing relations of power. The Soviet veto only 'was effective in excluding a committee of inquiry into the change of régime in Czechoslovakia. In all other cases it was by-passed in one way or another, so far as practical results are concerned'.[3]

Unlike the Soviet Union, the United States controlled the voting majority in the United Nations and thus could be confident in the basic direction of its policies.[4] The United States' failure to transfer some of the vast power that it had accumulated to the authority of the United Nations can have only one explanation. In the classic

[1] On March 17, 1948, Truman declared to Congress that 'one nation' and one nation alone had prevented the establishment of a 'just and honorable peace'. – Fleming, op. cit., p. 507 n.

[2] The Korean 'police action' is the exception that proves the rule. The two key decisions – to go into the war and to unify Korea by force – were taken unilaterally by the United States first, the United Nations being faced in both cases with a *fait accompli*. The lack of international support for the United States dominated and directed action is easily seen in the composition of the United Nations forces. cf. discussion of Korea, p. 114 and p. 123 n.4 below.

[3] John Maclaurin, *United Nations and Power Politics* 1951.

[4] 'In the years 1946–53 the General Assembly adopted over 800 resolutions. The United States was defeated in less than 3 per cent – and in no case where important security interests were involved. In these eight years only two resolutions supported by us failed of adoption.' – E. Gross in *Foreign Policy Bulletin*, September 15, 1954. In these years, the dictatorships of Nicaragua, Haiti, Paraguay, Honduras, Thailand, Taiwan, Venezuela, the Dominican Republic, Turkey, Greece and Peru voted with the US, 90 per cent of the time or more on non-colonial political questions. On the other hand, countries like Israel voted with the US only 57 per cent of the time while India voted with the US only 33 per cent – Riggs, *Politics in the UN*, 1958. For an account of American dominance in the UN in later years, see Conor Cruise O'Brien's *To Katanga and Back*, 1962.

manner of strong nation states America wanted that power, to exercise it by means and for purposes as she saw fit. Thus when it was within her ability to strengthen and effectively create a sorely needed international machinery, the United States chose to preserve the traditional power structure of nation states, and to enjoy her newly achieved predominance (supplanting Britain, Germany and Japan)[1] even if it meant aborting or rendering ineffectual the United Nations.

In the Fall of 1946, there had been some hopeful signs that the growing breach between East and West might still be healed. The peace treaties with the Nazi satellites (Italy, Bulgaria, Finland, Hungary and Rumania) had been agreed upon and signed, and for a few weeks the feeling of 'peace' was really in the air. The United States had ended a bone of contention by returning six hundred Danubian barges and ships to their Danubian owners (they had been impounded in Germany) while Bulgarian and Rumanian officials made statements welcoming American friendship and capital, and the United States and Czechoslovakia patched up their recently strained relations. 'The sun of peace is rising at last,' commented British Foreign Secretary Bevin in New York.[2]

Then, in the last days of January 1947, the worst snowstorm since 1894 descended on Britain and paralyzed her. Within four months, it was demonstrated to the world that where once the seat of mighty empire had stood, only a gaping power vacuum remained, so financially ruined as to be incapable of supporting army or navy,[3] the necessary instruments of her will. As a result, India, Burma, Palestine were cast loose from British rule (Palestine to United Nations administration); South Africa, Guatemala, Argentina, Iraq and Egypt challenged the shell of English power in one way or another without suffering reprisal.

This crisis led Britain to inform the United States on February 24, that she could no longer pay for her troops in Greece or continue aid to Turkey. On March 12, 1947, Truman went before Congress to announce the Truman Doctrine and to seek military and economic aid for the two countries, especially Greece where civil war was still

---

[1] For discussion of this predominance and the nature and use of this power, cf. pp. 86 et seq. below.

[2] Smith, op. cit., pp. 16–18; Fleming, pp. 429–30.

[3] 'For a short period at the end of 1947 it was down to a total active strength of one cruiser and four destroyers.' – Smith, p. 28.

raging. However, instead of proposing to assist in solving the genuine social and economic crisis of Greece, President Truman used the occasion of Britain's withdrawal to launch an ideological crusade against totalitarian régimes. Truman declared that every nation was faced with a choice between alternative ways of life.

> One way of life is based upon the will of the majority, and is distinguished by free institutions, representative government, free elections, guarantees of individual liberty, freedom of speech and religion and freedom from political repression.
>
> The second way of life is based upon the will of a minority forcibly imposed upon the majority. It relies upon terror and oppression, a controlled press and radio, fixed elections, and the suppression of personal freedoms. . . .

Taken in the abstract, the conflict of values expressed here is one of the most critical that political man has to face. In the context of the world of 1947, however, the statement was a vast oversimplification of a very complex set of choices in a very complex world system. In the context of the specific situation in Greece,[1] the best that could be said of Truman's antithesis was that it was irrelevant. Greece under Tsaldaris was quite obviously a totalitarian régime, and United States economic and military aid was clearly aid to totalitarian forces.[2]

This widely noted gap between Truman's rhetoric and the concrete reality at hand was hardly surprising since the Doctrine had been in Truman's mind a long time before it was announced. As early as the London Conference of Foreign Ministers in September 1945, he had decided to proclaim the existence of a world division and the United States' determination to crusade against one of the two parties. 'He made up his mind then that, when a fitting opportunity arose and one which Congress and the people would recognize as such, he would proclaim the new doctrine,' wrote Arthur Krock, the informed Washington columnist of the New York *Times*.[3] 'On several occasions he thought the time had come, but

[1] In Turkey as well, which was a dictatorship.

[2] The other key point in Truman's address, concern for the independence of Greece, can hardly be squared with the decision to grant the aid bilaterally, to by-pass the United Nations, see discussion below.

[3] New York *Times*, March 23, 1947, cited in Fleming.

some of his important advisors talked him out of it.' When the British informed the United States that they were withdrawing from Greece, a situation arrived which Truman found suited to his 'long held purpose', and Clark Clifford was set to drafting 'the global anti-Communist policy'.[1]

Such was the genesis of perhaps the major document in America's cold war offensive: an ideology waiting for a set of facts (and as it happened, the wrong facts) to confirm it. Small wonder that the scholarly Kennan was distraught at this version of containment.

The Truman Doctrine, of course, was more than mere rhetoric; it also postulated a *modus operandi* which embodied an important policy decision, namely, *to by-pass the United Nations.*

Four months earlier, the Food and Agriculture Organization (FAO) of the United Nations's Economic and Social Council had produced a complete plan for Greek reconstruction, which would not have been subject to any veto, because no veto existed in the Council. Moreover, the plan would not have precluded the sending of military aid to the country while it was still unable to stabilize itself under the reconstruction program.

But the Truman Administration was not interested in the United Nations at this point. Instead of transferring what had been a British sphere of influence into the hands of the United Nations, thereby extending the authority of the organization and acting to establish a new order in international affairs, the United States chose to *replace* Britain as a national power in that area.

The repercussions of this action were immediate and profound. On March 10, the Moscow Conference of Foreign Ministers had opened negotiations on the major problems confronting the two great powers. According to W. W. Rostow, Director of the State Department's Policy Planning Staff in the Kennedy and Johnson Administrations and from 1947 to 1949 special assistant to the Executive Secretary of the Economic Commission for Europe, the failure of this conference was the irreversible turning point in post-war relations with the Soviet Union. Wrote Rostow:

> The United States went to the Moscow meetings prepared with a range of clear detailed negotiating positions in order to establish

[1] cf. Fleming's long and important discussion of the Doctrine, pp. 433-76.

whether Soviet objectives were compatible with American
interests on the questions of German unity, German disarmament, and the end of the Austrian occupation.[1]

The delegation went 'prepared to stretch to the limit to meet legitimate Russian security interests in the structure of Germany and
Europe' in a mood 'of searching flexibility' and 'mature realization
of the consequence of failure in Moscow: a split Germany and
Europe the reunification of which was difficult if not impossible to
perceive through the mists of a dangerous and tense future'.

Here then was the key post-war moment, an effort by the
United States to go all out in a spirit of compromise to reach an
accord with the Soviets. Here, if at any time, the 'split' was preventable. But, alas, 'the position taken by the Soviet negotiators was
thoroughly unambiguous: Stalin refused to move toward a defin-
itive settlement in Europe'. Thus defeated in their carefully planned
move to prevent the tragic inception of the cold war, 'the Americans
came home from Moscow firm in the conclusion that the United
States should never again negotiate from a base of weakness'.
Reports of Europe's benighted economic condition then converged
'with the conclusions about Stalin's attitude and intentions drawn
from the Moscow Conference [to] set the stage for the Marshall
Plan'.[2]

The Marshall Plan, then, was conceived as a 'counter-offensive'
(Rostow's term) to the Soviet Union's moves in East Europe and as
a reaction to Stalin's decision, registered at the Moscow Conference,
to rebuff all gestures of compromise looking toward settlement of
the problems dividing Europe. In line with this partisan conception,
the Marshall Plan by-passed the United Nations Economic Commission for Europe which was composed of every European state
and gave no veto right to its members:

> . . . there was even in being an organization dedicated to European
> economic co-operation – the Economic Commission for Europe –
> *The ECE was, however, an organization of the United Nations,*

[1] *The US in the World Arena*, p. 208.
[2] ibid., pp. 208–9; 'On April 29, the day after his report to the nation on the
failure of the Moscow Conference, Secretary Marshall instructed the Policy
Planning Staff to prepare a general plan for American aid in the reconstruction
of *Western* Europe.' [Emphasis added]. – Rostow, pp. 209–10.

with Soviet and Eastern European countries as members. Its very existence posed a basic question. Should an effort be made to embrace all of Europe in a new enterprise of reconstruction, or should the lesson of the Moscow Conference be read as indicating that the only realistic alternative for the West was to accept the split and to strengthen the area still outside Stalin's grasp ?[1] [Emphasis added.]

The decision, of course, was to 'accept the split' and in effect to intensify it.[2] Central to Rostow's argument in placing the onus for this split on the Soviet Union, was his contention that at the Moscow Conference a serious and well planned United States gesture of compromise was met with intransigence. The United States response to this Soviet attitude was to adopt a cold war posture and launch a counter-offensive.

Given the circumstances in which Rostow's book was written, his thesis reflects apparently the then prevailing view within the State Department. The difficulty with this version of events is that it fails to take into account the fact that *it was precisely two days after the start of the Moscow Conference that Truman 'shouted' his 'war-cry'*[3] *of March 12 !* Howard K. Smith's eyewitness report records the catastrophic effect of the Truman Doctrine speech on the negotiations :

> Still in the glow of the settlement on the satellite peace treaties in New York two months before [the Russians] were determined to be charming, amiable hosts. Vishinsky, the official welcomer, wrung the hand of John Foster Dulles before photographers as though he were a visiting delegate to the League of Proletarian Advocates and not a Wall Street Fascist Beast. . . .

[1] ibid.
[2] On May 8, in a speech characterized by Truman as 'the prologue to the Marshall Plan'. Dean Acheson made clear the philosophy behind the proposal and its consistency with post-war US programs: 'These measures of relief and reconstruction have been only in part suggested by humanitarianism. Your Congress has authorized and your Government is carrying out, a policy of relief and reconstruction today chiefly as a matter of national self-interest. . . . *Free peoples who are seeking to preserve their independence and democratic institutions and human freedoms against totalitarian pressures, either internal or external, will receive top priority for American aid.*' [Emphasis in original] cited in Ingram op. cit., pp. 58–9.
[3] The phrase is from Louis J. Halle, *American Foreign Policy*, 1960, pp. 296–7. Halle was a State Department official.

In the first days of the conference Soviet press reports on it were thorough and free from their customary acid asides on Western motives. Molotov proved uncommonly conciliatory in the opening discussion on rules of procedure and yielded his own suggestions first to those of Marshall, then to those of Bevin.

The Russians undoubtedly assumed that all was well and that things would go according to prescription. They had learned the formula for procedure from the satellite negotiations and were prepared to follow it; but this time with more ease, for they knew the ropes: two years of haggling and pressuring until deadlock was reached, then settlement on that basis.

Stalin even told Marshall in the course of the conference that 'these were only the first skirmishes and brushes of reconnaissance forces. . . . After people exhausted themselves in dispute, they then recognized the necessity of compromise. . . . That compromises were possible on all main questions. . . . It was necessary to have patience and not become pessimistic. . . .' But patience was given no chance to do its work.

Right on top of the conference, two days after it opened, burst the bombshell of the Truman Doctrine. President Truman said, 'nearly every nation must choose between' the two worlds; it sounded like an ultimatum to the rest of Europe to be with us or to be counted against us. That wiped the smiles off the Russians' faces. While America prepared to move into Greece, Russia proceeded to button up Hungary, arresting democratic leaders to the accompaniment of angry diplomatic protests from the West.
. . . the four men sat down in a world in turmoil and tried to carry on as though it all had nothing to do with their conference. It was impossible.[1]

From this impasse Marshall returned to America with plans for strengthening the Western bargaining position, since, in the words of Rostow, 'it was useless to test Soviet intentions before self-evident Western strength and the development of alternatives to Soviet agreement had narrowed the realistic choices open to Moscow to a range of solutions compatible with the American interest.'

[1] Smith, op. cit., pp. 118–23.

In fact, however, there remained a 'schism' in the State Department 'in attitudes toward Eastern European and Soviet participation' in the projected Marshall Plan. Partly as a result of this schism, no official decision was taken to exclude the Communist and other East European states. Special care, moreover, was taken to provide the plan with a rhetoric which did not betray the more partisan intentions reflected in its structure. In his famous June 5 speech announcing the initiative, Secretary of State Marshall declared: 'Our policy is directed not against any country or doctrine but against hunger, poverty, desperation and chaos.'

For their part, the Soviets took a wait-and-see attitude and went so far as to allow Czechoslovakia, Poland and Yugoslavia to reach out 'toward Marshall's initiative and to the West'.[1]

Under the terms of the Marshall proposal, the European powers were to draw up their own program for European recovery, which the United States (a Republican Congress willing) would then finance. For the purpose of drawing up such a plan, the European powers met in the summer of 1947 in Paris. The Soviets were invited by the British but according to Rostow, 'Bevin and the British Foreign Office [as well as some American officials] were fearful that Stalin would agree and took no pains to create a hospitable atmosphere at Paris for Molotov'.[2]

Molotov arrived at the conference with a contingent of 89 economic experts and advisers. The Soviets, whose repeated three year request for a $6 billion credit from the United States had been 'lost' in Washington,[3] were cautious in their pre-conference statement to the British representative in Moscow.[4]

In the fateful two days that Molotov remained in Paris, he was presented with a plan drawn up by Bevin and Bidault based on the principle of integrating national economies. But 'integration in a single plan means that each nation must produce what it produces best. To Mr Molotov this looked like asking the Eastern countries to jettison their various national "plans" to industrialize, and to become instead the agricultural granary of the West; that would be

---

[1] Rostow, op. cit., p. 212.

[2] ibid., p. 211. One fear was that if the Russians accepted it, the US Congress would not finance it.

[3] Williams, op. cit., pp. 278-9.

[4] Ingram, op cit., p. 60.

the ideal integration. Tied to an industrial nation, an agricultural nation always becomes the weak dependent sister.'[1]

Molotov rejected the plan and walked out of the conference in a gesture of open hostility which stunned those who had seen the Marshall proposal, however mistakenly, as a step toward the restoration of European unity. The manner and nature of his rejection were characteristic of Soviet diplomacy in the period that followed:

> . . . – breaking off talks in a peeve, giving no explantaion save an acid, jargon-ridden attack on America that made little sense, leaping to the fantastic conclusion that the plan was a pattern for aggressive war against Russia and ordering Communists everywhere to sabotage the plan to the point of subverting their governments – . . .[2]

From the Soviet point of view, the challenge which the Marshall 'counter-offensive' presented to their interests was serious. It must be remembered that 'Eastern Europe in the early summer of 1947 had by no means reached full satellite status. A democratic government existed in Prague; in Warsaw all manner of Polish nationalists, inside and outside the Communist Party, had not yet been brought to heel; in Yugoslavia, unknown to the West. Tito . . . was stirring the Bulgarian and Hungarian Communists with ideas about a Balkan Communist alliance, quasi-independent of Moscow'.[3] The Soviet leaders had only to review the events of the previous spring in Western Europe to grasp the full meaning of Rostow's use of the adjective 'offensive' in connection with the Marshall initiative. For against the background of Europe's economic crisis, United States failure to channel its aid through international organizations had carried obvious implications. The crisis was 'above all a dollar crisis. The goods and supplies the world most wanted – wheat, meat, coal, steel, machinery – were only to be found in the Western Hemisphere and as the nations bought them eagerly, their dollars drained away . . . by the middle of the summer it was clear that either the United States would have to provide more dollars or the Western European nations would cease to be able to buy at all'.[4]

[1] Smith, p. 98.
[2] ibid., p. 99.
[3] Rostow p.212.
[4] Barbara Ward, *The West at Bay*, 1948, pp. 6–7.

In France, the socialist Premier Ramadier warned the country that the time would come when 'each credit will be dictated by political realities. A little of our independence is departing from us with each loan we obtain'. He proceeded to appeal to America for another credit.[1] In May 1947 Ramadier dismissed the Communists from his cabinet. The same thing happened in Italy. Soviet strategists would have been quick to note that an offer of Marshall Aid might tempt the non-Communist members of the ruling coalition in Czechoslovakia, for instance, to follow the French and Italian examples (although this was unlikely). In any case, the political significance of American economic power could not be ignored.

On July 2, Molotov left the Paris Conference; on July 10, a trade agreement was concluded between the Soviet Union and Bulgaria, on July 11 with Czechoslovakia, on July 14 with Hungary, on July 25 with Yugoslavia, on August 4 with Poland and on August 26 with Rumania.[2] This was an important step in the direction of the economic consolidation of East Europe; the political division of the continent came next.

In November, the newly activated Cominform, consisting of the Communist Parties of East Europe, Italy and France, issued a statement which in less veiled terms reiterated the substance of the Truman Doctrine, albeit from the other side of the curtain:

... Two opposite political lines have formed: On the one side the policy of the USSR and democratic countries directed toward undermining imperialism and strengthening democracy, on the other side is the policy of the USA and England directed toward strengthening imperialism and strangling democracy. ...

The Truman–Marshall plan is only a constituent part, the European section of the general plan of world expansionist policy carried on by the United States in all parts of the world. ...[3]

With the issuance of the Cominform statement, the lines for the cold war were clearly drawn. The Communist parties of Europe began a campaign to oppose the Marshall Plan by all means avail-

[1] Smith, op. cit., p. 156.
[2] Ingram, op. cit., pp. 63–4.
[3] cited in Schuman, *Russia Since 1917*, 1957, pp. 362–3.

able to them. The effect was to lend substance to fears of sabotage and subversion, to oppose a plan on which the economic revival of West Europe depended and thus to help thrust political power into the hands of the right wing everywhere. The decisive expression of these changes in the state of affairs and the shape of power was the Czechoslovakian *coup* in February 1948.

The very bloodlessness of this *coup* – performed without an execution, and with only a few arrests, and actively opposed neither by Foreign Minister Masyryk nor President Benes, the two most respected and powerful democrats in the country – ought to have indicated to the West that the *coup* was not necessarily a pattern for the rest of Europe, since no takeover there could have been carried out without a civil war. This consideration did not prevail, however, and the Communist seizure of power served to congeal those fears and attitudes which have dominated thinking in the West ever since. For the source of this reaction in Europe one has only to turn to the power vacuum created by the defeat of Germany and the collapse of the United Kingdom.

For the first time since the rise of the Bolsheviks, the Russians had emerged into Europe. 'Russian troops were garrisoned at the outskirts of Hamburg, once the greatest continental port, not a long cannon-shot from the Western seas.'

No nation ever held such extensive sway over Europe with the consent of the other great powers. Russia had directly annexed an area in Europe of about 250,000 square miles – an area larger than that of France, Switzerland, Holland, Belgium and Denmark together. Eight other Eastern European countries and parts of two more had become her satellites.[1]

This was not any Russia, which had extended itself so greatly, moreover, it was Stalinist Russia, Russia of the purges and the forced labor camps, Russia which had absorbed the Baltic states.

Thus poised over a prostrate continent with no other counterbalancing European power in sight, in the wake of massive strikes led by native Communist parties in France and Italy, the Soviets subverted the democratically elected, pro-Soviet Government of the

[1] Smith, op. cit., p. 38.

one central European state which had become the symbol of the whole disastrous slide into World War II.

If ever a symbol of appeasement existed, it was the sellout of Czechoslovakia by the Western powers at the Munich Conference in 1938. If ever there could be a psychological rallying point for the creation of a new European Army in the post-war years, it was a new blow against that unfortunate people. No extenuations, no careful analysis of the falseness of analogies between 1948 and ten years before, could erase, in the minds of the public, the seemingly incontrovertible image of history repeating itself.

The power of this event can perhaps be gauged by the reaction in Scandinavia. There, a formidable movement towards unification and neutralism had been growing. Denmark, Norway and Sweden had joined the Marshall Plan for compelling economic reasons. But when a 'Western Union' conference was held in Brussels (the plan had been announced in January 1948 by Bevin) they demurred, publicly declaring that they would not participate in a scheme condemned by Russia.

In Sweden, Dr Ernst Wigforss, the Minister of Finance, shocked Americans by a public statement saying that the danger in the cold war was not a Russian act of aggression so much as a possible forestalling attack by the United States. Then came the Czech *coup*.

The event sent a shudder through all Scandinavia. Almost overnight the mood of amicability toward Russia collapsed in all three countries. Laborite Prime Minister Gerhardsen of Norway – once considered a rabid Red himself – launched a bitter attack on Norwegian Communists in the Storting. On May Day 1948, the Swedish Socialist Premier, Erlander, followed this up. 'The *coup* in Czechoslovakia,' he said, 'was a testing time not only for Prague, but also for Stockholm.' It is a sign of the changing pressures of the times that the Danish upper house of Parliament, the Landsting, which had not held a foreign-policy debate for over a hundred years, held one after the Czech *coup*. A Copenhagen radio broadcast actually instructed citizens to report to the nearest police station any suspicious moves that might indicate an attempted seizure of power.[1]

[1] Smith, op. cit., p. 185.

Despite long-standing policies of pacifism and neutrality, 'a bill before the Swedish parliament to reduce military estimates was replaced by one asking for a fifty per cent increase in planes and a one hundred per cent increase in personnel for the air force.' Norway and Denmark followed suit, and in addition joined Nato when it was formed (Sweden maintaining her neutrality to give Russia no excuse for Sovietizing Finland).

Thus appearing as a verification of the most apocalyptic prophecies of those who feared and hated Soviet power, the *coup* in Czechoslovakia strengthened the hand of every die-hard anti-Bolshevik and extreme nationalist in the Western camp. In the wake of this event, the liberal-left entered into an alliance with the reactionary right from which neither it, nor the Western World has yet recovered. Russian aggression, though in areas behind the Iron Curtain, served to underwrite every catastrophic step taken in the West toward massive rearmament and to make possible the ascendancy of political figures like Dulles and Adenauer.

With the sides now clearly formed, the cleavage into armed military camps was merely a question of time, since the Soviets had accomplished for the West its chief and most difficult task: the marshalling of public opinion.[1] Even so, rearmament in countries like Britain proved a difficult and economically straining proposition. In the East, without the enormous over-productive capacity of the United States, it was disastrous. Forced to support a 1·6 million man army for Stalin's defenses, the hitherto impressive economic advance of East Europe[2] was halted and a period of intense hardship and Stalinist construction began, resulting in the revolts of 1956.

Before Nato, and before the rearming of East Europe, however, an event occurred which stripped the veil from some of the pretenses under which this more intensified phase of the cold war was to be waged. In June 1948, the great schism between Tito and Stalin occurred, and was followed by a vast purging of Titoist heretics in the Communist Parties of East Europe.

For the East, these events refuted Moscow's claims that its actions

---

[1] It is questionable whether even the Marshall Plan would have been passed by Congress without the impetus given by the Czech *coup*.

[2] East Europe, 'which lost twice as many lives and suffered almost twice as much damage in the war' as did West Europe, passed pre-war production levels first in the post-war period. – Smith, op. cit., p. 282; cf. also pp. 332–5.

were purely defensive in the interests of world socialism. The purging of men like Gomulka and the hundreds of thousands of Communist Party members accused of Titoism was nothing more than a purging of all politically effective nationalist elements in the now satellite nations. If the Soviets had been willing to tolerate a measure of independence and national development during the less hostile times of 1945–8, their answer to Western toughness was to put the defense of Russia above all other ends, even if it meant the brutal subjection of their own Communist allies.

On the other hand, the Titoist heresy and the responses it elicited, undercut, at the outset, the main justification for the Western military build-up, the creation of Nato and the rearming of the German war machine. For the failure of the Red Army or of any of the satellite armies to invade the renegade state ('I will shake my little finger – there will be no more Tito. Tito will fall.' Stalin had said) could mean only one of two things. Either the Soviets were not willing to invade a country presenting a 'strong national front – or, *already existing American military power*, was sufficient to deter Stalin from any armed aggression in Europe.[1]

Thus *before* Nato, *before* Western and West German rearmament, *before* the spiralling and debilitating arms race had seized hold of Europe, Communist power was adequately and effectively 'contained' by the greater and more vastly extended power of the USA. And this, it may be noted, was fully realized by American strate-

---

[1] Recently we have been provided with much more evidence that Stalin's conservatism would have prevented him from any armed agression in Europe. Six days after the Czech *coup*, Milovan Djilas was in the Kremlin witnessing the following conversation: 'Stalin then turned to the uprising in Greece: "The uprising in Greece will have to fold up. . . . Do you believe" – he turned to Kardelj [Vice-Premier of Yugoslavia] – "in the success of the uprising in Greece?"

'Kardelj replied, "If foreign intervention does not grow, and if serious political and military errors are not made."

'Stalin went on, without paying attention to Kardelj's opinion: "If, if! No, they have no prospect of success at all. What do you think that Great Britain and the United States – the United States, the most powerful state in the world – will permit you to break their line of communication in the Mediterranean? Nonsense. And we have no navy. The uprising in Greece must be stopped, and as quickly as possible." ' – *Conversations with Stalin*, 1962, p. 164. The Berlin Blockade, which lasted from June 1948 until May 1949 would have tended to confirm the above estimates. From the first the Russians limited their objectives and their means. They did not attempt to interfere with the airlift and they lifted the Blockade just at the time that the airlift would have ceased to be feasible.

gists, indeed by the very man who was the foremost proponent of a rearmed and re-militarized world, who went so far as to attempt to revive the military will of atom-blasted Japan. In March 1949, John Foster Dulles declared:

So far as it is humanly possible to judge, the Soviet Government, under conditions now prevailing does not contemplate the use of war as an instrument of its national policy. I do not know any responsible official, military or civilian, in this Government or any Government who believes that the Soviet Government now plans conquest by open military aggression.[1]

[1] Schuman, *Russia Since 1917*, 1957, p. 394; Dulles' statement is corroborated by more than half a dozen estimates of American leaders from 1946 to 1949 cited in the *Forrestal Diaries* (Forrestal was appointed Secretary of Defense in 1947): On June 10, 1946, Forrestal himself wrote that he thought the Russians 'would not move this summer – in fact, at any time'. On August 3, 1948, two months after the Berlin Blockade had begun, General Walter Bedell Smith, Ambassador to the Soviet Union, reported to the War Council his impression 'that the Russians do not want war'. As late as December 1950, six months after the start of the Korean War, it was reported that Admiral Alan G. Kirk, who replaced Smith as envoy to Moscow '. . . sees no signs in Moscow that Russia expects war now. . . . Currently Admiral Kirk detects none of the tell-tale signs of war that the experts watch for. For example, Soviet Army units are remaining at peacetime strength. No over-age classes are being called up. No extraordinary movements of troops or supplies have been detected. There is no drive in Russia to build bomb shelters or to restrict civilian consumption of critical materials. . . .' *US News and World Report*. And in a lecture at the Graduate Institute of International Studies in Geneva in May 1965, George Kennan, in essence, repeated Dulles' statement: 'It was perfectly clear to anyone with even a rudimentary knowledge of the Russia of that day [i.e. during the early cold war period] that the Soviet leaders had no intention of attempting to advance their cause by launching military attacks with their own armed forces across frontiers.'

CHAPTER VI

Retrospect

THE foregoing pages serve to make clear certain important facts that have been largely overlooked by most Western accounts of the cold war's origins. In particular, they show that as of April 23, 1945, the Russians found themselves faced with a new and unfriendly American leadership prepared to abandon the wartime coalition and to employ overt pressures against their former allies as soon as the war was actually over. In addition, the Russians could not fail to realize quickly that this new American leadership did not intend to offer aid to the Soviet reconstruction program, and that they would even go so far as to actively resist attempts to take, in reparations, the materials which the Soviets considered necessary to their task of rebuilding.

During this and the immediately preceding period, moreover, the Russian rulers witnessed an expansion of American power on a prodigious scale.[1] As a result of American victory in the war and the terms of the peace, the new areas of American dominance were 7,000 miles from her borders and included the strongest Asiatic power, Japan, and the source of power of the potentially strongest European nation, Germany. Since 1942, America had displaced Britain as ruler of the seas, including 'that most British of all waters',

[1] Some aspects of this power expansion certainly had an immediate and important post-war impact on Soviet thinking: 'In July 1945 President Truman . . . declared emphatically that the United States would not take one inch of additional territory as a result of the part she had played in winning the victory. An uproar arose in the Congress, and from American Army and Navy leaders. They protested that the United States must retain as her exclusive property all the strategic bases in the Pacific which American forces had captured. The President thereupon let it be known that he had not meant precisely what he had said. . . . The effect of these incidents was much more far-reaching than has generally been recognized. Many of these Pacific bases lay within a short distance of the Soviet Union's Siberian provinces. The United States' claim for permanent possession could only create deep-rooted suspicion on the part of the Soviet Government.' – Sumner Welles, op. cit., p. 365.

the east Mediterranean. By 1949, America was said to have a lien on some four hundred world-wide naval and air bases. This meant, 'that any empire linked to its motherland by water exists on American sufferance, as it did last century on British sufferance – a fact that need never be expressed to have a profound influence on its policies'. Pacts to standardize arms tied virtually the whole of North and South America to the United States. (The same arrangement was soon made with Western Europe.) This meant that it was nearly impossible for the attached nations either to enter or to stay out of war without the consent of the United States.

Partly as a consequence of the war and partly as a consequence of American initiatives, American economic penetration of the world reached tremendous proportions in the post-war period.[1] To mention but one area, America came to own concessions 'on nearly half the wealth of the Middle East', the vital land bridge of three continents. By grants and loans, 'the economic veins of a large part of the world [became] connected to America's pumping industrial and agricultural heart'. Many of the countries depended on America not only for aid, without which they would be worse off, but 'for naked survival'. 'By a decision on whatever grounds to reduce or cut off the flow, America could stop factories, cause riots and upheaval, break governments.'[2]

While United States leaders were prudent enough to limit their objectives in this period (and thus to avoid unnecessary reactions to their dominance) they were by no means inhibited about capitalizing on the power at their disposal, when they felt the necessity to do so. A case in point was the Italian election of 1948. This was the first post-war election in Italy and the Communist–Socialist bloc was given an 'even chance' by Western observers to win a 51 per cent majority. When the votes were in, the pro-Western Christian Democrats had 53 per cent of the ballots, a stunning victory, while the pro-Communist bloc polled but 30 per cent. 'The most important factor in the turning of the tide' [wrote Howard K. Smith] 'was the frank, open entrance of America into the campaign.'

[1] America's large economic expansion continued throughout the cold war. In 1950 total direct foreign assets of American corporations amounted to $11·8 billion. 'By 1963 this had grown to $40·6 billion, or 244 per cent, in thirteen years.' – *Monthly Review* January 1965. Figures from *Survey of Current Business* October 1964.

[2] The above account is taken from Smith, op. cit., pp. 70–1.

... The opening salvo was the dramatic joint proposal of America, Britain and France to Russia that Trieste – the former Italian port in the Adriatic, made a 'free city' by the peace treaty with Italy – be returned to Italy. ... After that event not a day passed without the anti-Communist majority of the press having a new, effective American gesture to put in its headlines. President Truman made Italy a badly needed gift of 29 merchant ships; gold looted from Italy by the Nazis was returned; the first Marshall Aid ships arrived and were unloaded amid ceremony and with a speech by the American Ambassador; the State Department announced that Italians who were known to have voted Communist would be denied that dream of all Italians, emigration to America; the War Department announced that American naval contingents in the Mediterranean would be strengthened; American occupation troops in Trieste held their first full-dress military parade since the war, complete with tanks and big guns; American and British warships anchored off Italian ports during the campaign. ...[1]

In March, Secretary of State Marshall bluntly told Italy and all other nations participating in the European Recovery Program (the Marshall Plan) that 'benefits under ERP will come to an abrupt end in any country that votes [*sic*] Communism into power'.[2] Given the dollar crisis in Europe, which had hit the Italians particularly hard, this threat alone might have sufficed to swing the elections.

In view of such open United States intervention, the Truman Doctrine's promise that it would be United States policy to support free peoples against external pressures and to 'assist free peoples to work out their own destinies in their own way' proved to be an empty one. These events, however, throw light on a far more significant reality than the failure of United States actions to conform to United States ideals. For the open but relatively peaceful manner in which the United States was able to intervene to protect its strategic interests, was a factor of key significance in the development of the early cold war.

The scene of the most interesting and historically important contrast between attempts by the United States and the USSR to

[1] Smith, pp. 204–6.
[2] Ingram, op. cit., p. 63.

extend their respective 'security zones' in this period, was Iran. The Iranian incidents, which occupied world attention from November 1945 until May 1946, deserve special attention, because they are generally held up as the first overt instance of the Soviet Union's remorseless post-war expansion.[1]

During the war, all three of the major allies had occupied Iran in order to assure wartime oil supplies to Russia; this seemed a prudent step in view of the Iranian Government's flirtation with the Nazis. After the war, it was agreed that all three should move out simultaneously, but the Russians stayed beyond the deadline. During this time, they fomented a rebellion against the central Iranian Government in the Soviet-occupied areas of northern Iran and set up a friendly 'autonomous' government there. By this pressure they were able to induce the central government to grant them oil-exploitation rights in northern Iran. Russian aims were to win oil resources to supplement the production of their own badly damaged Caucasian fields.

The Western powers condemned these actions in the Security Council and, in May, the force of public opinion induced the Russians to withdraw from Iran. Then the central Iranian Government sent troops to break up the autonomous Azerbaijan Government. With this accomplished the Iranian parliament denounced the oil agreement with Russia.

The sequel to these events is not so widely known. As the Russians left, the Americans moved in – not with troops and revolution – 'but silently with dollars in support of the *status quo*.' In addition to American funds, the Iranian Government received American Advisors, including military, and Iran became in effect 'an American satellite'. If America did not yet have military bases there, she could have them anytime she wished.[2]

The effect of this incident on Russian mentality can be easily guessed. The United States had achieved exactly the end that Russia had sought, but there was no way to make a case of it before the United Nations. Moreover, as one Western correspondent pointedly observed, 'this "defense" base that America had for the taking was six thousand miles from America, but on Russia's most sensitive border. Russia could legitimately adopt the question the

[1] cf. Stevenson, op. cit.
[2] This account is taken from Smith, op. cit., pp. 407–8.

West put to her: where does security end short of domination of the whole earth?' Thereafter, 'Russia fought tooth and nail to close her satellite nations to the "Iranian method" '.[1]

From this brief review of the scope and use of United States power in the initial post-war period, it can be seen that by early 1947 when the cold war became a public reality, the Russians had real cause for concern about United States intentions and the future employment of United States economic and military muscle. Then the bombshell of the Truman Doctrine was exploded, followed by the economic 'counteroffensive' of the Marshall Plan in Europe. It was at this point that the public phase of the cold war was really engaged by the Soviets as they responded to the Truman–Marshall initiatives by subverting the non-Communist governments of Hungary and Czechoslovakia, and by taking swift steps to fully integrate the economies and political structures of the East European countries and to reduce them to satellites in the service of their mobilization against the West. Even as late as 1948–9, the resistance to Sovietization within the East European communist parties themselves (let alone non-party groups) was so considerable as to require the purging of vast numbers of 'Titoists' and nationalist elements.

Putting the sequence of events in its proper perspective in this way, raises the inescapable question of the *casus belli* of the cold war itself: was the Sovietization of East Europe an inevitable development after the Yalta Agreements of February 1945? Or, was it rather the product of interacting post-war American policies and Stalinist responses? In other words, would Stalinist strategy, of itself, have led to the attempted Sovietization of East Europe, regardless of the policies of the post-war American leadership?

There are, it should be noted, preliminary grounds for supposing that United States policy was a very important and probably decisive factor in the post-war development of United States–Soviet relations. In the first place, preponderance of power gave the

---

[1] ibid., 'When Russia extends her security zone abroad, it almost inevitably requires an overthrow of the *status quo*, for the *status quo* of the world is capitalist; which means a lot of noise and ugly scenes. If America extends her zone of influence abroad, for the same reason – that the rest of the world is capitalist – it involves only supporting the *status quo*: no scenes, no noise.' – Smith, p. 93.

United States a flexibility and range of alternative that the Russians simply did not have. In the second place, there was a divergence in the highest levels of the United States administration over the options to be taken toward the Soviet Union after the war, and in fact, an established course, which had worked in the preceding period was replaced at the end of the war by an untried policy which did not.

What we have subsequently learned about events behind the Stettin–Trieste line in the years 1945–9 not only bears out the above preliminary assumptions but amplifies them. The importance of these facts for assessing United States foreign policy in the period justifies a brief review of the main outlines of what took place.

In the mid-1920s, Stalin's thesis of 'socialism in one country' became the dogma of the revolution and the guiding principle of Soviet foreign policy down through the end of World War II. Indeed, the wartime alliance was predicated on this concept. In the words of Isaac Deutscher, 'Soviet self-containment was the very premise of joint allied policy, written into the paragraphs and clauses of the Teheran, Yalta, and Potsdam Agreements.' The agreements divided spheres of influence between the Allies, allotting all of Eastern and much of Central Europe to Russia, while at the same time stipulating that this was to be the sphere of influence of Russia, not of Communism.[1]

'In retrospect,' observes Deutscher, 'it appears extraordinarily shortsighted of the great statesmen of the West to have believed that Russia's personality could be thus split and her national-power ambitions separated from her social and political outlook. But the illusion was not merely Roosevelt's and Churchill's. It was shared by Stalin.' It may be argued, of course, that Stalin's wartime attitude was deception on his part, his pledges of non-interference in the internal affairs of neighboring countries 'simply dust thrown into the eyes of his allies'. But, Stalin's deeds at the time lent weight to his vows, and 'both Churchill and Roosevelt had solid evidence that Stalin's policy was in fact geared to self-containment'.

They saw Stalin acting, not merely speaking, as any nationalist

[1] This account is taken from Isaac Deutscher, *Russia After Stalin*, 1953, pp. 74, et seq. cf. also Deutscher's *Stalin*, 1949.

Russian statesman would have done in his place – they saw him divested, as it were, of his communist character. He was approaching the problems of the Russian zone of influence in a manner calculated to satisfy nationalist Russian demands and aspirations and to wreck the chances of communist revolution in those territories.

He prepared to exact and did in fact exact heavy reparations from Hungary, Bulgaria, Rumania, Finland, and Eastern Germany. This, he knew, would make the name of communism as well as that of Russia odious to the peoples of those countries, to whom it did not even occur to distinguish between the two. With a zeal worthy of a better cause he insisted on slicing territories away from Poland, Hungary, and Germany, and on expelling many millions of citizens from their homes.

Stalin's policies in the initial post-war period thus made sense only if he assumed that these countries would remain capitalist, that is, 'if he had no design to impose Communist governments on them'. He expected, of course, that Russia would enjoy a position of diplomatic and economic 'preponderance' in neighboring countries ruled by 'friendly' governments, but he also expected them to remain essentially capitalist. 'If [Stalin] had been viewing those countries as future provinces of his empire, it would have been the height of folly on his part to insist on levying in the most unrelenting manner heavy reparations and enforcing expulsions.'

Stalin had become convinced in the inter-war period that the revolutionary potentialities of foreign Communism were nil. Accordingly, he did what he could to discourage the Communist parties from making bids for power and from jeopardizing his relations with his wartime allies:

... He urged the French Communists to take their cue from General de Gaulle at a time when they were the chief driving force behind the French Resistance. He urged the Italian Communists to make peace with the House of Savoy and with the government of Marshal Badoglio, and to vote for the re-enactment of Mussolini's Lateran pacts with the Vatican. He did his best to induce Mao Tse-tung to come to terms with Chiang Kai-shek, because he believed, as he said at Potsdam, that the Kuomintang was the only force capable of ruling China. He angrily remonstrated with Tito because of the latter's revolutionary aspirations, and demanded his consent to the restoration of the monarchy of Yugoslavia. . . .

He stared with incredulity and fear at the rising tides of revolution which threatened to wash away the rock of 'socialism in one country', on which he had built his temple. This so-called prophet of Marxism and Leninism appears at this moment as the most conservative statesman in the world.[1]

The subsequent post-war 'wrecking' of Stalin's policy of self-containment 'partly by forces beyond Stalin's control and partly by Stalin himself', is a complex story of which only a small but significant part is yet known. Of the European countries which became communist in this period, Yugoslavia was one that had not been allotted to the Soviet sphere of influence during the wartime negotiations, but was to have been a border zone between the British and Russian spheres. Stalin was therefore most interested in keeping the Yugoslav revolutionaries in check lest his relations with the allies be compromised:

> . . . For long he disparaged Tito's partisans and extolled the counter-revolutionery Chetniks of Drazha Mikhailovich as the alleged heroes of anti-Nazi resistance. The embittered Tito, still one of the most faithful agents of the Stalinist Comintern, implored him: 'If you cannot send us assistance, then at least do not hamper us.' Stalin, so Tito relates, 'stamped with rage' and tried to induce Tito to agree not merely to the restoration of the monarchy but to a possible British occupation of Yugoslavia. . . . Tito's unruly revolutionary moves were to Stalin a 'stab in the back of the Soviet Union'.[2]

---

[1] This picture of Stalin as conservative with regard to the world revolution is orthodox among sovietologists: 'From the bourgeois world, as from his political entourage in the world of communism, Stalin wanted only one thing: weakness. This was not at all identical with revolution. . . . Stalin did not want other states to be communist. He was concerned only that they should be weak, or that they should at least expend their strength not against him and his régime but against each other. . . .' – Kennan, *Russia and the West Under Lenin and Stalin*, 1960, p. 253.

[2] Deutscher, ibid.

Stalin's rage can be appreciated, for he was beginning to lose control over his own Communist parties, whereas he had always been confident that he could use them 'as pawns in his great diplomatic game of chess'. The pawns, however, were beginning to show 'a life of their own', and Stalin 'could not even lay hands on them'. Moreover, Stalin 'could not afford the odium of an open betrayal' of the revolution. To what extent in each individual case he merely yielded to the will of the pawns, pretending to move them, and to what extent he actually moved them himself, is still not known. Only the 'accident' of Yugoslavia's break with Moscow has revealed the information that we have. What is 'certain' however, 'is that as Stalin began reluctantly to identify himself with the rising forces of foreign communism his Western Allies also began to identify him with those forces. The Grand Alliance was giving place to the Great Enmity. Stalin then sought reinsurance against the West; and Communist régimes in the Russian sphere of influence promised to provide it. And then it was without a doubt he who moved the pawns.'

From Tito, himself, comes an even more explicit verification of the shape of this dynamic of forces; for as Deutscher reports, 'According to Tito, Stalin finally decided to bring Eastern Europe under close Soviet control in 1947, *at the time when the Truman Doctrine was proclaimed.*' [Emphasis added.]

The impetus to integrate and absorb East Europe at the time of the Truman Doctrine, however, did not stem only from the collapse of the alliance and, with that, Stalin's reasons for holding back these forces. As we have seen, the alliance was already dead by the fall of 1945. The pressure to fully integrate East Europe in the Soviet system after the Truman Doctrine seems rather to have come from the twofold desire to close East Europe to the 'Iranian method' and to facilitate the military defense of the Soviet Union.

To understand this latter tactic, we must add to the picture of American post-war power sketched earlier in this chapter, America's possession of the Atomic Bomb. Russian military leaders were likely to be impressed not merely by American possession of this weapon, and by its use against a defeated country, but by the emphasis in Western military theory on the efficacy of strategic air power, the much-touted doctrine of preventive war,[1] and the

---

[1] The most important government figure to publicly espouse the doctrine of preventive war was Secretary of the Navy Francis P. Matthews, who said on

effort to secure air bases on the perimeter of the Soviet Union.

Soviet responses to the possibility of atomic attack took several forms, including a crash program to produce nuclear weapons, a huge fighter defense program, a build up of land forces to provide 'their only possible military reply to the Western nuclear striking power' and maintenance of 'strict geographical secrecy over their land areas so as to deny target information to the Strategic Air Command'.[1]

Since the main military threat was from manned nuclear bombers, 'the greatest possible depth for air defence was vital. During the Second World War it was found that the efficacy of a fighter defence system increased rapidly with the depth of the defence zone'. Therefore, at the political level, 'the Soviet Union consolidated its forward military line by the political *coup* in 1948 in Czechoslovakia, and integrated the other satellite countries more closely into the Soviet defence system'.

> Support for the view that the communist *coup* in Czechoslovakia was not solely due to the desire to spread the borders of the Soviet world, but had at least a strong military foundation, is seen by noting that the USSR did not act similarly in Finland. The military difference is obvious. Czechoslovakia in the Western orbit would have greatly weakened Russia's military strength. Finland's geographical position made it unnecessary to stage a communist *coup* to keep her out of the Western military orbit. However, if Sweden had joined Nato, the Soviet military staff might have pressed for the full integration of Finland.[2]

Thus, the Truman Doctrine of a world divided into two opposing camps proved to be a self-fulfilling prophecy: given the mentality of

---

[1] P. M. S. Blackett, *Studies of War*, op. cit., pp. 151–2.
[2] ibid.

August 25, 1950: 'We should boldly proclaim our undeniable objective to be world peace. To have peace we should be willing, and declare our intention, to pay any price, even the price of instituting a war, to compel cooperation for peace ... [This] peace-seeking policy, though it cast us in a character new to a true democracy – an initiator of a war of aggression it would earn for us a proud and popular title – we would become the first aggressors for peace.' For other examples cf. Fleming, pp. 391–4.

the Russian leaders, the whole post-war United States policy of facing the Soviets with an 'iron fist' and 'strong language', while at the same time making it as difficult as possible for them to carry out the work of reconstruction, virtually ensured the 'expansion' that the policy, allegedly, had been designed to prevent.

PART TWO

Leader of the Free World: 1950-63

Human liberty is an abstraction which men of power have profaned. They have profaned this idea, not alone because they have violated it, but because they have invoked it.

BERTRAND RUSSELL

CHAPTER VII

Containing Conspiracy

There are in the country, semi-Trotskyites, one-eighth Trotskyites and
... people who from liberalism ... gave us help.

KARL RADEK

... men who could not see that what they firmly believed was liberalism
added up to socialism could scarcely be expected to see what added up to
Communism.

WHITTAKER CHAMBERS

The most brazen lie of the century has been fabricated by reckless dema-
gogues among the Republicans to the effect that Democrats were soft on
Communists. ...

HARRY S. TRUMAN

IN NOVEMBER 1946, the Republicans won the Congressional
elections for the first time since 1928. Most political analysts shared
the view of columnist Marquis Childs that 'the cry of communism
which was raised by Republicans from one side of the country to
the other' played a large part in the GOP victory. The Republicans,
Childs noted, were significantly assisted in establishing the 'Red
issue' by J. Edgar Hoover, who, one month before the elections, had
'let loose a resounding blast against Communists in the United
States saying more or less directly that they were at work at every
level and in every organization'.[1] Hoover said he would not be
concerned if it were only a matter of 100,000 Communists, but
'their satellites, their fellow-travelers and their so-called progressive
and phony liberal allies' constituted a threat.[2]

Just five months after the election, Truman acted to steal the

[1] Quoted in Fleming, p. 431.
[2] Quoted in Alan Barth, *The Loyalty of Free Men*, 1952, pp. 37–9; also in
Fleming, p. 431.

Republican thunder. On March 12, in his Truman Doctrine speech, he virtually declared war on the international Communist movement; thirteen days later, he initiated the internal phase of his strategy by issuing an order requiring 2,500,000 government employees to undergo a new security check. Under this order, the test of disloyalty was to be 'membership in, affiliation with, or sympathetic association with . . . any . . . organization, association, movement, group or combination of persons, designated by the Attorney General as totalitarian'. The President's motivation was scarcely veiled. 'Well, that should take the Communist smear off the Democratic party!' he said.

It seems not to have occurred to Truman that this stratagem would have the added effect of undermining the very basis of public trust. 'At one stroke of the pen the assumption that American citizens were loyal was destroyed. All government employees became second class citizens, living under the shadow of F B I dossiers whose contents could never be revealed to them on the ground of protecting secret informers.'[1]

Thus began the era of the loyalty oath. In 1947, Truman's executive order required loyalty boards to have 'reasonable grounds' for dismissal; by 1950 this was amended to read 'reasonable doubt' and in 1953 President Eisenhower set up new and even vaguer standards under which the question to be determined was whether the employment of a civil servant would 'be clearly consistent with national security'.

When Truman signed the order it applied only to 2,500,000 government employees, but soon afterwards it was extended to include 3,000,000 members of the armed forces and 3,000,000 employees of defense contractors. 'Thus at least 8,000,000 Americans are always under the shadow of having to prove their loyalty, if any anonymous, protected informer questions it. Including the families of 8,000,000, about 20,000,000 American citizens are subject to investigative procedures at any time. As people enter and leave investigated employment, the vast total of people who have secret police dossiers compiled about them increases year by year. . . .'[2]

By November 6, 1953, the wheel of suspicion had come full circle

---

[1] Fleming, ibid., p. 1067.
[2] Fleming, op. cit., p. 1068.

and the loyalty of the man who had initiated the loyalty check came under fire. On that date, Republican Attorney General of the United States, Herbert Brownell Jr., charged Truman himself with having knowingly harbored a Russian spy.[1]

To reduce a complex set of events to its simplest terms, McCarthyism, of which the Truman order proved to be the first major manifestation, was the domination of American political life by a Manichean orthodoxy. This outlook defined the world in terms of a vaguely conceived Soviet Communist Conspiratorial Evil, and a vaguely postulated American Anti-Communist Good. Its pervasiveness and potential for harm is inadequately indicated by merely citing the number of people who were summoned before investigating committees, or placed under the surveillance of a political police; the prime tèst of its success, like that of any other political orthodoxy, is the extent to which it succeeded in infiltrating the assumptions of its victims and even of its vigorous opponents.

President Truman was one of the prime targets of the Republican McCarthyists, and in self-defense, he occasionally showed courage and even some eloquence in resisting his critics:

> The demagogues, crackpots and professional patriots had a field day pumping fear into the American people. . . . Many good people actually believed that we were in imminent danger of being taken over by the Communists and that our government in Washington was Communist-riddled. So widespread was this campaign that it seemed no one would be safe from attack. This was the tragedy and the shame of our time.[2]

This was written during the height of the McCarthy period, and is typical in that it attributes major responsibility for this 'tragedy of shame' to the Republicans and totally ignores the fact that in essence the Democrats shared and promoted a similar outlook. In his own defense of the Truman Doctrine, to cite one instance among many,

---

[1] i.e. Harry Dexter White, an assistant secretary of the Treasury in the Truman administration and former executive director of the International Monetary Fund – the charges against White (who had died of a heart attack three days after denying that he was a Communist before a Congressional Committee in 1948) were never substantiated – Truman refused to answer the subpoena to appear before a Congressional Committee (in 1953) in connection with the case.

[2] *Memoirs* Vol. II, p. 291, cf. also pp. 270 et seq.

Truman revealed his basic McCarthyist orientation. 'The world reaction to it proved that this approach had been the right one. All over the world, voices of approval made themselves heard, while Communists and their fellow-travelers struck out at me savagely.'[1]

Thus the world is seen, by Truman, to be divided into two kinds of men, Communists and anti-Communists. Those who oppose the Doctrine, *ipso facto*, must be Communists, and conversely because Communists oppose the Doctrine, *ipso facto*, it must be good.

A glance at the record, however, shows that the Doctrine drew opposition from a considerable number of diplomats from non-Communist countries, the British Labor Party and many English newspapers, and from such American columnists as Walter Lippmann, William L. Shirer, Samuel Grafton, Drew Pearson, Thomas L. Stokes and Marquis Childs.[2] The Chicago papers, including, of course, the bitterly anti-Communist *Tribune*, 'were unanimous in opposition', while a Gallup Public Opinion Poll showed, on March 27, that 55 per cent of the people disapproved the Doctrine's bypassing of the United Nations. Even Russian expert George Kennan, expressed a strong dissent. 'To say that he found objection to it is to put it mildly' wrote Joseph M. Jones who was responsible for drafting the Doctrine. 'He objected strongly to the tone of the message and to the specific action proposed.' Kennan spoke to a number of people in the State Department, including Dean Acheson, in an attempt to stop the plan, but 'It was too late.'[3]

Thus the line was not so sharply or simply drawn. The issues were complex. Reading Truman's *Memoirs* one would never suspect that between the savagery of the Communist attacks and the world-wide 'voices of approval' there were any positions worthy of note. Yet the record shows that, outside the Communist movement, criticisms of a fundamental nature were raised, concerning issues which subsequently determined the course of the cold war.

But Manichean thinking leaves no room for such middle groups; it requires the establishment of an orthodox position in all spheres. And indeed while the loyalty oath served to establish orthodoxy for internal domestic politics, the Truman Doctrine itself sought to

---

[1] ibid., p. 106.
[2] D. F. Fleming, op. cit., pp. 448–55 et seq.
[3] Joseph M. Jones, *The Fifteen Weeks*, 1955, p. 155.

establish such an orthodoxy for the world: 'In my address I had said that every nation was now faced with a choice between alternative ways of life.' Truman had loftily divided the world into the two camps of democracy and totalitarianism (thereby excluding the large and all-important middle)[1] in practice, his program came down heavily on the side of the *status quo*. In outlawing revolution by 'armed minorities' the Doctrine in effect outlawed all revolution, for while authentic revolutions eventually gain at least the covert support of the people, they are begun and usually carried out by small groups of determined men.

In a prophetic manner, Walter Lippmann warned of the danger of the policy of global containment which the Doctrine also heralded. Pointing out that the United States did not possess the military manpower to circle the Soviet Union, Lippmann concluded that the policy could be implemented only 'indirectly' that is to say by 'recruiting, subsidizing and supporting a heterogeneous array of satellites, clients, dependents and puppets . . . around the perimeter of the Soviet Union.'

A diplomatic war conducted as this policy demands, that is to say conducted indirectly, means that we must stake our own security and the peace of the world upon satellites, puppets, clients, agents about whom we can know very little. Frequently they will act for their own reasons, and on their own judgments, presenting us with crises for which we are unready. The 'unassailable barriers' [erected around the perimeter of the Soviet Union] will present us with an unending series of insoluble dilemmas. We shall have either to disown our puppets, which would be tantamount to appeasement and defeat and the loss of face, or must support them at an incalculable cost on an unintended, unforeseen and perhaps undesirable issue.[2]

Unmindful of these pitfalls (now bearing the familiar names Korea, Viet Nam, Laos, Formosa . . .) Truman forged ahead with a program that essentially reflected the prescriptions of the Republican

---

[1] In preceding and subsequent policy statements, Truman and the US leadership identified 'free enterprise' with democracy, and any variety of socialism with totalitarianism.

[2] Lippmann, *The Cold War*, 1947, pp. 14–16.

right wing: defining the world in terms of Our Way of Life, by-passing the United Nations and taking an implacably 'hard line' towards the Soviet Union, while interpreting all attempts to alter the *status quo* by force as Communist, and therefore evil. But this did not save him from the criticism of his political opponents, who had only to accuse him of not prosecuting the anti-Communist cause with enough vigor. Their assaults mounted to a full scale, irresistible attack, when a massive breach was made through the wall of containment by titanic revolution in China. . . .

1948 was an election year in America and the first year of real cold war in Europe. The Czech *coup* came in February, the Berlin blockade followed in June, and Congress voted peacetime conscription for the first time in United States history. During the gathering heat of the election campaign, the Republican-dominated House Committee on Un-American Activities held widely publicized hearings to uncover Communist infiltration into the Federal Government. Among those named as Communists by Committee informers was Alger Hiss.

Hiss, a former State Department official in the Roosevelt administration, was head of the Carnegie Endowment for International Peace. He immediately denied the charges and lodged a $75,000 libel suit against his accuser, Whittaker Chambers. Meanwhile, Truman labeled the whole series of investigations a political 'red-herring', designed to take people's minds off the failures of the Republican controlled Congress during the preceding session.

It took two trials to convict Hiss of perjuring himself in denying a subsequent charge that he had committed espionage. He maintained his innocence to the end. The far-ranging significance of the case, however, had little to do with whether Hiss was, in fact, guilty or not;[1] its significance stemmed rather from its symbolism, the meaning that the event was made to assume by the mass media and by its occurrence in a charged political context:

. . . The joining of New Dealism and Communism in a troubled

[1] For doubts about the official verdict, cf. Fred J. Cook, *The Unfinished Case of Alger Hiss*, New York, 1957; also 'New Doubts on the Hiss Case – The Added Witness' by George Altman in *The Nation*, October 1, 1960, pp. 201–9.

American mind was easy, almost axiomatic. Was it not the New Dealers, like the Communists, who talked of uplifting the masses, fighting the businessmen, establishing economic controls over society, questioning the traditional in every part of living? Was it not the reformers at home who had called during the war for linking hands with the Bolsheviks abroad? Was not Alger Hiss just the type of which the New Dealers had been so proud?[1]

The years of the Hiss case proved to be the watershed of McCarthyism and the years of ascendance of the Republican Right Wing. Manichean McCarthyism (which pre-dated the senator who lent it his name) was the perfect conceptual framework for those nationalists who saw what they saw of world history in terms only of American successes and defeats. For these men the Russian explosion of an Atomic Bomb in 1949 was not the triumph of Russian effort, but a betrayal of the United States by American spies. It was 'our' bomb, and 'they', the Russians, had stolen it. The Chinese Revolution which burst with such shattering effect on the American consciousness in the same fateful autumn, was no Chinese achievement, but an American 'loss'. The thread which bound up this view of the world in the McCarthy epoch (and to a great extent still binds it) was the theory of conspiracy:

> The heart of the emotional drive behind this whole conspiracy theory lay precisely in the fact that it *was* a theory of conspiracy. The hated developments could all have been prevented, they were all the work of a few wicked men, operating behind a cloak of hypocrisy . . . The rise of Communism around the world did not result from long-running historical forces, the Red advances came from the Alger Hisses, who had contrived to bring them about.[2]

To the American nationalists, addicted as they were to the theory of conspiracy in an extreme form, the coincidence of the Chinese

---

[1] Goldman, *The Crucial Decade and After,* 1960, pp. 105, 119.
[2] Goldman, op. cit., p. 123. Hiss was a key target for the fulminations of the period because he had been at Dumbarton Oaks and at Yalta. Despite the record, Yalta had by this time become the symbol of American 'surrender', Roosevelt's concessions 'giving' Poland to the Soviets and 'permitting' them to become a Pacific power.

Revolution with the Hiss revelations was an especially unsettling experience. 'For many decades a feeling had been growing in America that the Asiatics were the special mission of the United States under the law of history.' As Senator Wherry told a wildly cheering crowd in 1940: 'With God's help, we will lift Shanghai up and up, ever up, until it is just like Kansas City.'[1] General Douglas MacArthur put the emotional and political essence of this position somewhat apocalyptically when he said during World War II:

> Europe is a dying system. It is worn out and run down, and will become an economic and industrial hegemony of Soviet Russia . . . The lands touching the Pacific with their billions of inhabitants will determine the course of history for the next ten thousand years![2]

The 'loss' of China was a blow of immense proportions to sensibilities such as these. In the panic which ensued, this nationalist right wing focused its fury on the only enemy within reach, the 'enemy within'. The architects and administrators of the ruptured policy of containment, Europe-oriented Democrats, largely East-Coast bred and Ivy League educated, were particularly vulnerable on a whole range of points, which found their superb expression in the symbol-rich figure of Alger Hiss. Dean Acheson, who was at the foreign policy helm, hence answerable above all others for the 'loss' of China, meshed neatly with the Hiss image (Acheson and Hiss were also long-time associates):

'I look at that fellow,' exploded Senator Hugh Butler of Nebraska, 'I watch his smart-aleck manner and his British clothes and that New Dealism, everlasting New Dealism in everything he says and does, and I want to shout, Get out, Get out. You stand for everything that has been wrong with the United States for years.'[3]

Another target was General George C. Marshall who had been Chairman of the Joint Chiefs of Staff during the war and had served as Secretary of Defense and Secretary of State under Truman. The President had referred to him as the 'greatest living American', but this did not faze McCarthy. Marshall, of course, had been connected

---

[1] ibid., p. 116.
[2] John Spanier, *The Truman–MacArthur Controversy*, 1959, p. 67.
[3] Goldman, op. cit., p. 125.

with the Truman policy in the Far East, and the Marshall mission to China had tried to bolster the hopelessly doomed régime of Chiang Kai-shek, by convincing him to form a government with the Communists on terms favorable to the Nationalists.

In a sixty-thousand word speech on June 14, 1951, McCarthy charged that Marshall had been part of 'a conspiracy so immense, an infamy so black, as to dwarf the history of man . . . (a conspiracy directed) to the end that we shall be contained, frustrated and finally fall victim to Soviet intrigue from within and Russian military might from without'.[1]

Other China experts in the State Department who had supported similar plans for avoiding loss of American prestige and interest in China, were charged in McCarthy's speech with having thrown their full weight 'in the balance of the conspiratorial, subversive Reds against our ally, the Government of China'.[2]

The success of the McCarthy onslaught may be gauged by the fact that both Acheson and Marshall were driven to vow to the Senate that they would not even consider the recognition of Red China, in fact, that the United States would not *ever* do so! And indeed the policies established during that period have remained through three subsequent Administrations, the essential China policies of the United States. This basic continuity of policy (albeit in a special area) is difficult to reconcile with the view, held by many, that McCarthyism was simply a temporary aberration of a particular, Republican section of American society, rather than a specific manifestation of a fundamental United States approach to the cold war. It is certainly true, for example, that McCarthy and his associates wreaked havoc with the State Department *after* the Republican victory in 1952, but consider what had happened to the China Service in the last years of the Truman Administration:

The basic burden of the reporting of the China Service in the critical years (1944–9) was that, in the inevitable clash between the Chinese Communists and Chiang Kai-shek, Chiang would be the loser. This correctness in judgment has resulted, however, not in honor either collectively or individually to the China Service.

---

[1] Goldman, op. cit. p. 213. cf. also Richard H. Rovere, *Senator Joe McCarthy*.
[2] *Congressional Record*, June 14, 1951, Vol. 97, pp. 6556–6602.

China has gone Communist. In some fashion the men of the China Service were held responsible. The China Service, therefore, no longer exists. Of the twenty-two officers who joined it before the beginning of World War II, there were in 1952 only two still used by the State Department in Washington. Most of the rest were still serving the American government, but not . . . where their intimate knowledge of a China with whom we were desperately at war in Korea might be useful.[1]

Thus before McCarthy ever achieved the advantage of Republican power, the Democrats had dissolved the service of the men who had 'lost' China, as though, in fact, they were somehow responsible. It can be argued, of course, that the Democrats did this to 'forestall' a McCarthy attack, i.e. purely as a 'defensive' maneuver, and this was certainly Truman's motivation in 1947 in launching the loyalty oath. But in that case it proved rapidly suicidal, for in order to take this line of defense, the Democrats had to (and in fact were ready to) share and articulate essentially the same basic premises as the Republicans. With no clear alternative picture of the forces behind the events, why should the American people not have believed the Republican charge that the Democrats were responsible for the 'mess'?

The China issue – and the fate of Dean Acheson – respresent a classic case in point. The State Department issued a *White Paper*, in August 1949, predicting that China would soon fall to the Communists and defending the Administration's China policy. In the preface, Acheson wrote:

It has been urged that relatively small amounts of additional aid – military and economic – to the National Government would have enabled it to destroy communism in China. The most trustworthy military, economic, and political information available to our

---

[1] Theodore H. White, *Fire in the Ashes*, 1953, p. 375. Dean Acheson in violation of his own regulations fired John Stewart Service (in 1951) from his post in the Far East division of the State Department, despite the fact that at the time Acheson fired him, Service had been cleared eight times: once by grand jury, once by a Senate investigating committee, and six times by loyalty security boards. In 1957 the US Supreme Court reversed this expulsion, restoring Service, to job, rank, security and back pay (Fleming, op. cit., p. 883).

Government does not bear out this view. . . . The only alternative open to the United States was full-scale intervention in behalf of a Government which had lost the confidence of its own troops and its own people.[1]

Declaring that the Chiang Kai-shek régime was corrupt, inefficient, and purblind to the just aspirations of the masses of the Chinese people, Acheson concluded that 'the ominous result of the civil war in China was beyond the control of the government of the United States. . . . *It was the product of internal Chinese forces*, forces which this country tried to influence but could not.'[2] [Emphasis added.]

In reviewing the last stages of Chiang's fall, the White Paper cites foreign service memorandums which emphasize that the Kuomintang in 1943-4 was pursuing a suicidal course in the face of the Japanese invasion, while the Communists were following paths which were 'historically and evolutionarily sound'. For while Chiang insisted on pressing the civil war against the Communists, the Communists were fighting, against the Japanese, a war 'agressively waged by a totally mobilized population'. This mobilization was made possible by 'an economic, political and social revolution'; for the first time, the people had 'been given something to fight for'. Because of this 'mass support, mass participation', the Communist movement had expanded to include 850,000 square kilometers and 90 million people. The Communists, concluded the memorandums, 'are in China to stay. And China's destiny is not Chiang's but theirs.'[3]

The collapse of Chiang in 1949 came swiftly after the long twenty-two year Communist effort. Whole cities and armies surrendered with barely any resistance, while masses of Chiang's troops deserted to the Communist forces. The years of fantastic Kuomintang corruption, brutality, disregard for human life, reluctance to defend against the Japanese invader and above all, resistance to the agrarian revolution had taken their inevitable toll.

---

[1] General Joseph Stilwell, commander of US forces in China during World War II, wrote in 1944. 'We were fighting Germany to tear down the Nazi system – one-party government supported by the Gestapo . . . China, our ally, was being run by a one-party Government [the Kuomintang], supported by a Gestapo [Tai Li's organization] . . . To reform such a system it must be torn to pieces . . .'

[2] Department of State, *United States Relations with China, 1944-9*, 1949.

[3] *White Paper*, pp. 565, 566, 567 and 573; cited in Fleming, pp. 566-7.

Yet, some Americans, spurred by the nationalist right wing, insisted on seeing this historically momentous event as a palace conspiracy, an Oriental version of the Czech *coup*, a disaster wholly preventable by increased arms aid. That this would rapidly become the predominant American view was assured when Acheson retreated from the position of the White Paper – the only ground on which to base a sound defense of the Administration as well as a sound China policy – and adopted the simplistic McCarthyist theory of conspiracy, albeit in a somewhat more refined form.

On February 16, 1950, seven days after McCarthy's famous attack on the State Department, in Wheeling, West Virginia, Acheson delivered an important policy address. One of the first official policy statements after the explosion of Russia's Atomic Bomb in the fall, it outlined the State Department's program to meet the changed conditions of the world situation.[1] For those like Winston Churchill, who was urging that the time had come to sit down with the Soviets and try to control the developing arms race and end the cold war,[2] Acheson had little, if any sympathy:

> We hear it said that if we could only get Harry Truman to 'get his feet under the same table' – that is the phrase used – with Joe Stalin, we would be able to iron out any international difficulty. . . . We must realize, however, that the world situation is not one to which there is an easy answer. The only way to deal with the Soviet Union, we have found from hard experience, is to create situations of strength.[3]

In the new atomic context, creating situations of strength could only mean building an H-bomb bigger than the Soviet's A-bomb. To justify this intensified arms race, Acheson conjured up an image of an enemy so cunning and so 'deadly serious' that indeed 'we could lose without ever firing a shot'. The evidence as to the nature of this mysteriously powerful foe was provided by the Chinese Revoltuion:

---

[1] cf. Fleming, pp. 528–32 for a discussion of these statements and of alternative proposals current at the time.

[2] ibid., p. 530.

[3] Acheson, *Strengthening the Forces of Freedom*, pp. 15–16.

. . . The Communists took over China at a ridiculously small cost. What they did was to invite some Chinese leaders who were dissatsified with the way things were going in their country to come to Moscow. There they thoroughly indoctrinated them so that they returned to China prepared to resort to any means whatsoever to establish Communist control. They were completely subservient to the Moscow régime. . . . These agents then mingled among the people and sold them on the personal material advantages of Communism. . . .[1]

This was indeed a revised explanation of China's revolution (a bare half year after the issuance of the White Paper). Acheson was now using the weight of his authority to propogate a version of historical events that no one with his experience in world affairs could possibly believe, namely, that after twenty-eight years of revolutionary struggle (twenty-two in bloody civil war), the Chinese Communist leaders would simply turn over the reigns of power, in a land of 500 millions, to non-Chinese rulers, men who had not even participated in the long struggle and who, at crucial points, had even opposed it. Yet, the only Communist leader in East Europe whose party had achieved power without the intervention of the Red Army, namely Tito, had already found subservience to Stalin an intolerable burden. Moreover, Tito's situation was infinitely weaker *vis-à-vis* Moscow than Mao Tse-tung's, not least because Mao had been the actual ruler of tens of millions in the Communist held areas for many years before winning power in all of China.

Indeed the absurdity of Acheson's revised version of Chinese history was underlined by the spectacle of Stalin's continued blindness to the character and potential of the Revolution. Even after the war when it was clear to most observers that Chiang was finished, Stalin did not think much of the prospects of Chinese Communism. When the Chinese Communists sent representatives to Moscow shortly after Japan's defeat, Stalin 'told them bluntly that [he] considered the development of the uprising in China had no prospect.'[2] He advised the Chinese Communists to join Chiang's Government and dissolve their army. They agreed to do so, went back to China and 'acted quite otherwise'.

[1] op. cit., p. 16.
[2] Vladimir Dedijer, *Tito*, 1953, p. 322.

Throughout the war, moreover, the Russians had sent their war aid to China to the Kuomintang, not to the Communists, and the Kuomintang used this material in their war against the Communists. After the war, the Russians looted Manchuria, China's industrial heartland, creating deep grievances and arousing a storm of protest among the Chinese populace.[1] Sino-Soviet differences were known to the foreign service and reported by them. Yet on May 18, 1951, Assistant Secretary of State for far Eastern Affairs, Dean Rusk (who had never been in the Far East) declared:

> The Peiping régime may be a colonial Russian government – a Slavic Manchukuo on a larger scale. It is not the Government of China. It does not pass the first test. It is not Chinese. It is not entitled to speak for China. . . . The National Government of the Republic of China [Formosa] . . . more authentically represents the views of the great body of the people of China.[2]

How the Chiang régime, after two years of rule on Formosa, represented 'the great body of the people of China', when in 1949 while it was still in possession of the mainland, Dean Acheson described it as a government which 'had lost popular support',[3] Rusk did not explain.

The statements of Rusk and Acheson revealed quite clearly the new 'fundamental' assumptions on which United States policy towards China was based. Here in black and white was the theory of monstrous conspiracy, and no other. There was no recognition of vast historical forces sweeping across China, forces which the Chinese Communists over a twenty-year period had organized, marshalled and led, against a hopelessly despotic, corrupt régime.

Moreover if 'the Communists took over China at a ridiculously small cost', as Acheson had come to say they did, then it became relevant to ask, why with its billions in aid, with its armies actually on the mainland amounting to 100,000 men, its technical advisors and missionaries, the United States Government couldn't 'save' China, as it had 'saved' Greece. This is, in fact, exactly what the

---

[1] Fleming, pp. 573–4, 576.
[2] Rusk's speech is printed in the *MacArthur Hearings,* pp. 3191–2, 1951.
[3] Acheson, op. cit., p. 164.

Republicans did ask, with devastating effect. (Acheson to this day is regarded by some as the man who 'lost' China.) But their question could never have been so devastating to the administration, and McCarthyism would never have been the powerful threat that it was (and remains), if it had not been supported in its basic thesis and world view by the very people whom it attacked, the presumably sophisticated proponents of containment.

For what was the theory of containment, as enunciated and practised by the Truman Administration, if not an 'answer' to the threat of a world *conspiracy*, rather than of a world *revolution*? The model invoked by United States leaders was the seizure of power by minority Communist Parties in East Europe (in the shadow of the Red Army); the Truman Doctrine and the Marshall Plan seemed reasonable measures for preventing a similar fate in West Europe. But the world revolution rising out of Africa, Asia and South America was of a different order of magnitude, and no Marshall Plan or Truman Doctrine could stem the revolutionary tide, because they could not, indeed would not support the changes in social relations which were necessary to make possible any alleviation of the misery of these impoverished, non-industrial and semi-feudal areas.

Against the (abnormal) background of Communist takeovers in East Europe,[1] the myth of the conspiratorial nature of what was, in fact, a world revolution sank popular roots, and in McCarthyist terms, the Enemy became: International Conspiratorial Communism. This international conspiracy was seen as nothing more than a clique of gangsters – the Kremlin gang – operating without any purpose but to perpetuate power, without any designs, but to extend their domination, without any capabilities, but the capabilities for subversion and suppression. In this view Communist dictatorships (regardless of country) were vulnerable, as any dictatorship was vulnerable, to a strong push at the top. In this view, also, power from the outside would undoubtedly generate revolutionary power within, for the dictatorship rested on a base of human suffering and nothing more. Thus the theory of containment, mounted on a theory of conspiracy, gave way to a new and dangerous logic: the logic of liberation.

[1] On the distorting influence of the East European events see discussion Chapter XXVI below.

CHAPTER VIII

Containment into Liberation: Korea

This chapter is for Inso, whose bitterness will never be assuaged but whose spirit remains unbroken.

The Koreans were not the first to learn that, while freedom is precious, 'liberation' is a high price to pay for it.

SIR ANTHONY EDEN

KOREA was occupied in 1945 by the Soviet Union and the United States in accord with their agreements at Cairo, Yalta and Potsdam.[1] By August 10, most of North Korea was in Russian hands. American troops landed in South Korea on September 8, and the United States proposed a demarcation line at the 38th Parallel.[2] Based on the exigencies of a military situation, the choice of the 38th Parallel as a line of demarcation was particularly unfortunate, because Korea's Japanese-built industries lay in the north, while the bulk of her population resided in the south. A disinterested policy would have spurred attempts to remove foreign forces at this early stage, while encouraging unification at once. But at the Moscow Conference in December 1945 (without consulting the Koreans) the Foreign Ministers decided that Korea should be held as a joint trusteeship for five years by the occupying powers.

After forty years of Japanese occupation, Korea was eager and

---

[1] W. D. Reeve, *The Republic of Korea*, 1963, p. 23; Reeve was in Korea from 1952–6, most of the time as advisor to the Prime Minister of the South Korean Government. His book was written under the auspices of the Royal Institute of International Affairs. On the ensuing events, cf. Fleming pp. 589–660, on which this account draws heavily.

[2] Dean Acheson testified in the *MacArthur Hearings* (Part 3, p. 2104) that the division at the 38th was recommended by the Secretary of War, was approved by the Joint Chiefs of Staff, by the State–Army–Navy–Air Force Coordinating Committee, and by the President.

ready in 1945 to reassume the tasks of self-government. A nation-wide resistance movement existed which had organized revolutionary committees throughout Korea upon Japan's surrender. Although Communists were members of nearly all of these committees (they were the only party with a nation-wide membership), the committees themselves contained representatives of all groups. In the important province of Cholla Nam Do, the committee was headed by a pro-American Christian pastor.[1]

A representative assembly of these Committees of Preparation for National Independence was held in Seoul on September 6, and formed a national government with jurisdiction over all of Korea, North and South. 'If the People's Republic exhibited radical tendencies, it only reflected with reasonable accuracy the views of the Korean majority.'[2] Two days later, the American occupation force, headed by General John R. Hodge, landed, ignored the People's Republic Government which had just been formed, made use instead of Japanese and quisling elements, and on October 5 appointed an Advisory Council which contained many 'well known collaborators'.[3]

In these little-known events of the immediate post-war period are buried the seeds of the Korean tragedy. At the other end of the globe, during these years, the wartime alliance was giving way to the cold war, the effect of which in Korea was to preclude the possibility of a unified effort to bind up the nation's wounds.

On October 10, the United States Military Government in Korea (USAMIGIK)[4] proclaimed itself to be the only government in South Korea and called for an end to the pronouncements of 'irresponsible political groups'. These acts 'crystalized a large part of Korean thinking into an anti-American mold' and made the people feel that 'the liberators had become the oppressors'.[5] When a Congress of the People's Republic met on November 20, 1945, and

[1] E. Grant Meade, *American Military Government in Korea*, 1951, pp. 69–72. Meade was a member of the American Military Government.

[2] ibid. These radical views included 'the call for unification, land reform, the ousting of Japanese collaborators, wide extension of the suffrage, and the formation of cooperatives'. – Reeve, op. cit., p. 24.

[3] ibid., pp. 59–62.

[4] It should be noted that not a single member of the USAMIGIK spoke Korean. Alfred Crofts, 'Our Falling Ramparts – the Case of Korea', *The Nation*, June 25, 1960, p. 545. Crofts himself was a member of USAMIGIK.

[5] Meade, op. cit.

refused to dissolve itself, General Hodge declared its activities unlawful. On February 14, 1946, a Representative Democratic Council, sponsored by the United States Military Government and headed by the just-returned Syngman Rhee (who had spent thirty-seven of his seventy years in the United States)[1], was formed. This council was heavily rightist,[2] based on the landlords, capitalists and other conservative elements, and leading liberals refused to participate.[3]

By May 1946, when the Soviet and American members of the Joint Commission were failing to reach agreement on unification, the jails in the American zone were 'filled to the rafters' with opponents of the Rhee régime.[4] The reason for the deadlock between the occupying powers was simple. While the United States had set up its own puppet régime in the South, the Russians had acted to achieve similar control in the North. Instead of ignoring the native Korean Government, however, the Russians took 'extreme care' to keep themselves in the background, making sure at the same time that the Communist wings within the government councils would be able to establish their control. A government was formed, headed by Kim Il-Sung, a leading Korean Communist and revolutionist against Japanese rule. In March, 1946, Kim's Government carried out a land reform, dividing one-half of the existing land between 725,000 landless peasants; this act promoted a feeling of loyalty for his régime from the start.[5]

In the South, the American Military Government issued a decree two years after the Northern reform under which roughly 700,000 acres of former Japanese holdings were sold to 600,000 tenant families. This reform was so popular that nearly all candidates in the election of May 10, 1948 campaigned for further distribution of privately owned lands. But the Rhee Government delayed a new land reform law repeatedly; meanwhile, tenants were being forced by

[1] Crofts, op. cit. 'In mid-October, USAMIGIK welcomed Syngman Rhee, Director of the wartime Korean Commission in Washington. ... His return attracted little general attention, though from the first he seems to have won the favor of collaborationist groups.'

[2] Crofts, 'Before the American landings, a political Right, associated in popular thought with colonial rule, could not exist; but shortly afterward we were to foster at least three conservative factions.' cf. also Reeve, p. 25.

[3] George M. McCune, *Korea Today*, 1950, pp. 47–52.

[4] Mark Gayn, *Japan Diary*, 1948, p. 431.

[5] McCune, op. cit., pp. 51–2; 201–7.

their landlords to buy the plots they tilled on unfavorable terms or be evicted.[1]

Thus, 'the unhappy Koreans, who only wanted to be rid of all foreigners, rapidly became two countries with very different social outlooks, both halves of the nation suffering great economic hardship from its artificial division'.[2]

On November 14, 1947, in the face of failure by the United States and the Soviet Union to reach agreement on Korean unification, the UN General Assembly created a United Nations Temporary Commission on Korea to expedite its independence. The Soviet Union refused this Commission permission to enter North Korea, and eventually it was decided to hold an election in South Korea alone. This decision was opposed strongly by the Australian and Canadian representatives. It was also opposed by the middle-of-the-road and leftist groups in South Korea on the grounds that a separate election would divide the country permanently, and that, moreover, a free atmosphere did not exist. 'Only the Rightists favored the separate election.'[3] The Communists and Rightists formed terrorist bands before the elections (to be held on May 10, 1948) and in six weeks prior to the balloting, 589 people were killed. The Rightists won a heavy victory and the UN Commission certified that the results 'were a valid expression of the will of the electorate in those parts of Korea which were accessible to the Commission'. Not too many parts could have been accessible to the Commission, however, as they had only thirty people to observe the elections. A contrary view holds 'that the elections were not in fact a free expression of the Korean will'.[4]

On December 12, 1948, the UN General Assembly passed, by 41–6, a resolution declaring the Rhee Government to be 'a lawful government having effective control over that part of Korea where the Temporary Commission was able to observe . . .; that this Government is based on elections which were a valid expression of the free will of the electorate of that part of Korea . . .' and further, 'that this is the only such [i.e. lawful and freely elected] Government in Korea'. The resolution, it should be noted, did *not* give backing to the Rhee Government's subsequent claim to be the only legitimate

[1] ibid., pp. 133–8.
[2] Fleming, op. cit., p. 592.   [3] ibid., p. 592. Reeve, pp. 26–7.
[4] McCune, op. cit., pp. 229–30.

government for the *whole* of Korea, but only purported to deal with
the question of the proper government in that part of Korea open
to observation by the Temporary Commission.[1]

Despite its UN sanction, the Rhee Government was so unpopular
as to make its ability to survive doubtful.[2] Moreover, the tip of the
Korean Peninsula was not strategically vital. These realities led
American strategists to place it outside of the United States defensive perimeter, which ran from the Aleutians through Japan to the
Philippines. As late as January 1950 Secretary of State Acheson
publicly defined this perimeter as excluding Korea, a statement
which later evoked heavy Republican criticism as having invited the
North Korean invasion.[3]

By 1950, the United States was faced with a considerable dilemma.
Operating under the mutually dependent theories of conspiracy and
containment, the Truman Administration had found it virtually
impossible to 'explain' to the satisfaction of the American people the
'loss' of China, a situation which the right wing was exploiting to
the full. Now, new difficulties loomed. Inevitably, the Chinese Communists would attempt to complete their revolution by destroying the
remaining Kuomintang forces which had sought refuge on Formosa.

The United States could choose to intervene in Chinese affairs,
to defend Chaing, thus driving the wedge deeper between the new
China and American interests (at this time Acheson was farsighted
enough to perceive that there were basic areas of conflict between
Russia and China which could be exploited.)[4] Or it could elect to
stand by while the Communists disposed of the hopelessly corrupt
and ruthless Nationalist remnants.

---

[1] Reeve, op. cit., p. 27.

[2] It should be noted that the Franchise Law (passed on June 27, 1947) was
restrictive, debarring the large group of illiterates, for example. As a result, the
government was dominated by 'landlords and members of the old aristocracy'
(Reeve, p. 31). Two rebellions broke out in 1948, in Yosu and Cheju Do. 'While
every allowance must be made for government nervousness in the face of
rumours of imminent invasion from the north, the "near-extinction of civil
liberties" which followed the [Yosu] rebellion, as well as such strong-arm
methods as the razing of villages on "a vast scale" after an uprising in Cheju Do
in April 1948, gave the régime a fascist stamp.' – Reeve, p. 32, cf. also Fleming,
p. 592.

[3] cf., for example, campaign speech by Eisenhower, *Time*, October 6, 1952.

[4] John Spanier, *The Truman–MacArthur Controversy and the Korean War*,
1959, pp. 51–61. Spanier also deals with the Republican thrusts at this policy
and the resulting inflexibility in the American position.

Acheson's statements, in January 1950, excluding Formosa as well as Korea from the United States defense perimeter can be seen as an attempt to justify Chiang's collapse from a strategic point of view. Indeed, on December 23, 1949, the State Department had sent a private circular to diplomats abroad preparing them for the fall of Formosa and for the non-intervention of the United States. The right wing went into action immediately. On January 2, former President Hoover and Senator Taft demanded the use of the Navy to defend Chiang and, on January 3, the contents of the confidential circular were leaked to the public from Tokyo.

On January 5, the Administration reaffirmed its stand in a written statement which declared that, 'The United States has no predatory designs on Formosa or any other Chinese territory. . . . Nor does it have any intention of utilizing its armed forces to interfere in the present situation. The United States Government will not pursue a course which will lead to involvement in the civil conflict in China.'[1] Moreover, Acheson declared that this was not basically a strategic decision but had to do 'with the fundamental integrity of the United States and with maintaining in the world the belief that when the United States takes a position it sticks to that position and does not change it by reason of transitory expediency or advantage on its part'. Acheson was referring to the fact that the United States had promised at Cairo, Yalta and Potsdam that Formosa would be returned to China, i.e. to the government in control of the mainland.[2]

Within six months the non-intervention policy was reversed – and the solemn wartime pledges to restore Formosa to China were broken. In the face of mounting attack by the Republican and Democratic right wing, Acheson survived by 'trading policy for time', as Walter Lippmann observed.

In May, Senator Tom Connally, Chairman of the Senate Foreign Relations Committee, said in an interview that many people 'believe that events will transpire which will maneuver around and present an incident which will make us fight. That's what a lot of them are saying: "We've got to battle some time, why not now?"'

---

[1] Spanier, op. cit., p. 55.
[2] ibid.
[3] Cited in Fleming, pp. 593–4, cf. also I. F. Stone, *The Hidden History of the Korean War*, 1952, p. 22. Stone's main thesis is that MacArthur, Dulles, Chiang and Rhee provoked the Korean War.

Among those who had a clear interest in an incident which would call forth American military intervention were the threatened Chiang and Rhee.

Rhee's stake in a possible involvement of United States military forces in the defense of South Korea was great. On May 30, less than four weeks before fighting broke out, Rhee was decisively defeated in the elections. 'The régime was left tottering by lack of confidence, both in Korea and abroad.'[1] In the face of a deteriorating political position, both Rhee and his Defense Minister for months had been threatening to invade North Korea, declaring that they were ready to 'take Pyongyang within a few days' and 'do all the fighting needed'.[2] Indeed, according to the syndicated right wing columnist, Holmes Alexander, Secretary of State Acheson 'never was quite sure that Rhee did not provoke the Red attack of 1950'.[3] At MacArthur's headquarters on that fateful day, John Gunther reported 'one of the important members of the occupation [was] called unexpectedly to the telephone. He came back and whispered, "A big story had just broken. The South Koreans have attacked North Korea!" '[4]

The United States, recognizing Rhee's unreliability, had taken the precaution to arm the South Korean Army with light weapons for defensive purposes only[5] so as to remove any temptation to invade North Korea. This, however, did not rule out provocation. If the North did initiate hostilities, moreover, it is something less than believable that MacArthur's Military Intelligence was entirely unaware of the imminence of the attack, as is generally reported. (The command in Tokyo is supposed to have been 'taken utterly by surprise' as was President Truman and the Administration. And this in turn is cited to explain why no counter-buildup was ordered

[1] *US News and World Report*, July 7, 1950, p. 29. Cited in Fleming, p. 594. Reeve, p. 42: 'As the election campaign progressed, there were more and more arrests of candidates and their supporters for violating the National Security Law; nevertheless the results showed that most of the electorate preferred candidates not openly associated with the parties of the old Assembly, for 133 independents were elected out of a total of 210 members. . . . the President's supporters . . . fell from 56 to 12.'

[2] Fleming, op. cit., p. 654.

[3] ibid.

[4] John Gunther, *The Riddle of MacArthur*, 1951, p. 166.

[5] Department of State, *U.S. Policy in the Korean Crisis*, pp. 21–2.

to protect the Parallel.) But, MacArthur's intelligence chief, Major-General Charles A. Willoughby has disparaged this 'alleged "surprise" of the North Korean invasion', saying that 'The entire North Korean Army had been alerted for weeks and was in position along the 38th Parallel.'[1] According to John Gunther, the attack was launched from four points and consisted of 70,000 men and 70 tanks, which he considered must have taken a month to six weeks to organize. Thus many agonizing questions about the triggering of this war will have to await a time when further evidence becomes accessible.

If the relative availability of data makes it possible to gain insight into the dynamics of the situation in Washington and the Far East prior to the outbreak of the war, the scarcity of parallel information makes it exceedingly difficult to know the factors at work on the other side of the dividing line. Yet hindsight, and the inevitably wider perspective that distance brings to the view of a once tense political situation, casts serious doubt on the basic Western thesis that the North Korean invasion was directed by the Kremlin as part of a general plan of remorseless expansion.

First, this objective hardly required a major military move because, as Acheson acknowledged subsequently, 'the Communists had far from exhausted the potentialities for obtaining their objectives through guerilla and psychological warfare, political pressure and intimidation'.[2] This was amply demonstrated by the results of the May election and the approaching demise of the Rhee régime.

Kremlin strategy was also known to be conservative at this time and to be highly sceptical of 'adventuristic' moves, a factor which would have been especially important considering the fluid situation in the South. In fact the Communists lost four concrete advantages as a result of the war's outbreak, including 'a favorable rearming ratio; the neutrality of certain people; the element of surprise; and the imminent recognition of Red Chinese delegates by the United Nations'.[3] Indeed, the thesis of Kremlin direction cannot be squared with the fact that the Soviet Union opted to boycott the UN at precisely that time in protest against Taiwan's presence on the

[1] Cited in Fleming, p. 599.
[2] Cited in Fleming, p. 599; *MacArthur Hearings* (Part 3), pp. 1990–91.
[3] Wilbur W. Hitchcock, 'No. Korea Jumps the Gun', *Current History*, March 1951.

Security Council. If the Kremlin had planned the invasion, it is difficult to understand why they did not postpone the attack for one month until the Russian delegate would have been chairman of the Security Council and could have frustrated any proposed moves until the North Koreans had defeated the ill-equipped South Korean Army.[1]

Nor was the North Korean Army adequately equipped to carry out an invasion in September 1950 as Joseph Alsop reported from Korea. The United States did not possess air control over the battlefield. There had been many occasions when 'even two enemy intruder fighters, attacking the interminable lines of our transport moving over the appalling Korea roads in broad daylight would have been enough to produce a twenty-four hour tangle' and we would 'have lost our foothold in Korea'. But no enemy planes ever came because the Russians were not 'prepared to play the game at all'.[2] Even Soviet propaganda was caught napping by the attack. Communist papers were scooped on the outbreak and had no ready story of explanation, an unlikely pass had the invasion been carefully planned.

A former member of the United States Military Government in Korea, analyzing these and other facts inconsistent with the Western thesis, concludes that the attack on South Korea was ordered by Kim Il-Sung of North Korea, not only without instructions from Moscow, but without its knowledge. The immediate event triggering Kim's decision may have been the fact that three envoys sent to Seoul on June 11 to discuss unification had been arrested, and probably shot. A new Russian arms shipment had recently arrived, Rhee had been repudiated at the polls and a bumper rice crop was waiting in the South for the first time since World War II.[3]

Whatever the war's origin, it is very clear that there were elements of genuine civil conflict in the Korean situation which gave it a dynamic of its own. This is borne out by the fact that within weeks of the outbreak of fighting,

[1] ibid., summarized in Fleming, pp. 606–8.

[2] New York, *Herald Tribune*, September 29, 1950. cf. Walter Lippmann, New York *Herald Tribune*, October 5, 1950, for similar views.

[3] Hitchcock, op. cit., cf. also Fleming's discussion of this article and other points, pp. 604–8. cf. Spanier, op. cit., p. 15 et seq., especially p. 29 for official American estimates.

... three-fourths of South Korea was overrun. The invaders' Russian tanks could easily have been stopped in the hills by a resolute defense; ... Communist doctrine had little appeal to a population familiar with the grim reports of Northern refugees. But millions of South Koreans welcomed the prospect of unification, even on Communist terms. They had suffered police brutality, intellectual repression and political purge. Few felt much incentive to fight for profiteers or to die for Syngman Rhee. Only 10 per cent of the Seoul population abandoned the city; many troops deserted, and a number of public figures, including Kimm Kiu Sic,[1] joined the North.[2]

When the fighting broke out, a cable was sent by the UN Temporary Commission on Korea to the UN's Secretary General declaring that what looked like a full-scale war was in progress, but assessing no blame for the origin of the fighting, even quoting the North Korean radio claim that the South Koreans had invaded during the night and were being pursued south. The report suggested a meeting of the Security Council.[3] With this cable (and no other) before it, the Security Council adopted a United States resolution condemning the armed attack on the Republic of Korea, demanding an immediate withdrawal of North Korean forces to the 38th Parallel and calling on all members to render every assistance to the UN in the execution of this resolution.[4] The question of responsibility for the war was thus 'answered', with few facts, by the West's built-in majority in the Security Council, and the juridical ground work for the subsequent 'police action' laid.

[1] Kimm Kiu Sic, along with Kim Koo, Lyuh Woon Hyeung and Rhee, was one of the leading figures in South Korea's political life. American-educated, he had formed a party in opposition to the left of center Republic of Lyuh Woon Hyeung. Kim Koo, 'the most distinguished of the returning *émigrés*' whose government-in-exile had kept 35,000 troops in the field with the Chinese Nationalist Army, sought peaceful unification with the North until he was assassinated in the South in 1949. Lyuh Woon Hyeung was assassinated in the South in 1947.

[2] Crofts, op. cit.

[3] Fleming, op. cit., p. 601; Spanier, op. cit., pp. 35–6.

[4] Spanier, p. 39. The countries taking part in the police action were Australia, Belgium, Canada, France, Greece, Turkey, the Netherlands, New Zealand, the Union of South Africa, the United Kingdom, Thailand, the Philippines, Colombia and Ethiopia.

On June 27, President Truman ordered 'United States Air and Sea forces to give the Korean government troops cover and support'.[1] He also commanded the Seventh Fleet to interpose itself between Formosa and China (reversing the policy of non-intervention in the Chinese Civil War) and increased military assistance to the Philippines and to the French troops seeking to maintain their colonial dominance over the rebelling Vietnamese. On the same day, the United States called upon the Security Council to invoke sanctions against North Korea; the Council responded by recommending 'such assistance to the Republic of Korea as may be necessary to repel the armed attack and to restore peace and security in the area'.[2] This resolution passed, attaining just the necessary seven votes (of eleven) required by the Charter. Yugoslavia voted 'no' because she thought the Council did not have enough information, while Egypt and India abstained.

The haste with which these steps were taken was somewhat extraordinary since, as Fleming notes, 'up to this time enforcement of the United Nations Charter had not been a compelling motive in Washington'.

The UN was brushed aside in Greece, and independent action taken to defeat the Communist guerillas. In Indonesia the United States had brought strong moral pressure to bear on the Netherlands in the Security Council, but no troops and planes were sent to fight the Dutch when they defied a UN cease-fire order. Nor did the United States mobilize the UN to save the infant Israeli Republic when five Arab states invaded Palestine in 1948 to overturn by force the partition plan adopted by the UN General Assembly. Defiance of the UN could not have been more flagrant, but the United States moved no troops and planes to save the victims of Hitler's hate who had gathered in Israel and who appeared to be on the point of being destroyed by the armies of UN members converging on them from all sides. In the end Israel was saved by her own heroic fighting, with arms obtained largely from communist Czechoslovakia.

[1] State Department *White Paper*, op. cit., pp. 21–2.
[2] Security Council, Official Records, 5th year, Doc. 5/1501. cf. Fleming, p. 601.

The US gave no armed support to Israel as the ward of UN.[1]

In any case the UN condemned the North Koreans but never heard their side of the story. To be sure, the Security Council was correct in ordering the withdrawal of the invading North Korean troops from South Korean soil, and in taking steps to force them to do so when they disregarded the order. But after the *status quo* had been restored, it was incumbent upon the UN to hear both litigants in the dispute and to render judgement as an international organization and court. Unfortunately, by the time the *status quo* had been restored and the North Korean armies were returned to North Korean territory, the UN action was firmly under the control of forces unleashed by America's cold war crusade.

On July 12, 1950, with the North Korean forces racing southward towards Pusan, the House of Representatives applauded Congressman who urged that the cities of the North Koreans be atom-bombed unless they withdrew in a week's time.[2] On July 31, General MacArthur visited Chiang Kai-shek on Formosa to confer on the defense of the island. Upon his return to Tokyo MacArthur praised Chiang whose 'indomitable determination to resist Communist domination arouses my sincere admiration. His determination parallels the common interests and purpose of Americans, that all people in the Pacific should be free – not slaves'.[3]

The determination to emancipate the slaves on the other side of the 38th Parallel (and in MacArthur's mind there seems never to have been a doubt that China itself would have to be liberated – soon) led to the key decision in the Korean War, what Fleming has charitably called 'the cardinal error in our foreign policy to date [1960]'. This was the decision to 'liberate' North Korea.

On September 15, MacArthur had landed the marines at Inchon, from where they began to break the North Korean offensive, until on September 30, with the enemy in full retreat, they reached the 38th Parallel. On October 1, MacArthur issued an ultimatum to the

[1] Fleming, op. cit., pp. 603-4.
[2] Cited in Fleming, p. 609, New York *Herald Tribune*, July 13, 1950, along with a number of other cries for 'a showdown' with Russia.
[3] Spanier, op. cit., p. 71.

North Koreans to lay down their arms and cease hostilities 'under such military supervision as I may direct'.[1]

As Dean Acheson had recently observed, the 'one difference which is just about impossible to negotiate is someone's desire to eliminate your existence altogether'. MacArthur's call for North Korea's unconditional surrender merely ensured the continuation of hostilities.[2] Indeed, MacArthur's troops were already preparing to set foot upon North Korean soil.

MacArthur's invasion of North Korea had been fully authorized more than two weeks earlier (on September 11) by President Truman. On September 26, the Joint Chiefs informed MacArthur that his 'military objective is the destruction of the North Korean armed forces' – a more ambitious objective than restoration of the *status quo ante* – and in pursuit of this authorized him to 'conduct military operations north of the 38th Parallel'.[3]

On September 30, United States Ambassador Warren Austin presented the United States' position to the UN. 'The aggressor's forces should not be permitted to have refuge behind an imaginary line. . . . The artificial barrier which has divided North and South Korea has no basis for existence in law or in reason.'[4]

On October 1, South Korean forces under MacArthur's command crossed the 38th Parallel and advanced rapidly to points deep in North Korean territory.[5] Six days later, a full month after President Truman had authorized such action, the UN General Assembly approved an American–British resolution which sanctioned, but did not mandate, the northward invasion. The UN invasion of North Korea was, of course, a travesty of basic UN principles.

> It meant that the United Nations were no longer concerned only to repel the invasion and clear South Korea of the enemy. They were now committed to war against the North Koreans, to the invasion of North Korean territory. And they were carrying out

[1] Fleming, p. 615.

[2] Cf. Spanier, op. cit., p. 91.

[3] Courtney Whitney, *MacArthur: His Rendezvous with History*, 1956, p. 397. Cited Spanier, p. 95.

[4] Spanier, op. cit., p. 88. The barrier had been proposed, of course, by the United States. See above p. 114.

[5] UN Documents, S/1840, S/1843. Cited in Fleming, p. 617, and Spanier, p. 100.

this undertaking without first hearing the North Korean case. They were abandoning the principle of attempting to settle the dispute by peaceful means, and were now resorting to force. They were now participants in the dispute, allies of one of the parties to the dispute.[1]

If the UN attempt to unify divided Korea by force at this time was unjustifiable as well as inappropriate because of the character of that body, the United States' role similarly lacks justification. For to seek, as the United States did, to unify Korea by force, was to do exactly what the North Koreans were judged to be so wrong in attempting to do. As President Eisenhower said to Syngman Rhee, in June 1953, to dissuade the latter from breaking the imminent truce: 'It was indeed a crime that [North Korea] invoked violence to unite Korea. But I urge that your country not embark upon a similar course . . .'[2] Thus, in 1953, Eisenhower unwittingly underscored the culpability of United States' actions two years before.

In any case, had the United States-controlled UN forces stopped at the 38th Parallel, the UN's chief objective, as expressed in its June 27 resolution, would have been accomplished, and the principle of collective security would have been dramatically and effectively defended. As it was, *four-fifths* of all American casualties occurred *after* the original UN aim of re-establishing the *status quo* had been achieved. Assuming similar proportions for North Korean, Chinese and United Nations casualties, the attempt to 'liberate' North Korea, a project clearly beyond the jurisdiction of a United Nations organization, resulted in 4,000,000 casualties.[3] Korea itself lay in ruins from end to end, its fields awaste, its industrial centers smashed by American bombs, its villages burned, its people deeply scarred and once again left under the heel of military occupation

[1] Ingram, p. 196. The United States contention that there was only one Korea, that North Korea did not exist, that the 38th Parallel was an 'artificial barrier' having 'no basis for existence in law or reason' cannot be squared, of course, with the original UN resolution calling on the North Koreans to withdraw behind the barrier.

[2] *Time*, June 29, 1953, p. 19.

[3] Fleming, p. 656. A significantly smaller, but equally appalling estimate is given in R. Leckie, *The Korean War*, 1962: 2,415,601 total casualties, exclusive of North Korean civilians.

and dictatorship, the nation more hopelessly divided than before.

This was the terrible price paid for a military operation justified by the United States in terms of preventing 'future attacks'. ('The aggressor's forces should not be permitted to have refuge behind an imaginary line because that would recreate the threat to the peace of Korea and the world.'[1]) The same doctrine was invoked to justify the attempt to drive the North Koreans beyond the Yalu, even after their armies had been smashed;[2] and the same reasoning underlay MacArthur's proposed strategy to bomb Manchuria. Indeed, the same reasoning would have justified a campaign to eliminate threats to the peace all the way to Moscow. Containment, which was, after all, a military and not a diplomatic doctrine, could never be satisfied until it had passed into liberation. The best defense, under a military definition of reality, is always an offense. For the military objective is the elimination of the opponent, not the establishment of a *modus vivendi* with him.

That the crossing of the Parallel had dubious legality, was clear from the actions of American leaders themselves. On September 30, when United States forces had reached the 38th Parallel, MacArthur wired Secretary of Defense Marshall that he intended to issue a directive to the Eighth Army to liberate the North under the June 27 UN resolution. Marshall cabled back: 'We desire that you proceed with your operations without any further explanation or announcement and let action determine the matter. Our government desires to avoid having to make an issue of the 38th Parallel until we have accomplished our mission.'[3] This message reportedly caused even MacArthur to 'raise his eyebrows . . . MacArthur could appreciate the President's natural inclination to present the other United Nations governments with a *fait accompli*'.[4]

The strategy was eminently successful. South Korean troops crossed the frontier on October 1, and on October 7 the General Assembly provided, perforce, the necessary sanction. India and six other Afro-Asian nations abstained because it 'would impair faith

---

[1] Spanier, op. cit., p. 88. Statement of Warren Austin, US delegate to the UN.

[2] ibid., p. 123.

[3] ibid., p. 100; Whitney, p. 399.

[4] Whitney, op. cit., p. 399. Spanier thinks this '*fait accompli*' was actually the work of some 'leading Western powers' including Britain. Cf., op. cit., p. 100.

in the United Nations if we were to authorize the unification of Korea by force against North Korea after [resisting] North Korea's attempt to unify Korea by force against South Korea'.[1] The United States resolution to sanction action in the North was carried 47–5, a dubious victory since the United States had in its pocket the votes of the South American bloc representing 40 per cent of the Assembly, the West-European powers heavily dependent on the United States financially, and such other US dependencies as Turkey, Thailand, Formosa and the Philippines.

If moral and legal considerations were negligible factors in the United States decision to cross the Parallel, power considerations were more seriously weighed. The main question, of course, was whether China would enter the war.

Dean Acheson thought they would not. 'Now I give the people in Peiping credit for being intelligent enough to see what is happening to them,' he said on September 10. 'Why they should want to further their own dismemberment and destruction by getting at cross purposes with all the free nations of the world who are inherently their friends and have always been friends of the Chinese as against this imperialism coming down from the Soviet Union I cannot see. And since there is nothing in it for them, I don't see why they should yield to what is undoubtedly pressure from the Communist movement to get into the Korean War.'[2] Despite the rapid accumulation of intelligence reports indicating Chinese preparations, Acheson maintained this posture of naïve incredulity.

In fact, even after the Chinese had entered the war, Acheson declared that 'no possible shred of evidence could have existed in the minds of the Chinese Communist authorities about the intentions of the forces of the United Nations. Repeatedly, and from the very beginning of the action, it had been made clear that the sole mission of the United Nations forces was to repel the aggressors and to restore to the people of Korea their independence'.[3] In other words, the Chinese were to trust these friendly armies to liberate Korea right up to their border and stop there, and to protect Chinese interests in the Yalu dam and power complexes which supplied

---

[1] *Time*, June 29, 1953.
[2] Spanier, op. cit., p. 99.
[3] ibid., p. 97.

F.W.C.—E

China's industrial heartland with electrical power. That the Chinese remained unconvinced seems hardly surprising.

Of course 'assurance after assurance was offered to Peking'[1] after US–UN forces had crossed the 38th Parallel to the effect that China's interests would be respected. But the Chinese could cite impressive chapter-and-verse to justify little faith in such promises. On January 5, 1950, for example, President Truman had declared in a written statement that 'The United States has no predatory designs on Formosa. . . . Nor does it have any intention of utilizing its armed forces to interfere in the present situation.' Six months later, he interposed the Seventh Fleet between Formosa and the mainland and began a military and economic aid program to Chiang's Army. On July 10, 1950, Acheson himself said that the United States was fighting in Korea 'solely for the purpose of restoring the Republic of Korea *to its status prior to the invasion from the North*'.[2] Three months later, the United States was doing precisely what Acheson had declared it would not do, that is, seeking by force to alter the previous *status quo*.

On October 23 (a month before China entered the war), a spokesman for the United States First Corps announced that 'foreign troops would be halted forty miles south of the Yalu'. Forty-eight hours later, the plan was denied by the Eighth Army in Korea and MacArthur's headquarters, which felt that such action would 'establish a new "Thirty-eighth Parallel" . . . It would also offer a North Korean Government a segment of territory where it might freely reorganize for new blows against the Korean Republic'.[3]

Thus, it did not require that the Chinese leaders be paranoid to interpret United States' actions in terms of classic aggression. And indeed, on November 28, a Chinese spokesman at the United Nations made this charge, saying that the Chinese people 'know fully well that the United States Government has taken this series of aggressive actions with the purpose of realizing its fantatical devotion of dominating Asia and the world. One of the master-planners of Japanese aggression, Tanaka, once said: to conquer the world, one

---

[1] ibid., p. 120.

[2] Spanier, op. cit., pp. 88–9, State Department Bulletin XXIII (July 10, 1960), p. 46. Emphasis added.

[3] Spanier, op. cit., p. 123. 'Headquarters did not explain how an almost totally defeated enemy would rebuild his army for such a strike.'

must first conquer Asia; to conquer Asia, one must first conquer China; to conquer China, one must first conquer Korea and Taiwan ... American Imperialism ... plagiarizes Tanaka's memorandum, and follows the beaten path of Japan's imperialist aggressors!'[1]

In terms of MacArthur's actions, at least, the accusation was not so far-fetched. The Supreme Commander had declared in Seoul, Korea, in August 1948:

> This barrier [the 38th Parallel] must and will be torn down. Nothing shall prevent the ultimate unity of your people as free men of a free nation ... The manner in which those issues are resolved will determine in large measure not only the unity and well-being of your people, but also of the future stability of the continent of Asia.[2]

This could only mean the destruction of Communist power. 'The lands touching the Pacific' MacArthur had declared earlier 'with their billions of inhabitants will determine the course of history for the next ten thousand years!'

Eventually, MacArthur had to be relieved of his post to prevent him from spreading the war to China by enlisting the forces of Chiang Kai-shek and bombing Manchuria. Upon his return home, he was given a demonstration of popular support never before witnessed in the United States.

At the beginning of October, as United Nations armies invaded North Korea, the Chinese leaders warned publicly that China would not 'supinely tolerate the destruction of its neighbor'. But the US-led advance continued relentlessly. In the last half of October, 250,000 Chinese troops were reported massing along the Korean frontier. By the end of October, the first Chinese 'volunteers' had been taken prisoner.[3]

On November 5, after a Chinese strike which sent a United Nations army into retreat,[4] MacArthur still contended that the

---

[1] Spanier, op. cit., pp. 86–7.
[2] John Gunther, op. cit., p. 169, cited in Fleming, p. 595.
[3] At the MacArthur Hearings, General Collins, Chairman of the Joint Chiefs of Staff, declared that intelligence concerning the Chinese intention to intervene during this period was 'voluminous'. Cf. Fleming, p. 616 n. Also Spanier, pp. 114–15.
[4] Spanier, op. cit., pp. 118–19.

Chinese probably would not officially enter the war.[1] Even in his last fatal attack which brought the Chinese in 'with both feet' he felt that his boldness would convince Peking that Korea's fate had already been settled, particularly since he had publicly announced that the 'new and nerve-shattering experiences' of a modern army's fire power and low-level strafing had demoralized the Chinese Communist forces.[2] MacArthur operated at this time – and throughout the war – on this thesis which he had expressed with utmost candor. '. . . it is in the pattern of the Oriental psychology to respect and follow aggressive, resolute and dynamic leadership.'[3]

After the November 5 setback at the hands of the Chinese forces, 'abrupt calm' developed on the battlefront, and a series of diplomatic moves began. Britain strongly urged the United States to permit the Chinese to occupy a buffer zone; Churchill supported the endeavor.[4] Meanwhile, the Chinese were scheduled to arrive at the United Nations in New York. On November 22, 'well informed sources' in Washington indicated that agreement on a plan for a buffer strip along the Manchurian border was near and awaited 'primary approval of its military details by General of the Army, Douglas MacArthur'. Final agreement was expected momentarily.[5]

Then, on November 24, *the day the representative of the Chinese Communist Government arrived in New York* to participate in the United Nations Security Council debate, MacArthur launched a 100,000-man offensive towards the Yalu River. 'He launched it knowing there were at least 100,000 men facing him in front and 40,000 guerillas behind him. He also knew that the size of his assaulting force was inadequate for a frontal attack; he therefore split his attacking army in two [the wings were so far apart and liaison between them was so difficult that it was established through Tokyo instead],[6] thereby creating an attractive and fatal vacuum in the middle of his line.'[7]

---

[1] ibid., p. 121. The Chinese were claiming at this point that their troops were volunteers.

[2] ibid., p. 122.

[3] Cited in Fleming, p. 612: New York *Times*, August 29, 1950.

[4] Cited in Fleming, p. 621: New York *Times*, November 14, 1950; New York *Herald Tribune*, November 16, 17, 1950.

[5] Fleming, p. 621.

[6] ibid , p 621.

[7] Spanier, op. cit., p. 122 (emphasis added).

In the light of this, MacArthur's move could have had only one objective: to prevent a peace settlement and to provoke China into entering the war.[1] He was entirely successful. The Chinese openly and massively entered on November 26. The United Nations armies were cut to ribbons. The point of no return had been reached; the real bloodletting and destruction had begun. As the decimated United Nations forces moved South through December and January, they adopted a scorched earth retreat leaving millions of Koreans homeless and hungry.

At his press conference November 30, President Truman stated that 'we will take whatever steps are necessary to meet the military situation.' When asked if that included the Atomic Bomb, he said: 'that includes every weapon we have' and added that 'there has always been active consideration of its [the Atomic Bomb's] use'.[2]

The Chinese response to MacArthur's attack convinced the National Security Council, according to the Alsops, that the Soviet Union (!) had moved the 'time of utmost peril' when it would be ready for major aggression up from 1953–4 to 1950–51, so that the United States government leaders 'expect major Soviet aggression now, today, tomorrow, next month, next spring, next summer'. It was no use 'pretending that much can be accomplished' before the crisis, but every man and weapon 'will surely be needed somewhere, somehow and soon'.[3]

The Chinese, 'dizzy with success', crossed the 38th Parallel south in late December, committing the same fault as that of the United Nations forces before.[4] They were stopped and stalemated in mid-January. The New Year brought world-wide appeals for negotiation from such leaders as the Pope and nine ministers of the British Commonwealth. The problem of peace, they said, was that of removing the causes of war; of easing tension and promoting understanding; and of 'being at all times willing to discuss our differences

[1] Neither our own policy nor that of the United Nations required his mad dash to the Manchurian Border, 'and this MacArthur knew . . . The decision was his; it was provocation'. – McGeorge Bundy, 'Appeasement, Provocation and Policy', *The Reporter*, January 9, 1951; cited in Fleming, p. 622.

[2] Truman, *Memoirs*, II, p. 395.

[3] Fleming, p. 626.

[4] Ingram, op. cit. Chou En-Lai recognized the existence of a 'boundary' when on October 1, 1950, he announced that his government 'would not stand idly by when the territory of its neighbour [North Korea] was wantonly invaded'.

without foolishly assuming that all attempts to secure peace are a form of appeasement'.[1]

But US leaders were hardly in a state of mind to concern themselves with the discussion of differences. They were off on a new, solemn, freedom-advancing crusade: *to brand China the aggressor*. On December 20, Herbert Hoover demanded that the United Nations 'declare Communist China an aggressor' and on January 5, the United States sent notes to 29 governments warning that the United Nations might collapse (!) unless China were so branded. Nehru cautioned that such a branding would 'bolt and bar the door to a peaceful settlement in the Far East' but this did not faze the American leaders.

On January 19, the House of Representatives, with only two dissenting votes, passed a resolution demanding that the United Nations name China an aggressor and bar it from membership. Four days later, the United States Senate passed a similar resolution.

On January 11, a proposal for the withdrawal of all foreign troops 'by appropriate stages' and for a conference between the Great Powers had been introduced in the United Nations and was being discussed. The Chinese had sent a reply to this proposal which the United States termed a rejection. But most of the Arab–Asian bloc and some of our European allies held that it was not a rejection, but a bargaining step.[2]

United States pressure on the United Nations to act built up to the point where 'United States Ambassador Austin refused to agree to a forty-eight-hour postponement in the debate to allow the Indian delegate to get information which the latter thought was vital to the decision'. (James Reston.) The Indian delegate, Sir Benegal Rau, wanted the time to get added information concerning a new two-step settlement proposal from Mao Tse-Tung which had been sent through the Indian Government in response to a direct appeal from Nehru.

In the debate that followed this proposal the United States maintained its demand for action against the Chinese, opposing and defeating an Asian–Arab resolution proposing talks. Finally, the United States rammed through the resolution declaring China an

[1] Fleming, p. 630.
[2] *The Nation*, January 27, 1951; also cf. Fleming, p. 631.

aggressor, the Western Allies, as the *Wall Street Journal* put it, voting 'under the lash'.[1]

These events reminded Walter Lippmann of September, 1950 when Mr Acheson 'ordered Mr Austin to mount his white charger and lead the hosts of righteousness across the 38th Parallel' having no clear idea of what would follow after the United States had lined up the votes. Noting the Asian opposition, Lippmann called the vote a 'self-inflicted defeat' because the United States had 'used the whole apparatus of the United Nations to make a spectacular demonstration that Asia is not with us'.[2]

The United States then switched from its offensive in the United Nations to a military crusade on the battlefield, calling its new Korean policy 'Operation Killer', slaughter without end and without purpose, which, as Pearl Buck wrote, 'lost us what we cannot afford to lose – the mind of man in Asia'.[3]

But the actual destruction of the Korean peninsula had preceded the Chinese entry. General Emmet (Rosie) O'Donnell, who was head of the Bomber Command in the Far East, put it succinctly: 'I would say that the entire, almost the entire Korean peninsula is just a terrible mess. Everything is destroyed. There is nothing standing worthy of the name. . . . Just before the Chinese came in we were grounded. There were no more targets in Korea.'[4]

When the Chinese came into the war, General O'Donnell wanted to use the A-bomb on them at once. 'They'll understand the lash when it is put to them.'[5] The US–UN forces did not get to use the A-bomb, but they did experiment with a new weapon in Korea:

[1] 'None [of the European nations] could afford to alienate the US in a show-down', commented the *Journal*, 'but few hid their opposition'. – Cited in *The Nation*, February 10, 1951. cf. Sherman Adams, *Firsthand Report*, 1961, p. 127: In 1954, when the British were pressuring the Eisenhower Administration to recognize China, and support its admission to the UN as a measure which would reduce tension and the danger of war, Eisenhower demurred saying: 'How can we agree to admit to membership a country which the UN has branded an aggressor?'

[2] Cited in Fleming, p. 632.

[3] Cited in Fleming, p. 633: Pearl Buck, 'What Asians Want', *Christian Century*, June 27, 1951. cf. also James Michener in *Life*, June 1951: 'Never in our national history have we been so feared and despised . . . China, India, Burma and Indonesia today condemn us as reactionary and imperialistic. We . . . are ourselves branded as willful aggressors.'

[4] I. F. Stone, op. cit., p. 312.

[5] Cited in Fleming, p. 630.

napalm (jellied gasoline). The effects of these bombs were described by the Korean correspondent of the BBC.

> In front of us a curious figure was standing a little crouched, legs straddled, arms held out from his sides. He had no eyes, and the whole of his body, nearly all of which was visible through tatters of burnt rags, was covered with a hard black crust speckled with yellow pus . . . He had to stand because he was no longer covered with a skin, but with a crust-like crackling which broke easily . . . I thought of the hundreds of villages reduced to ash which I personally had seen and realized the sort of casualty list which must be mounting up along the Korean front.[1]

After it was all over, *Time* magazine summed the human cost of the war to the Koreans in macabre (but for that magazine, not uncharacteristic) terms:

> The war to save Korea has also killed 400,000 [South] Korean civilians, left 500,000 homes wrecked beyond repair. One-fourth of all Koreans are homeless, and 100,000 are orphans; all are underfed. In North Korea, 40 per cent of all habitations are destroyed, and of military targets – factories, power plants, etc. – UN airmen agree there is not much left to destroy . . . South Korea, likewise, is a war-wrecked shell:[2] 75 per cent of its mines and textile factories are out of action, two-thirds of its schools unusable. But out of disaster has grown a tough army of 16 divisions, and a sense of manhood.[3]

One cannot even say that the reckless waste of human life caused by the attempt to 'liberate' North Korea advanced Western security interests. In fact, the invasion of North Korea cost the West dearly in the power struggle:

[1] René Cutforth in the Manchester *Guardian*, March 1, 1952. Cited in Marzani op. cit.

[2] Cf. Fleming, p. 615 n: 'Seoul was recaptured on September 30 [1950] and the liberators received a cool welcome because of the damage done to every part of the city by planes and artillery. Army and Marine commanders protested that the damage and heavy casualties were useless. They contended that "a triumphal entry into the city" was ordered "as soon as possible and we gave it to them, but it cost us and the Koreans plenty." ' – New York *Times*, September 9, 1950.

[3] *Time*, June 29, 1953, p. 18.

. . . The final stalemate was a victory for the Communist powers, because Oriental troops had thrown back and held the troops of the greatest power in the West, with full control of the air at its disposal . . .

China was built up into a major military power. Her peasant troops out-dug us, fought us on fully equal terms and learned to use every kind of weapon except atomic bombs, including jet planes . . . She was welded closely to Russia, to her great profit in military and industrial development, and to the long term gain of both countries . . .[1]

If Western security was hardly advanced by the protracted war, neither was freedom. For those South Koreans who survived to live under the Rhee régime, life was hardly 'free' after the struggle was over. Rhee's concern for Korean welfare can be guaged by his persistent opposition to a negotiated settlement which would have meant the ending of bloodshed. His resistance to the truce was broken down only under US pressure and with the assurance that economic and military support would be forthcoming to his government afterwards.

After the war, Rhee visited the United States and pressed home the cause of 'liberation'. Addressing a joint session of Congress on July 28, 1954, he called on the United States to join him in a war on Red China. In Philadelphia, Rhee urged the United States to overcome its fear of the atomic age and stand up to Russia as the 'positive and fearless' leader of the free world.[2]

Back in Korea, Rhee moved relentlessly against his opponents. On October 14 he proposed to reduce the number of newspapers by 85 per cent because they were too critical of his administration. On November 28, he forced through the Assembly an amendment to enable him to remain as president for life. An attempt by his henchman to prevent the clerks from announcing that the proposal was one vote short of the necessary two-thirds majority produced a fist fight, but the life term for Rhee went through.

Rhee's police machine held the people in a firm grip,[3] which he

---

[1] Fleming, p. 656.
[2] Cited in Fleming, p. 653. New York *Times*, July 29, August 1 and 2, 1954.
[3] South Korean 'justice' under Rhee has been described by William J. Lederer in *A Nation of Sheep*, 1961: 'Once in Seoul I was present when a Korean thief

maintained in 1958 and 1959 by ejecting the growing opposition from parliament and jamming through additional "laws" to perpetuate his rule'.[1] In the spring of 1960, 'a wave of popular unrest' sparked by student demonstrations, toppled Rhee from the pedestal where the United States had put him.

The new government of John M. Chang which introduced some limited but necessary reforms, was soon succeeded by a military *junta*, after a successful *coup d'etat* on May 16, 1961. In a Seoul dispatch on January 31, 1963, the veteran correspondent A. M. Rosenthal described a growing struggle for power within the *junta*, and the effort of United States officials to prevent the outbreak of civil war (in the South). As for the United States attitude towards the military *junta* itself, Rosenthal observed:

> Ever since the *coup* the United States has been working hard for the success of the *junta* Government. This was calculated risk. It involved sacrificing the respect of some Koreans, who bitterly accused Washington of financing a dictatorship.
>
> But the United States believed that the *junta* Government, particularly General Park, represented the only available choice for building stability and progress and moving gradually into a relatively free society.[2] With Communist North Korea within binocular range of United States troops stationed here, the country's stability is a military as well as a political matter.

If such thinking had any possible validity fifteen years before, when the United States Military Government helped Syngman Rhee

---

[1] Fleming, pp. 653–4.

[2] But cf. E. W. Wagner, 'Failure in Korea' – *Foreign Affairs*, October 1961, p. 133. 'The record of the first months of military rule offers little hope that here at last is the kind of leadership South Korea has been crying for. . . . All executive, legislative and judical powers are lodged in General Parks' Supreme Council for National Reconstruction. Not only the National Assembly but all deliberative bodies, down to the village level, have been disbanded and all elected officials discharged.' Cf. also Reeve, op. cit., pp. 151 et seq. 'Administratively the *junta* brought into being a more authoritarian régime than that of Rhee.'

---

was caught stealing a pair of pants from an army truck. Brought before the Korean magistrate, the culprit was called upon to confess. He pleaded innocent. One by one, the magistrate had the thief's fingers broken in an effort to make him confess. He never did . . . They are a fierce lot, these Koreans.' (p. 54).

to form a police state in the South,[1] subsequent history had made this line of reasoning possible only for the self-deceived or the deeply cynical. For years of police state rule had left the country economically as well as politically in ruins.

Despite two and a quarter billion dollars in United States economic grants since 1954, unemployment in 1960 was estimated to be as high as 25 per cent of the labor force. Gross national product was less than 2 billion and per capita income well under 100 dollars. Exports averaged 20 million dollars per year. The average farm household, consisting of over six members, worked just two acres of land and 40 per cent of farm families had to subsist on one acre or less.[2]

By contrast, the Communists' reconstruction effort since the end of the Korean War had achieved some notable successes:

True, the North Korean authorities publish economic information in a form calculated to impress; but confirmatory evidence from other sources lends credibility to many North Korean claims. In some key areas, such as output of electric power, North Korea has approached the per capita levels of Italy or Japan. Production in all sectors of the economy has surpassed previous totals, in most cases by wide margins, and an unusually rapid pace of economic growth has been attained. The fruits of this advance have been utilized to give the 10,000,000 inhabitants of North Korea a higher standard of living than they have ever known. And as these people have never lived under free institutions as we know them, the harsh features of Communist rule must seem less crucial to them than their material progress.[3]

Indeed, according to the distinguished Cambridge economist, Professor Joan Robinson, 'All the economic miracles of the postwar world are put in the shade by [North Korea's] achievements.'[4]

These facts, while relatively unknown in the West, have not been missed by Koreans. Some 70,000 Korean residents in Japan have chosen repatriation to North Korea.[5] Moreover, 'all but a fraction of

---

[1] Wagner, op. cit., pp. 129–30.
[2] ibid., pp. 130–1.
[3] ibid., p. 132.
[4] 'Korean Miracle' *Monthly Review* January 1965.
[5] ibid., p. 128.

those accepting repatriation to the north originated in the South. The choice they have made, therefore, in a very real sense reflects their judgement as to which half of the divided peninsula offers the better hope for the future'.[1]

In a tragic afternote to all the destruction wreaked upon this unhappy land and underscoring the total failure of United States policy there, Professor Wagner concludes, 'The Communist threat to South Korea today is the threat of subversion by invidious comparison. In the long run South Koreans will not choose between Washington and Moscow but between Seoul and Pyongyang.'[2]

---

[1] Wagner, op. cit., p. 132–3.

[2] ibid., p. 135. Wagner is Assistant Professor of Korean studies, Department of Far Eastern Languages, Harvard University. cf. Joan Robinson op. cit.: '. . . great pains are taken to keep the Southerners in the dark. The demarcation line is manned exclusively by American troops, down to the cleaners, with an empty stretch of territory behind. No southern eye can be allowed a peep into the North. There is no postal connection. *This* wall is not opened at Christmas for divided families to meet.'

CHAPTER IX

Viet Nam

It makes no difference who says that our objective is peace, even if he be the President of the United States. Our actions speak louder than words; and our actions in Asia today are the actions of warmaking.

... ever since 1954, when the United States did not sign the Geneva accords but instead started down the road of unilateral military action in South Viet Nam, we have become a provocateur of military conflict in Southeast Asia and marched in the opposite direction from fulfilling our obligations under the United Nations Charter....

SENATOR WAYNE MORSE
August 5, 1964

ON APRIL 11, 1951, President Truman removed MacArthur for insubordination in his continuing effort to extend the Korean War to China. Acutely aware of the military unfeasibility of expanding the conflict,[1] Truman committed the United States to a limited, and hence a stalemated conflict, which would achieve at four times the original human cost precisely the results that had been gained by September 30, 1950.[2]

This decision to limit the war, that is, to be content with containment and forego liberation, was successfully attacked by Republicans as defeatist, a retreat from the Democrats' own 'war' against Communism in Europe. As Senator Taft declared:

... my quarrel is with those who wish to go all-out in Europe, ... and who at the same time refuse to apply our general program and strategy to the Far East. ... [In Korea] the Administration refused to fight that war with all the means at its command, on

[1] cf. Spanier, p. 240 et seq.
[2] ibid., p. 146.

the theory that we might incite Russia to start a third world war.
But in Europe we have not hesitated to risk a third world war
over and over again . . .[1]

MacArthur's own defense of his aggressive policies was based on
the central justifying principle of America's cold war against Communist 'expansion', and it is no accident that 60 per cent of the
public supported him in this moment of his career:[2]

> . . . history teaches with unmistakable emphasis that appeasement
> but begets new and bloodier war. It points to no single instance
> where the end has justified that means – where appeasement has
> led to more than a sham peace. . . . Why, my soldiers asked of me,
> surrender military advantage to an enemy in the field? [pause]
> I could not answer.[3]

MacArthur put his ace card down on the conspiracy side of the
domestic political table: 'I have always been able to take care of the
enemy in my front,' he said, 'but have never been able to protect
myself from the enemy in my rear.'[4]

Against this charge of 'sell-out' which the Republicans exploited
to the full, Truman erected the Democratic defense. In the words of
General Bradley, MacArthur would have involved the United
States 'in the wrong war, at the wrong place, at the wrong time, and
with the wrong enemy'. But Truman could not or would not carry
through the logic of his conflict with MacArthur, which would have
involved settlement of the Korean War. This could be accomplished
only after the election of President Eisenhower, on the same terms
that Truman could have had many months and several hundred
thousand casualties earlier.[5]

[1] ibid., p. 161.

[2] Goldman, op. cit., p. 203.

[3] Spanier, p. 216; It is important to note that MacArthur's attitude towards
China was also in keeping with the expectations of containment and Communist
collapse: 'I don't suppose there is a year in China that from 5 to 10 million
people don't die of starvation or of the results of malnutrition. It is an economy
of poverty, and the moment you disrupt it, you will turn great segments of its
population into disorder and discontent (50 million people might starve as the
result of his plans, MacArthur later estimated) and the internal strains would
help to blow up her potential for war. . . .' – Spanier, op. cit.

[4] Spanier, op. cit., p. 95.

[5] 'President Truman and Secretary Acheson, . . . never seemed able to afford

It is one of the ironies of this period that while Eisenhower's nomination was a victory for the moderate wing of the Republican party, his election to the Presidency brought the right wing to power. Actually, the Manichean assumptions on which the global war against communism was firmly based in the American mind virtually assured the ascendance of the right. Confronting an absolute and uncompromising evil, a tough, fearless, absolute position would eventually carry decisive weight. It was the moderate Eisenhower whose first inaugural address set a precedent by beginning with a prayer ('Our government makes no sense, unless it is founded in a deeply felt religious faith – and I don't care what it is.') and went on to state America's vision of the cold war apocalypse in classic terms:

> Here, then is joined no argument between slightly differing philosophies. This conflict strikes directly at the faith of our fathers and the lives of our sons. No principle or treasure that we hold, from the spiritual knowledge of our free schools and churches to the creative magic of free labor and capital, nothing lies safely beyond the reach of this struggle.
> *Freedom is pitted against slavery; lightness against the dark.* [Emphasis added.]

On a less cosmic plane, a fundamental Republican aim was to cut government expenditures. This seemed to conflict with the commitment to global containment, which could be managed only by a huge armament budget. The solution to this problem, and to that presented by the public's desire to 'keep the boys home', was a new military strategy which its author, John Foster Dulles, dubbed *massive retaliation.*[1]

In 1947 Walter Lippmann had foreseen that the military requirements of containment would put intolerable strains on American capabilities:

> American military power is distinguished by its mobility, its

[1] Rostow, op. cit., pp. 301–6.

---

to make peace on the only terms which the Chinese would agree to, on the terms, that is to say, which Eisenhower did agree to. The Democrats were too vulnerable to attack from ... the whole right wing of the Republican Party.' – Walter Lippmann, cited in Spanier, p. 270.

speed, its range and its offensive striking force. It can only be the instrument of a policy which has as its objective a decision and a settlement . . . it is not designed for, or adapted to, a strategy of containing, waiting, countering, blocking, with no more specific objective than the eventual 'frustration' of the opponent.

The Americans would themselves probably be frustrated by Mr X's policy long before the Russians were.[1]

When, five years later, Lippmann's prediction proved true, John Foster Dulles came forth with his plan for a 'maximum deterrent' at a 'bearable cost'. Reasoned Dulles:

Policies that do not defend freedom in Asia are fatally defective.

How do we defend it? Obviously we cannot build a 20,000 mile Maginot Line . . .

The answer in Dulles' view was that the free world must develop the will and organize the means to retaliate against 'open aggression by Red Armies', so that wherever it occurred, 'we could and would strike back where it hurts, by means of our own choosing'.[2]

An unkind convergence of circumstances, however, conspired to rob Dulles' theory of its credibility before he could put it into practice. Though Dulles first set forth his views before the 1952 election, it was only on January 12, 1954, that he was able to enunciate the doctrine as a United States policy. He did this one month before the French General Navarre launched his plan for 'victory' in Indo-China which the United States had demanded as a condition of increased aid. Six months earlier, however, Russia had dropped her first H-bomb.

More than a thousand times as powerful as the Hiroshima A-bomb, the H-bomb rendered the United States and particularly its allies with their large population centers and proximity to Russia even more vulnerable than the Soviet Union. Thus, by the time Dulles announced his policy of 'massive retaliation', it had become, in the words of P. M. S. Blackett, 'militarily absurd' (not least, because of the size of the Soviet's nuclear stockpile). This did not prevent the Secretary of State from invigorating the policy of massive retaliation with the strategy of 'brinkmanship', nor from

[1] *The Cold War*, pp. 13–14.
[2] *Life*, June 16, 1952, pp. 66–7.

attempting to avoid, block, disrupt and negate efforts to stabilize, and pacify the international situation in the years when he was at the foreign policy helm.[1] Such policies and the attitudes which supported them, led George Kennan to declare that Americans had become 'wholly absorbed with power values to the point where they are impatient of any discussion of international affairs that tries to take account of anything else'.[2] This 'over-militarization' of American thought and its consequences were nowhere more evident than in United States policy in Viet Nam.[3]

When World War II ended, Viet Nam was a colony of France. Unlike Britain, which gave independence to India, Burma and Ceylon, France sought to maintain Vietnamese subjection with the aid of the puppet emperor Bao Dai, who had collaborated with the Japanese. The resistance to Japanese occupation had been spearheaded by the Communist Ho Chi Minh and his guerrilla army. By the end of the war, Ho's Vietminh had become 'a broad national movement uniting large numbers of Vietnamese regardless of their politics, and reaching down into the masses'.[4] This same view was expressed by Edwin O. Reischauer, Ambassador to Japan in the Kennedy Administration, who wrote that the 'whole history of the Communist Vietminh revolt . . . indicates that it rested more heavily on nationalism for its mass support than on Communist dialectics'.[5]

On September 2, 1945, a Declaration of Independence modelled on the United States document was issued by Ho's national congress and Bao Dai was forced to abdicate. Ho's Republic was soon recognized by France as a 'free state' and a referendum was scheduled to determine whether the three parts of Viet Nam should be united. The South contained the bulk of France's investments, and it soon became apparent that the French were determined to separate this section from the rest of the country. They also insisted on controlling the army and diplomacy of Viet Nam, as well as its currency and economy.[6]

[1] Chalmers Roberts, 'The Pious Truculence of John Foster Dulles', *The Reporter*, January 23, 1958.
[2] New York *Times*, March 24, 1954.
[3] cf. Fleming, pp. 661–704.
[4] Ellen J. Hammer, *The Struggle for Indo-China*, 1954, pp. 84–6.
[5] E. Reischauer, *Wanted: An Asian Policy*, 1955, p. 253.
[6] Hammer, op. cit., pp. 190, 173. Seton-Watson, *The Pattern of Communist Revolution*, p. 312.

Under these conditions, fighting broke out and the French installed Bao Dai in a puppet régime. In 1951, The New York *Times* (February 12) reported that Ho's Army contained about 70,000 lightly armed men, 20 per cent of whom were Communists, the rest strong nationalists. The French, for their part, were able to continue the struggle only because of American financial and military aid, which had assumed prodigious proportions. Against the lightly armed Vietnamese the French used artillery and napalm (supplied by the Americans) which made civilian casualties 'inevitable'.[1]

In 1951, Senator John F. Kennedy visited the Far East and on his return wrote:

> In Indo-China we have allied ourselves to the desperate effort of a French régime to hang on to the remnants of empire. There is no broad, general support of the native Vietnam Government [i.e. of Bao Dai] among the people of that area.[2]

By February 1954, a rapidly deteriorating military situation prompted the French to agree to negotiate a settlement, and a peace conference was scheduled to convene at Geneva on April 26. Before the conference met, however, a last ditch United States-sponsored effort to retrieve the French military position was attempted, as the French parachuted 20,000 of their best troops into a valley in the heart of enemy-held territory known as Dienbienphu. As General Navarre launched this offensive, the United States leadership was already holding top level conferences to devise means of strengthening the French so as 'to prevent a negotiated peace'.[3]

On March 14, Navarre's troops were predictably assaulted by a Vietminh Army of 25,000 to 45,000, and the American leadership grew tense. Admiral Radford, Chairman of the Joint Chiefs of Staff (who had previously told a Congressional Committee that Red China had to be destroyed even if it required a fifty-year war) argued for the use of 500 planes to drop tactical A-bombs on Vietminh troops to prevent the fall of Dienbienphu. (He and Dulles were overruled on this by Eisenhower.) If China openly came into the

[1] New York *Times*, April 13, 1952, cited in Fleming.
[2] Kennedy, *Strategy of Peace*, 1960, p. 89.
[3] Hanson Baldwin, New York *Times*, February 7, 1954, cited in Fleming.

picture, Peking was to be given atomic treatment.[1] On March 29, Dulles declared that Communist domination of Indo-China and Southeast Asia 'by whatever means [*sic*] would be a grave threat to the whole free Community'.[2] In Saigon, South Viet Nam, United States officials agreed that there had been a marked increase in anti-American feeling. Five different groups of non-communists were listed as uniting against growing American 'interference'.[3]

And American 'interference' was growing. On April 7, Eisenhower explained to the public the strategic importance of Indo-China by citing the 'falling domino' principle: the fall of Indo-China would lead to the fall of Burma, Thailand, Malaya and Indonesia; India would then be hemmed in by communism and Australia, New Zealand, the Philippines, Formosa and Japan would all be gravely threatened.[4] A more immediate source of Eisenhower's willingness to come through with the enormous aid required to maintain France's empire was later revealed by Sherman Adams, Eisenhower's 'chief of staff':

The French were opposed to the European Defense Community because they could not put aside their natural aversion to building up once more the military power of Germany. . . . With the support of the National Security Council, Eisenhower increased the American share of the cost of the Indo-China war from $400 million to $785 million, or virtually the whole expense of the French military operation. Behind this decision was the hope that picking up the check in Indo-China would help to win approval of the European Defense Community Treaty in Paris.[5]

On April 16, 1954, when it had become obvious that the French forces at Dienbienphu were hopelessly trapped, Vice-President Nixon declared that if the French withdrew, the United States would have to send troops. For making this statement, he was, in Adams' words, 'doomed in Congress for "whooping it up for war" '. Dulles quickly issued a statement that the use of American soldiers in Southeast Asia was 'unlikely'.[6]

[1] C. Wright Mills, *The Power Elite*, 1956, p. 211.
[2] New York *Times*, March 30, 1954, cited in Fleming.
[3] New York *Times*, April 4, 1954, cited in Fleming.
[4] Sherman Adams, *Firsthand Report*, p. 121.
[5] ibid., p. 120.   [6] ibid., p. 122.

As a matter of fact, [continues Adams] two weeks earlier, at a Sunday night meeting in the upstairs study at the White House Eisenhower had agreed with Dulles and Radford on a plan to send American forces to Indo-China under certain strict conditions. It was to be, first and most important, a joint action with the British including Australian and New Zealand troops, and if possible, participating units from such Far Eastern countries as the Philippines and Thailand so that the forces would have Asiatic representation. . . .[1]

The Vietnamese and the American people were spared this second Korea by the refusal of the British (Sir Anthony Eden, backed by Winston Churchill) to accept a plan which they considered militarily unfeasible because the United States was not willing to commit enough land forces to make the operation successful. Eden and Churchill were sceptical of unsupported air and naval power.[2]

Of no small significance was the timing of the plan for intervention. In ten days the peace conference was scheduled to meet in Geneva. The French were anxious to reach a settlement[3] because the catastrophe at Dienbienphu had demoralized their armed forces. The French people were clamoring for the end of a war that, among other things, was killing annually as many French officers as the French military academy graduated. Moreover, a settlement might open the way to a profitable economic relationship under conditions of peace.

The British were anxious to achieve a settlement that would stabilize the area and 'ensure an effective barrier as far north of [Malaya] as possible'.[4] As for the Russians, it was Eden's view, as co-chairman of the conference with Molotov, that the Soviet Foreign Minister was 'genuinely anxious to reach a settlement'.[5]

The Chinese and Vietnamese (who disagreed not only with the Russians on certain issues, but with each other) were also coopera-

<hr />

[1] ibid., p. 122.

[2] Sir Anthony Eden, *Full Circle*, 1960, pp. 104–5.

[3] Bidault, the first French Premier to negotiate, would have preferred other alternatives, but Mendes–France who replaced him as Premier was pledged to achieve peace within thirty days or resign.

[4] Eden, op. cit., p. 87.

[5] ibid., p. 121.

tive, as were the other member states of the Indo-Chinese peninsula. The only participant who was unimpressed by the importance of stabilizing this troubled area and ending the brutal eight-year war, was John Foster Dulles.

Dulles, who 'scrupulously avoided even looking in the direction of Communist China's premier',[1] left the conference in the middle of the negotiations and sought to boycott the final settlement by refusing to sign it. Two weeks before the Geneva Agreement was concluded, President Eisenhower told a news conference, 'I will not be a party to any treaty that makes anybody a slave; now that is all there is to it.'[2] The United States, however, was outmaneuvered by Molotov and Eden who agreed that, 'in order to eliminate the problem of signature, the declaration should have a heading in which all the participating countries would be listed.' This included the United States.[3]

Dulles' lack of interest in the peace settlement (he was anxious among other things, to implement his design for a Southeast Asia Treaty Organization) was not surprising considering his pre-Geneva activities. On February 18, 1954, the agreement to hold the Geneva Conference had been reached. Two months later, and three weeks before the peace conference was to meet, according to Eden,

> The American Government ... approached the French and ourselves with a new proposal. This was to the effect that all countries concerned should issue, before Geneva, a solemn declaration of their readiness to take concerted action under Article 51 of the United Nations Charter against continued interference by China in the Indo-China war. We were informed that the proposed warning would carry with it the threat of naval and air action against the Chinese coast and of active intervention in Indo-China itself.[4]

On April 12 and 13, two weeks before the opening of the conference, Dulles had formal talks with Eden, and again raised the proposal for intervention. This time the ultimatum to China (hence,

[1] Marquis Childs, *Eisenhower: Captive Hero*, 1958, p. 203.
[2] *Time*, July 12, 1954.
[3] Eden, op. cit., p. 142.
[4] ibid., p. 92.

the pretext of Chinese intervention) was omitted from the plan:

> On the question of intervention, Mr Dulles was convinced that Indo-China was the place for such action, should it become necessary, provided that two requirements could be met. First, an unequivocal declaration by the French Government of independence for the Associated States, and secondly, the placing of the conflict on an international basis. . . . I was not convinced by the assertion which Mr Dulles then made, that the situation in Indo-China was analogous to the Japanese invasion of Manchuria in 1931 and to Hitler's reoccupation of the Rhineland.[1]

On April 26, the Peace Conference began, but Dulles was not a man to be easily diverted from his path:

> The issue of intervention continued to dog us during the opening stages of the conference. As soon as I arrived in Geneva, Mr Dulles came to see me to learn the British attitude to the United States proposal. I told him once more that if a settlement were achieved at the conference, the United Kingdom would be prepared to join in guaranteeing it. If the conference failed, we would be ready to examine the situation afresh, but we were not ready to take part in armed intervention now.[2]

Having worked so hard to destroy the peace conference before it started, and having taken so desultory an interest in its actual proceedings, Dulles then proceeded to undermine the settlement that was reached and, with it, the stability that had been sought. This negative United States course was of considerable significance particularly because the Geneva Agreement seemed to offer hope of a genuine effort at an international *détente*.

In June, Winston Churchill spoke out on the East–West conflict in terms which were a marked contrast to the strategic assumptions of the United States. 'To jaw-jaw is always better than to war-war . . .,' he declared. 'I am of the opinion that we ought to have a try for peaceful coexistence, a real good try. . . . I do beg you to give them the chance to grasp the prospects of great material well-being and I

[1] Eden, op. cit., p. 97.
[2] ibid., p. 108.

am rather inclined to think, if I had to make a prediction, that they will not throw away such an opportunity.'[1]

America's global crusade, however, was formulated in strictly military terms of victory and surrender, which provided for no such evolutionary concepts as were behind the course that Churchill was suggesting. US policies placed a premium on strength and stability, and thus inevitably on dictatorial and military régimes and the maintenence of the social and economic *status quo*. In this context, post-Geneva events in South Viet Nam followed a predictable pattern.

The armistice agreed upon (July 21) divided Viet Nam substantially at the 17th Parallel, and provided for free elections within two years to re-unify the country, a provision which the United States endorsed.[2] It was generally believed that the Vietminh would win the all-Vietnamese elections.[3] Speaking on the floor of the Senate in the previous April, John F. Kennedy had expressed this consensus:

> Despite any wishful thinking to the contrary, it should be apparent that the popularity and prevalence of Ho Chi Minh and his following throughout Indo-China would cause either partition or a coalition government to result in eventual domination by the Communists.[4]

Thus faced with an overwhelmingly popular opponent, the United

[1] Fleming, pp. 693–4.

[2] On July 21, Under-Secretary of State Walter Bedell Smith, speaking for the US delegation said: 'In connection with the statement in the declaration concerning free elections in Viet Nam my Government wishes to make clear its position which it has expressed in a declaration made in Washington on June 29, 1954, as follows: "In the case of nations now divided against their will, we shall continue to seek to achieve unity through free elections supervised by the UN to insure that they are conducted fairly. With respect to the statement made by the representative of the State of Viet Nam, the US reiterates its traditional position that peoples are entitled to determine their own future and that it will not join in an arrangement which would hinder this." ' – *Department of State Bulletin*, August 2, 1954, p. 162.

[3] cf. Fleming, p. 694. In his memoirs *Mandate for Change*, 1964, Eisenhower wrote: 'I have never talked or corresponded with a person knowledgeable in Indo-Chinese affairs who did not agree that had elections been held as of the time of the fighting, possibly 80 per cent of the population would have voted for Ho Chi Minh.'

[4] Kennedy, p. 88.

States embarked upon a course to prevent the elections, and re-unification, from taking place.

On January 17 and 22, 1955, C. L. Sulzberger reported the first stages of a Franco-American conflict over Viet Nam. The United States was trying to seal off the North from the South, by boycotting the economy of the North and threatening to blacklist French business which pursued a contrary policy. French policy was 'directly opposite' to that of the United States whose only justification for being in Viet Nam at all was to assist France. Jean Sainteny[1] was 'working for good political and economic relations with the Communist régime'. The French wished 'to keep a big foot in the door which we seek to slam'. For the French believed that the South would be taken over by the Communists in the 1956 elections, but that the Russians and Chinese could not supply much economic aid and a good market for France could be preserved.[2]

During this period prior to the reunification elections, the United States was working through the new régime of Ngo Dinh Diem, who had been installed by Bao Dai at the behest of Dulles on June 16, 1954, a month before the final agreement at Geneva. Diem, a Catholic, had been in the United States from 1950 to 1953 'where his presence and fitness for office appears to have been noticed by the influential Cardinal Spellman'.[3] The French made no secret of their dislike for Ngo Dinh Diem,[4] but having put him into power, the United States threw its full weight behind him (and his family) and he stayed. Diem's popularity as a leader may be gauged by Senator Mike Mansfield's report on the 'unbelievably grave' situation in South Viet Nam in 1955:

> During those unpredictable days, almost the only thread that linked the multiplicity of forces in Viet Nam was their general agreement that Ngo Dinh Diem must go.[5]

[1] For a brief account of the Sainteny mission cf. Donald Lancaster, *The Emancipation of French Indo-China*, 1961, pp. 364–7. This study was written for the Royal Instute of International Affairs.

[2] New York *Times*, January 17 and 25, 1955, dateline Paris, cited in Fleming.

[3] Lancaster, op. cit., p. 327 n. For an account of Spellman's involvement, see R. Scheer 'Hang Down your Head Tom Dooley', *Ramparts*, Jan–Feb. 1965.

[4] Sulzberger, New York *Times*, June 8, 1955, cited in Fleming.

[5] *Problems of Freedom*, ed. W. Fischel, 1961, p. lx – This is a symposium of official and semi-official views on 'Free Viet Nam'.

Diem prevailed, however, and on June 8, 1955, C. L. Sulzberger reported that the premier would not agree to South Viet Nam's participation in the all-Vietnamese elections provided for in the Geneva Agreement. Ngo Dinh Diem objected 'even to the very thought of such a vote'. Evidently the United States had found its Syngman Rhee for South Viet Nam. Later appeals by the Viet Minh to the Geneva Chairmen Molotov and Eden were of no avail,[1] and the elections were never held.

Ngo Dinh Diem's victory over his opposition which included not only the army, but 'the vast majority of those Vietnamese whose services on behalf of the nationalist cause would seem to have entitled them to play some part in the creation of an independent state'[2] was not difficult to explain. For despite the fact that the political chances of a Roman Catholic mandarin from Hué who displayed 'a congenital inability either to compromise or to act' appeared to be slight, Diem held a trump card. This was the assurance of 'unqualified and unfaltering American support'. With this support, Diem was able to consolidate his control within three years.[3] The results of this consolidation were summed up by the correspondent for the London *Times* and the *Economist*, who was an eyewitness to the events:

> ... Instead of uniting it, Diem has divided the South. Instead of merely crushing his legitimate enemies, the Communists, he has crushed all opposition of every kind, however anti-Communist it might be. In doing so, he has destroyed the very basis on which his régime should be founded. He has been able to do this, simply and solely because of the massive dollar aid he has had from across the Pacific, which kept in power a man who, by all the laws of human and political affairs, would long ago have fallen. Diem's main supporters are to be found in North America, not in Free Viet Nam. ...[4]

The consolidation of Diem's control also meant the replacement

[1] Lancaster, op. cit., pp. 370–2; cf. also Fleming, p. 699.
[2] Lancaster, op. cit.
[3] ibid., pp. 346–7.
[4] David Hotham in *Viet Nam: The First Five Years*, Lindholm ed., 1959, p. 346–9.

of French by United States influence in the South. During the fiscal year 1957–8, American aid to Viet Nam supported the whole cost of the Vietnamese armed forces, nearly 80 per cent of all other government expenditures and almost 90 per cent of all imports. Nor was this all:

> In terms of personnel, American commitments are equally far-reaching. USOM [US Operations Mission] provides for American technical help in every field of activity. Michigan State U., under a million-dollar-a-year contract to ICA [International Co-operation Administration] runs the administration school and trains the police; US educators write the country's textbooks.; . . . and a vast US Military Assistance Advisory Group – its exact size classified but including well over a thousand officers and men – trains the Vietnamese Army, Navy and Air Force.[1]

On June 1, 1956, Senator Kennedy addressed a conference of the American Friends of Viet Nam and declared that the United States must offer the Vietnamese people 'a political, economic and social revolution far superior to anything the Communists can offer – far more peaceful, far more democratic, and far more locally controlled'. But the United States failed to achieve a single one of these goals under the Eisenhower or Kennedy Administrations.

In 1959 David Hotham wrote:

> What has been done in the South to capture the imagination of the masses there? Almost nothing! Four years after Dien Bien Phu, three years after Diem's rout of the sects, and with $250 million a year pouring into the country, scarcely a single house has been built, land reform has hung fire, not a new industry has been created to speak of.[2]

The United States, it should be noted, did attempt to induce Ngo Dinh Diem to carry through a land reform, though the effort was half-hearted and the reform which came to nothing would not

---

[1] Bernard Fall, 'Anti-Americanism: Will South Viet Nam be Next?' *The Nation*, May 31, 1958, p. 490. The presence of the US Military Advisory group 'including well over a thousand officers and men' was a clear-cut violation of the Geneva agreements.

[2] *Viet Nam*, p. 360.

have changed much. Prior to this program, there were 600,000 land-less peasants in South Viet Nam;[1] 2½ per cent of the landowners owned 50 per cent of the land while 70 per cent owned only 12½ per cent. When Diem's agrarian reform became effective in 1959, the landless population remained landless, but a maximum rent had been set, amounting to 25 per cent of their crop.

United States advisors were apparently satisfied with this step, but the peasants in areas formerly occupied by the Viet Minh, which had carried out its own reform, were not: 'In these areas . . . landlords had sometimes not collected rent for as long as eight years. Therefore, landlords looked upon Diem's contract program as a means to assure them a rental of at least 25 per cent of the crop. On the other hand, tenants in these areas resisted the program, since they had been paying no rent at all.'[2]

Actual land redistribution was not really a part of the program. In October 1956 Diem limited the amount of acreage that could be owned to 100 hectares. He exempted from this rule 'substantial holdings in rubber' and other 'industrial crops' such as tea, sugar cane, cocoa, etc.[3] In the end only 2,600 of 50,000 landlords were affected.[4] The excess land was bought by the government to be sold to peasants who could afford to pay from $57 to $170 a hectare,[5] considerable sums in a country with an annual per capita income of under $100. Even with the program completed United States advisors admitted that two-thirds of the tenants would remain tenants, but concluded that 'The complete abolition of tenancy is neither feasible nor desirable if low rentals and real security of tenure can prevail.'[6]

In point of fact, neither low rentals nor security of tenure pre-vailed under the Diem program[7] and in 1959 reactivated elements of the Viet Minh resumed the rebellion. In 1960 a National Libera-tion Front was formed (dubbed 'Vietcong' by the Americans). The

[1] *Problems of Freedom*, ed., W. Fishel, p. 162.

[2] *Viet Nam*, op. cit., Price Gittinger, a Specialist in Agrarian Reform with the US Operations Mission in Saigon, 1955–9, p. 202.

[3] *Viet Nam*, op. cit., p. 204.

[4] *Problems of Freedom*, p. 169.

[5] ibid., p. 170.

[6] Wolf Ladejinsky, Land Reform Expert and Technical Consultant at the Presidency in Free Viet Nam – *Problems of Freedom*.

[7] cf. Gittinger in *Viet Nam*, op. cit. Most tenants pay 33 per cent or more and 'the clauses relating to tenure have proved difficult to enforce'.

composition of the Front was predominantly non-Communist,[1] a fact reflected in its program, which called for the setting up of a democratic multi-party régime, but the Communists were probably a dominant influence. As Diem's military position deteriorated, the Administration in Washington changed and a new assessment was made of the situation in South Viet Nam. Acting under advice from General Maxwell D. Taylor and W. W. Rostow, President Kennedy took steps to escalate the American military commitment in the troubled country. American troops were increased twelve-fold and rocket carrying helicopters and counter-guerrilla warfare methods were introduced into the fighting.

With these developments the war entered a more savage phase. In 1962, the United States Army flew 50,000 sorties, strafing, bombing, and blistering entire areas with napalm fire bombs.[2] On June 19, the New York *Times* reported that nearly 1,400 villages had been destroyed. In an attempt to deprive the Vietcong of its food supplies, chemical warfare was employed to destroy crops and livestock, with resulting hardship for the peasant populations among whom the Vietcong were housed.[3]

> This is a dirty, cruel war – as dirty and as cruel as the war waged by French forces in Algeria which so shocked the American conscience. Currently the weekly toll of dead, including noncombatants, runs at 500.[4]

[1] cf. statement by Barry Zorthian of USIS in *Life*, November 27, 1964, also New York *Times*, Int. Ed., December 6, 1964. cf. also Dennis Bloodworth in The London *Observer*, February 21, 1965: 'For the past eleven years the United States has backed a succession of quasi-dictatorial, sometimes oppressive, régimes in Saigon that were despised or even hated by the Vietnamese people. . . . Most Vietcong guerrilla leaders are not Communists but genuine Nationalists who fought with the Vietminh and against the French colonial forces in the Indo–China war solely to win independence for Vietnam. . . . Sources in the Liberation Front itself have confirmed that only 10 per cent of their followers are Communists.'

[2] New York *Times*, Int. Edn., February 9, 1963; November 20, 1962: 'Some say that Americans fly 30 per cent of the combat missions. Some say it is even more.'

[3] New York *Times*, Int. Edn., March 21, 1963; April 10, 1963: 'I raise my voice . . . not only because I am in profound disagreement with American objections to social change in Indo-China, but because the war which is being conducted is an atrocity. Napalm jelly gasoline is being used against whole villages, without warning. Chemical warfare is employed for the purpose of destroying crops and livestock and to starve the population.' – Bertrand Russell.

[4] Toronto *Telegram*, cited in *The Nation*, January 19, 1963.

By the end of 1962, it was reported that the 10–20,000 active rebels (their reserve support was estimated at 100,000) ruled 80 per cent of the southern delta's population of 10 million and dominated 90 per cent of the land mass.[1] A *Nation* editorial drew the obvious conclusion, declaring: 'By now it should be perfectly clear that American forces in South Viet Nam are engaged not in protecting "freedom", but in the essentially ugly business of suppressing a massive peasant insurrection against the Diem régime.'[2]

The assumption behind this conclusion, namely, that the rebellion was drawing its strength from primarily indigenous forces, was confirmed by General Paul D. Harkins, head of United States military forces in Viet Nam. At a press conference in the Spring of 1963, Harkins was reported as saying that 'the guerrillas obviously are not being reinforced or supplied systematically from North Viet Nam, China, or any place else. He said they apparently depend for weapons primarily on whatever they can capture.'[3]

The indigenous quality of the revolt, and hence the impossibility of isolating the guerrillas from the population by physical means, led to the failure[4] of the chief stratagem introduced by the Kennedy Administration. This was the 'strategic hamlet' program, adopted from the British (who had used it successfully in Malaya) and administered in South Viet Nam by the President's brother, Ngo Dinh Nhu. Under this program, rural villages were 'fortified' in an

[1] ibid., 'Still more important . . . the rebels have managed to reduce the movement of rice from the delta by a fourth in just two years.' Lower but equally impressive figures were admitted by US officials after the fall of the Diem régime.

[2] November 3, 1962.

[3] Washington *Post*, March 6, 1963; cf. also report by David Halberstam New York *Times*, March 6, 1964: 'No capture of North Vietnamese in the South has come to light.' A *White Paper* released by the State Department in early 1965 sought to contradict this picture, and to establish North Vietnamese 'aggression' in South Viet Nam during this period. But a comparison of figures in the *White Paper* with Pentagon figures for captured Vietcong weapons, shows that of 15,100 arms captured from the Vietcong in the years 1962-64, only 179 or slightly more than 1 per cent were not either home made or of US origin. The *White Paper* figures on infiltration from the North, while virtually unsubstantiated in any case, specifically identify only six native North Vietnamese 'infiltrees' in the three years' See 'A Reply to the White Paper', *I. F. Stone's Weekly*, March 8, 1965.

[4] Of the 400 hamlets in the key provinces of Deak Zong and Long An, 'United States civilians estimate that about 20 per cent are politically and military viable. Other sources put the figure at 10 to 20 per cent.' – New York *Times*, Int. Edn., November 21, 1963.

effort to make them politically and militarily impregnable. In the rice-rich Mekong Delta, to cite but one area, 'tens of thousands of peasants were forced to leave their homes and ordered to help build new villages surrounded by barbed wire barricades.'[1] By May 1963 eight million villagers were living in these hamlets. Even United States officials admitted that the charge that the strategic hamlets were 'concentration camps' built by 'forced labor' was 'all too accurate in many instances'.[2]

Political control in the hamlets was patterned along the totalitarian lines which the Diem régime had already established in the metropolitan areas under its domination. Conditions in Free Viet Nam as of 1962 were summed up by the exiled anti-Communist leader of the Vietnamese Democratic Party, Tran Van Tung, in the following terms:

> In eight years in office Diem has not effected one reform requested by the United States and desperately needed by the Vietnamese. Instead he has purged himself of all capable anti-Communist leaders, imprisoned 50,000 anti-Communist Vietnamese nationalists, stripped the populace of all rights and freedoms, forced the people into cruelly administered concentration camps, murdered many score innocent families in the name of 'anti-Communism' and let the Communist Vietcong control and terrorize the country right up to the city limits of Saigon! ... Hated and feared by 80 per cent of the people, continuing domestic policies that would shame Hitler, Diem stays in power only because of United States support.[3]

Tran Van Tung's reference to continuing United States responsibility for Diem's rule was echoed in slightly different form by a

[1] New York *Times*, Int. Edn., December 3, 1963.

[2] ibid. 'It is certainly an ironic way to protect the peasant masses from Communism – to herd them behind barbed wire walls under police control, to subject them to intensive indoctrination, to burn their villages. Poor as the Vietnamese are, they are not domestic animals.' – Tran Van Tung in Democratic Party of Viet Nam report September 1963 – quoted in *Extract of Data Compiled on War in Vietnam*, Bertrand Russell Peace Foundation.

[3] Letter of Tran Van Tung to New York *Times*, dated Paris, October 12, 1962. Tortures, patterned on the French practices in Algeria were also a technique employed by the Diem régime against civilian dissenters as well as against the Vietcong. – cf. New York *Times*, Int. Ed., November 9, 1963.

high State Department official while visiting the country in March 1963. 'The thing that bothers me about this Government,' he said, 'is that the only people who are for it are Americans.'[1] Two months later, a series of events was initiated, which deprived the Diem family of its United States support and thus brought about its downfall.

The predominantly Catholic Diem régime had, for several years, persecuted the Buddhist majority, some 70 per cent of the population. On May 8, 1963, a demonstration was held in the Buddhist Center of Hué to celebrate the Buddha's birthday and to protest the government's ban against flying the Buddhist flag. When the people had assembled, the leaders of the demonstration were advised that the gathering was illegal. Soon government trucks with soldiers arrived and as the crowd began to disperse in terror, the troops opened fire killing nine persons, including seven women and children. One West German psychiatrist who was present during the incident wrote later:

I am one of the very few European witnesses of what today is being called 'the Buddhist monks' revolution. At Hué, the religious capital of the Buddhists of Indo-China, I saw machine-guns opening fire on the crowds and killing children. I also saw troops using poison gas to attack students demonstrating near a pagoda.[2]

The government promptly denied responsibility for the attack and declared that the nine had died at the hands of the Vietcong.[3] Faced with an intransigent official attitude, the Buddhist revolt began to grow and to become the spearhead for other dissident non-Communist elements. On June 11, an aged Buddhist priest, Thich Quang Duc, burned himself to death in a gesture of protest which called world attention to the situation in Free Viet Nam. As the 'revolt' gathered strength, the government reacted with sterner measures. On August 21, the Buddhist pagodas were raided by Ngo

[1] New York *Times*, Int. Edn., September 11, 1963.
[2] London *Observer*, August 18, 1963.
[3] New York *Times*, September 11, 1963, Int. Edn., contains a long account of the crisis.

Dinh Nhu's special security forces (financed and trained by the CIA, at a cost of $250,000 per month[1]) who dragged the nuns and priests from the temples, beat them and carried them to prison in trucks.[2] Diem put the country under martial law, appointing General Ton That Dinh military governor of Saigon, and imposed an eight-hour nightly curfew.

At this point, the United States began, in vain, to exert pressure on Diem to dissociate himself from the anti-Buddhist excesses and to purge Ngo Dinh Nhu and his wife (an outspoken supporter of the repressions) from the inner circles of government. A new Ambassador, Henry Cabot Lodge, was appointed to replace the pro-Diem Nolting, and President Kennedy publicly declared that 'in the last two months the [Diem] government has gotten out of touch with the people'. This trend could be reversed, he added, 'with changes in policy, and perhaps with personnel'.

On August 30, President de Gaulle suggested that the only viable solution for Viet Nam was to free the country of foreign influences and to provide for its reunification under a neutral government. This proposal, which was in basic accord with the provisions of the Geneva Agreements of 1954, had been previously advanced both by the Vietcong and Ho Chi Minh, and was reaffirmed by them after this statement.

Actually, the French had already begun in secret to take steps to implement their proposal. Contacts were made between Diem and Ho through the French Ambassador, M. Lalouette, to discuss the possibility of declaring Viet Nam neutral and of calling for the withdrawal of United States military personnel. In late August, Lalouette brought Ngo Dinh Nhu together with the Polish representative on the International Control Council for further discussion of this proposal, and later Nhu's representatives met North Vietnamese agents at a coastal town north of Saigon.[3]

To long-time observers of the Vietnamese situation, these moves were not difficult to comprehend. As the *Economist*'s David Hotham had written six years earlier, 'The story of Viet Nam for thirty years has been its national struggle for independence. ... The

---

[1] New York *Herald Tribune*, Int. Edn., September 9, 1963.
[2] *Newsweek*, September 2, 1963.
[3] Roger Hagan in *The Correspondent* (Cambridge Mass.), November–December 1963.

overriding motive in Free Viet Nam is not, and never has been, anti-Communism; it is nationalism. By imposing the cold war strategy on Viet Nam, making it a Free World–Communism issue, the West has fitted it with a pattern which is against the whole drift of Viet Nam's recent history. It is like putting mushrooms under cement to stop them growing, but in the end they grow through.'[1]

Washington reacted to de Gaulle's public proposal for reunification and neutralization with deep resentment, and it was noted in the press that the French President had made the same proposal, with no result, two years before[2]. On the other hand, the recent events had not failed to impress Washington, which was paying $1·5 million per day to Diem to continue the war to suppress the Vietcong. On the very day that de Gaulle proposed his solution, it was reported that United States officials responsible for Vietnamese policy had decided 'that no government that includes Ngo Dinh Nhu and his wife can win the war against Communism and that the Nhus cannot be separated from the government'. According to highly informed diplomatic sources, the United States was therefore 'ready to initiate action that might lead to the overthrow of the Government'. 'Americans [it was reported] are already known to have been contacting key people in the military recently.'[3]

On November 1, 1963, after a series of United States diplomatic pressures, the régime of Ngo Dinh Diem was toppled by a military *coup d'etat*'[4] Both Diem and his brother were shot.

The *coup* was carried out by men who had been Diem's most faithful Generals, including Ton That Dinh, military governor of Saigon during the Buddhist crackdown, and Tran Van Don, son of a wealthy landowner and chief of the Joint General Staff. The leader of the Generals was Duong Van Minh, whose zeal in aiding Diem to crush his opposition during the years 1955–7, had made him a 'hero to the American military'. He later fell into disfavor with Diem 'for being too close to General Maxwell Taylor, then Mr Kennedy's personal military advisor, and now chairman of the Joint Chiefs of

---

[1] Viet Nam, op. cit., p. 361.
[2] New York *Times*, Int. Edn., August 31, 1963.
[3] New York *Times*, Int. Edn., August 31, 1963.
[4] For a detailed inside account cf. New York *Times*, Int. Edn., November 7, 1963.

Staff'.[1] The man appointed to be Premier of the new régime was Nguyen Ngoc Tho, a Buddhist who had been Ngo Dinh Diem's Vice-President and before that had served in official posts under the French colonialists and the Japanese occupation forces. The new régime promptly made it clear that there would be no consideration of reunification with the Communist North.

Within a short time, however, it was readily apparent that the new American-backed régime would have no more success in stemming the tide of rebellion than had the former one. Nine years earlier, on April 6, 1954, Senator John F. Kennedy had pointed out with great wisdom the lesson of the previous nine-year war effort by the French. 'I am frankly of the belief,' he said, 'that no amount of American military assistance in Indo-China can conquer an enemy which is everywhere, and at the same time, nowhere, an enemy of the people which has the sympathy and covert support of the people.' In November 1963 it was difficult to perceive any signs that the lesson had been learned.

[1] London *Sunday Times*, November 3, 1963.

CHAPTER X

Guatemala

Any nation's right to a form of government and an economic system of its own choosing is *inalienable*. . . . Any nation's attempt to dictate to other nations their form of government is *indefensible*.

DWIGHT D. EISENHOWER
April 16, 1953

ON JUNE 16, 1954, the United States put Ngo Dinh Diem into power in South Viet Nam. Two days later, on June 18, Colonel Carlos Castillo Armas invaded the Central American Republic of Guatemala from neighboring Honduras, in an effort to overthrow the constitutionally elected government of Jacobo Arbenz. Ten days later, a decade of social democracy in Guatemala was over, and a decade of dictatorship and right-wing rule had begun.

On June 14, Clement Attlee declared in the House of Commons:

The fact is that this was a plain act of aggression, and one cannot take one line on aggression in Asia and another line in Central America. I confess that I was rather shocked at the joy and approval of the American Secretary of State on the success of this *putsch*.[1]

Secretary of State Dulles had ample cause for joy at the success of the *putsch*, which in his words, added 'a new and glorious chapter to the already great tradition of the American States . . .'[2] because it was planned, financed, armed, and protected against United Nations action by the United States Government itself.[3] Responsibility for the *coup* was widely attributed to the United States, of

[1] HM Stationery Office, *Parliamentary Debates, Commons*, Official Report, 5th Series, Vol. 530 (1954), cols. 489–90.
[2] Department of State, *Intervention of International Communism in Guatemala*, 1954, p. 33. Hereafter referred to as *White Paper*.
[3] Wise and Ross, *The Invisible Government*, 1964, pp. 165ff.

course, but the precise details were not revealed until nine years later when Republican Thurston B. Morton appeared on television and cited the Guatemalan success while criticizing President Kennedy's failure to achieve similar results in Cuba.

> As Morton recalled the scene, President Eisenhower reviewed the Central Intelligence Agency's plans for toppling the régime of Guatemalan President Jacobo Arbenz Guzmán. Then Ike said: 'I want all of you to be damn good and sure you succeed.'
>
> Besides Morton, those present included Secretary of State John Foster Dulles and Secretary of Defense Charles E. Wilson, ... as well as Allen Dulles, then Director of the CIA, and the Joint Chiefs of Staff ...
>
> ... Ike is close to Morton ... and probably won't quarrel with Morton's recollection that the general declaimed:
>
> 'When you commit the flag, you commit it to win.'[1]

The justification for overthrowing the democratically elected Arbenz government (in the 1950 elections Arbenz received 267,000 of the 370,000 votes cast) was that 'international communism' had gained a 'political base' in the hemisphere there. Actually, neither Secretary of State Dulles nor any other top official claimed directly that Guatemala was a Communist State; this omission was not accidental since Arbenz' reform program was modelled on Mexico's. Nor did Dulles claim it was a police state which denied political freedoms. Indeed, in the State Department's *White Paper: Intervention of International Communism in Guatemala*, Arbenz is indicted for allowing *too much* political freedom:

> The President's public speeches and actions indicate him as a leftist influenced by Marxist thought and an extreme nationalist, but he has not defined his personal ideological orientation towards communism ... his official position might be defined as one of denying that his government is Communist while simultaneously defending the freedom of Communists to organize and engage in politics as any other citizens. He thus, publicly, at least, implicitly accepts the Communists as an authentic domestic

---

[1] *Newsweek*, March 4, 1963.

political party and not as part of the world-wide Soviet Communist conspiracy.[1]

The extent of Communist penetration of Guatemalan society and organized political life, during the ten-year democratic period (the Party was in fact outlawed until 1952), if anything, has been over-studied and documented (even to the point of citing the fact that Arbenz' personal library contained works by Marx and Lenin),[2] and needs no recounting in detail here. It is important, however, to assess what these studies do and do not show.

The Communist Party of Guatemala, even at its height in 1954, could not be properly called a mass organization. According to the State Department *White Paper*, its strength in May, 1954, was estimated at 3,000 to 4,000 in a country of 3 million people, having been smashed in 1932 and not reformed even on a clandestine level until September 28, 1947. The average age of the party's Central Committee was twenty-six.[3] Moreover, it had little electoral strength, holding only four of the fifty-six seats in Congress.[4] No Cabinet members were Communist, so the decisive levers of power (in particular, the police and the army) were out of their hands.[5]

However, the Communists did have important posts in certain administrative bodies of the government,[6] and had considerable,

[1] *White Paper*, p. 69. '. . . we have maintained inviolate the respect for democratic principles which involves the adequate guarantee of all beliefs, opinions and forms of organization of all, of absolutely all the social sectors and classes. ' – Arbenz.

[2] The most thorough study is *Communism in Guatemala*, by Ronald M. Schneider for the Foreign Policy Research Institute, University of Pennsylvania, 1959.

[3] *White Paper*, p. 47.

[4] Schneider, p. 185.

[5] Compare this with the extent to which the army was represented in the government: 'In 1954 the President of Congress and seven other deputies, the Chief of the National Agrarian Department, the Director General of Highways and all the twenty-two Departmental Governors were army officers.' – Schneider, p. 43. Two Ministerial posts were also held by officers. 'Even as staunch a non-Communist as Colonel Elfego Monzon was kept by Arbenz as Minister without Portfolio to satisfy the more conservative officers that this was no radical government.' – ibid.

[6] The Communists were represented mainly in the bureaucracies having to do with education, propaganda, social security and agrarian reform. In the latter, in which their influence was most heavily felt, they held some two dozen of 350 posts. – *White Paper*, p. 70. According to Secretary of State Dulles, 'They [the

though not unlimited personal influence on Arbenz himself. In a private discussion with the officer corps (in June 1954) over the question of Communists in the government bureaucracy, Arbenz quoted Peron to the effect that 'Communism was like strychnine, beneficial in small doses but highly dangerous in large quantities'.[1] In a nation 70 per cent illiterate, with only 5 per cent of the population possessing a high school education,[2] the Communists were useful in supplying Arbenz with advocates and administrators of the agrarian reform program. According to the American political scientist, Philip B. Taylor, 'Arbenz . . . was quite sympathetic to Communist activities but under the best of contrary circumstances the ousting of Communists from their positions in the government would have been extremely difficult and would have stripped the government of its trained, though not necessarily efficient, bureaucrats.'[3]

Some insight into the relation between Arbenz' sympathy for Communist activities and his desire to promote an agrarian reform is offered by Dr Ronald Schneider, a political analyst for the State Department. It is well to remember that prior to the Agrarian reform, 2 per cent of the land owners owned 70 per cent of the arable land, while two-thirds of all land owners held only 10 per cent of the cultivated land area. (Twenty-two families owned 1,250,000 acres.) The purpose of Arbenz' agrarian law (as stated in the law itself) was to 'liquidate feudal property . . . in order to develop . . . capitalist methods of production in agriculture and prepare the road for the industrialization of Guatemala'[5]:

[1] Schneider, op. cit., p. 317.

[2] *White Paper*, p. 41.

[3] Philip B. Taylor, Jr, 'The Guatemalan Affair: A Critique of United States Foreign Policy', *The American Political Science Review*, publication of the American Political Science Association, September 1956, p. 788.

[4] *White Paper*, p. 36.

[5] *The Nation*, July 31, 1954, 'Counter-revolution: Guatemala's Tragedy', Bernard Rosen. Rosen taught history and economics at the American School in Guatemala City for several years, and in 1952, conducted a State Department Seminar for Guatemalan teachers.

Communists] dominated the social security organization . . .' – *White Paper*, p. 31. But according to the *White Paper*, p. 71, 'The Guatemalan Institute of Social Security (IGSS) appears to be a stronghold of the "non-party" Communists . . .'

When Arbenz decided in 1953 to press forward with agrarian reform as the keystone of his program, the 'progressive' land owners who had formed the right wing of Arbenz' support had to be bludgeoned into line to give the legislation their reluctant support, but the Communists furnished in Gutiérrez the leading Congressional exponent of agrarian reform and could truthfully say that they had been working on the problem for almost five years . . . As many of the deputies of the revolutionary parties proved somewhat hesitant in their support, the stock of the Communists rose in Arbenz' eyes. Through their control of the labor movement they held out to him an efficient arm for the implementation of agrarian reform and mobilization of *campesino* support. . . .[1]

Even the Communist control of the labor movement in the Guatemalan context did not mean the kind of power it would have meant in other countries, as Schneider points out:

The events of the last week of the Arbenz régime showed that Communism in Guatemala had not developed into a successful popular movement. Although they exercised great influence through the key positions which they had attained in the country's rather simple political structure, the Communists had not found sufficient time to build a broad base or to sink their roots deeply . . . when the showdown came in June, 1954, only a . . . small number of workers were ready or willing to act . . .[2]

Thus the Communists were a party with influence, as long as their program coincided with Arbenz', but they had no substantial base of power. Real political power lay, in Guatemala, as in most Latin American countries,[3] in the hands of the army. And the army was openly and actively anti-Communist.[4]

Arbenz himself was an army man, and, in the crisis, rather than

---

[1] Schneider, op. cit., pp. 36–7.

[2] ibid., pp. 317–18. The Communist party's influence in the various political parties of the revolutionary coalition and among the peasant population was also without depth.

[3] cf. the authoritative study by Edwin Lieuwin for the Council on Foreign Relations: *Arms and Politics in Latin America*, 1961.

[4] Schneider, op. cit., pp. 316–17.

risk civil war (as the Communists urged), he resigned in favor of Colonel Diaz, Army Chief of Staff.[1] Diaz went to United States Ambassador Puerifoy, who was 'coordinating the rebellion from within'[2] and offered to outlaw the Communist party,[3] but Peurifoy wasn't interested. He wanted his own candidate, General Elfego Monzon, a rightist,[4] and Diaz was escorted from the meeting at gunpoint.[5]

Since Arbenz appointed the Communists to what positions they did have in the government bureaucracy, it is important to note that even his power would soon end, when his term in office was completed (1957) and that the electoral strength of the opposition (some 105,000 of 235,000 votes in the January 1953 Congressional elections) was considerable.[6] Moreover, there was no move towards the end of the Arbenz régime to place Communists in positions of power. And without either army support or a mass base, the prospects for an imminent bid for power by the Communists were not, in any meaningful sense, good.

If the Communist party of Guatemala was not in a position to make a serious bid for power,[7] what changes in Guatemalan society necessitated the CIA *coup d'etat*? The answer is revealed in the history of social democracy in Guatemala.

In 1944, the dictatorship of General Guillermo Ubico was overthrown, and replaced by a revolutionary military *junta* composed of Jorge Toriello, an influential businessman, Javier Araña, a tank commander (assassinated in 1949), and Jacobo Arbenz, an army captain and substantial landowner. The *junta* set up elections which were won in December by a social democrat and schoolteacher, Juan

---

[1] Schneider, op. cit., p. 312. Reviewing their mistakes in 1955, the Communists felt that they had relied too heavily on the middle class, which proved unable to withstand 'imperialist pressures'. '. . . In addition, the party leaders felt that they had placed too much faith in Arbenz' revolutionary determination. The PGT (CP) criticized his "typically bourgeois attitude" in underestimating the role which the masses could play and relying too greatly on the army.' Manuel Fortuny, the Secretary General and chief liaison between the Communists and Arbenz, was stripped of all his offices within the PGT, p. 319.

[2] Tad Szulc and Karl Meyer, *The Cuban Invasion*, 1962, p. 75.

[3] According to an AP dispatch cited in *The Nation*, July 10, 1954.

[4] *Time*, July 12, 1954; Schneider, op. cit., p. 43.

[5] *Time*, July 12, 1954.

[6] Schneider, op. cit., p. 303.

[7] Even if Arbenz had been a Communist, this would still have been true, since a military *coup* could have relieved Arbenz of power at any time.

José Arévalo, who received 255,000 of the 295,000 votes cast. Arévalo immediately embarked on a program of social reform and industrialization to transform the two-crop backward economy[1] and to make living conditions more tolerable. Among Arévalo's reforms were abolition of forced labor on the plantations and raising of the minimum wage to twenty-six cents a day:[2]

> It is a mute testimony to the stagnation and backwardness of Guatemala under Ubico that as essentially moderate a program as that supported by Arévalo should be thought of as radical or even 'Communistic' by the Guatemalan employers. . . .
>
> More than two dozen abortive attempts to overthrow the government occurred in the first four years of his [Arévalo's] term, as well as several more serious ones in 1949–1950.[3]

In addition to the opposition of domestic vested interests, Arévalo had to contend with the more powerful economic interests of United States companies. For example, according to a United Nations' report, because of 'labor difficulties', but mainly in 'anticipation of policies subsequently adopted through the Agrarian Reform Law of 1952', the United Fruit Company acted to curtail its own operations.[4] Since only 10 per cent of the company's assets (reported at $579,342,000) were situated in Guatemala,[5] this did not entail a significant reduction of its own profits. On the other hand, the Guatemalan economy was heavily dependent on United Fruit production. In 1948, 7·7 million stems of bananas represented 41 per cent of Guatemalan exports. By 1952, the number of stems had declined to 1·5 million, a drop of 80 per cent.

Similarly, laws designed to allow Guatemala to exploit its natural resources (e.g. the constitutional provision that 51 per cent of any company exploiting oil must be nationally owned and that only

[1] Bananas and coffee accounted for 90 per cent of Guatemala's $76 million exports. Ninety per cent of the electricity of the country was concentrated in the capital city. Four-fifths of this electricity was supplied by a foreign company. – *Foreign Capital in Latin America*, report of the United Nations' Department of Economic and Social Affairs, New York, 1955, p. 97.

[2] C. Wright Mills, *Listen Yankee*, 1960, p. 69.

[3] Schneider, p. cit., p. 21 n.

[4] United Nations' report, p. 97.

[5] New York *Times*, July 4, 1954; cited in Taylor, p. 798.

refined products could be exported) met with decisive opposition:

> Several companies which were engaged in petroleum prospecting discontinued their activities subsequent to the passage in 1949 of a petroleum law which they considered unfavorable. No foreign petroleum company is reported to have applied for a concession since that time.[1]

Because of their power, the foreign companies had been able to gain considerable concessions from previous Guatemalan régimes, to maximize the returns on their 108 million dollars worth of holdings. For example, the United Fruit Company and the International Railways of Central America (Guatemala's primary transportation system – controlled by United Fruit[2]) 'were exempt from taxes on business profits, except on those resulting from the sale of consumer goods in company stores'. A third United States-owned enterprise, the electric power company, was taxed at 5 per cent of the net profit from the sale of electric energy and 2 per cent of the gross sale of energy.[3]

Given these limitations, the Arévalo régime (and its successor under Arbenz) was able to make some strides towards the economic development of Guatemala:

> Under Arévalo and later Arbenz, Guatemala moved rapidly into a period of bourgeois reform. A new constitution gave the people the civil rights enjoyed in advanced Western nations. Labor and peasant organizations were legalized. Steps were taken to diversify the agriculture of the country. . . . A government sponsored institute was established, . . . to aid capitalists who wished to expand their enterprises or start new ones. . . .[4]

Five days before the Presidential elections of 1950, a right-wing

[1] United Nations Report, op. cit., p. 97.
[2] ibid., p. 99.   [3] ibid.
[4] *The Nation*, July 31, 1954, op. cit. Also, United Nations Report, op. cit., p. 100. 'In 1948, the Government established the Institute for the Development of Production. . . . with an initial capital of $6·5 million. The Institute may establish enterprises of its own or participate in private enterprises with equity capital. The Institute investment in an enterprise is to be sold when the business is firmly established. The Institute is already operating some enterprises and has planned the establishment of others.'

coup, led by Colonel Carlos Castillo Armas, was broken and Armas put in jail; he escaped shortly afterwards. Arbenz won the election, defeating General Ydigoras Fuentes. Being a military man and a landowner, Arbenz was expected to be more conservative than his predecessor. The expectation proved unfounded as he raised the minimum wage to $1·08 a day and in 1952 enacted a program of land reform.

It was an action taken under the terms of this land reform which precipitated the first friction between Guatemala and the United States. In particular, it was the expropriation of idle land owned by the United Fruit Company, which in the past had 'bribed politicians, pressured governments and intimidated opponents to gain extremely favorable concessions' for itself.[1]

In March 1953, the Arbenz Government expropriated 234,000 of 295,000 acres of uncuitivated land owned by United Fruit in the Tiquiaste area near the Pacific coast. The compensation offered the company ($600,000 in 3 per cent, twenty-five-year bonds) was based on the value set on the property in 1952 for tax purposes 'by the owner himself'.[2] This compensation was termed 'unacceptable' by United Fruit, which did not like either the sum suggested nor the terms of payment (in bonds). At this point, the government of the United States intervened diplomatically on behalf of the threatened company, claiming that the compensation offered did not conform to the 'minimum standards of just compensation prescribed by international law. . . .'[3]

In April 1953, the United States took action, filing a claim of $16 million against Guatemala for the expropriated properties, of which $9 million was supposed to represent the damage to properties not expropriated, resulting from the expropriation of the other acres.[4] In August 1953, Guatemala started proceedings to expropriate 173,000 of 263,000 United Fruit acres at Banañera, near the Atlantic coast.

The reaction of Latin America to the United States' role in this dispute and the US response have been described by Professor Dozer, a former government official who served with several United States agencies in Latin America during the years 1941–56:

[1] Schneider, op. cit., pp. 48–9.
[2] United Nations Report, op. cit., p. 98.
[3] United Nations Report, op. cit.
[4] ibid.

'The North American government,' sharply declared the generally pro-United States *El Pais* of Montevideo [May 29, 1954], 'in
pressuring the government of Guatemala to accept the conditions
demanded by the United Fruit Company. . . . under a leprous
contract[1] concluded the 30th of April 1923 under the dictatorship
of General Lazaro Chacón . . . is returning to a policy which will
alienate the sympathy of the continent and rouse a clamor of
disapproval.' . . .

As the United States undertook to line up other anti-
Communist nations to embargo arms shipments to Guatemala
and imposed an economic squeeze on that government by withdrawing its already limited technical assistance, it roused further
protests. To these protests the State Department replied, first,
that it was no more concerned with the United Fruit Company
than with any other United States interest in a foreign country
and, second, that it was not intervening in the internal affairs of
Guatemala, but was merely trying to check the aims of the Soviet
Union in this hemisphere.[2] (New York *Times*, June 19, 1954.)

The State Department's disclaimer notwithstanding, the United
States was soon to show a somewhat greater concern for the United
Fruit Company than it had for some other United States interests in
foreign countries. One explanation which has been offered for this
fact is that John Foster Dulles was both a stockholder and long-time
corporation counsel for the United Fruit Company, and was legal
adviser to the company in drawing up the contracts of 1930 and 1936
with the Ubico dictatorship.[3]

In March 1954, the Tenth Inter-American Conference of the
Organization of American States met at Caracas, Venezuela and was
attended by all the American republics except the little democratic
state of Costa Rica, which refused to attend in protest against the
dictatorship of the host government.

Dulles addressed the Conference several times and was rewarded

---

[1] United Nations Report, op. cit., p. 98. 'The operations of the large foreign
enterprises in Guatemala have traditionally been regulated by concession contracts ranging up to ninety-nine years in duration, exempting the companies
from the provisions of any future legislation that may conflict with their terms.'

[2] Donald M. Dozer, *Are We Good Neighbors?* 1959, p. 342.

[3] Cited by Taylor, op. cit., p. 791 n. Jorge Toriello, *La Batalla de Guatemala*
(Mexico, 1955).

by the passage of his resolution delcaring that 'the domination or control of the political institutions of any American State by the international communist movement, extending to this Hemisphere the political system of an extra-continental power, would constitute a threat to the sovereignty and political independence of the American States.' . . .[1]

Dulles was successful in passing his resolution but he did so in the face of considerable uneasiness and some opposition. A number of delegates felt that 'the condemnation of a particular type of political arrangement in the Americas – even one abetted or inspired from outside the hemisphere – was difficult to reconcile with the principle of non-intervention in internal affairs'.[2]

Still others felt that the primary problems of Latin America were social and economic rather than merely political:

'Our peoples expect something more than a new way of fighting Communism,' said a Bolivian delegate; 'something appropriate to improve their welfare and progress.' In the absence of constructive economic and social measures, mere opposition to Communism might even 'give it prestige and . . . spread it.'[3]

Summing up reactions, one political scientist commented:

It is significant that those who sprang to Dulles' support in the debates following the presentation of the resolution were not the democratic nations but the authoritarians, Venezuela, the Dominican Republic, Cuba, and Peru. (New York *Times*, March 3 and 4, 1954.) Guatemala's Foreign Minister, Guillermo Toriello, denouncing the Dulles' proposal as '. . . the internationalization of McCarthyism . . .' received twice the ovation that Dulles did.[4] (New York *Times*, March 6, 1954.)

Toriello, correctly assessing that the resolution was directed at Guatemala, declared that the policies of his government conformed

[1] *White Paper*, pp. 8–9.
[2] Richard P. Stebbins, *The US in World Affairs*, 1954, published under the auspices of the Council on Foreign Relations, 1956, p. 376.
[3] Stebbins, op. cit., p. 373.
[4] Taylor, op. cit., p. 791.

to 'the economic resolutions adopted by the United Nations . . . with regard to economic development, agrarian reform, capital investment, social policy, and the exploitation of natural wealth and resources in behalf of the people.'[1] But these non-Communist efforts to modernize Guatemala's semi-feudal economy, said Toriello, had been twisted into a 'Communist threat against the Americas' because they infringed upon the interests of certain United States business concerns in Guatemala 'which were holding back progress and the economic development of the country'. These concerns were not paying equitable taxes, Toriello charged, and the pressures applied by the United States on their behalf violated the principle of non-intervention and represented a return to the policies of the ' "big-stick" and the lamentable "dollar diplomacy" '.[2]

Despite Toriello's defense and the sympathy it engendered, only Guatemala voted against the proposal, while Mexico and Argentina abstained.[3] A delegate from Uruguay said: 'We contributed our approval without enthusiasm, without optimism, without joy, and without the feeling that we were contributing to a constructive measure.' (New York *Times*, March 16, 1954.)

With the 'juridical' case in hand, a new situation arose over what Dulles described at a news conference on May 25, 1954, as a 'massive shipment of arms from behind the Iron Curtain'.[4] The construction given to this arms shipment to justify the CIA-engineered invasion of Castillo Armas' forces is revealed in Edwin Lieuwen's study, *Arms and Politics in Latin America*:

> The shipment of Soviet-bloc arms to Guatemala gave the ousted pro-Arana army exiles, now led by Colonel Carlos Castillo Armas, their opportunity to return, for it provoked the United States government, which saw its vital strategic interests in jeopardy, to counter the Russian move by sending armaments to Guatemala's neighbors [Nicaragua and Honduras – the arms

[1] cf. United Nations' resolution 626 (VII) of the General Assembly.

[2] For text, cf. OAS 10th Inter-American Conference Document 95 (English), SP-23, 5 March 1954. Also, Toriello, op. cit.

[3] New York *Times*, March 7, 1954. 'They were willing to applaud [Toriello] since it cost them nothing. But not many were willing to vote against the United States when they might have to get up later in the conference and ask for economic aid.'

[4] *White Paper*, p. 12.

were sent by air. D. H.],[1] which quickly found their way into the hands of Castillo.[2]

Lieuwen's account and Dulles' statement are misleading on several scores. First, the 'massive' shipment consisted of one Swedish ship, the M/s *Alfhem*.[3] The arms were not 'sent' to Guatemala as is implied; (nor is there any evidence that it was a a 'Russian move') they were bought by Guatemala for $10 million.[4] Moreover, the idea of a threat to vital United States strategic interests (at his news conference, Dulles suggested that the arms might be intended to develop a Communist strongpoint dominating the Panama Canal)[5] is hard to fathom since underdeveloped Guatemala with its 3,000,000 people is 1,000 miles and four countries away from the Panama Canal and at the time had neither a Navy nor an Air Force, its Army consisting of less than 8,000 men.[6] Wrote Sir Anthony Eden:

It seemed to me that their [i.e. United States] fears of a communist 'build-up' in Guatemala were probably exaggerated, and our reports were that the supplies were mainly, if not entirely, small arms.[7]

Even so, the Guatemalan Government's decision to buy Czechoslovakian arms might have portended a new direction in Guatemalan policies, since no significant trade with the Soviet bloc had existed prior to this.[8] But even this interpretation is not possible since it was not choice which sent the Guatemalan Government behind the Iron Curtain for arms, but necessity:

[1] H. Stark, *Modern Latin America*, Florida, 1957, p. 245.
[2] Szulc and Meyer, p. 93.
[3] *White Paper*, p. 12; cf. Dulles' remaining remarks at this news conference. Also, p. 95.
[4] Betty Kirk, 'US in Latin America – Policy of the Suction Pump', *The Nation*, October 5, 1957.
[5] Taylor, op. cit., p. 794 n.; cf. New York *Times*, May 26, 1954.
[6] Lieuwen, op. cit., p. 210; Eden, *Full Circle*, p. 136.
[7] Sir Anthony Eden, op. cit., p. 134.
[8] During this week of the Armas invasion, former President Arévalo was interviewed in Buenos Aires and indicated his support for the Arbenz Government. Said Arévalo: 'There is not a single Russian in my country today, but there are 25,000 Americans. Perhaps it would be advisable to look among them for secret and dangerous Communists.' – *The Nation*, June 26, 1954.

For years the Guatemalan government had been vainly seeking to purchase arms, first in the United States, then from other sources. Finally Arbenz looked behind the Iron Curtain for help. Major Alfonso Martinez ('an opportunist non-Communist' – *White Paper*, p. 70), a long-time crony of the President, left Guatemala for Europe early in January 1954. . . . Martinez went to Switzerland to negotiate payment for Czech arms which were to be shipped from Stettin, Poland, by a devious route on board a chartered Swedish ship, the Alfhem.[1]

The fact that it was in January 1954 that the Arbenz Government finally felt it necessary to go to Czechoslovakia for arms is understandable, because it was on January 30 that it first announced in a formal communiqué that a plot had been prepared to invade Guatemala and overthrow the régime. Several Central American States were charged with complicity in the plot[2] as was 'the government of the North', United Fruit, and several individuals, among them Castillo Armas and General Miguel Ydigoras Fuentes. In the previous October, John Peurifoy had been appointed Ambassador:

> It seems clear from the circumstantial evidence presented by journalists concerning the period from his arrival to the outbreak of the civil war between Castillo Armas and the Arbenz government that the United States did little to disabuse Arbenz' opponents of the notion that North American aid, moral and/or military, would not be lacking when the need arose. . . . Flora Lewis, writing for the New York *Times Magazine*, July 18, 1954, says of Peurifoy: 'It was perfectly clear that his instructions and his purpose had one simple theme: "Get rid of the Reds." '[3]

One final observation on the arms episode must be noted. In his

[1] Schneider, op. cit., p. 309. Also, Eden, op. cit., pp. 134–5, 'Like the United States, we had . . . placed an embargo on the delivery of arms to Guatamala . . . our arms embargo had been in operation for several years and the control was efficient.'

[2] Taylor, op. cit., p. 793 n., cites Donald Grant of the St Louis *Post-Dispatch:* '. . . this writer . . . was . . . an eyewitness to many of the decisive events. Exiled Guatemalans, the Governments of Honduras and Nicaragua, the United States Departments of State and Defense, the Central Intelligence Agency, the United States National Security Council and other agencies and individuals were involved.'

[3] Taylor, op. cit., p. 793.

news conference the week after the shipment, Secretary of State Dulles seemed to find great significance in the secrecy which surrounded the operation:

> One cannot but wonder why, if the operation was an aboveboard and honorable one, all of its details were so masked.[1]

Certainly, in the context of widely held respect for international law and freedom of the seas, such a clandestine operation would justify genuine suspicion. Unfortunately, such respect does not seem to have been widespread at this time:

> In May 1954 . . . Sir Roger Makins, our Ambassador in Washington, was told by Mr Dulles that the United States Navy had been ordered to establish what amounted to a blockade of the Guatemalan coast. Any suspicious vessels were to be searched for arms, with the permission of the Governments concerned if there was time to obtain it, and Mr Dulles asked for our cooperation. He said that, whatever the law might be and the formal view we might take, he hoped that we would in practice agree to whatever action was necessary in order to prevent further arms reaching Guatemala.
>   I thought this a strange way of phrasing a request from one democratic Government to another. . . .[2]

Ironically, United States protest against the arms shipment produced a solidarity of public opinion behind the Guatemalan Government, that, according to the New York *Times'* correspondent, Sydney Gruson, surprised the government leaders themselves.[3]

On November 19, the United States set up a military mission in Nicaragua to train the armed forces of the Somoza dictatorship; on April 23, a Mutual Security Treaty was signed with Nicaragua, and on May 20, with Honduras. On May 19, Nicaragua broke off diplomatic relations with Guatemala and sought to call a meeting of the Foreign Ministers of the OAS under the provision of the Caracas resolution. As the pressure mounted, the Guatemalans sought to avoid a showdown and, on May 23, proposed that Presidents

[1] *White Paper*, p. 12.
[2] Eden, *Full Circle*, p. 134.
[3] May 24, 1954; Taylor, op. cit., p. 794 n.

Eisenhower and Arbenz discuss the friction over the United Fruit Company and other private United States interests in an effort to improve relations between the two nations.

The United States response was to airlift material to Nicaragua and Honduras ('enough arms and other military equipment to fit out an infantry battalion in each country');[1] on May 27, 'three B-36 bombers paid a "courtesy call" on Managua, the Nicaraguan capital'.[2] On June 8, in a press conference, Secretary of State Dulles rejected the notion that the issue between Guatemala and the United States was the United Fruit Company and other private interests:

> . . . [this] is a totally false presentation of the situation. There is a problem in Guatemala which affects the other American states just as much as it does the United States, and it is not a problem which the United States regards exclusively as a United States–Guatamala problem.

On June 8, the Guatemalan Government declared itself in a state of siege.

On June 18, Castillo Armas invaded Guatemala from his base in Honduras with two hundred men and six United States' planes (four F-47 fighters and two C-47 cargo planes) and US pilots to fly them.[3] The fighting, by all accounts, was desultory. Castillo's unopposed planes did the greater part of the damage, while his invasion forces were 'contained' after penetrating twenty miles, by regular units of the army.[4] The following day, the Guatemalan representative to the United Nations requested that the Security Council be called into

[1] Dozer, op. cit., p. 342.

[2] Taylor, op. cit., p. 795.

[3] *Time*, July 12, 1954. According to this source, the cost of the invasion was perhaps as much as $5 million, or more than the amount sixteen of the twenty republics had received in economic assistance in 1954. A similar pattern was followed in the Cuban invasion of April 1961, as recounted in the New York *Times*, Int. Edn., March 13, 1963: 'It became known today that the four American airmen who died in the 1961 Bay of Pigs invasion of Cuba were the crewmen of two B-26 bombers shot down April 18 during combat missions over the island. Authoritative informants said the report of the crash of a C-46 cargo aircraft over the Caribbean was merely a "cover story" issued at the time to conceal the fact that Americans flew combat missions during the invasion.'

[4] Schneider, op. cit., p. 311.

session in an effort to bring pressure on Honduras and Nicaragua, and thus deprive the rebels of their base.[1] Arbenz apparently failed to take into consideration the fact that the President of the Security Council, who would be responsible for implementing such action, was, at the time, United States delegate Henry Cabot Lodge.

A French-sponsored resolution calling for an immediate termination of bloodshed was passed on June 20. After no action had been taken, Guatemalan Foreign Minister Toriello wrote Lodge on June 22 asking that the Security Council take steps to implement the resolution. Lodge replied:

> . . . the Soviet Union . . . has crudely made plain its desire to make as much trouble as possible in the Western Hemisphere . . . many persons will wonder whether the whole imbroglio in Guatemala was not cooked up precisely for the purpose of making Communist propaganda here in the United Nations. This I am sure Mr Toriello would not want.[2]

Lodge's suggestion that Castillo's invasion might be part of a Communist conspiracy could hardly be taken seriously and, in fact, he rejected Toriello's plea on quite different grounds:

> The fact that it has become increasingly plain that the situation in Guatemala is clearly a civil – and not an international war – makes it even more appropriate that the Security Council should not intervene further.

Lodge's contention that the conflict was an internal affair and therefore outside the jurisdiction of the United Nations echoed in principle an earlier Soviet position with regard to the 1948 *coup* in Czechoslovakia. But the evidence available to the United Nations made clear that Castillo's forces had been marshalled in Honduras and had crossed the Guatemalan frontier with the knowledge and acquiescence of the Honduran Government, which 'was in fact performing an act of aggression against Guatemala'.[3]

Yet, when the Guatemalan Government put its complaint

---

[1] ibid., p. 312.
[2] *White Paper*, p. 18.
[3] New York *Times*, June 18, 1954, cited in Taylor, op. cit., p. 789 n.

against Honduras and Nicaragua before the Security Council, Ambassador Lodge continued to insist that 'the information available to the United States thus far strongly suggests that the situation does not involve aggression but is a revolt of Guatemalans against Guatemalans'.[1]

Anxious to keep the issue out of the United Nations, the United States contended that Guatemala should take its case first to the regional Organization of American States 'where the situation can be dealt with most expeditiously and most effectively', and where, as Eden acknowledged, 'Guatemala was likely to be in a minority'.[2] A draft resolution to refer the matter to the OAS, however, was killed by Soviet veto. In the debate, Lodge said:

That will be the second veto by the Soviet Union in three days. We had veto No. 59 on Friday, and now we are going to have veto No. 60 on Sunday. And, vetoing what? Vetoing a move to ask the Organization of American States to solve this problem, to try to bind up this wound in the world and then report back to the Security Council. ... I say to you, representative of the Soviet Union, stay out of this hemisphere and don't try to start your plans and your conspiracies over here.[3]

Meanwhile, the position of the Arbenz régime was deteriorating. Dissident and conservative elements in the army[4] were manifesting signs of disloyalty:

On Friday the 25th the President instructed his loyal Chief of the Armed Forces, Colonel Carlos Enrique Díaz, to furnish arms to the revolutionary[5] parties and mass organizations. Arbenz felt secure in the belief that 'counting on the armed populace, we

[1] *White Paper*, p. 14.
[2] Eden, op. cit., p. 136.
[3] *White Paper*, pp. 16–17.
[4] Schneider, op. cit., p. 315: 'Considering the fact that many of the older officers were conservatively inclined, that others saw the traditional privileged position and political influence of the army endangered by the extensive changes which were taking place [one of the original doctrines of the revolution of 1944 was *civilismo*, the elimination of the army as a political force – D.H.] ... it was not surprising that when the crisis came, the army was not willing to stand squarely behind the régime.' Also cf. Lieuwen, op. cit.
[5] i.e., the Revolution of 1944.

would be perfectly able to fight, not only the invaders, but also against our own treacherous army'. He was shaken to receive a report from Colonel Díaz on Saturday that the other officers would not allow him to fulfill the order to equip the civilians.[1]

On that same Friday, the Security Council *refused to place on its agenda* a request by Guatemala for action in its behalf. The vote against the inclusion of the item was 5–4. France and Britain abstained. The Soviet Union, New Zealand, Lebanon and Denmark voted in favor of considering the Guatemalan plea, which the United States, Taiwan, Turkey, Colombia and Brazil voted against.

The fact that the two Latin American countries on the Council voted with the United States when even such a staunch United States' ally as the United Kingdom felt it could not in good conscience[2] do so may seem puzzling. A glance at the internal situation in these countries, however, makes it apparent why their governments, like those of Taiwan and Turkey, should have been amenable to the United States' position. For at the time of the vote, the normal susceptibility to United States pressures (usually economic) of these countries was enhanced by the fact that the Colombian Government had been overthrown a year earlier by the army dependent on United States' aid, and the Brazilian Army, also beefed up with United States' equipment and funds, was on the point of deposing President Vargas.[3]

In arguing against the inclusion of the Guatemalan complaint on the Security Council's agenda, the United States once again contended that the United Nations must not supersede existing regional organizations.[4] It is one of the ironies of history, of course, that within two years, much to the dismay of the United States, the Soviet Union would be claiming that a regional body to which *it* belonged (the Warsaw Pact) was fully competent to deal with a 'domestic' problem in one of its member nations (Hungary).[5]

---

[1] Schneider, op. cit., p. 312.
[2] cf. Eden, op. cit., pp. 136–7.
[3] Lieuwen, op. cit., pp. 231, 88, 76.
[4] *White Paper*, pp. 18–19, 22–3.
[5] This kind of eventuality was foreseen by Attlee: 'There is a principle involved and that principle was the responsibility of the United Nations. I think it was a mistake in these circumstances to try to hand over to a regional body. We might also have to talk of handing over to a regional body in other parts of the world and I do not think we would like the results very much.'

The United Nations' vote occurred on Friday the 25th. On Sunday, Toriello visited Ambassador Peurifoy and suggested that the war could be ended in fifteen minutes 'if a military *junta* were formed and accepted'. Toriello said that he himself would resign, but he urged that President Arbenz be kept in office. Peurifoy replied that he felt the only solution was 'a clean sweep of the Arbenz Government'.[1] That day Arbenz resigned in favor of his Army Chief of Staff, Díaz. But Peurifoy considered Díaz 'no change' and got in touch with the rightist Colonel Monzon. On Monday, Díaz saw Peurifoy at armed forces headquarters and offered to outlaw the Communist Party,[2] but Peurifoy was unmoved. Thereupon, the Chief of Staff was escorted at gun point from the meeting by other army officers and Colonel Monzon announced that Díaz had resigned and that he was replacing him. This was an 'authentic change', and Peurifoy energetically set to work arranging for peace talks (with Castillo) in San Salvador.[3]

However, the peace talks in San Salvador did not proceed very smoothly and Peurifoy was soon called to preside over the formation of the 'revolutionary' *junta*, which he managed as successfully as he had everything else.

Thus ended the nine and one-half years of the Arévalo-Arbenz program.[4] Tribute has been paid to the fruits of this program by the scholar who has sought to document the State Department's case:

. . . Anti-Communism had become the single unifying theme of the various opposition groups, but it was relatively meaningless

[1] Cited in *The Nation*, July 10, 1954.
[2] ibid.
[3] *Time*, July 12, 1954.
[4] It is one of the sad commentaries on the cultural default in the West during the cold war period that although more than 300 books on the historic Hungarian revolution have been printed in the English, French and German languages, not a single Guatemalan account of the intervention in Guatemala appears to have been translated into these key tongues. Among those available are: Guillermo Toriello (Guatemalan Foreign Minister), *La Batalla de Guatemala*, Mexico, 1955; Raúl Osegueda (Minister of Education), *Operación Guatemala* $$ *OK* $$ Mexico 1955, Luis Cardoza y Aragon, *La Revolucion Guatemalteca* Mexico, 1955, and former President Juan José Arévalo's *Guatemala, La Democracia y el Imperio*, Montevideo, 1954. Arévalo's 1956 political fable about the United States and the twenty Latin American Republics has been printed in English under the title, *The Shark and the Sardines*, by Lyle Stuart, New York, 1962

to the Guatemalan masses, who were interested primarily in a fuller and more satisfying life. While Guatemalans in general had enjoyed more freedom during the 1944–54 period than ever before, the working class had particular reason to feel loyal to the revolutionary régime. For the first time in Guatemalan history labor enjoyed the right to organize freely, bargain collectively and strike. Never before had they felt free to speak out openly and voice their feelings without restraint, much less be confident of gaining a sympathetic hearing from the government. The lower classes enjoyed the novelty of living in a new atmosphere, officially fostered, in which they were treated with a measure of respect and dignity.[1]

Statistics tell an equally impressive story. Of twelve Latin American republics,[2] Guatemala achieved the highest annual increase in *per capita* national income over the nine-year period – 8·5 per cent – despite an annual population increase of 3 per cent (also the highest). The average *per capita* income growth for these countries was less then 3 per cent. Capital investment increased annually by 10·8 per cent during 1945–53 (third highest), industrial production by 6·0 per cent during 1950–5 (also third highest), while its cost of living rose only 2·8 per cent annually during 1945–55 (as compared with 17·2 per cent in Argentina, 13·0 per cent in Brazil, and 24 per cent in Chile), all despite the handicap of a fall in exports (as a result of the difficulties with United Fruit) of 1·9 per cent per year during the ten-year period.[3]

Throughout the period of friction between Guatemala and the United States, the Guatemalan Government contended that the issue at hand was the interference of foreign business interests in the economic development of Guatemala and the United States' narrow interpretation of the rights of those interests. In his June 30 address, Secretary of State Dulles called this an attempt by 'the Guatemalan

[1] Schneider, op. cit., pp. 302–3.
[2] Argentina, Brazil, Chile, Colombia, Cuba, Dominican Republic, Ecuador, Mexico, Panama, Peru, Venezuela, Source, *Latin American Highlights*, The Chase National Bank, September, 1956.
[3] '. . . over the whole period since the counter-revolution of 1954, the growth of the Guatemalan economy has lagged behind that of many other Latin economies and has barely kept pace with a 3 per cent per year population growth'. M. Brower, *The Correspondent*, Winter 1965.

Government and Communist agents throughout the world . . . to obscure the real issue – that of Communist imperialism – by claiming that the United States is only interested in protecting American business'.[1]

> . . . A prosperous and progressive Guatemala is vital to a healthy hemisphere. The United States pledges itself not merely to political opposition to Communism but to help to alleviate conditions in Guatemala and elsewhere throughout the hemisphere. Thus we shall seek positive ways to make our Americas an example which will inspire men everywhere.[2]

To create this example, the United States poured 90 million dollars into Guatemala in loans, guns and subsidies within two years[3] (compared to six hundred thousand dollars in the previous ten years).[4] The acts of the United States-sponsored Castillo Armas Government during the first two years of 'liberation' were highly revealing in terms of the real issues in the struggle.

To 'inspire men everywhere', the *junta* first suspended the agrarian reform and disfranchised the 'illiterate masses', meaning some 70 per cent of the people.[5] 'Hastening to recognize Trujillo and Franco, dissolve Congress, . . . levy a "liberation tax" and pass a law against "dangerous thoughts", the Colonel proceeded to restore all the lands expropriated from United Fruit and to abolish the tax on all interest, dividends and profits payable to investors living outside

---

[1] 'Miguel Ydigoras Fuentes, however, reports that he was approached in the following terms by US agents, while in exile in 1954: 'A former executive of the United Fruit Company, now retired, Mr Walter Turnbull, came to see me with two gentlemen whom he introduced as agents of the CIA. They said that I was a popular figure in Guatemala and that they wanted to lend their assistance to overthrow Arbenz. When I asked their conditions for the assistance I found them unacceptable. Among other things, I was to promise to favor the United Fruit Company and the International Railways of Central America; to destroy the railroad workers labor Union; . . . to establish a strong-arm government, on the style of Ubico. . . .' Ydigoras, *My War with Communism*, pp. 49–50, 1963.

[2] *White Paper*, pp. 32–34.

[3] Betty Kirk, op. cit.

[4] $10·2 million was also given to help Guatemala build its section of the inter-American highway.

[5] *The Nation*, July 17, 1954.

the country – as a result of which, $11 million cascaded into the lap of a single foreign-owned company . . . .'[1]

Within six months, Castillo began softening the nation's oil laws by presidential decree to make it possible for petroleum to be extracted by anybody and exported in the crude state and thus resold to Guatemala as gasoline. Predictably, the big United States companies rushed in to file applications for oil rights. A subsidiary of Signal Oil was awarded the first concession – rights to 671,000 acres. Within two years, concessions had been solicited for more than half the area of Guatemala.[2]

Similarly, Castillo reversed the Arbenz–Arévalo labor program. The process was begun when the new régime relieved every labor official in the country of his office. In order to start up again, a union had to choose leaders acceptable to the dictatorship. As a result, working conditions reached a shocking state, with government tribunals 'striking down labor's most respectful pleas as Communist agitation', and with landowners 'seizing the property of the peasants by burning them out'.[3] 'The Castillo Armas régime,' wrote two United States experts in the field, 'in spite of the good intentions of the President [!], was a brutal dictatorship. Hundreds and perhaps thousands of peasants and workers were killed in a wave of revenge on the part of employers and landlords, who felt that they had been mistreated during the Arévalo–Arbenz period.'[4]

In the summer of 1957 Castillo Armas was assassinated by a 'fanatical Communist' and an election was held. When a 'moderate' civilian candidate won the October election, 'the military-led, rightist political faction stirred up so much resistance that the armed forces felt obliged to nullify the election and to re-establish the *junta.* Then in early 1958, the conservatives led by General Miguel Ydigoras Fuentes, having won on their second try, made the General president.'[5] It was General Ydigoras, a former Minister in the

---

[1] David Graham, 'Liberated Guatemala', *The Nation*, July 17, 1956.

[2] During this period the Eisenhower Government successfully exerted pressure on the governments of Panama, Nicaragua, Bolivia, Cuba, Costa Rica, and Guatemala to change their laws to favor foreign capital. – Betty Kirk (correspondent for the Manchester *Guardian*), op. cit.

[3] Graham, op. cit.

[4] Charles O. Porter and Robert J. Alexander, *The Struggle for Democracy in Latin America*, 1961, p. 70.

[5] Lieuwen, op. cit., p. 165.

detested Ubico dictatorship, who in 1960 allowed the CIA to use Guatemala as a base for the training of the counter-revolutionary Cuban invasion forces, other Latin American countries having refused the use of their territory for such purposes.[1]

In the end of March 1963, Ydigoras was himself overthrown by a right-wing military *coup*. The threat which this *coup* was purported to meet was the announced return of former president Juan Jose Arévalo to run in the forthcoming presidential elections.[2] As Ydigoras had been 'constitutionally elected' the Kennedy Administration cut off aid momentarily, but relented when the *junta* promised to hold new elections in the 'future', and thus allowed Guatemala to return to the 'alliance of free governments'.

[1] New York *Times*, October 14, 1962.
[2] New York *Times*, Int. Edn., April 1 and 2, 1963.

CHAPTER XI

Iran–Greece–Turkey

We've done some damn good things – in the economy, especially, and overseas too – Iran and Guatemala. . . .

EISENHOWER, 1956

IN the cold war campaigns in Guatemala, Viet Nam and Korea, the United States either used its power directly to oppose social and economic change, or lent its support to those social forces most strongly committed to the maintenence of the *status quo*. By its support of the ruling classes and élites, in these countries, whose rule rested on great economic and social injustice, the US insured that its support would maintain in power politically repressive régimes as well. In this way US foreign policy failed to meet the challenge inherent in US ideals. This same failure moreover, – for essentially these same reasons – chracterized the US program, in those countries within the Western orbit where the cold war had had its origins.

Back in November 1945, it had become evident that Russia was making an effort to retain control of the province of Azerbaijan in North Iran; Russian occupation troops not only failed to withdraw within a designated time-span, but supported an autonomy movement and went so far as to stop Iranian troops from entering the province. The aim of these Russian moves seemed to be control of Iranian oil reserves. Strong diplomatic pressure by the United States forced the Soviets to withdraw from Iran, after securing an oil concession on a 51–49 division of profits, 'a basis highly embarrassing to the British who turned over to Iran only about 20 per cent of their gains'.[1] However, when the Soviets withdrew, the Iranian Parliament refused to ratify the agreement.

On May 1, 1951, three days after Dr Mohammed Mossadegh had

---

[1] Fleming, p. 345.

been elected Prime Minister, the huge billion-dollar British owned Anglo-Iranian Oil Company was nationalized. The Iranian people, Mossadegh declared, were opening 'a hidden treasure upon which lies a dragon'.[1] The teeth of this dragon were soon shown, as Iranian oil, which until then had provided a major part of Iran's foreign exchange earnings, found itself virtually boycotted in the West. Mossadegh's attempts to make deals with independent United States' companies were frustrated by the State Department; 'the international oil cartel held firm – and Iran lost all its oil revenues'.[2]

In the resulting financial crisis, the United States provided some aid ($1·5 million in 1951 for a technical rural-improvement program, $15 million in 1952, which was used mainly to make up Iran's foreign exchange shortages) and thus manifested its differences with the British:

> . . . It seemed to the United States a reckless policy to allow the situation to deteriorate, as they considered it would if Mossadegh were left without any help.
>
> Our reading of the situation was different. I did not accept the argument that the only alternative to Mossadegh was Communist rule. I thought that if Mossadegh fell, his place might well be taken by a more reasonable Government with which it should be possible to conclude a satisfactory agreement.[3]

These Anglo-American differences were not resolved until the election of Eisenhower in 1952, and the appointments of John Foster Dulles and his brother, Allen Dulles, to the posts of Secretary of State and Director of the CIA. Within seven months, the Mossadegh Government was overthrown by a United States planned and directed *coup d'etat*.[4]

In view of Dulles' interests in the United Fruit Company in Guatemala a year later, it is interesting that the Anglo-Iranian Oil Company was financed by the Industrial Bank of Iran. This bank,

---

[1] Eden, *Memoirs*, p. 194.

[2] Fred Cook, 'The CIA,' *The Nation*, June 24, 1961.

[3] Eden, op. cit., p. 201.

[4] Fred Cook, op. cit. cf. also Fleming, p. 926. cf. also Wise and Ross, *The Invisible Government*, pp. 110 ff.

in turn, was formed in the early 1900's by Baron Reuters and others, including J. Henry Schroeder & Co., the international German banking house with which Allen Dulles was later connected.[1] Frank C. Tiarks, one of Allen Dulles' fellow directors in the Schroeder banking enterprises, served also as director of Anglo-Iranian Oil, and Sullivan and Cromwell, the legal firm in which the Dulles brothers were partners, was the long-time legal counsel of Anglo-Iranian Oil.[2]

As a result of the US engineered *coup*, the British lost their oil monopoly and Iranian oil was turned over to a four-nation consortium, England, France, Holland and the United States (whose cut was 40 per cent) to exploit under an agreement with the Iranian Government similar to other Middle East oil agreements.[3] The Iranian Government further agreed to pay $70 million compensation to the Anglo-Iranian Oil Company in settlement of all claims (as a result of the abortive nationalization).[4]

The money to pay this claim presumably came from funds which the United States began to pour into the country immediately after the success of its *coup* of August 19. These funds, which came as part of the mutual security program, amounted to $5 million per month for the next three years, ostensibly 'to make up deficits in Iran's government budget'.[5] A Congressional committee reported in 1957, however, that with $300 million per year in restored oil revenues, Iran should have been capable of financing its own government and development programs without any United States aid. The reality of the matter was that 'Iran's CIA-installed government was so corrupt that the national treasury constantly teetered on the brink of bankruptcy' and that it was this corruption that was responsible for the ever-mounting deficits.[6]

---

[1] 'The parent firm ... was headed by Baron Kurt von Schroeder ... the Baron played a key role in the accession to power of Adolf Hitler. It was in his villa at Cologne on January 7, 1933, that Hitler and von Papen met and worked out their deal for the Nazi seizure of power. ...' – Cook, op. cit.

[2] Cook, ibid.

[3] Eden, and Wise and Ross, op. cit. The CIA chief who managed the *coup* 'later left the CIA and joined the Gulf Oil Corporation as "government relations" director in its Washington office. Gulf named him a vice-president in 1960.'

[4] Eden, op. cit., p. 218.

[5] Cook, op. cit.

[6] Cook, ibid.

... Our hundreds of millions of dollars have done virtually nothing for the people of Iran; they have enriched only the grafters and widened the gulf between the very rich and the abysmally poor. The Congressional committee in 1957 found literacy so low in Iran that, even in the cities, some estimates placed it at not more than 7 per cent. ... [It was] reported in 1960 that some families were still living on the produce of a single walnut tree, that tiny children worked all day at the looms of rug factories for 20 cents or less.[1]

Much of United States aid to Iran – some $500 million – went to support the 20,000-man Iranian Army. Expressing concern about the purpose of this army, Senator Hubert Humphrey exclaimed: 'Do you know what the head of the Iranian Army told one of our people. He said the Army was in good shape, thanks to US aid – it was now capable of coping with the civilian population. That Army isn't going to fight the Russians. It's planning to fight the Iranian people.'[2]

Iran was not the only country where oil seemed to be a determining factor in United States policies. On January 5, 1957, President Eisenhower addressed Congress with a proposal which became known as the Eisenhower Doctrine, an extension of the Truman Doctrine to the Middle East. Eisenhower asked Congressional approval of authority for the President to use armed force in the Middle East 'to secure and protect the territorial integrity and political independence of such nations requesting aid against overt armed aggression from any nation controlled by International Communism'. The words are memorable in light of the situation in which the Doctrine was later invoked.

On July 15, 1958, the United States marines were landed in Lebanon, accompanied by 'a vast American armada' which suddenly appeared off the port of Beirut.[3] The reasons for the landing were the *coup* in Iraq, which had deposed the pro-Western Nuri es-Said, and a state of non-shooting civil war in Lebanon, which was endangering the rule of President Chamoun.

Chamoun had rigged the election of June 1957 to secure a par-

---

[1] ibid.
[2] ibid.
[3] Fleming, p. 920.

liament that would approve his acceptance of the Eisenhower Doctrine. The rigging was so successful, that 'almost every important opposition figure' found himself outside the parliament, which, it was believed, would accede to Chamoun's wish to change the constitution permitting him to rule another term, if not for life. The Patriarch of the Maronite Christians summed up the results as 'forty years' work ruined in a month, a country divided against itself'.

Chamoun's acts 'threw the country into a strange state of civil war. Armed rebellion erupted in Beirut on May 12. A major pipeline was cut and the United States Information Library was burned. The government promptly alleged that foreign agents were behind it and appealed to the United States to save it.'[1] Dulles decided immediately to send troops if required. Before long, 'half' of the capital and 'half' of the country was 'in hostile hands', under various rebel leaders; it was, according to the London *Sunday Times* a 'calculated defiance of authority by at least half of the population.'

At the same time as these events, Colonel Karim Kassem took power in Iraq. At first there was 'strong consideration' among United States government leaders of 'military intervention to undo the *coup* in Iraq'.[2] United States Ambassador Gallman received a message from the State Department advising him 'that Marines, starting to land in Lebanon might be used to aid loyal Iraqi troops to counter-attack'. But no one could be found in Iraq to collaborate with. Everybody was for the revolution.'[3]

> The gulf between rich and poor was a standing incitement to revolt. . . . The hatred of Nuri [es-Said] and of the land-owning Arab Sheiks and Kurdish Aghas who made up his party was pathological. There were two other objects of universal execration: the 50/50 oil agreement made with the Iraq Petroleum Co. in 1952; and the Baghdad Pact.[4]

---

[1] Fleming, ibid.
[2] New York *Herald Tribune*, July 21, 1958; cited in Fleming, p. 922.
[3] Fleming, ibid.
[4] General H. G. Martin in *Middle Eastern Affairs*, March 1959; cited in Fleming, ibid. 90 per cent of Iraq is illiterate, the average life-span is twenty-six years and *per capita* income is less than $90 per year. The Baghdad Pact was formed in 1955 and included the United States, Great Britain, Turkey, Iran, Pakistan and Iraq. Iraq withdrew in 1959 and the pact was renamed CENTO.

These then were the 'threats' which precipated the US landings in Lebanon. 'This action . . .' wrote Sir Anthony Eden afterwards, 'was unquestionably against the terms of the [United Nations] Charter as interpreted at the time of our intervention at Port Said. Since the United Nations observers were already on the spot and proclaiming that the motives for Anglo-American intervention did not exist, it was rather more heinous.'[1]

When the landings in Lebanon took place, the United States and the British governments announced that they would not invade Iraq unless the government of that country failed, as the New York *Times* reported, to 'respect Western oil interests'. In the formulation of C. Wright Mills: 'Thus did the power élite attempt, in official language, "to assure the independence and integrity of these two small countries", or, in the unofficial terms of the *Times*' reporter, Dana Adams Schmidt: "to restore Western prestige generally in the Middle East and to stabilize the friendly oil-producing governments in Saudi Arabia and the Persian Gulf region".'[2]

[1] Eden, op. cit., p. 578.
[2] Mills, *The Causes of World War III*, 1958, pp. 65–7. In his account, Mills cites an important Congressional document confirming the view that the issue was not communism but oil. On February 8, 1963, Kassem was toppled by another *coup*. This time there were no Western landings. Just prior to the *coup* Kassem had announced the formation of a national oil company to exploit the oil areas he had recovered in 1961 from foreign oil interests (amounting to 99 per cent of their concessionary areas). In a special interview with *Le Monde*, four days before the *coup*, Kassem revealed that he had received a note from the US State Department, threatening him with sanctions, unless he changed his attitude. According to the Paris weekly *L'Express* (February 21, 1963) 'The Iraqi *coup* was inspired by the CIA. (cf. also *Le Monde* February 12.) The British Government and Nasser himself . . . were aware of the *putsch* preparations. The French Government was left out.' The British had stipulated that the new Government must abandon any claims to Kuwait and must not proceed with the plans to exploit the oil in the areas recently recovered by Iraq. The Americans obtained agreement that 'the liquidation of the Communist Party would be achieved only through martial courts and not by summary executions'. (The Iraqi Communist Party had been outlawed under Kassem and was under open attack towards the end of his rule.) In fact thousands were massacred in the weeks following the *coup*. Supporting the evidence given by *L'Express* and *Le Monde*, was the fact that the first statement on the new régime's intentions towards the oil monopoly came not from Baghdad, but from Washington. In the midst of the three day fighting and at a time when the new Iraqi foreign minister had limited himself to statements in favor of non-alignment and 'against imperialism', US officials reassured newsmen that the new government 'is not interested in nationalizing the gigantic Iraq Petroleum Co.' (*Christian Science Monitor*, February 13). And on February 12, *Le Monde* reported from

If Eisenhower's extension of the Truman Doctrine seemed to jar with the avowed intentions of the latter ('to support free peoples who are resisting attempted subjugation by armed minorities or by outside pressures'), its results – the shoring up of dictatorial régimes and the maintenance of socially backward *status quo* – were virtually identical. For, after a decade of United States involvement in Greece and Turkey, it was apparent that little else had been accomplished.

To Greece, with its population of 9 million, the United States sent $1,593 million in economic aid between 1946 and 1958, of which only $37 million was in loans. This was three times the outright economic grants given to either India or Latin America in the same period. During these years, moreover, military aid to Greece amounted to another $1,238 million. The use to which all this aid was put, however, was limited by the social outlook of those elements into whose hands the British and Americans had placed political control of the country. Thus, the *New Leader* reported in 1958 that,

Economic stability and fortunate circumstances have not . . . had the same meaning for all Greeks. So far, the circumstances have all favored the interests of the privileged classes, whose sole care has been further self-enrichment. The interests of the workers, artisans and employees have been constantly sacrificed to 'stabilization'. The Rightist régimes in power have given the former everything they want, while demanding only sacrifice from the latter.[1]

As for Greek freedom, *Amnesty* reported in 1963:

About 60,000 political exiles have had their citizenship taken away from them. Public meetings are restricted and the press can be prosecuted for 'slander', a term widely interpreted. The

[1] Manolis Korakas, 'Greek Communists Stage a Comeback', *New Leader*, May 26, 1958.

Washington: 'While the events of 1958 prompted the US to send 10,000 marines to Lebanon, the present *coup* is not regarded as a menace to US interests; on the contrary, it is regarded as a pro-Western re-orientation in the Middle East.' – The above is taken from information compiled by the Iraq Students Association, United Kingdom.

radio is entirely controlled by the Government, and conscientious objectors are subjected to very harsh régimes. . . .

. . . all those who [have] been engaged in any protests against the Government have to have 'Certificates of Social Opinion', issued by the police in order to get work. This applie[s] not only to work in the public service, but in private firms as well. Even the children of [political] prisoners [have] to produce Certificates if they [want] to go to the University.[1]

To Turkey and its 27 million people, $1,158 million in economic aid and $2 billion in military aid between 1946 and 1960 brought similar results. In the spring of 1960, student demonstrations precipitated the fall of the United States-supported Menderes dictatorship. The *Economist*, on June 4, 1960, pointed out that the Turkish Government had kept a huge army of 500,000 men mobilized, without making any contribution 'to the much needed capital investment in roads, schools, dams, irrigation and drainage'. As for the peril to Turkey, the *Economist* noted,

The real threat is implicit in the fact that the Turkish-speaking Soviet citizens on the other side of the frontier have a standard of life which is nearly twice that of the mass of Anatolian peasants. Again, while the vast majority of Turks in Turkey are illiterate and higher education (despite American efforts) is extremely scanty, there is little or no illiteracy among the Soviet Turks and their higher education is advancing at an astounding pace. Moreover, in Turkmenistan agricultural investment now rates high priority amid an accelerating industrial development.[2]

As Walter Lippmann astutely observed in 1958: '. . . we delude ourselves[3] if we do not realize that the main power of the Communist states lies not in their clandestine activity but in the force of their example, in the visible demonstration of what the Soviet Union has

[1] *Amnesty*, No. 4, 1963 Report of Reg Sorensen, M.P.
[2] Cited in Fleming, p. 1028.
[3] 'History records that our aid programs to Turkey and Greece were the crucial element that enabled Turkey to stand up against heavy-handed Soviet pressures, Greece to put down Communist aggression and both to recreate stable societies and to move forward in the direction of economic and social growth.' President Kennedy's Message to Congress on the Foreign Aid Program, New York *Times*, April 3, 1963.

achieved in forty years, or what Red China has achieved in about ten years.'[1]

In 1961, in the wake of the invasion of Cuba, Lippmann expanded upon the other half of this proposition saying,

> I venture to argue ... that the reason we are on the defensive in so many places is that for some ten years we have been doing exactly what Mr K[hrushchev] expects us to do. We have used money and arms in a long, losing attempt to stabilize native governments which, in the name of anti-communism, are opposed to all important social change. This has been exactly what Mr K's dogma calls for – that communism should be the only alternative to the *status quo* with its immemorial poverty and privilege.[2]

The correctness of Lippmann's characterization of the mutual security program is revealed in the fact that one-quarter of outright United States grants in the period 1946–61 went to five countries – Turkey, Greece, South Korea, South Viet Nam and Formosa – all right-wing dictatorships opposed to social change, and, with the exception of Formosa,[3] all hopelessly backward economically. With combined populations of only 75 million people, the countries received $8·7 billion in economic aid, or more in grants than war-ravaged Europe,[4] without its having any significant effect – again excluding Formosa – on their economies. Militarily, they received $7·9 billion in arms,[5] more again than Western Europe ($7½ billion – $4 billion of which went to France, $2½ billion for her war against the

---

[1] Walter Lippmann, *The Communist World and Ours*, 1959, pp. 36–7.

[2] Cited in *The Nation*, June 24, 1961, p. 534.

[3] Although it is unable to stand on its own feet economically, after Japan it has the highest *per capita* food consumption in Asia – but it has always had this.

[4] Not all European aid went to war-ravaged sectors, however. Spain, for example, received more than one billion dollars in economic aid, and $500 million in military grants. In April 1963, President Kennedy said, 'no peacetime victory in history has been as far-reaching in its impact, nor served the cause of freedom so well, as the victories scored in the last seventeen years by this nation's mutual defense and assistance programs.' Yet, in 1963, *Amnesty* reported that 'In Spain, one could not speak about personal freedom, but only about persecution. ... Spain [is] a police state in every sense of the word.' (Report of Ernest Davies, former Under-Secretary of Foreign Affairs, Great Britain.)

[5] Korea's $1·7 billion does not include the Korean War period.

Indo-Chinese alone)[1] and 36 per cent of the non-European total. This money has put almost 2 million men under arms, or more than twice the number of men the United States has under arms, relative to its population. If China were to arm in equal proportion to *its* population, this would mean a standing army of 20 million men.

The disproportionate size of these armies is most evident in the 600,000-man army of Chiang Kai-shek (Formosa's population is 10 million). This army is an army of occupation in the literal sense of the word, since it seized power in Formosa in the late 1940s at the cost of tens of thousands of lives, destroyed the existing Formosan Government and still excludes native Formosans from holding national office. The 600,000-man force is not necessary for the defense of the island, moreover, since the United States Seventh Fleet effectively performs that service. Likewise, the 600,000-man Korean army holds the balance of political power in Korea, but it is the 50,000 United States troops and the power behind them which effectively defend the 38th Parallel.

On June 20, 1958, Senator Fulbright raised his voice against the undiscriminating United States military aid program, as he grimly pointed out that 'for the next fifty years' most of the blood-letting in the world 'will be traceable to military equipment of US origin'. But Fulbright's attempt to get the emphasis shifted from military to economic aid was unsuccessful.[2]

On January 25, 1959, as United States Congressmen raised cries against the executions of some 500 accused torturers and murderers of the 20,000 Cubans who had been killed by the Batista régime[3]

[1] A sizeable amount also supported France's war against Algeria. For a critical analysis of United States military aid programs, cf. Edgar S. Furniss, Jr, 'Some Perspectives on American Military Assistance', Center of International Studies, Princeton University, 1957, pp. 29–39.

[2] Fleming, p. 1088.

[3] 'How come, [the Cubans] asked, American Congressmen and editorial writers had not protested against the gouging of eyes, the cutting of testicles, and the slicing of women's breasts in the Batista jails? How come nothing was said when every morning the people of Santiago found their sons, husbands and brothers dead and mutilated in doorways and public squares. Why had the deaths of thousands of persons under the Batista régime been accepted in silence while American tourists gaily flocked to Havana's casinos and night clubs.' – Szulc and Meyer, *The Cuban Invasion*, pp. 32–3.

('What Castro and Agramonte [Cuban Foreign Minister, and later exile] ought to do is drop on their knees before their Maker and ask for forgiveness', declaimed Senator Wayne Morse on January 14), Chester Bowles reminded Americans that during the Batista dictatorship, 'our tanks, planes, and small arms brought death to the rebels and their families, manufactured in American factories, paid for by American taxpayers and shipped to Cuba by the American Government'.

The American Republic had come a long way indeed since the days when Metternich had complained, that 'In fostering revolutions wherever they show themselves, in regretting those which have failed, in extending a helping hand to those which seem to prosper, [the Americans] lend new strength to the apostles of sedition and reanimate the courage of every conspirator.' [1824.]

CHAPTER XII

Cuba

You killed women and children in Playa Giron [Bay of Pigs]. You bombed the first decent houses, the first schools, the first hospitals of Cubans who never before, during the long American protectorate over Cuba, had a roof, an alphabet, or their health. And you did it in the name of liberty, democracy and free enterprise. What do you want us to think of these nice-sounding words when in their names a population is murdered and the first proofs of concrete welfare are destroyed ? We think the same as Simon Bolivar did 150 years ago: 'The USA seems destined by Providence to plague us with all kinds of evils in the name of liberty.'

CARLOS FUENTES
Mexican Novelist

. . . from the moment it was clear to American policy-makers that Fidel Castro was bent on carrying through a genuine social revolution, it became the overriding aim of Washington's Cuba policy to overthrow his régime.

HUBERMAN AND SWEEZY

US HOSTILITY to the Cuban revolution before Castro's victory was not confined to military aid to Batista.[1] In the first week of December 1958, William D. Pawley, a former US diplomat who knew Batista personally, proposed a plan for preventing Castro from coming to power, to a group of State Department and CIA officials. His idea was to persuade Batista 'to capitulate to a caretaker government unfriendly to him but satisfactory to us, which we could immediately

---

[1] A US arms embargo went into effect in the Caribbean in March 1958, but the US Military Mission was not withdrawn and Great Britain continued to supply Batista with arms. – Lieuwen, pp. 268–9.

recognize and give military assistance to in order that Fidel Castro not come to power'. The proposal was cleared through to Dulles, who apparently approved it over the telephone. Pawley flew to Havana to see Batista, and spent three hours with him on the night of December 9, but Batista refused the offer.[1]

The victory of the revolution did not change the United States attitude towards it. Batista fled the country on January 1, 1959, and Castro announced the formation of a government with Manuel Urrutia Lleo as President. The next day, American officials allowed the press to refer to their 'apprehension' about Cuba's future under Castro. Various American business interests were also reported to be antagonistic, and the discredited pro-Batista US Ambassador Earl T. Smith was kept at his post until January 10. The United States did not recognize Cuba's new government until January 7, 'and it does not seem that it would have been beyond the realm of decorum for Washington to send a special emissary with the note'.[2]

When Ambassador Smith resigned, Castro publicly noted the occasion saying, 'I am under the impression, that the United States is changing its attitude toward Cuba and will remove the things that caused friction [in the past], but that is for the United States to say.' There was no direct answer from the United States, but the new Ambassador, Philip Bonsal, was not appointed until January 21. He did not arrive in Havana until February 19, 1959, or six weeks after Ambassador Smith's resignation. That this was an act designed specifically to show US displeasure with the Castro Government was publicly revealed as early as January 15, 1959, when the press reported that pressure on Castro had been considered by the government (because of the executions of Batista lieutenants) and that it had been decided that the proper action to take would be to delay the sending of a new Ambassador.[3] Moreover, the appointment itself made it clear that the United States was not very interested in removing 'the things that caused friction':

[1] Hearings before the Sub-Committee of the Senate Judiciary Committee to Investigate the Administration of the Internal Security Act, etc., Part 10, Washington GPO, 1961, cited in Wm. A. Williams, *The US, Cuba and Castro*, 1962, pp. 33–4; this, and Scheer and Zeitlin's, *Cuba: Tragedy in Our Hemisphere*, 1964, are by far the best accounts of the substantive issues involved in the Cuban revolution and US–Cuban relations.

[2] Williams, ibid., pp. 34–5.

[3] ibid., p. 37.

The crimes of the Batista Government were not merely against the persons and property of Cuban citizens . . . the cesspool of corruption under Batista proves to be immeasurable. Scarcely a transaction, a contract or a concession was negotiated here without incredibly large percentages going to Batista and his entourage. The telephone company [US owned] got its rates raised with a pay-off to the régime of $3 million, according to documents found. . . . No wonder the populace on November 1 smashed telephone coin-boxes.

And now a US Ambassador who . . . for much of his life . . . was an officer of this same Cuban telephone company. . . . And in a revolutionary situation such as exists here![1]

United States hostility to the Cuban revolution at its inception was thus in evidence, despite the general consensus among authorities that, 'for a substantial period of time, the aggregate morale of the Cuban revolution was democratic, anti-dictatorial and anti-Communist' and that in its hour of success it should have been encouraged and 'given every assistance'.[2] The search for the source of official attempts to check the revolution in its early stages, and the readiness of the State Department to be rid of it entirely, is not an academic one, moreover, since as Karl E. Meyer and Tad Szulc in their authoritative study of the subsequent invasion of Cuba have pointed out, 'The invasion plan was in some sense a logical extension of prevailing attitudes to a revolutionary situation.'[3]

Two sources for initial US antipathy to the revolution suggest themselves immediately, namely, the fear of Communism and the fear of social reforms which would create an 'unfavorable climate' for US investments, as in Guatemala.

Fear of Communism can quickly be dismissed because as Edwin Lieuwen has noted, 'During the first six months of the Castro régime, little trace of Communism was detectable in the revolution-

---

[1] Carleton Beals in *The Nation*, January 31, 1959. Another step which the US took in the Caribbean and which the Cubans interpreted as a sign of revived US interventionary intentions was the sending of a military mission to the ruthless Duvalier régime in Haiti. – cf. Lieuwen, pp. 290–1.

[2] A. A. Berle, Jr, 'The Cuban Crisis', *Foreign Affairs*, October 1960.

[3] *The Cuban Invasion*, New York, 1962; Szulc is a member of the Washington Bureau of the New York *Times* and Meyer is on the editorial staff of the Washington *Post*.

ary coalition.'[1] 'In the trade union elections held in March 1959, the workers overwhelmingly backed David Salvador and other members of the *July 26* movement against the Communist candidates, *who lost heavily in all the 3,800 posts up for election.*'[2] As late as May 21, 1959, Castro said publicly:

> The tremendous problem faced by the world is that it has been placed in a position where it must choose between capitalism, which starves people, and communism, which resolves economic problems, but suppresses the liberties so greatly cherished by man. Both Cubans and Latin Americans cherish and foster a revolution that may meet their material needs without sacrificing those liberties. . . .[3]

The second possible source of US hostility – fear of the revolution's effect on US Economic interests – had a more substantial basis in fact. To begin with, US citizens controlled 80 per cent of Cuba's utilities, 90 per cent of the mines, 90 per cent of the cattle ranches, almost 100 per cent of the oil refining industry, 50 per cent of the public railways, 40 per cent of the sugar industry, and 25 per cent of all bank deposits. Cuba ranked fourth in Latin America in *per capita* income and third in US investments. US firms received 40 per cent of the profits on sugar, a crop which accounted for 80 per cent of exports; their total earnings on direct investments amounted to $77 million (1957), but they employed only 1·08 per cent of the Cuban population.[4] The balance of payments from 1950 to 1960 had been favorable to the US with regard to Cuba to the extent of $1 billion.

As for Castro's revolutionary program, it had not been set out in detail (revolutionary programs never are, for the obvious reason that support for the revolution must be maximized), but it embodied a firm commitment to the Cuban Constitution of 1940. If he had been successful in his first revolutionary attempt, he said in court in 1953, 'The first revolutionary law would have restored sovereignty to the

---

[1] Lieuwen, p. 276; 'known Communists had no official posts in either the primary or secondary echelons of government'.

[2] Javier Pazos, in *Cambridge Opinion 51* (emphasis added).

[3] Quoted in C. Wright Mills, *Listen Yankee*, 1960, p. 98.

[4] Williams, pp. 21–2.

people and proclaimed the Constitution of 1940 as the true supreme
law of the state, until such a time as the people would decide to
modify it or to change it.'

Now the Cuban Constitution, unlike its US counterpart does not
emphasize political rights as the first thing to be guaranteed and the
last to be taken away. The emphasis of the Cuban document is
rather on the social development of the country in preference to and
if need be at the expense of political freedoms. The Constitution
'defines the state as the agent of, and charges it with responsibility
for, economic developemnt, social welfare and justice, and the
recovery and protection of Cuban national sovereignty'.[1]

The October 12, 1940, issue of *Business Week* perceived the full
implications of this Constitution, both with regard to Cuban
society and to US–Cuban relations, and did so twenty years before
the event:

> Whether or not it is ever enforced, Cuba's spectacular new
> charter has created a powerful implement for social and economic
> reforms. . . . Sudden and drastic enforcement of the new regula-
> tions is not anticipated. Cuba is too closely tied to the United
> States both economically and politically.[2]

'It would have been difficult to put the truth any more neatly,'
comments William Appleman Williams, '*The Cuban Constitution of
1940 could not be put into operation without disrupting the basic
substance and tone of traditional American–Cuban relations.*' [Em-
phasis in original.] Indeed, the reduction of American power
(though not specifically named) was an explicit directive in the
Constitution (e.g. cf. Article 90: 'The law shall restrictively limit
acquisition and possession of land by foreign persons and companies,

---

[1] Williams, op. cit., p. 64. This has been ignored by Theodore Draper (*Castro's
Revolution: Myths and Realities*, 1962) and others, as has the fact that elections
were postponed for two years by the full revolutionary coalition (not simply
Castro). According to the Constitution, all political rights 'may be suspended
in all or in part of the national territory, for a period not greater than forty-
five caldendar days, whenever the security of the State may require it'. Clearly,
the forty-five days can be indefinitely extended by interrupting the ban for
twenty-four hours every six weeks. No schedule of elections is established by
the Constitution. For a discussion of the framing of the Constitution cf.
Williams, pp. 55 et seq. For text, cf. Scheer and Zeitlin, op. cit.
[2] Cited in Williams, pp. 67–8.

and shall adopt measures tending to revert the land to Cuban ownership.' See also Articles 3, 88, 272, etc.)[1]

When Castro came to power with the intention of implementing the Constitution, Cuba was in the throes of a social disaster, the direct result of decades of corrupt tyrannical régimes under US tutelage. Six hundred thousand Cubans were unemployed, as many proportionally as were unemployed in the US during the great depression. Half the population did not have electricity, and three and a half million Cubans lived in huts, shacks and slums without sanitary facilities. In the cities, rents represented almost one-third of family incomes. Almost 40 per cent of the population was illiterate; 100,000 persons suffered from tuberculosis and 95 per cent of the children in rural areas were affected by parasites. Only $1\frac{1}{2}$ per cent of the landowners controlled 46 per cent of the total area of the nation, while 85 per cent of the small farmers paid out almost a third of their incomes in rent.[2]

Castro's list of priorities for dealing with Cuba's problems were stated by him in his 1953 speech:

The problem concerning land, the problem of industrialization, the problem of housing, the problem of unemployment, the problem of education, and the problem of health of the people; these are the six problems we would take immediate steps to resolve, along with the restoration of public liberties and political democracy.

The first steps of the revolution were the investment of $250,000 in housing, schools, recreation facilities and other public works. Salaries were raised, electric power rates cut, rents decreased by as much as 50 per cent and a tax reform was introduced. In February, Castro specified 'the principal point of our economic program – industrialization at the fastest possible rate'.[3] It is to be noted that he did not then embark upon a program of forced industrialization, but confined himself to reforms that immediately improved the prospect of Cuban life. None the less, these reforms 'dismayed the

[1] ibid., p. 64.

[2] Castro speech before the UN, September 26, 1960. cf. Scheer and Zeitlin, op. cit., Chapter 1.

[3] Cited in Williams, p. 85. cf. Scheer and Zeitlin, Chapter 3.

conservatives and the middle-of-the-roaders. ... Money has tightened and no investments are being made.'[1] This reaction of capital served to intensify the already severe depression. Since Cuba's reserves were at a low $70 million, the need for capital to enable the government to foster industrialization was great, and it was partly for this reason that Castro came to the United States in April 1959.

Castro, of course, did not get the loan he was seeking,[2] and this proved to be a decisive turning point in the revolution. After two rounds of talks between Cuba and the International Monetary Fund, the loan was rejected on grounds significant not only for the revolution in Cuba, but for the development programs of the under-developed areas generally. The loan was turned down, because 'the Castro Government [had] not shown itself prepared yet to accept a stabilization program.'[3] Such a program had been demanded by the Fund and accepted by the Frondizi Government of Argentina during December 1958 and January 1959; 'a dramatic fall in consumption, unemployment, wage cuts, strikes, police action ... followed in inevitable progression.'[4]

It was thus clear that 'Castro could obtain aid, but only by acquiescing in terms (credit restraint and a balanced budget)[5] that would prevent him from carrying through the social revolution by denying him the use of the tool of deficit financing for handling industrialization and agrarian reform, and by imposing economic controls that would be very apt to stir popular unrest against his government. The stabilization conditions, in other words, were basically designed to preserve the Cuban *status quo*,[6] allowing only

[1] New York *Times*, April 4, 1959, cited in Williams.

[2] The whole question of this loan is very involved, and Castro's attitude towards it had certain intensely ambiguous elements, among these, his bitter sense that it would mean surrendering some of Cuba's sovereignty at the outset. The interplay of forces within the coalition and the various choices presented to the coalition are carefully considered in Williams' account as are the criticisms of Castro made by Rivero, Pazos and Fresquet, and repeated by Draper, pp. 91 et seq. cf. also Scheer and Zeitlin, op. cit., pp. 85 et seq.

[3] New York *Times*, April 26, 1959, cited in Williams.

[4] Paul Johnson, 'The Plundered Continent', *New Statesman*, September 17, 1960.

[5] New York *Times*, April 22, 1959.

[6] These conditions apply generally to US aid to underdeveloped countries and thus their intent goes way beyond preserving just the *Cuban status quo*.

a few fringe reforms to be put into operation.' If, however, Castro chose to go forward with the revolution, he would have to 'adopt a controlled economy' (as one US Government economist noted) and subject the Cuban people to severe hardships.[1]

Rebuffed in his requests for a loan, Castro went to the Economic Council of the Organization of American States which was meeting in Buenos Aires and, on May 2, delivered a speech on the problems faced by Latin Americans in seeking to transform their countries. His speech was 'restrained and generous towards the US'. He examined each of the various opportunities for development finding them inadequate (e.g. increased trade, but the US maintains a high tariff wall; available loans, but they require stabilization programs, etc.). As an alternative, he asked the United States to lend Latin American countries $30 billion, repayable in ten years. He admitted that this would require new sacrifices from already burdened US taxpayers, but he asked that it be made for two reasons: to help the people of Latin America and to avoid forcing Latin America to choose between no (or retarded) development and development under tyrannies of the Right and the Left. His request was dismissed as ridiculous in the United States.[2] Two years later, President Kennedy inaugurated the Alliance for Progress, a program of aid to Latin America amounting to $10 billion over a ten-year period but tied to stabilizing (hence *status quo* preserving) fiscal policies.

Upon his return from Buenos Aires, Castro found his government and programs under attack from the Conservatives and Communists. He moved first to rebuff the Communist challenge. Bluntly and angrily on May 8 and 16, he dissociated himself from the Communist Party and its ideas and programs. Subsequently in June, he acted to block Communist influence in the labor movement.[3]

On May 17, the day after his second assault on the Communists, Castro promulgated an Agrarian Reform Law which he had had a decisive hand in formulating and which was more radical than

[1] Williams, op. cit., p. 102.
[2] Williams, op. cit., p. 109. A partial text of Castro's speech is contained in Scheer and Zeitlin, op. cit., pp. 89–90. The full text has been printed as *Plan for the Advancement of Latin America*, Havana, 1959.
[3] Williams, p. 112; Scheer and Zeitlin, Chapter 6.

anticipated.[1] Hard hit were not only the large US companies, three of whom together lost over one million acres, but also many Cuban landowners. The agrarian reform split the revolutionary coalition. In the words of Edwin Lieuwen, it 'precipitated a break between the moderates and the left and turned the revolution, at least in part, into a class struggle, between the proletariat and the people with property. During June–July 1959, the moderates, including President Manuel Urrutia and five middle-group cabinet officers, were forced out of the government, and replaced by radical leftists. As expected, there followed during the latter half of 1959, a series of defections, conspiracies, terrorist acts, and counter-revolutionary movements on the part of the moderates.'[2]

In this situation, the revolution moved left; a people's militia was built up and an intelligence organization created. As of July, however, Castro had made no move towards accepting extensive support from the Communists, although he had appointed individual party members to government posts.

There is evidence that at this time Castro made another effort to obtain a loan. On August 9, American officials were reported to feel that the Cuban economic crisis had Castro 'in a box'. A loan would, of course, ease the crisis, but 'the United States would make such a loan only if the Castro régime agreed to the kind of stabilization program that the International Monetary Fund has worked out with other nations in similar trouble.'[3]

On October 14, the United States delivered a second note to Cuba opposing the expropriation and other provisions of the Agrarian Reform Law. In the wake of this note, the revolutionary coalition underwent a further crisis and Felipe Pazos was replaced by Che Guevara as President of the National Bank, Manuel Ray resigning as Minister of Public Works.[4] On December 17, Castro

---

[1] Draper has raised some questions about this law in connection with Castro's commitment to the Constitution of 1940 (pp. 31–3); for Williams' reply, see Williams, pp. III et seq.

[2] Lieuwen, op. cit., pp. 271–2 of Scheer and Zeitlin, Chapter 5.

[3] New York *Times*, August 9, 1959; cited in Williams, pp. 131, 133.

[4] This crisis was intensified by the arrest and sentencing of Major Huber Matos on charges of treason. For Draper on the Matos affair, cf. pp. 65–7; for Williams' reply, cf. pp. 121–38. This was also the period of the Salvador affair, which has been seriously misreported. For the correct version of this event, see Scheer and Zeitlin pp. 301–2.

predicted that in 1960, Cubans would have to 'defend the revolution weapons at hand'.

In February 1960, a trade pact was signed and on May 7 diplomatic relations were resumed with the Soviet Union. In June, US-owned oil companies in Cuba refused to refine Soviet crude oil and the US congress authorized President Eisenhower to cut the Cuban sugar quota. On July 7, the sugar quota – Cuba's economic life-line – was cut. On July 9, Khrushchev declared that the USSR would use rockets to halt any US military intervention in Cuba. On July 10, the Soviet Union agreed to purchase all 700,000 tons of sugar cut from Cuba's quota. In the light of this sequence of events it is hardly surprising that most Latin Americans blame the US for forcing Castro into Soviet hands.[1]

The first overt US protest against a revolutionary reform instituded by the new Cuban Government, had been its note on the agrarian law of June 11, 1959; this was long before Castro's revolution had become involved with the Soviet Union, and months before the premier had forged any kind of alliance with the Communists. The note warned that Cuba's right to expropriate foreign-owned property was 'coupled with the corresponding obligation for prompt, adequate and effective compensation'. But, obviously no country that is poor and developing has the funds for 'prompt, adequate and effective compensation'.

Hence, the US demand, as Williams points out, was relevant only as a vehicle for the implied threat that the United States would resort to other means if its formal injunction were not honored. The United States made it clear in the note that it would 'seek solutions through other appropriate international procedures' if Cuba did not

[1] See, for example, James Reston's interview with the anti-Castro President of Mexico, López Mateos (New York *Times*, December 12, 1962) in which Reston reports that the Mexican leader 'blamed the US for forcing Fidel Castro into the Communist camp. ... Castro, he said, was in deep economic trouble after replacing Batista as head of the Cuban Government. He was, said the Mexican President, like a drowning man in the pool, who sought help from the American side, but every time he splashed over to our side of the pool, "we stepped on his fingers" and eventually to save himself, Castro, according to López Mateos, went over to the Communist side. Moreover, López added, there was a time in the Cuban crisis, when the Cuban revolution could have been saved without communism, but when Mexico, Brazil and Canada tried to mediate and arrange a compromise, the Eisenhower Administration, he insisted, refused to cooperate, and thus created the Havana–Moscow alliance,'

meet the American conditions.[1] Castro knew, of course, that his offer to pay compensation in twenty-year bonds at about 4 per cent with the amount based on the evaluation provided by the US firms themselves for Cuban tax purposes, would not be acceptable to the United States. It was a reasonable compensation offer, but the same terms had been rejected as unjust by the United States in connection with Guatemala's agrarian reform and the United Fruit Company.

Indeed, the Guatemala experience served as a lesson and guide on both sides, for 'while CIA Officials privately assured the Eisenhower and then the Kennedy administrations that Cuba *would* become another Guatemala, Castro began warning publicly as early as March, 1960 that his country *would not* be a Guatemala'.[2] Castro's intelligence network must have been quite efficient, for it was precisely in March 1960 (two months before Cuba resumed diplomatic relations with the USSR, and four months before the confiscation of any further US properties)[3] that President Eisenhower authorized the invasion plan.[4]

An invasion had been first proposed by Vice-President Richard Nixon, in April 1959, after an interview with Castro.[5] The fact that Nixon understood what was involved in such an operation, in terms of international law, was made clear on October 21, 1960, when he

[1] Williams, op. cit., pp. 127–8; A few nights after receiving the note, Castro went on TV and said that it was 'an insinuation that served to awaken our people'. 'There are only two groups I recognize in Cuba: those who wholly support the revolution and those who are joining the reactionaries.' – *Time*, June 22, 1959.

[2] Szulc and Meyer, p. 74.

[3] This was in explicit retaliation for (1) the failure of the American oil companies to refine Soviet crude oil, (2) US cuts in the sugar quota. In May, the Cuban Government made overtures to discuss the deteriorating situation; the US declined the offer. Williams, p. 143.

[4] Szulc and Meyer, p. 77. 'What was the situation in Cuba in March 1960? A private Princeton opinion institute reported two months *later* that 86 per cent of the Cuban people firmly supported Castro. *Bohemia*, whose editor left Cuba in July, published in June the results of a poll estimating at least 80 per cent of the people in support of Castro. . . . Communist influence in Cuba was still inconsequential. Diplomatic relations between Cuba and the USSR were not yet established. *Diario de la Marina*, *Bohemia* and *Prensa Libre* all were publishing. In other words, the US had been working to overthrow a popular non-Communist nationalist government that tolerated a hostile opposition.' – Scheer and Zeitlin, op. cit., p. 215.

[5] Draper, p. 62; 'But . . . in the spring of 1959, the bulk of Cuban exiles in the US were repentant or unrepentant *Batistianos*.' – p. 63.

debated John F. Kennedy on television in the presidential campaign, and 'opposed' an invasion (in order to provide a cover for the one in process, according to his later account), citing the UN Charter and five treaties with Latin America banning intervention in the internal affairs of other countries.[1]

On April 3 1961, the State Department released a *White Paper*,[2] written by Arthur Schlesinger, Jr, which took a strong stand against foreign interventions. The following day, April 4, a meeting of the National Security Council was held to render judgement on the CIA's proposed invasion plan. Attending the meeting were Allen Dulles, Richard Bissell (CIA), General Lemnitzer, Secretary of State Rusk, Secretary of Defense McNamara, A. A. Berle, Jr, Arthur M. Schlesinger, Jr, McGeorge Bundy, Assistant Secretary of State Mann, Assistant Secretary of Defense Paul Nitze, Secretary of the Treasury C. Douglas Dillon, and Senator William J. Fulbright, Chairman of the Senate Foreign Relations Committee.

The one dissenting voice at the pivotal meeting was that of Senator Fulbright.[3]

That night, President Kennedy made the decision to go ahead with the invasion plan.[4] Only three weeks earlier, he had concluded a speech on his proposed 'Alliance for Progress' for Latin America, with the words:

[1] Cited in Szulc and Meyer, p. 69; Nixon omitted other laws that would have been violated by such a plan (and were indeed violated); e.g. US Code, Title 18, Section 960, provides for prosecution against anyone who 'knowingly begins . . . or provides or prepares a means for' a military expedition against a country with which the US is at peace. Szulc and Meyer, p. 110.

[2] An analysis of this *White Paper*, is contained in Scheer and Zeitlin, Appendix 3.

[3] Williams, op. cit., pp. 152–3. 'In perhaps the single most perceptive and courageous action of his distinguished career, Senator Fulbright bluntly told the President that he was mistaken on moral and pragmatic grounds. He did this not once, but twice. Fulbright's performance was a magnificent display of statesmanship – both absolutely and by comparison with the performance of such liberals as presidential assistant Arthur M. Schlesinger, Jr. As with others, Schlesinger in the crisis valued his future influence more than his present morality. Schlesinger's failure is particularly striking because he has so diligently and haughtily criticized the Communists for just that scale of values – and also because [as a historian] he has stressed the moral issue of slavery in explaining the coming of the American Civil War.'

[4] Szulc and Meyer, pp. 112–13.

Let us once again awaken our American revolution until it guides the struggles of people everywhere – not with an imperialism of force or fear – but the rule of courage and freedom and hope for the future of man.

The *White Paper* also declared the United States' 'profound determination to assure future democratic governments in Cuba full and positive support in their effort to help the Cuban people achieve freedom, democracy and social justice. . . .' But Secretary of State Dulles had expressed similar determinations towards Guatemala, and it had only been in the concrete results of the 'revolution' that the Guatemalan people were able to ascertain what such words really meant. Although the abortive invasion did not provide similar 'hard' evidence with which to evaluate the contents of these statements, the facts available do not leave in doubt either the outcome, if the invasion had been successful, or the intentions of those who organized it.

The program of the Revolutionary Council headed by Dr Miró Cardona was announced on March 22, 1961. One provision in particular clarified the position of the Council towards Cuba's social revolution:

> We emphatically assure those who have been unjustly dispossessed that all their assets shall be returned.[1]

At the same time, the left wing of the Revolutionary Council, the MRP, headed by Manuel Ray, maintained a separate position on two points, namely, that foreign owned utilities that had been nationalized would remain so, and foreign banks as well. In the end, Ray's group, which constituted the underground inside Cuba, and thus would have provided the focal point for any uprising within the country, was not even notified when the invasion took place[2]. The CIA left nothing to chance in shaping *its* revolution:

> . . . On January 18, [1961] the rebel troops in the Guatemalan camps were summoned by the CIA agents in charge and informed that the new military leadership of the anti-Castro army was

[1] Cited in Szulc and Meyer, p. 107.
[2] ibid., p. 119.

being placed in the hands of officers enjoying the special confidence of the United States. These officers . . . were Captain Artime, Captain José P. San Román and Captain Miguel Villafaña. . . . San Román was a former officer in the Batista Maestra region. . . . Villafaña . . . a rightist. . . .

Other officers identified with the right-wing school of thought, including *Batistianos*, were given command of numerous units. . . .[1]

In the opening months of 1961, a CIA appointed group under Joaquín Sanjenís acquired considerable power within the invasion operation:

This power was reputedly used to eliminate from the preparations most of those who had cooperated with Castro in the early days of the revolution and who held reasonably progressive or liberal views. The foremost target was Manuel Ray's MRP . . .

In the Guatemalan camps, more than 200 troops who had objected to the January *coup d'état* were arrested on the spot. . . .[2]

With the leadership of the invasion forces safely in the hands of men free even from the taint of liberalism, the CIA might have rested, assured of the outcome of their revolution.

But even the pre-invasion purges were not enough, apparently for the CIA operatives and their Cuban business and political friends. There was still one more arrangement in the dark to assure that a post-Castro régime contained no troublemakers. . . . This top-secret project was known as 'Operation Forty', . . .[3]

'Operation Forty' was intended as a civilian–military government that would 'move in on the heels of the invading army and take control of the national and local governments before the underground fighters [i.e. Ray's MRP] could realize what was happening'. The men who were to make up these governments 'at best can be called unreconstructed anti-revolutionaries'.

[1] ibid., p. 92.
[2] ibid., pp. 93, 94.
[3] Szulc and Meyer, pp. 95–6; it is interesting to note how these authors absolve by omission any US businessmen and *their* political friends from exercising influence on what was, after all, a US planned and dominated operation.

'Operation Forty' had a second task, namely, assassinating political leaders who stood in the way. 'It was reported that the project included a hand-picked task force of professional killers who were to eliminate obdurate elements which might oppose a return to the good old days. In the confusion of battle, such killings could go unnoticed and the victims depicted as Communists.'[1]

Thus, as in Guatemala previously, and for much the same economic reasons, the United States had organized, planned and directed a 'genuine counter-revolution'.[2] Moreover, this counter-revolution was not an isolated aberration of policy, but a logical extension of prevailing US attitudes towards the Cuban revolution and towards social revolutions in general.

[1] ibid.

[2] Even without the CIA precautions this would have been the case. It cannot simply be argued, moreover, that President Kennedy's ignorance of some of the CIA's maneuvers absolved him from responsibility. In January 1963, Kennedy welcomed back these same counter-revolutionary invasion forces and holding up a Cuban flag, said: 'I can assure you that this flag will be returned to this brigade in a free Havana.' Moreover, the replacement of Allen Dulles by John A. McCone as head of the CIA represented no change in the political and social outlook of the CIA at all.

CHAPTER XIII

The US and the World Revolution

... on the issue of social justice, where does the US stand today?
This question is a world-wide one; but Latin America is the field in
which the US is going to be put to her acid test.

ARNOLD TOYNBEE
February 1962

... The role of Job does not behoove a revolutionary. Each year by
which America's liberation may be hastened will mean millions of
children rescued from death, millions of minds freed for learning,
infinitudes of sorrows spared the peoples. ...

'Declaration of Havana'
February 4, 1962

'BY far the greatest and most significant thing that is happening in
the World today,' Arnold Toynbee told a Latin American audience
in 1962, 'is a movement on foot for giving the benefits of civilization
to that huge majority of the human race that has paid for civilization,
without sharing in its benefits, during the first five thousand years of
civilization's existence.'[1]

The roots of this world-wide movement for social justice, according to Toynbee, lay in the historical failure of the middle-class or
bourgeois revolutions to spread their benefits to the 'depressed
majority' of mankind. To be sure, these revolutions broke the
power of the 'small oligarchy of big landlords' which had monopol-
ized human wealth until then, and at the same time increased the
productive power of the whole community. But as its 'reward', the
middle-class 'appropriated almost the whole of the increased

---

[1] Arnold Toynbee, *The Economy of the Western Hemisphere*, 1962, pp. 3–4.

production which the first phase of the Industrial Revolution ... generated; and, in consequence, the great majority of mankind ... experienced no appreciable change for the better as a result of the middle-class revolution. From the majority's point of view, what has happened has been merely the replacement of a landlord oligarchy by a middle-class oligarchy'.[1] It is this situation that has sparked the movement for 'social justice' which has grown to such immense proportions in the present era.[2]

Where does the United States stand with regard to the issue of social justice, which is 'the first item on the present agenda of at least three-quarters of the human race?'[3] The answer to this question is by no means academic. In the post-war period, as most clearly evidenced in US actions in Greece, Turkey, Iran, Guatemala, South Viet Nam, South Korea, Lebanon, Laos and Cuba, and less obviously elsewhere,[4] the US has acted as a world-wide 'policeman standing guard over vested interests'. 'If the United States were to dedicate herself irrevocably to the cause of wealth and vested interests,' declared Toynbee in 1962, 'I believe that History would sweep the United States out of the path of its onward march.'[5]

Whether the US has committed itself irrevocably to this anti-revolutionary role is not a question to be answered here. But in view of the pronouncements of the Kennedy Administration during the brief period of the New Frontier, it is important to consider whether in fact any significant steps were taken to embark on a new and radically different course in defense of social justice.

---

[1] ibid., pp. 20–21.

[2] It was, for example, Nehru, and not Mao Tse-Tung who said: 'Inevitably, we are led to only one possible solution – the establishment of a socialist order, firstly within national boundaries and eventually in the world as a whole, with controlled production and distribution of wealth for the public good. ... It is clear that the good of a nation or of mankind must not be held up because some people who profit by the existing order object to change. If political institutions or social institutions stand in the way of such a change they have to be removed.' – Cited in M. Edwardes, *Asia in the Balance*, 1962, p. 191.

[3] Toynbee, op. cit., p. 53.

[4] E.g. in Spain: '... American military accords with Spain have supplied, for a full decade, the economic strength to save the Franco régime from bankruptcy. To Americans, such action may mean merely a detached strategic realism, free of all political intent. To Spaniards, it means the foreign decision that has decisively defined their political life.' – Emmet John Hughes in *Newsweek*, September 9. 1963.

[5] Toynbee, *The Economy of the Western Hemisphere*, p. 54.

The area of policy where such a new initiative would have been most clearly manifest was foreign aid; and indeed, in a special message to Congress March 22, 1961, the President proclaimed the beginning of a 'Decade of Development' and declared, 'the fundamental task of our foreign aid program in the 1960s is not negatively to fight Communism: its fundamental task is to help make a historical demonstration that in the twentieth century, as in the nineteenth – in the southern half of the globe as in the north – economic growth and political democracy can develop hand in hand.'

This reformulation of the goal of the US foreign aid program (from 'mutual security' to 'economic assistance') was important for two reasons: first, because social justice clearly could not make much progress without a corresponding expansion of economic productivity, and second because during the previous decade, the foreign aid program had not included economic growth as one of its serious goals. This last point was emphasized in figures quoted by a member of the special committee appointed by the President to review foreign aid in 1963. According to this source, $45 billion or *ninety per cent* of foreign aid expenditures (which totalled $50 billion) after the Marshall Plan was in 'military' aid. $30 billion of this was spent directly on military equipment. 'Of the remaining $20 billion, about 85 per cent was also military in that these funds were made available to support the budgets of nations mainly on the periphery of the Iron Curtain that have undertaken a scale of military effort far greater than they can afford. Korea, Taiwan, Pakistan and Turkey are examples.'[1]

This leaves about $5 billion, of which $3·5 billion has gone for development loans. The remaining $1·5 billion, or about one-half of one per cent of all foreign aid funds, has been spent on technical assistance in the fields of training, health, education and welfare.[2]

Since US aid went to about ninety countries, the $5 billion earmarked for development obviously did not amount to more than a token gesture. To implement the President's new program (to preempt the Communist revolutions by demonstrating the superiority

[1] Howard Rusk, New York *Times*, Int. Edn., April 5, 1963.
[2] ibid.

of democratic 'revolutions' in attaining social justice), the existing program would have to be vastly expanded and the new goals adopted and adhered to by Congress. Neither event came to pass.

In early 1963, the President appointed the Committee to Strengthen the Security of the Free World, under the leadership of General Lucius D. Clay, a right-wing Republican, to review the foreign aid program. He did this in the hope that the bi-partisan committee would forestall attempts, then being made, to pare down the size of the aid appropriations. The Clay Committee, however, recommended a $500 million *cut* in Kennedy's current request of $4·9 billion. The Committee further proposed that aid be discontinued to those countries which were not important to United States 'security' and that no aid should be given to help establish 'government-owned industries and commercial enterprises which compete with existing private endeavors'.[1]

Kennedy fully endorsed these proposals, including the $500 million cut, in a speech to Congress on April 2.[2] Shortly afterward it was reported that the President's hasty retreat had so undermined his supporters, that Congressional leaders were predicting an additional cut of $1 billion when the bill came up for passage.[3] In fact, the foreign aid budget was cut by $1·5 billion[4] or by about 40 per cent of the original Kennedy request, thus ending any possibility that a significant contribution to the economic development of the underdeveloped world would be forthcoming from this quarter.

Indeed, when the actual cuts were being made in November, Kennedy defended his program not from any new vantage point, but in wholly traditional terms. Ninety per cent of the foreign aid program, he pointed out, was spent on US products (accounting for 12 per cent of US exports);[5] foreign aid, he added, created 500,000 jobs and made possible the maintenance of 3·5 million allied troops along the Communist perimeters.[6]

[1] New York *Times*, Int. Edn., March 17 and 25, 1963.
[2] In defending the proposed bill against further possible cuts, he noted that the US was spending only 0·35 per cent of its national income on economic assistance to other countries.
[3] New York *Times*, Int. Edn., April 4, 1963.
[4] London *Sunday Times*, December 22, 1963; New York *Times*, Int. Edn., December 23, 1963.
[5] London *Sunday Times*, December 22, 1963.
[6] New York *Times*, Int. Edn., November 9, 1963.

At the time of the Clay Committee recommendations, Congressional opinion was surveyed by the New York *Times* and the views recorded carried important implications, not only for the future of aid, but for Toynbee's question about vested interests. According to the *Times'* account, Senator George D. Aiken, dean of Senate Republicans and a steadfast internationalist, uttered a stream of 'buts' about the aid program, 'that form a composite picture of the disenchantment that many one-time foreign aid supporters have developed':

> But why shouldn't we concentrate our effort on the Western Hemisphere and certain other areas where we have mutual interests:
>   But why should we have any responsibility in Africa?
>   But why should we pay for economic aid to the Congo where we have practically no investment? Why should we, in effect, guarantee their [the Belgian and the British] investment?[1]

Senator Aiken's concern for US interests in the Western Hemisphere makes it appropriate, at this point, to turn to the second major initiative of the Kennedy Administration with regard to the critical issue of social justice. It was on March 13, 1961 that President Kennedy launched the Alliance for Progress,[2] declaring: 'Let us transform the American continents into a vast crucible of revolutionary ideas and efforts . . . an example to all the world that liberty and progress walk hand in hand.'

As many recognized at the time, the Alliance was a long overdue proposal. In fifteen post-war years, less US economic aid had gone to the whole poverty stricken continent of Latin America than went to Franco Spain in the first dozen years of the mutual security program there (1951–63). The impetus for this change in US attitudes was, of course, the leftward shift of the Cuban revolution,[3]

---

[1] New York *Times*, Int. Edn., April 4, 1963.

[2] Alliance for Progress funds, it should be noted, were only cut by 25 per cent in the new foreign aid appropriations. – New York *Times*, Int. Edn., December 23, 1963.

[3] It was only in July 1960, after the cut in the sugar quota and the confiscation of US properties were announced, that Eisenhower proposed a special Latin aid program, the forerunner of Kennedy's Alliance. Eisenhower immediately made

which followed the return of Castro from his trips to the United States and to the Buenos Aires conference where he had asked in vain for development aid.

In a private interview shortly before his death, President Kennedy candidly discussed the motivation behind the new policy. 'I believe there is no country in the world . . .' he told Jean Daniel, 'where economic colonization, humiliation and exploitation were worse than in Cuba, partly as a consequence of US policy during the Batista régime. I believe that, without being aware of it, we conceived and created the Castro movement, starting from scratch. I also believe that this accumulation of errors has put all Latin America in danger. The whole purpose of the Alliance for Progress is to reverse this fatal policy.'[1]

Before examining the Alliance to see whether in fact it did represent a reversal of previous policy, it will be useful to sketch the situation in Latin America which made a dramatically expanded program necessary.

With an annual *per capita* income of under $200, Latin America easily qualifies as one of the world's 'underdeveloped' regions. As in most areas which have been historically subjected to economic imperialism, the countries of Latin America are primary producers of raw materials. Their economies, in the main, are dominated by the production of a single crop and lack the industrial bases and modern infrastructures necessary to achieve self-sustaining growth.

The land, which ought to be a primary source of wealth in this area ('more cultivable high yield tropical soil than any other continent, at least three times as much agricultural land *per capita* as Asia')[2] is kept unproductive by the *latifundia* system which dominates the continent. The nature of this system is expressed in the simple fact that 10 per cent of the population of Latin America

---

[1] London *Observer*, December 8, 1963.
[2] Paul Johnson, op. cit., *New Statesman*, September 17, 1960.

---

clear that aid would not be available to Cuba, nor would it be on anything like the scale of the Marshall Plan. The self-interested character of this project was transparent. Senator Mike Mansfield called the gesture 'a callous attempt to purchase favour in Latin America at a time when we are specially desirous of obtaining it'. Latin Americans immediately dubbed the $500 million program 'Fidel Castro Plan' and responded with the remark 'Gracias Fidel'. – Szulc and Meyer, op. cit., p. 63.

owns 90 per cent of the land.[1] The large estates, or *latifundia* are mostly held in reserve by their owners and used for speculation; the shall plots of *minifundia* are too small to be economically productive, indeed scarcely feed the families which till them.

Illiteracy on the continent, as a whole, is above 50 per cent, sanitation and housing conditions are hopelessly below the minimum adequate levels, and the annual death toll due to curable diseases is of staggering proportions. Moreover, the economic situation, which is the root of this misery, is rapidly deteriorating.

Since 1952 there has been a general and steady decline in the world price of raw materials which has drastically affected the area's income. Coffee, for example, yields six Latin American countries (including giant Brazil) more than one-half of their foreign revenues. Trade statistics show that a drop of one cent per pound in the price of green coffee annually means a loss of $50 million to Latin American producers. Since 1954, the price of coffee has been more than halved.[2] Indeed, the Committee of Nine of the Inter-American Economic and Social Council (a key agency of the Alliance) conservatively estimates that since the period 1950–3, the loss to Latin America due to the fall in export prices and the rise in import prices (for capital goods) has been approximately $1·5 billion *per annum*.[3]

Mainly as a result of this loss of revenues, the average annual growth rate for the area has declined sharply since 1940–50 when it was 3·5 per cent, *despite* a net influx of foreign capital between 1955 and 1961 of $8 billion.[4] Thus, in 1960–61, the year before the Alliance, the growth rate for Latin America hardly went above 1 per cent (in the immediately preceding years it was even lower). At the same time, the population of the area was increasing at a yearly rate of 2·8 per cent.

To cope with this situation the Alliance, whose formal Charter was signed at Punta del Este on August 17, 1961, proposed during the next ten years to utilize $20 billion in foreign capital (including $10 billion in US Government funds and $300 million annually in US private capital investment) and $80 billion in capital provided by the Latin Americans themselves, to finance an economic growth of

[1] Toynbee, op. cit., p. 31.
[2] New York *Times*, April 29, 1963.
[3] Report of September, 1962.
[4] New York *Times*, November 13, 1962.

2·5 per cent. An essential element in the success of this plan, formally recognized as such by the Alliance Charter, was the carrying out of those social and economic reforms necessary to free the productive forces of the continent.

In the main, these reforms called for the alleviation of the most glaring inadequacies in diet, housing and health, the improvement of agriculture through diversification, broadening of land ownership, expansion of cultivable acreage and increasing of modern farming techniques, the expansion of industries, the elimination of illiteracy and education of technicians, the enlargement of existing systems of transportation and communications, assurance of fair wages and satisfactory working conditions, reform of tax laws, stabilization of the prices of basic exports, and acceleration of the economic integration of Latin America.

With few exceptions, this same program was prescribed for Cuba by the Foreign Policy Association in 1935, by the World Bank in 1950, and by the United States Department of Commerce in 1956.[1] One can understand, therefore, the comment of Arnold Toynbee (who restricted his observation to a single, but in his view critical item on the agenda): 'Perhaps,' he said, 'it does need a revolutionary explosion of fifty-megaton power to blow up the . . . road-block that has hitherto obstructed both economic and social progress in Latin America so grievously.'[2]

In his speech, President Kennedy stressed the absolute necessity of social reforms, if the goals of the Alliance were to be achieved:

> For unless necessary social reforms, including land and tax reform, are freely made – unless we broaden the opportunity for all our people – unless the great mass of Americans share in increasing prosperity – then our alliance, our revolution and our dream will have failed.

With regard to land reform, observers like Toynbee were even more specifically categorical: 'In Latin America, agrarian reform is the *necessary starting-point* for political, economic, and social change alike.' (Emphasis added.) Writing in 1962, Toynbee also noted that 'the resistance to the redistribution of the *latifundia* has, so far been

[1] cf. Huberman, and Sweezy, *Cuba: Anatomy of a Revolution.* 1960, pp. 108–9.
[2] Toynbee, op. cit., p. 34.

astonishingly and distressingly successful'.[1] Thus, after two years, land reforms 'were on the books in 10 countries' but 'no substantial progress had been made in practice'.[2] Of these ten countries, moreover, five had had land reform programs prior to the Alliance for Progress. (Mexico, since 1917, Bolivia and Guatemala since 1953, Venezuela since 1954 and Colombia since 1961). The experience of these countries, and two in particular, Guatemala and Venezuela, suggested an even more negative outlook than the figures alone indicated.

In Guatemala, as we have seen, the US Government frustrated the beginnings of really effective land reform. Toynbee, it should be noted, saw a great deal of promise in the fact that since 1954, 'the United Fruit Company has . . . handed over a large part of its land reserves . . . to the present counter-revolutionary régime for continuing . . . the colonization work that the previous revolutionary régime had initiated. This is a prudent recognition of the persisting force, in Guatemala, of the demand for social justice'.[3] But according to one student of agrarian reform, 'at the rate at which land was distributed in Guatemala in the post-Arbenz years (1955–61), it would take 148 years for all peasant families to receive some land – if there were no population growth in the meantime'.[4]

The Venezuelan program, which was much heralded in some quarters, showed similar results. In March 1963, *Time* Magazine reported that 50,000 families received 3·5 million acres of land under the Betancourt program. However,

> In a report recently published jointly by the Venezuelan National Agrarian Institute, the Ministry of Agriculture, the Agrarian Bank and the National Planning Office, it appears that in the last 25 years, all put together, no more than 1·4 million acres have been distributed to 35,622 families. . . . On the other hand, it is true that 3·5 million acres were expropriated and paid for, often at exorbitant prices and in cash amounts in excess of the maximum prescribed by law.[5]

[1] Toynbee, ibid., pp. 30–31.
[2] New York *Times*, Int. Edn., August 18, 1963.
[3] Toynbee, op. cit., p. 13.
[4] Andrew Gunder Frank, 'Varieties of Land Reform', *Monthly Review*, April 1963.
[5] ibid.

One characteristic of the Betancourt program of land reform and of land reforms in general promoted by the US (e.g. abortively in South Viet Nam) is that they are mainly *resettlement* programs. They do not involve the break-up of large estates, but the buying of virgin lands, their reclamation, and the transfer of peasant populations to these previously uninhabited areas. Aside from the callousness involved in transferring indigenous peasant populations from the soil to which they have been attached for centuries, such 'reforms' have serious economic and political drawbacks. In particular, they do not break the political power of the oligarchs. Hence, the oligarchs are able to resist adequate land-taxation and land-utilization.

> For these reasons [writes Toynbee] a frontal attack on the *latifundia* would surely have to be made for the sake of economic efficiency and fiscal equity, even if all the landless agricultural workers and all the owners of economically non-viable *minifundia* could be provided for by the opening up of potentially rich virgin lands.[1]

Tax reform presents a similar story. To be sure, as of June 30, 1963, eleven Latin American countries had passed new tax laws to increase revenues. It would be somewhat utopian, however, to expect the same ruling groups that opposed land reform (even with compensation) to impose significant new taxes on themselves:

> [In Guatemala] the new income tax law stands in lieu of an old business profits tax that went as high as 44 per cent. But where the old tax was simple and had relatively few loopholes, the new is riddled with holes. American experts and local lawyers agree unanimously that business has reaped a bonanza with this 'tax reform' because it will be paying less this year than the years before under business-profits tax.[2]

Even where reforms were not as fraudulent as this, taxes could not be raised too high (the most radical reform, in Ecuador, called for a 15 per cent tax on corporate profits) without conflicting with a major

---

[1] Toynbee, p. 34.
[2] Sidney Lens, 'Building on Quicksand', *The Commonweal*, November 1, 1963.

objective of the Alliance, namely 'to stimulate private enterprise'. For one of the chief lures for private foreign capital is the extremely low tax-rate throughout the area.

If the Alliance failed to stimulate the enactment of significant reforms, it is not surpirisng that the minimal goals of economic growth were not approached either. Indeed, in 1962, Latin American growth, taken as a whole, actually declined to 0·5 per cent, which was less than the 1961 levels and only one-fifth the modest Alliance goal of 2·5 per cent. The 1963 figures were expected to be even lower.[1] Moreover, eleven nations were in the grip of inflation, private foreign investment had declined (despite 'guarantees' to investors against revolution and expropriation), and the foreign debt had attained 'grave proportions' in some of the countries. Such was the picture drawn by the President of the Inter-American Development Bank.[2]

In November 1963, the respected democrat and former President of Costa Rica, José Figueres, drew attention to inequities in the world market system, dominated by 'rich nations', and isolated them as a major source of the problems faced by the underdeveloped world. Ten years earlier, a coffee-producing country like Brazil bargained for 90 cents a pound for its coffee. This price was not out of proportion to what poor countries paid for a 'jet ticket or an international telegram'. Indeed, studies had shown that '50 to 60 cents for the different grades' of coffee were 'minimum' levels required for the development of the coffee countries.[3] The present price, noted Figueres, was 37 cents below the World Coffee Agreement. 'This,' he exclaimed, 'is the stabilization of hunger!'

Nor were prices the only area of the world market system that produced inequities. 'Advancing technology in consumer goods' increased the expenses of the poor countries without improving their income. 'Tariffs in the developed countries' and improperly administered foreign investment (i.e. in primary goods rather than commodity goods and services) were largely responsible. 'Generally,'

---

[1] New York *Times*, Int. Edn., December 23, 1963.
[2] New York *Times*, Int. Edn., November 12, 1963.
[3] In regard to Brazil's foreign debt, which Herrera had described as having attained 'grave proportions', Figueres noted that 'In coffee alone a difference of 20 cents a pound . . . on the amount of bags actually exported during the last seven crops would represent for Brazil the total amount of its foreign debt – about $3 billion.'

Figueres concluded, 'the poor countries are treated today as the European workers were a century ago.'

'It is becoming more and more absurd,' he added, 'for the rich nations to use their strong bargaining power *vis-à-vis* the poor nations, treating them as "equals" in a "free market", unintentionally exploiting them, and then trying to compensate with aid and good advice.'[1]

The Finance Minister of Colombia had made a similar analysis a year earlier, pointing out that his country had lost two to three times as much foreign income from falling coffee prices as it had received in Alliance for Progress credits. Until there was a long term world coffee pact, Señor Mejia had asserted, 'the help that is given to us, however generous it may be, will not be blood to vitalize our economies, but simply tranquilizers to avoid total collapse'.[2]

These appeals (and many others having the same import) failed to stir any major moves by the US to stabilize world commodity prices; instead, on the occasion of the São Paulo Conference to evaluate the first two years of the Alliance, President Kennedy urged those who were discouraged to remember the condition of Europe at the outset of the Marshall Plan. The comparison, however, cut two ways.

At a symposium held in June 1962, Felipe Herrera, President of the Inter-American Development Bank (one of the key agencies of the Alliance) also referred to the reconstruction of war-torn Europe, but with the contrary intention of warning his listeners against making facile analogies. First he noted that the Marshall Plan was aimed at the reconstruction of developed economies, whose productive capacity had been partially destroyed by war. Second, the Marshall Plan represented only a part of total US aid to post-war Europe, some $10·3 billion of $24 billion given between 1945 and 1951. 'During a six-year period, therefore, the flow of US public resources to Europe averaged some $4 billion per year. In the case of the Alliance for Progress, the flow of US public funds during the decade of the 1960s, is expected to total some $10 billion or an average of $1 billion each year.' Furthermore, Herrera noted, 'approximately 90 per cent of the total funds invested in the Marshall

[1] Letter to New York *Times*, Int. Edn., December 23, 1963.
[2] New York *Times*, April 23, 1962.

Plan was in the form of outright grants, the 10 per cent remaining consisting of loans.' In the Alliance for Progress, only 30 per cent of the funds invested were to be in the form of outright grants, while 70 per cent were to consist of loans.[1]

A difference omitted by Herrera, but significant none the less, was the attitude of the aid recipients towards the success of the project. The feeling among members of Latin America's economic élite was summed up for a Congressional Committee in May, 1962, by a US businessman:

> The absence of confidence by Latin America's business élite and ruling groups is vividly demonstrated by their own export of capital which, over the past decade, has been in excess of $10 billion. In passing, may I say that this $10 billion represents the amount of flight capital in numbered bank accounts in Switzerland alone. My New York banker friends tell me that the amount of flight capital on deposit in New York, or invested in American securities or bonds, is probably equal to another 10 or 12 billion dollars.[2]

This absence of confidence by Latin America's business élite was in effect a standing confession of its disinterest in imposing reforms on itself which were necessary to make the Alliance work. And, indeed, more than one observer pointed out that the dependence of the Alliance on such men was in large measure responsible for its failure to produce reforms:

> We have been pushing for a 'revolution' from the 'top-down' rather than from the 'bottom-up'. We have been asking the oligarchs to sign their own death warrants by agreeing to land reform, tax reform, and other innovations that will depress their own status. They have replied to our proddings by ruse and fraud.[3]

But why, it seems appropriate to ask, did the US insist on pushing

[1] Wm. Manger, Ed., *The Alliance for Progress: A Critical Appraisal*, 1963, pp. 45–7.
[2] *Congressional Record*, 87th Congress, May 10 and 11, 1962. Cited in *Monthly Review*, October 1962.
[3] Sidney Lens, op. cit.

for a 'revolution' from the 'top-down'? The answer of Alliance sponsors – that the Alliance was seeking to buy a revolution without having to pay the price of violence – could hardly stand in the face of such massive indifference to reform as was evidenced from the very beginning by the Latin American oligarchies.[1] For in Latin America the *status quo* itself is violence, the over-all infant mortality rate being four times that of the US, the deaths due to curable diseases numbering in the tens of thousands per year and those from hunger (not to mention premature old age nor the executions carried out by political police in such Alliance countries as Nicaragua and Haiti) adding equally shocking figures to the somber toll.

The reason for the United States' unwavering refusal to encourage the already present tides of revolutionary populism[2] to sweep the oligarchs away, may be seen in two little noted aspects of the Alliance program. For these two aspects preclude by their very nature any radical land and tax reform, or rapid economic growth. Moreover, by precluding what have been proclaimed as two of the three major goals of the Alliance (political freedom being the third), they suggest that there may be, in fact, some more important purposes which the program serves.

The first of these two blocks to Latin American progress is a section of the US Foreign Assistance Act of 1962 which is designed to forestall any radical land or tax reform aimed at US corporations abroad. Since US corporations have large investments in every important area of Latin America, any such injunction is of fundamental significance.

According to Section 620(*e*) of the Act, the President is instructed to cut off all foreign aid to any country which either nationalizes or places excessive tax burdens upon corporations operating in its territory, over 50 per cent of whose stock is owned by US citizens; the President may continue aid to such countries only if 'equitable

[1] It was also hardly credible in view of the US attempt to launch a civil war in Cuba in April 1961.

[2] 'In a real revolution today, in Latin America at least, the local Communists are to the right of the revolution. . . . The Communist parties in Latin America generally go for "popular fronts", and "national democratic coalitions", and so on. They haven't got sufficient popular support to make a revolution and so they sacrifice immediate revolutionary action – even thought – . . .' C. Wright Mills, *Listen Yankee*, p. 107.

and speedy' compensation is given, or rescinding of the taxes takes place within six months.[1]

Under the terms of this Act, the $3 million aid program to Ceylon was terminated in the spring of 1963, six months after that country had nationalized several oil companies owned by US citizens. The Ceylon Government had offered to pay compensation for the companies in bonds, but both the amount and form of the payment was termed unacceptable by the companies, and hence aid was ended.[2]

The importance of the Act for the Alliance for Progress was made crystal clear even before the Ceylonese case when the Government of Honduras passed an agrarian reform law on September 30, 1962, that would have affected land owned by the United Fruit Company, which dominated the economy of the republic.[3] The United Fruit Company was disturbed, among other things, by the fact that payment would be interest bonds and not cash. Of course, no underdeveloped country can possibly pay 'promptly' or in cash; indeed, the whole aim of land reform within the context of a national development program is to earn the capital for which, in the present, there is such a desperate need. Thus it is highly significant that when the Honduran question was raised in the Senate on October 2, the Senators who spoke, unanimously supported the viewpoint of the United Fruit Company; the liberal Senator Wayne Morse, chairman

---

[1] The criteria guiding the US Government and the US Congress in judging such disputes, particularly with reference to the key terms 'equitable' and 'excessive' are obviously of major importance. Sobering information about these criteria is revealed in the following news item which appeared in the New York *Times*, December 26, 1963, under the heading 'Alliance Facing Problem in Peru. Nationalization threat may snag US aid plans': 'The United States is faced with a problem in putting the Alliance for Progress to work in Peru. Should the united States provide substantial new aid funds for a promising economic and social development program in a country engaged in an unresolved dispute with an American-owned oil company? The International Petroleum Company, a subsidiary of Standard Oil of New Jersey, is faced by nationalization. The Peruvian Senate voted last week to nationalize the company unless it accepts a plan involving a $50 million "bonus" payment to the Government to stay in business here for 20 more years. The company, which lists assets here of $200 million, has balked at this plan, which entails new taxes. . . . *The United States position is that it will accept any solution satisfactory to the company.* Officials here . . . are concerned . . . over the possible effects on the investment climate of the outcome of the dispute and of *Congressional reaction in the United States to any action the company regards as unfair.*'

[2] New York *Times*, Int. Edn., February 9 and April 9, 1963.

[3] The following account is based on N. Gordon Levin, Jr, 'Our Men in Honduras'. – *Dissent*, Autumn, 1963.

of the all-important Sub-Committee on Latin American Affairs, expressed their consensus when he said:

> The Senator from Iowa [Hickenlooper] pointed out that it is contemplated that some script or bond or paper may be offered in payment for this property. Mr President, there is only one compensation that means anything, and that is hard, cold American dollars.[1]

In view of the fact that it is an announced aim of the Alliance to revolutionize the continent, and to do this by promoting land reform, diversification of agriculture and rural development through co-operatives, it does not seem far-fetched to expect that the Alliance itself would make funds available to the Government of Honduras in order to compensate the United Fruit Company. It is of further significance, therefore, that Morse's remarks made painfully evident that such a conception of the Alliance would be unthinkable, even to liberal Congressmen.

> . . . We must make clear to American investors that if there is a seizure of their property they will get fair compensation. If they do not get fair compensation, we do not propose to take American tax dollars and pour them into any country by way of foreign aid, so that they will in effect get a double take – the property of American investors and the taxpayer's money.

Far from retreating from this position, in the following year Congress added a new amendment, making any country which terminated contracts with US companies ineligible for foreign aid. The amendment was aimed at the nationalist governments of Peru and especially Argentina, where oil concessions granted illegally by the Frondizi Government in 1958, were cancelled by the newly elected Illia Government in 1963.[2]

If the Alliance had built into it resistance to land and tax reforms (not to mention national development of national resources, since a large proportion of Latin America's resources are exploited by foreign private firms), there was an equally forbidding structural

[1] Levin, ibid., *Congressional Record*, 87th Congress, Second Session, pp. 20457–60.
[2] New York *Times*, Int. Edn., November 12 and 16, 1963.

block to economic growth. This block was the emphasis (shared by the US and the banks of the Alliance) on monetary stability, meaning balanced budgets. For this kind of stabilization, as was pointed out in regard to Cuba earlier, ruled out 'the use of the tool of deficit financing for handling industrialization and agrarian reform'. The result of such stabilization on economic growth was noted in a New York *Times*' report (International Edition, March 25, 1963) on Colombia, which in the early days of the Alliance had been singled out as a prospective 'showcase' country:

> . . . if the US has shown strong interest in helping Colombia, a main reason has been her relatively stable currency. Aid from abroad is deemed essential to the country's development.
>
> What is now being realized, however, is the difficulty and even the contradictions involved in an austerity policy in an underdeveloped country that is trying to grow.
>
> One diplomat observed recently, that the US and the International Bank for Reconstruction and Development had pressed the Government to balance its budget as a condition for helping it with development funds.
>
> But to cut spending by the 1 billion pesos of the annual [Government] deficit would be to cut back the national product – because of the multiplying effect government spending has – by 10 to 15 per cent.

This evident concern for preventing any inflationary pressures (even economically 'healthy' ones) is motivated, of course, by a primary concern for creating the proper climate for foreign investment, as indeed the *Times*' article implied. But to stress the climate for foreign private capital to the point where it conflicts with the claims of national integrity and economic growth can only be understood in the context of the Alliance's own priorities. It is here that some light is finally thrown on the negative stance the US had, in practice, taken towards radical reforms and deficit financed economic growth, as well as its insistence on making a 'revolution' from the top down, no matter how reactionary the top might show itself to be.[1]

---

[1] Eighteen million dollars in Alliance funds, for example, were committed to Somoza of Nicaragua in the first two years of the Alliance. The Somoza family

In an address before the 4th Annual Institute on Private Investments Abroad and Foreign Trade, May 31, 1962, the US Co-ordinator of the Alliance, Teodoro Moscoso, made clear the priorities of the program:

> ... I would say as emphatically as I can that private enterprise – local and foreign – must respond if the Alliance is to succeed ... must respond by building the factories, the marketing and the service companies which are the manifestations of mature, developed economies. If the private sector fails, then our own public aid programs will have little effect. We may build some impressive monuments in the decade of Alliance development – dams and highways and schools; but unless the great impetus of the Alliance carries over into the private sector ... unless the private and corporate savings of Latin America find their way into productive reinvestment rather than into Swiss banks and high living – then I fear that the great hopes born of the Charter of Punta del Este will be deeply disappointed.

In other words, the government-to-government aspect of the program, or public aid, is designed to build the infrastructure for a developed economy, while the role of private capital is to develop it.

This is borne out by a breakdown of the aid given, for example, to Mexico in the first two years of the Alliance. Of \$700 million committed, \$345 million was in the form of stand-by credits to

---

had run Nicaragua as its private preserve since 1936 when General Anastasio Somoza first established his dictatorship. In these years (according to a study made for the Council on Foreign Relations) 'he used his monopoly of the means of violence to promote the interests of his family. By systematic graft he accumulated vast commercial and agricultural holdings, making the Somoza's one of the wealthiest families in the Americas.' In this same period, the population has remained 70 per cent illiterate, *per capita* income below \$200, living conditions sub-human (55 of every 100 Nicaraguan children dying before their fifth birthday) and democracy non-existent. There was no reason to expect that the Somoza family (the General was assassinated in 1956, the sons have taken over) would change merely because the Alliance sponsors proclaimed in vague terms the necessity for 'reform'. Meanwhile Alliance and pre-Alliance aid (including extensive military aid) certainly helped to stabilize the Somoza régime. Cynics may well observe, however, that the Somozas earned their US aid money by their active cooperation in the Guatemalan coup and their provision of Nicaraguan territory for the Bay of Pigs invaders in 1961.

bolster the peso, which could be drawn upon only in a grave monetary crisis. Another $80 million in credit was specifically for US exporters engaged in trade and $14 million went to private borrowers through the Export–Import Bank. Finally, $266 million was promised for development projects (health, housing, schools, water systems, roads, etc.).[1] It should be noted, perhaps, that of $1,500 million disbursed in the first two years of the Alliance, $600 million was in the form of loans from the Export–Import Bank, i.e. loans for the purpose of buying US products, and $150 million was furnished in the form of surplus food, under the 'Food for Peace' scheme, 'a program which frequently operates on the basis of dumping, causing incalculable harm to local producers'.[2]

In yet another speech, this time before the Detroit Economic Club on April 1, 1963, Mr Moscoso reiterated the basic philosophy of the program from a slightly different point of view. Dealing with what he called the myth that 'all that Latin America needs is a friendly climate for private enterprise ... and the job that the Alliance for Progress is trying to do will be done, Moscoso said: 'This view disregards the need for building roads, ports, power plants and communications systems which must be built at least in great part with public funds and which in many areas are a prerequisite for the effective and profitable investment of private capital.'

Latin America had, of course, a very bitter experience with regard to private capital and the dearth of an infrastructure, which Mr Moscoso did not mention.[3] To cite a typical example, in Guatemala in 1954, 90 per cent of the electrification was in the capital city.

---

[1] *Hispanic-American Report*, April 1963, Stanford. In November 1963, two Alliance loans to Mexico were announced to deal with the 'crucial Mexican housing problem'. 'Both loans will be made to the ... Government lending agency, and will be used to finance a housing trust fund. The money will be distributed to private lending institutions for loans to future homeowners.' – New York *Times*, Int. Edn., November 28, 1963. The Alliance built 140,000 new homes in its first two years. But according to an OAS Report (1953), 80 per cent of the rural population of Latin America lived in housing that met none of the minimum hygiene requirements – cf. Manger, op. cit., p. 33. The housing deficit, in the words of the New York *Times* is 'unmeasurable' and 'increases by an estimated one million units annually, or twelve times faster than what the Alliance has been able to provide'. Int. Edn., August 18, 1963.

[2] Alonso Aguilar, *Latin America and the Alliance for Progress*, (pamphlet), 1963. Aguilar is Professor of Economics at the University of Mexico.

[3] Scheer and Zeitlin, op. cit., pp. 29–33.

Four-fifths of the electric power of the country was generated by a US owned electric company which refused to take the risks involved in bringing electricity to the rest of the country. In Brazil, the US-owned telephone company was so inefficient that in 1962 there were 700,000 people on waiting lists for telephones.[1] When Governor Leonel Brizola of the state of Río Grande do Sul expropriated a telephone company belonging to IT&T, resolutions in the House and Senate were offered calling for a halt in aid. The issue was finally settled between the central Brazilian Government and the US when 'adequate' compensation was agreed upon.

It should be clear from the foregoing that the Alliance for Progress was conceived with a double rather than a straightforward single commitment. Its double commitment was to develop Latin America *through* the influx of private capital and to utilize public funds only in areas which were not directly profitable or where the risks for private enterprise were too great. Moreover, where there was conflict between the means (private capital) and the ends (economic development), it was inevitable from the very structure of the program, that the latter, that is, the 'goal' itself, would be sacrificed. And indeed, at the São Paulo Conference to review the first two years of the program,[2] one Brazilian delegate noted the new US legislation against nationalization of US foreign-based oil companies and said, 'It proves one fact, social reforms and private investments don't mix.' In recognition of this fact, it was decided that Alliance loans would be channeled through one inter-American agency which would direct them toward strictly economic development projects; social reforms would not be a prerequisite. As one Brazilian commentator concluded; 'The *Alianza* was born in Punta del Este and died in São Paulo.'[3]

It was not only in regard to social reforms that the emphasis on private investments raised conflicts within the structure of the program, and thus questions about its real priorities. For the expansion of US private investments, which the Alliance sought to promote, was not likely to mean an influx of capital into the area, as intended. Indeed, far from it. During the period 1950–1963, the *net* capital flow from US overseas corporations, generally, to the US

[1] New York *Times*, March 31, 1962.
[2] *Newsweek*, November 25, 1963.
[3] ibid.

was $17·4 billion.[1] The *net* flow from Latin American based US corporations in the years 1951–61 was $4 billion.[2] In other words, US private investments in the underdeveloped world generally, and in Latin America in particular, acted as suction pumps, depriving the capital-starved economies of these countries of precisely that essential component of growth, which economic aid programs like the Alliance were supposed to supply. Clearly, emphasis on preserving and expanding these investments could only represent an aim independent of (and in conflict with) the proclaimed Alliance goal of promoting economic growth in Latin America. In the priority scale of US policy makers moreover, it was inevitable (and already plainly manifest) that between the two goals, Latin American growth must play a subordinate and mainly supporting role.

Thus, while the Alliance for Progress involved tactical changes from past programs in Latin America, its strategic aim – preservation of vested interests, and of the stake of US private capital in particular – was no different. Only by seeing that the primary function of the Alliance was to defend private US vested interests in Latin America, moreover, is it possible to understand the total failure of the United States to honor a cardinal principle of the Alliance program: the commitment to political freedom. United States' failure in this regard prior to the promulgation of the Alliance concept had also been complete. 'While presenting itself as the defender of political democracy in Latin America,' wrote one committed cold war scholar, 'the United States supported virtually every military tyrant who came upon the scene (or was there already) between 1945 and 1960.'[3]

The reason for this support is not difficult to divine. As a dependably 'conservative' social force, the army in Latin America is a guarantor of economic and social, if not political stability. Surely, the $700 million in US military aid to Latin America since World War II[4] could not seriously be explained in the official terms of 'hemisphere defense'. In 1955, the exiled Colombian Liberal Party Leader Eduardo Santos made an eloquent plea in the United States

---

[1] *Survey of Current Business*, October 1964, cited in 'Foreign Investment', *Monthly Review*, January 1965.

[2] UN Economic Conversion for Latin America, Report of May 1963.

[3] Robert J. Alexander, 'Latin American Communism', *Soviet Survey*, August 1962. Parentheses in original.

[4] *Time*, October 11, 1963.

against the further dissemination of arms in Latin America. 'Against whom are we Latin Americans arming ourselves ?' he asked. 'What we are doing is building up armies which weigh nothing in the international scale but which are Juggernauts for the internal life of each country. Each country is being occupied by its own army.'[1]

Santos' plea had no noticeable effect on US policy; the arms flow to Latin America continued, and by 1960 more than one observer was ready to conclude that 'even where [democracy's] ceremonies are tolerated, the army is the ultimate arbiter'; '. . . where the Left has won elections, the fruits of office have turned into bitter ashes. We have already seen, in Argentina, a so-called extreme left government [Frondizi's] operating a police tyranny to pursue a policy of deflation dictated by foreign bankers. Much the same could be said of Venezuela, where the triumphant electoral victory of President Betancourt's left-wing *Accion Democratica* has been followed by social stagnation and heartbreaking disillusion.'[2]

Against the background of traditional US support for military dictatorships in Latin America, the Alliance for Progress proclaimed itself to be a new departure. It was to be 'an alliance of free governments' designed to work 'to eliminate tyranny from a hemisphere in which it has no rightful place'. In his Alliance speech, President Kennedy singled out the people of Cuba and of Trujillo's Dominican Republic for special solicitations as sufferers under dictatorial régimes. (The President might well have cited the military dictatorships in Haiti, Nicaragua, El Salvador and Paraguay, but chose instead to include them as Alliance partners.)

This endorsement of political freedom – despite its initial equivocation – was no mere rhetorical rallying point, but had a strategic importance. For, as was later reported, 'President Kennedy had evolved the notion that unless economic development is carried out along with democratic rule, no valid case can be made against the short-cut totalitarian practices of the Marxist–Leninist Cuban régime and, therefore, the west has nothing to offer Latin America ideologically to counter Communism.'[3]

[1] Cited in Lieuwen, op. cit., pp. 238–9. cf. p. 190 above.
[2] Johnson, *New Statesman*, September 17, 1960; cf. Lieuwen, *Arms and Politics in Latin America* for extensive documentation of the army's role in Latin politics.
[3] Tad Szulc in New York *Times*, Int. Edn., December 23, 1963.

Despite the critical value which thus attached to democratic means, President Kennedy found it expedient to recognize and lend support to five of the seven military *coups* against constitutional régimes which took place during his brief tenure, President Johnson recognizing the other two within a month of his assumption of office.[1]

One of these *coups* was against the democratic reform government of Juan Bosch in the Dominican Republic. The reaction not only of the Johnson Administration[2] in giving support to the *coup*, but of a significant section of the US élite in approving this support, was most revealing. Bosch had been 'freely and fairly elected' President[3] of the Dominican Republic, after the assassination of Trujillo in 1961 had brought an end to his thirty-year dictatorship. Bosch was inaugurated in February 1963 and deposed in September. Just after the *coup*, the New York *Times* described him editorially as 'a left-of-center intellectual in line with the democratic left represented by such leaders as President Betancourt of Venezuela and Governor Muñoz Marin of Puerto Rico'. Bosch, the editorial said, had 'tried to move too fast in transforming a rigidly autocratic social and economic structure, based on a business, landowning and military élite, into a popular and democratic régime'.[4]

Bosch was so willing to proceed with democratic reform, that the

---

[1] The *coups* were in El Salvador (January 1961), Argentina (March 1962), Peru (July 1962), Guatemala (March 1963), Ecuador (July 1963), Dominican Republic (September 1963), and Honduras (October 1963). Typical, was Peru: 'Between 1945 and 1960 the US supplied Peru with $83 million for "hemisphere defense" . . .; in fiscal 1962–3, despite the premises of the Alliance for Progress, military grants to Peru were almost doubled. . . . Symbolically enough, a US-supplied Sherman tank broke down the gates of the Pizarro Palace, and the officer who led the assault and arrested the seventy-two year old President Prado, was Colonel Gonzalo Briceno, a graduate of US Ranger School at Fort Benning, Georgia.' – Professor Samuel Shapiro, 'Peru and the Alianza' in *Studies on the Left*, Vol. III, No. 2, 1963.

[2] The difference between the Johnson Administration and the Kennedy Administration at this point was nil. There were no important changes in the State Department and it is unlikely that Johnson would have overruled them on an important matter like this. According to the *Times* editorial of September 26, Bosch had 'seemed to be losing, in recent months, the once enthusiastic support of the United States'. There is no question but that this was a result of the tempo of his reforms and the fact that he had made 'powerful enemies' among the Dominican élite.

[3] New York *Times*, Int. Edn., September 26; Bosch's victory was 'overwhelming'.

[4] New York *Times*, Int. Edn., September 26, 1963.

Alliance for Progress 'set out to make the Dominican Republic a shining example of how to help a one-time dictatorship turn into a thriving democracy'. Alliance funds to Bosch's Dominican Republic were among the largest *per capita* to any country in Latin America. Then came the rightist *coup*. Immediately, guerrillas emerged in the countryside[1] and the US was faced with the choice of throwing its support behind the new régime or letting it fall.[2]

Initially the Kennedy Administration broke diplomatic relations, halted economic and military aid and withdrew all its personnel. But faced, a few months later, with the prospect of a popular and possibly *fidelista* revolution, the US chose to throw its weight behind the new régime. In Latin America, both Colombia and Venezuela – 'the most successful democratic governments in the Alliance' – served notice that they would not follow suit and grant their recognition. Colombia, according to the *Times*, indicated that she would not march with the US 'on policies representing a return to the political philosophies of the Eisenhower era'.[3]

Equally significant was the argument in support of the resumption of relations offered by the New York *Times*. Only three months after its first evaluation of the Bosch presidency, the *Times* explained that 'President Bosch, who had every element of Dominican society, business and politics with him when he took office, had alienated every one of them in his seven months' administration. . . . Moreover, within thirty-six hours of the *coup*, the officers had turned the government over to a civilian triumvirate, aided by other civilians. . . . These civilians – honest, able, patriotic and friendly to the United States – *represent the traditional white, landowning and business élite.*' The *Times* concluded: 'Normal relations with the rest of the hemisphere should save the situation for the present moderate and relatively democratic [*sic*] government. There is no time to lose in sending aid.'[4] [Emphasis added.]

These events serve to underscore what the preceding analysis has made plain: the primary concern of US policy in Latin America is

---

[1] New York *Times*, Int. Edn., December 23, 1963.

[2] It would then have the choice of several powerful initiatives (all stemming from its geo-political situation) as it had in the first months of the Castro revolution.

[3] New York *Times*, Int. Edn., December 23, 1963.

[4] New York *Times*, Int. Edn., December 18, 1963.

to maintain social stability. For so long as the traditional Latin American ruling groups maintain their power, US vested interests are served. To be sure, certain reforms should and must be made in order that the system itself be preserved. In the words of President Kennedy: 'those who possess wealth and power in poor nations must accept their own responsibilities. They must lead the fight for those basic reforms which alone *can preserve the fabric of their own societies*. Those who make peaceful revolution impossible will make violent revolution inevitable.'[1] [Emphasis added.]

On the other hand, two years of the Alliance had revealed that only the most minimal reforms would be tolerated by either the Latin American oligarchies or the US Congress. When any Latin American government attempted to step beyond the bounds of minimal reform, it would find itself toppled by a military *coup*.[2] The United States would then be called upon to provide support for the basically unstable (because unpopular) political replacement. The US could be counted on to provide the necessary support (as seven *coups* in three years testified) because the US élite still had a greater fear of social instability with its promise of far-reaching reform, than the prospect of political dictatorship and the immemorial poverty and suffering of the *status quo*.[3]

---

[1] Speech of March 13, 1962, on the first anniversary of the Alliance.

[2] On December 25, Senator Wayne Morse announced that he planned to investigate the circumstances of Bosch's overthrow. 'Mr Morse ... said there was a "substantial body of evidence" that certain United States business interests helped finance the military *coup*.' – New York *Times*, Int. Edn., December 26, 1963.

[3] Within months of its advent, the Johnson Administration resolved the tension between the Alliance's reformist tactics and ideology, and its conservative strategic goals. It did so, simply by abandoning the former in favor of what it described as a pragmatic approach. On March 18, 1964, the new Assistant Secretary of State for Inter-American Affairs, Thomas C. Mann, outlined the four main purposes of US policy in Latin America, including economic growth, protection of US investments, non-intervention in the internal political affairs of the hemisphere's republics and opposition to Communism. The incompatibility of these last two points was only an apparent one, at least in the context of the interpretation given them by the State Department. Elaborating his position, Mr Mann made clear that 'non-intervention' was to mean toleration for 'anti-Communist' military *coups*, even against constitutional régimes. 'Mr Mann was quoted as saying that he had difficulty in distinguishing between Presidents Adolfo López Mateos of Mexico, Victor Paz Estenssoro of Bolivia and Alfredo Stroessner [dictator] of Paraguay.' (New York *Times*, Int. Edn., March 20, 1964.)

Two weeks later, on April 2, a rightist *putsch* in Brazil ousted the mildly reformist, but mainly opportunist constitutional régime of Joao Goulart. Twelve hours after the new provisional government took office, headed by an Army General, President Johnson sent his 'warmest wishes' and a tender of 'our intensified cooperation'. The next day Secretary of State Rusk implausibly hailed the military *coup* as a 'move to insure the continuity of constitutional government'.

The Johnson Administration's return to pre-Kennedy Latin American policy was further accompanied by a change in the personnel administering the Latin American program. On May 4, 1964, the last of the top-level Kennedy men, Teodoro Moscoso, 'who for two years personified the Alliance goals' (New York *Times*) resigned. 'His resignation,' commented the *Times*, 'comes at a time of growing disenchantment in Latin America and among Latin American Alliance officials in Washington over the present conduct of the program by the United States. The consensus in those quarters is that the alliance as conceived by Mr Kennedy, no longer exists.' – New York *Times*, Int. Edn., May 5, 1964.

PART THREE

Under the Sword of Damocles
1945-63

Comrades, to put it in a nutshell, as I have already said during the session of the Supreme Soviet of the USSR, it is not advisable to be in a hurry for the other world.

NIKITA KHRUSHCHEV

I. Containment and Liberation

If it explodes, as I think it will, I'll certainly have a hammer on
those boys [the Russians].

HARRY S. TRUMAN, on the eve of the first atomic test

. . . the main element of any United States policy toward the
Soviet Union must be that of a long-term patient but firm and
vigilant containment of Russian expansive tendencies . . .
. . . the United States has it in its power to increase enormously
the strains under which Soviet policy must operate, . . . and . . .
to promote tendencies which must eventually find their outlet in
either the break-up or the gradual mellowing of Soviet power.

'MR X' – GEORGE KENNAN

In our conflict with Russia a policy of settlement . . . would aim
to redress the balance of power, which is abnormal and dangerous,
because the Red Army has met the British and American armies
in the heart of Europe. . . .
A genuine policy would, therefore, have as its paramount
objective a settlement which brought about the evacuation of
Europe. . . . American power must be available not to 'contain'
the Russians at scattered points, but to hold the whole Russian
military machine in check, and to exert a mounting pressure in
support of a diplomatic policy which has as its concrete objective
a settlement that means withdrawal.

WALTER LIPPMANN

CHAPTER XIV

The Division of Europe

As long as there is a great disparity of power which makes negotiations seem to be unnecessary to one side, that causes them to believe that they can accomplish their purposes without it.

DEAN ACHESON

THE perspective of history is a sobering one. Viewed from the distance of a later time, events are no longer infused with the hysteria issuing from an unknown and uncharted future. For that future has since unfolded itself and freed us from those fears which time has proved unfounded. Thus we do not suffer as contemporaries did, from the distorting apprehension of calamities that did not occur, or of roads that might have been embarked upon, and that we now know were not taken. And because of this, we see the past more clearly.

Time has aided us in another way, for it has given us an understanding of the larger flow of history, so that events and issues which seemed decisive when they happened, can now be seen as mere waves in a larger tide.

In the sober light of a historical perspective, moreover, we can look back upon the courses which statesmen adopted and compare them with those courses which they avoided. We can identify not only the dangers which they chose to stress, but the opportunities which they disregarded. It is these comparisons, which allow us to measure men's performances in the past, and to gauge, whenever possible, their intent. In this way history can indeed become a 'secular conscience', and in being so, a guide to more successful futures.

In a remarkable series of articles, published in September 1947,[1] Walter Lippmann analyzed the basic problem that was then leading the world into cold war, criticized the Anglo-American attempt to cope with it, and suggested an alternative approach. At the heart of

[1] Walter Lippmann, *The Cold War*, 1947.

the conflict, as Lippmann saw it, was the presence of three outside armies (Russian, American and British) on the continent of Europe:

> This is the problem which will have to be solved if the independence of the European nations is to be restored. Without that there is no possibility of a tolerable peace. But if these armies withdraw, there will be a very different balance of power in the world than there is today, and one which cannot eaily be upset. For the nations of Europe, separately and in groups, perhaps even in unity, will then, and then only cease to be the stakes and the pawns of the Russian-American conflict.
>
> *The material cause and reason of the conflict will have been dealt with.* [Emphasis added.]

The armies were not withdrawn, the European countries continued to be stakes and pawns in the Russian–American conflict, the independence of these nations (particularly those of East Europe) was not restored and there was no tolerable peace. Responsibility for this pass in world history is complex, but much can be learned about the nature and origins of the course which events subsequently took, by examining the response of the Western powers to the problem that the armistice had posed, and by contrasting it with the alternative strategy that Lippmann had himself suggested.

> The terms of the problem were defined at Yalta in the winter of 1945. There, with a victory over Germany in sight, Roosevelt, Churchill and Stalin made a military settlement which fixed the boundaries where the converging armies were to meet, and were to wait while the governments negotiated the terms of the peace which would provide for the withdrawal of the armies. The crucial issue in the world today is whether the Yalta *military* boundary, which was intended to be provisional for the period of the armistice, is to become the *political* boundary of two hostile coalitions. [Emphasis added.]

It was Lippmann's contention, that as long as the military boundary remained in effect, a corresponding political boundary could not help but emerge. Western policy, he felt, must be oriented with an eye to this reality and, in particular, must concentrate its energies on negotiating peace treaties which would mean the withdrawal of the occupying armies. If and when the treaties of peace were agreed to for Germany and Austria, Lippmann reasoned, they would have to contain 'definite stipulations for the withdrawal of the armies of occupation':

> In some form or other, at some time or other, no matter what supervision and control are imposed upon, what guarantees are exacted from Germany, and exchanged among the Allies, these Treaties of peace will fix a time when the Red Army, . . . can no longer as a matter of legal right, remain in central and eastern Europe. . . .

'This,' Lippmann stressed, would be 'a wholly different kind of commitment from those which were made at Yalta and at Potsdam, and were then violated.' Over such agreements, and concerning such questions as to what is democracy and what is a free election, 'it is possible to differ honestly and to differ dishonestly'. But an agreement 'to evacuate an army' must either be carried out or violated. 'It is not a matter which can be hidden behind an iron curtain. It is a matter of plain and quite obvious fact.'

It was possible, of course, that Russia would not agree to a settlement which meant the evacuation of Europe. If her purpose was the domination of Europe and a large part of the world, she would never agree. For the military evacuation of Europe would not be a 'tactical maneuver' but would be 'a strategic change in the balance of power':

> For once the Red Army had been withdrawn behind the frontiers of the Soviet Union, it could not re-enter Europe without committing an obvious act of military aggression, which would precipitate a general war. . . .

The withdrawal of the Red Army was, therefore, the acid test of Soviet conduct and purpose 'incomparably clearer, more definite and more practical than whether or not they observe the Yalta Declaration in countries liberated from the Nazis but still occupied by the Red Army'. For agreements like Yalta did not change the balance of power. 'But the evacuation of a continent would change the balance of power.'

The Kremlin would understand this, and the United States therefore 'must expect it to exact the highest price it can obtain for what would be a deep reduction of its present power and influence in Europe, or, if it means to conquer Europe, to obstruct any settlement which meant that the Russian armies must evacuate Europe'.

Soviet intentions were never put to Lippmann's acid test. No attempt was made to ascertain if the Russians had any price for withdrawing, whether in terms of economic aid for their reconstruction program, or in terms of security guarantees, written into a German settlement.

Instead of the course urged by Lippmann, Western leaders continued along the path which they had embarked upon earlier, namely, 'a diplomatic campaign to prevent Russia from expanding her sphere, to prevent her from consolidating it, and to compel her to contract it'. This diplomatic campaign was launched by Truman on April 23, 1945, with his tongue-lashing of Molotov and pressed in the open, beginning with Byrnes' statement on the Bulgarian elections two weeks after the explosion of the Atomic Bomb. By the end of the Moscow Conference, in December 1945, negotiation implying any concession had become synonymous with appeasement. 'Roll-back' was then the policy, if not yet the word of the hour.

This diplomatic offensive to prevent the Soviet Union from consolidating or expanding its sphere of influence, and to compel her to contract it, was doomed from its inception because, according to Lippmann, 'until the Red Army evacuated eastern Europe, none of these objectives could be achieved'.

Had the West seen clearly the significance of the military situation, they would not have committed the United States to anything in eastern Europe while the Soviet government had the power to oppose it, while the United States had no power to enforce it. ... It would have been far better to base our policy on the realities of the balance of power; ... to have concentrated our effort on treaties of peace which would end the occupation of Europe.

In referring to 'the realities of the balance of power', Lippmann implied, though he did not explicitly say so, that the approach adopted by Anglo-American leaders was based rather on legalistic and moral considerations, in a manner having deep roots in the traditional conduct of American foreign affairs. To this idealism, Lippmann was opposing a policy based on a realistic appraisal of the power situation.

It is not important, in assessing this conception of the dispute, to enter the general debate among American historians as to whether American foreign policy was ever in fact based purely on moral and legalistic considerations.[1] For in the period 1945–9, and particularly after the explosion of the Atomic Bomb, the power advantage of the United States *vis-à-vis* the Soviet Union was taken by most American leaders to be overwhelming. This explains, as Lippmann's generous implication in regard to the proponents of containment and diplomatic roll-back does not, why the policy of compelling rather than negotiating (that is, bargaining for) the contraction of Soviet power was paradoxically formulated by such 'realists' as Dean Acheson, Averell Harriman, James V. Forrestal and George Kennan.

Forrestal's views have special significance because he was instrumental in Kennan's rise, in promoting the idea that diplomacy (meaning negotiation) was useless for dealing with the Soviets, and in forging the 'tough' policy in the first place (he was the only advisor at the White House meeting prior to Molotov's visit who thought it would be better to have 'a showdown with them now than later'.) He anticipated, perhaps even inspired, the specific actions in Greece and Turkey, which were later embodied in the Truman Doctrine. He was, moreover, the first United States Secretary of Defense (a post created in 1947) and was instrumental in setting up the National Security Council under whose aegis the direction of foreign policy came, in late 1947.

In a letter to Chan Gurney, chairman of the Armed Services Committee, Forrestal formulated his view of the European and world situation in succinct terms. The letter is dated December 8, 1947:

As long as we can outproduce the world, can control the sea and

---

[1] cf. George Kennan, *American Diplomacy 1900–1950*, and W. A. Williams, *The Tragedy of American Diplomacy* for contrasting views.

can strike inland with the atomic bomb, we can assume certain risks otherwise unacceptable in an effort to restore world trade, to restore the balance of power – military power – and to eliminate some of the conditions which breed war.

The years before any possible power can achieve the capability effectively to attack us with weapons of mass destruction are our years of opportunity.

Another 'realist' view, of the same year, and based again on a deep-going confidence in the world power of the United States, was noted by Forrestal in his diary of July 15, 1947:

Met with Mr Bernard Baruch, Eisenhower, Patterson [Secretary of War] after lunch. Baruch feels that we must begin to use immediately all possible economic measures in our relations with Russia. By this he means pre-emptive and preclusive buying of scarce commodities. He would, for example, buy the entire surplus of the Cuban sugar crop. He would also buy coffee and send gold to other countries in exchange for their raw materials . . .[1] [The cut here is in the original.]

The key elements of US power, as seen by Forrestal and Baruch and obvious to anyone, were atomic monopoly and preponderance of economic power; control of all the seas, the world's largest fleet, and a worldwide network of hundreds of bases made these powers globally operative. It is not to be overlooked, moreover, that a lack of these elements constituted the basis of Soviet weakness; indeed, Baruch's proposal depended on the dual assumptions that the US had the capacity to carry out such a program *and* that preclusive buying of raw materials would have a significant effect on the Soviet economy.

It is not surprising, therefore, to find that Lippmann began his assault on the policy of containment, not with a critique of legalistic attitudes, but by examining the assumption that the Soviet Union was weak, even collapsing, and did not *have* to be dealt with as a major power. Lippmann initiated his whole analysis with these words:

We must begin with the disturbing fact that Mr X's conclusions

[1] Forrestal, op. cit., p. 291.

depend upon the optimistic prediction that the 'Soviet power . . . bears within itself the seeds of its own decay, and that the sprouting of these seeds is well advanced,' that if 'anything were ever to occur to disrupt the unity and the efficacy of the Party as a political instrument, Soviet Russia might be changed overnight [*sic*] from one of the strongest to one of the weakest and most pitiable of national societies;' and 'that Soviet society may well [*sic*] contain deficiencies which will eventually weaken its own total potential'.

Of this optimistic prediction Mr X himself says that 'it cannot be proved. And it cannot be disproved'. Nevertheless, he concludes that the United States should construct its policy on the assumption that the Soviet power is inherently weak and impermanent, and that this unproved assumption warrants our entering 'with reasonable confidence upon a policy of firm containment . . .' (Emphasis in original.)

Having pinpointed Kennan's estimate of the weakness and impermanence of Soviet power as the orienting basis of Kennan's strategy, Lippmann declared:

I do not find much ground for reasonable confidence in a policy which can be successful only if the most optimistic prediction should prove to be true. Surely a sound policy must be addressed to the worst and hardest that may be judged to be probable, and not to the best and easiest that may be possible.

Here is the heart of the dispute.

Now the significance of the 'X' article in the shaping of United States foreign policy must not be overlooked. Kennan was the Director of the newly formed Policy Planning Staff of the State Department.

Thus, as Lippmann noted in the introduction to his analysis, once Mr X was identified as George Kennan, 'Mr X's article was no longer just one more report on the Soviet régime and what to do about it. It was an event, announcing that the Department of State had made up its mind, and was prepared to disclose to the American people, to the world at large, and of course also to the Kremlin, the estimates, the calculations and the conclusions on which the Department was basing its plans.'

It takes little imagination to speculate on the considerations and possibilities that might have been entertained by United States (and British) leaders at the time. Given a working estimate that the Soviet régime was on the brink of collapse, the necessity for achieving a compromise settlement would recede into the background. With the atomic monopoly of the west intact, and expected to remain so for five to ten years, certain risks could be taken. The situation presented Western leaders with the opportunity, among others, to be rid of a hated and feared régime, ideology and social system,[1] ruled by a group of men who were at best difficult to live with, and at worst constituted a formidable threat to Western interests, in many eyes, to Western survival.

Against the advantages of the 'hard line' of containment, moreover, there were certain disadvantages, from the standpoint of the American leadership, in seeking a negotiated settlement which would end the occupation of Eastern Europe. In the first place, any settlement to have been acceptable to the Soviets, would have had to offer them substantial benefits, as Lippmann pointed out, to compensate for what would have been 'a deep reduction of [their] present power and influence in Europe'.

But any compensation for Soviet loss of power in Europe must have entailed the strengthening of Soviet power at home. And this was something that American leaders had been reluctant to do, even before the Second World War had ended.[2] On January 3, 1945, the Soviet Government had filed its first formal request for a post-war credit. Molotov's memorandum asked for long-term credits to the amount of $6 billion, to be paid back over thirty years at two and one-quarter per cent.

The memorandum was given to Ambassador Harriman, who advised Washington at the time, that the US ought to do everything it could to assist the Soviet Union to develop a sound economy by credits. For he explained that he was convinced '. . . that the sooner

---

[1] Of these three, the régime itself was probably an insignificant factor. For although the rhetoric of the cold war would indicate otherwise, the way in which Western leaders actually conducted the war can only lead to the conclusion that they considered political repression and terror in other countries (so long as they were non-Communist) to be lesser evils, if indeed, they considered them to be evil at all.

[2] It was not true of such men as Donald Nelson, one-time head of the War Production Board, and others, but their views did not prevail.

the Soviet Union can develop a decent life for its people the more tolerant they will become'.[1] Unfortunately this far seeing advice was neither heeded in Washington,[2] nor maintained by Harriman. Three months later, in April, Harriman described the 'enormous plans' for Russian industrial expansion, and mentioned their request for a $6 billion credit to start on these vast projects, but he dropped the question as to whether 'our basic interest might better be served by increasing our trade with other parts of the world rather than giving preference to the Soviet Union as a source of supply . . . our experience has incontrovertibly proved that it is not possible to bank general good will in Moscow and I agree with the Department [of State] that we should retain current control of these credits in order to be in a position to protect American vital interests in the formulative period immediately following the war.'[3]

Initial reluctance to bolster the Soviet system was undoubtedly re-enforced by the policy (and predictions) of containment, which looked towards a strangling of Soviet power from without rather than a fostering of healthy forces from within. Moreover, concentrating on Western build-up, it must have been felt, would bolster forces whose friendship was certain, while at the same time exerting strong pressures on the Soviet Union to divert much of its energies to a counter build-up, particularly in East Europe, where it was busy taking by force what it could not borrow from the West. Thus the policy of containment promised to be doubly advantageous, strengthening the West, while encouraging Soviet power, which was already dangerously strained, to over-extend and perhaps over-strain itself, thereby precipitating its final collapse.

Such expectations proved false, however, and Soviet power strengthened itself (at a severe human cost) while tightening its grip on East Europe. Against the fact that a reconstructed Western Europe did not become Communist, therefore, would have to be weighed (if one were to make such a judgement) the fact that Eastern Europe did, an eventuality that might not have occurred if a settlement, meaning withdrawal, had been reached.

[1] Feis, *Churchill, Roosevelt, Stalin*, p. 646.
[2] Secretary of the Treasury Morgenthau agreed with this view and the Treasury rushed in to propose that the US lend $10 billion at 2 per cent, but Morgenthau was shortly eased out of his post.
[3] Forrestal, op. cit., p. 41.

In gauging to what extent *in fact* Western leaders did not follow Lippmann's approach to settlement because they expected and indeed wished to promote Soviet collapse, it is useful to focus on a few concrete and crucial policy statements and proposals, which engage the substantive issues of the early cold war. In particular, it will be necessary to determine whether Western appeals to the Soviet Union for cooperation towards the making of a settlement were merely specious, or whether they contained genuine overtures to the Soviet rulers to recognize their own self-interest in an Atomic Age, in international stability and peace.

One of the most striking statements in Kennan's article, and certainly the one most likely to prove tempting to any strategist, was the remark cited by Lippmann that if 'anything were ever to occur to disrupt the unity and the efficacy of the Party as a political instrument, Soviet Russia might be changed overnight from one of the strongest to one of the weakest and most pitiable of national societies'.

Regardless of whether Winston Churchill was struck by this line in Kennan's analysis, its logic did not escape him. In a major foreign policy statement at the Conservative Conference in October 1948, he said:

The 14 men in the Kremlin, who rule nearly 300 million human beings with an arbitrary authority never possessed by any Czar since Ivan the Terrible, and who are now holding down nearly half Europe by Communist methods, these men dread the friendship of the free civilized world as much as they would its hostility. If the Iron Curtain were lifted, if free intercourse, commercial and cultural, were allowed between the hundreds of millions of good-hearted human beings who dwell on either side, the power of this wicked oligarchy in Moscow would soon be undermined and the spell of their Communist doctrines broken. Therefore, for the sake of their own interests and of their skins, they cannot allow any intercourse or intermingling.[1]

Now any program which sought a settlement in Europe, meaning

[1] Winston Churchill, *Europe Unite*, 1950, p. 411.

withdrawal, and hence the liberation of East Europe, would have to recognize the self-interest of the Soviet rulers. Therefore, it is disconcerting to hear Churchill, but a few paragraphs later, lay down as a *precondition* for a parallel agreement, on the control of atomic weapons the following stricture:

> Above all, let them [the Soviets] throw open their vast regions on equal terms to the ordinary travel and traffic of mankind. Let them give others the chance to breathe freely, and let them breathe freely themselves. No one wants to take anything they have got and that belongs to them away from them.[1]

The last part of this statement can hardly have been offered ingenuously, since Churchill had just informed his listeners that opening Russia's borders would take *everything* the Soviet rulers had away from them.

Although the decisive connection between the atomic energy question and the problem of a settlement in Europe is not evident from the above quotes, the full formulation of Churchill's position in this speech makes not only that connection clear, but also reveals Churchill's conception of the world power balance.

> I hope you will give full consideration to my words. I have not always been wrong. Nothing stands between Europe today and complete subjugation to Communist tyranny but the atomic bomb in American possession. If the Soviet Government wish to see atomic energy internationalized and its military use outlawed, it is not only by verbal or written agreements that they must reassure the world but by actions, which speak louder than words. Let them release their grip upon the satellite States of Europe. Let them retire to their own country, which is one-sixth of the land surface of the globe. Let them liberate by their departure the eleven capitals of Eastern Europe which they now hold in their clutches . . .[2]

---

[1] ibid., p. 413.

[2] ibid., pp. 412–13. The *eleven* capitals presumably include those of the Baltic states. Among the strictures which follow is the absurd and impossible command 'Let them cease to foment the hideous protracted civil war in China.' Stalin had already tried to stop Mao, who led more than 90 million Chinese at this time, since a weak China was more in his interest than a strong one. But he had no power in this situation, cf. Vladimir Dedijer, *Tito*.

Settlement of the question of the European peace is envisioned here as a unilateral evacuation by the Soviet Union of its hard won military positions. Churchill did not, of course, expect this to be accomplished by the power of his rhetoric, or his appeal to principle (particularly since the Russians had a rather vivid image of the extent of his own commitment to the principle of independence in Greece). Obviously, the Atomic Bomb was for Churchill such an absolute weight in the power balance that a settlement in Europe would only have required the formulation of demands by the West, and the Soviets would have had little choice but to acquiesce or face destruction. Withdrawal would be achieved by a show of strength (*use* of strength would not be necessary) rather than negotiation. In the same speech, Churchill makes this objective clear:

> No one in his senses can believe that we have a limitless period of time before us. We ought to bring matters to a head and *make* a final settlement . . . The Western Nations will be far more likely to reach a lasting settlement, without bloodshed, if they formulate their just demands while they have the atomic power and before the Russian Communists have got it too. I am therefore of opinion that our Party is bound to support *any firm measures* which the Government is found capable of taking . . .[1] [Emphasis added.]

'Such a policy,' as Blackett observed,[2] 'could only be carried out by the clear threat of preventive war.' Moreover, given the view that the Soviet Union must be backed down by a show of strength, it is not surprising, that in the same speech Churchill urged the cessation of 'the endless trials of Germans who were connected with the former Nazi régime', especially 'these aged German Field-Marshals and Generals' not only on 'soldierly, juridical and humanitarian' grounds, but because 'how foolish, how inane – I might almost say insane – it is to make a feature of such squalid long-drawn vengeance when the mind and soul of Germany may once again be hanging in the balance between the right course and the wrong.'[3]

The difference between Lippmann's view that Western policy must seek to *negotiate* a withdrawal, and the view that Western

---

[1] ibid., pp. 414–15.
[2] P. M. S. Blackett, *Atomic Weapons and East–West Relations*, 1956, p. 86.
[3] Churchill, op. cit., p. 416.

policy must seek to *compel* a withdrawal ought to have stemmed, if our suppositions have been correct, from differing assessments of the power situation, in particular, of the capabilities of the Atomic Bomb. Western statesmen, as we have seen, clearly acted as if their atomic monopoly were such a powerful trump card as to enable them to wait until the political and economic situation in Europe would permit them to 'bring matters to a head and make a final settlement'.

On the other hand, Lippmann had written an analysis of US atomic capabilities as early as 1946 which, in effect, denied the practicability of preventive atomic war against the Russians and thus seriously questioned the feasibility of an ultimatum policy:

No atomic bombardment could destroy the Red Army; it could destroy only the industrial means of supplying it. The Russian defence to atomic attack is therefore, self-evident; it is to over-run continental Europe with infantry, and defy us to drop atomic bombs on Poland, Czechoslovakia, Austria, Switzerland, France, Belgium, the Netherlands and Sweden. The more we threaten to demolish Russian cities, the more obvious it is that the Russian defence would be to ensconce themselves in European cities which we could not demolish without massacring hundreds of thousands of our own friends.[1]

It is by no means insignificant, that the only cabinet member to actively oppose the Truman–Byrnes diplomatic offensive, Henry Wallace, held precisely the same estimate for precisely the same reasons, which he set forth in his famous letter to Truman in 1946.[2]

To Administration leaders, beguiled by the newly evolved policy of creating 'situations of strength',[3] however, even the explosion of the Soviet A-bomb did not compel a shift from optimism to realism. In a major address[4] in Berkeley, California in March 1950, Acheson

[1] Cited in Blackett, *Military and Political Consequences of Atomic Weapons*, p.74.
[2] ibid.
[3] On June 1, 1950, Lippmann wrote that no close observer in Washington could fail to feel that 'the Administration's foreign policy has during the past year created the impression here and abroad, that it places virtually complete dependence on military and material power', cited in Fleming, p. 539.
[4] All of the top State Department political officials contributed to it, according to the *New York Times*, March 19, 1950, cited in Fleming, p. 531

countered appeals from many quarters to resume high level discussions with the Soviet Union, in light of the changed situation.

It was evident from Acheson's remarks, that the Administration did not hold the general view that the power situation had, in fact, significantly changed. The Russians could not have had a large nuclear stockpile, nor extensive means to deliver nuclear bombs to the continental US.[1] Moreover, the US had already begun plans for an H-bomb, which would be a thousand times more powerful than than the A-bomb. In any case, Acheson's view of coexistence with the Soviets as expressed in his speech did not indicate that he suspected that a situation was rapidly developing in which such a course would be a compelling necessity.

Like Churchill before him, Acheson set forth the steps which the Soviet Union would have to take unilaterally to 'permit [*sic*] the rational and peaceful development of the coexistence of their system and ours'. The steps included change of their position on the UN and outstanding peace treaties, withdrawal from East Europe, agreement to 'realistic and effective' arrangements for control of atomic weapons, stopping the efforts of the national communist parties to overthrow régimes in any country which is outwardly friendly to the Soviet Union and stopping the distortion of motives of others through false propaganda that speaks of a 'capitalist encirclement' and of the US craftily and systematically plotting another world war. As James Reston observed, if the Soviets accepted these conditions 'they would virtually cease to be Communists'.[2] Once again the Soviet Union was being asked to surrender its position as a condition for entering serious negotiations. It was being asked to 'cooperate' not in making a compromise settlement, but in securing the achievement of Western objectives.

Acheson's continued confidence, his disinterest in attempts to settle the conflict with Russia, his apparent lack of concern for the growing consolidation of the division of Europe, cannot be explained merely by the extent to which American officials discounted the immediate significance of the Soviet nuclear test, however. For to put the Soviet achievement of nuclear capability five to ten years in

---

[1] Blackett, *Atomic Weapons and East–West Relations*, pp. 49–53.
[2] March 19, 1950, cited in Fleming, p. 531.

the future as they did,[1] would be to offer a strong argument in favor of negotiations in the present, while the United States still had its immense nuclear advantage as a bargaining factor. Such an argument would be undermined, on the other hand, if the Soviet power position was expected to decline, as indeed the containment thesis had predicted. The failure of American leaders to attempt to capitalize their immense power advantage in the early cold war years through negotiation, can only mean that they expected to achieve their purposes without negotiation. (The same conclusion is reached by a sympathetic critic of the Achesonian doctrine of 'negotiation from strength', who has written: 'The hope held out in Acheson's words is of agreements registering acceptance of a situation that has been changed by other means. . . .'[2])

This is also the conclusion reached by the historian William Appleman Williams, proceeding from slightly different considerations:

The emphasis [of American leaders] on open-door expansion [in regard to the Marshall Plan and the Truman Doctrine] and the assumption of the inevitable downfall of the Soviet Union suggest that American leaders were not motivated solely by fear of Russian expansion. Their plan for dealing with the possibility that the Soviet Union would accept the Marshall Plan indicated this. Kennan thought the possibility could be handled, even if it materialized, by requiring Russia to divert resources from its own recovery to the aid of Western Europe . . . viewed in the light of his assumption [in the 'X' article] that American power would force Russia to give way, Kennan's advice on how to 'play it straight' suggests that American leaders thought it was basically a matter of time until the Russian problem was solved. Their

---

[1] In December 1948, Forrestal wrote: 'The Russians cannot possibly have the industrial competence to produce the atomic bomb now, and it will be five or even ten years before they could count on manufacture of it in quantity.' – Forrestal, p. 495–6.

[2] Coral Bell, *Negotiation from Strength*, 1962, p. 22; '. . . negotiation from strength was not a new doctrine but . . . it made explicit an aspiration that had been implicit in Western policy since 1947.' p. 28. Bell's thesis is that the democratic US was never politically able to muster the strength necessary to make this 'revisionist' doctrine effective. ('Revisionist' in the sense of seeking to revise the *status quo* through pressure.)

continued remarks discounting the probability of Russian attack point in the same direction.[1]

In introducing the specter of Soviet expansion as a possible motivation for American policy, Williams touches on what is probably the main point of resistance to the above line of argument. In fact, however, the whole orthodox conception of American policy towards the Soviet Union as a policy of response, is undermined by a careful consideration of the pivotal events of this period between the explosion of the Soviet A-bomb and the war in Korea.

At this moment in cold war history, the American defense budget was at the low post-war level of $13 billion (still, however, more than 30 per cent of the $39·5 billion budget). The Russians had ended their blockade of Berlin the preceding May and thus eased their pressure against the weakest point along the Nato front in Europe. The Nato pact itself had been signed and ratified and the first American arms aid sent to the member countries.

Not only was the Western position in Europe stronger than it had been during the previous four years, but a consensus of responsible observers had seen in the approaching end to American atomic monopoly an opportunity to open serious negotiations to halt the arms race and pacify the cold war conflict. In addition to Lippmann, Senators Tydings and MacMahon (chairman of the Joint Committee on Atomic Energy) called for imaginative diplomatic action, while the New York *Herald Tribune* editorialized (in February) that there was a feeling among 'millions of Americans that there must be a new approach to the Soviet Union in order to close the horrible vistas' ahead. At the same time, Harrison Salisbury was allowed to report from Russia that some Moscow diplomatic quarters believed that the Soviet Government was prepared to meet the US in 'a two-power effort to solve the major problems confronting both countries, including the question of atomic controls'.[2]

It was in this context that Acheson firmly and publicly shut the door to negotiations towards a constructive settlement, while in Washington a secret decision was taken to embark on a massive rearmament program. Before considering this latter development,

---

[1] Wm. A. Williams, *The Tragedy of American Diplomacy*, pp. 179–80.
[2] Fleming, pp. 527 and 528.

however, let us dwell a little more on the historical turn which events took in the spring of 1950, and on the orthodox interpretation of them.

The failure 'to grasp the opportunities for a constructive peace settlement' in the spring of 1950,[1] had dire consequences for the future course of the cold war. Indeed, the really intractable problems attending a European settlement may be said to date from this period. For by the time a substantial, if half-hearted attempt to negotiate issues had been made at Geneva in 1955, the Korean War had intervened, the American defense budget had quadrupled in size, and German rearmament within the structure of Nato was well under way.

This disastrous chain of events is easily assimilated into orthodox western accounts of the cold war, in a way which preserves the 'defensive' character and responsive nature of American policy. According to this version of history, the North Korean invasion of South Korea was the first stage in a new program of Soviet expansion, inspired by the Kremlin's recent acquisition of the Atomic Bomb. In the circumstances, the 325 per cent increase in the American defense budget in the next two fiscal years (so that it surpassed the *total* budget prior to the increase) is comprehensible. The same argument would explain the urgency with which US leaders sought to have Western Germany rearmed within the Nato alliance, rather than neutralized and armed defensively on the pattern of Austria. The trouble with this orthodox view, quite apart from the fact that Acheson had already begun his campaign for West German rearmament in 1949, and that Soviet responsibility for the North Korean invasion is still by no means clearly established, is that the American decisions to maintain their opposition to a negotiated settlement and to quadruple the peacetime military budget were taken *at least two months prior to the invasion of South Korea.*

These crucial policy decisions were made in accord with the broad strategy prescribed by a National Security Council Paper (NSC-68), initialled by President Truman in April 1950, which dealt with

---

[1] '... the truth is that the Democratic Administration by its intransigent attitude is failing to grasp the opportunities for a constructive peace settlement, while the Republicans are, if anything, doing more to harden the Administration against an understanding with Russia.' – So wrote the conservative David Lawrence on April 3, 1950; cited in Fleming.

international relations, particularly with respect to the Soviet Union. The paper, described by Acheson as 'one of the great documents in our history' held that there was a basic and probably permanent incompatibility between Communist and democratic philosophies, '. . . that will keep the Communist and non-Communist worlds in conflict into an unforeseeable future [the words are those of the New York *Times* account]'.[1] In this situation, the document held, the US could pursue one of four alternatives (none of which, of course, entailed entering negotiations). 'It could do nothing beyond what it already was doing, it could abandon its international commitments and retreat behind "fortress America", it could attempt to forestall danger with a preventive war, or it could undertake a massive re-building of its own and the free world's defensive capabilities and adopt an unflinching "will to fight" posture toward its enemies.' This latter course was chosen in the NSC document, which said, in elaboration, that 'The nation should think of arms cost in an order of magnitude of $50 billion annually [as opposed to the present $13 billion].'[2]

Thus, in a period of relative international tranquility, amidst admonitions from many distinguished sources to open negotiations towards a settlement of the European and nuclear problems, the US leadership not only reaffirmed the strategic decisions of 1945-7 against negotiations and the use of diplomacy, but opted also for military rearmament on a scale never before witnessed in peacetime.

The secret character of the NSC document puts a severe limit on the conclusions which can be safely drawn from reports of its contents. One seemingly inescapable conclusion, however, is the emptiness of the orthodox view which sees American policy in this period as consisting of responses to Soviet strategies. For while the Korean conflict may have played a role in making possible the actual American military buildup, the *policy decision* to increase the military posture fourfold – with all the consequences that that entailed for the problem of divided Europe – was strategic and not defensive in character.

[1] New York *Times*, Int. Edn., April 13, 1964.
[2] Post-war US military budgets were as follows: 1945–$81·2 billion; 1946–$43·2 billion; 1947–$14·4 billion; 1948–$11,771 billion; 1949–$12·9 billion; 1950–$13 billion; 1951–$22·444 billion; 1952–$43·9 billion; the years are fiscal years.

As long as the NSC document remains secret, the full range of motives behind this plan to quadruple a military posture which had already 'contained' Soviet power in Greece, Turkey, Iran and Berlin – insofar as it needed containing – must remain obscure. But if we focus our attention on the Nato build-up in Western Europe, a major element in the strategy of American policy at this time, becomes clear.

Nato had been formed in 1949 not so much to provide a force capable of containing a Soviet land aggression, as to provide a 'trip-wire' which would involve the United States and engage US nuclear power. Thus Nato was intended to have only 22 divisions against some 180 estimated Soviet divisions, and could not have prevented the Red Army from marching swiftly to the sea. Then, in February 1952, four years after the Czech *coup* and six months after truce talks had begun in Korea, the Nato allies met in Lisbon and approved a plan which would provide 50 divisions by the end of 1952, 70 by the end of 1953 and 97 by the end of 1954.[1] These quotas were never filled, because the European powers were unimpressed by the immediacy of any threat and were content to rely on the US deterrent if any should arise. One must assume these countries had adequate military intelligence forces, and thus that there was in fact no immediate threat to their security. What then was behind the urgency of the build-up?

The answer to this question lies in an understanding of how the build-up would have altered Nato's function:

A build-up of ground forces on even a lesser scale [than planned] ... began to provide a somewhat new conception of Nato's military meaning. Europe's ground forces might not be able alone to meet and defeat a fully mobilized ground attack by the Soviet Union; but, on the other hand, Nato was clearly a force *which could obstruct a march from East Germany to the Channel.*[2] [Emphasis added.]

One corollary of Nato's new meaning would be to preclude the Soviet's use of its deterrent, i.e. occupation of Western European

---

[1] W. W. Rostow, *The United States in the World Arena*, p. 332.
[2] ibid.

cities, and would therefore make Russia vulnerable to nuclear attack. This change in Nato's military meaning, thus was well tailored to fit in with plans for creating a situation of strength in which the Soviet Union could be served with an ultimatum:

> The action, as opposed to the deterrent, value to the West of its nuclear power was most in evidence during the last years of the West's effective nuclear monopoly – say from 1950–4. This was the period of the Western doctrine of 'massive retaliation', though the term was not used till the end of the period, and of the political concept in influential circles of the United States of 'roll-back', 'liberation' and the 'year of decision'. In this concept *the year of decision was to arrive when Western rearmament on land had gone far enough for the West to be able to repulse a Soviet counter-thrust into Europe. When the West had acquired this adequate strength on land, it would be able to use its nuclear power to force the Soviet Union to accept the Western terms or be bombed.* These terms were generally held to include the freeing of the satellites and the unification of Germany within the Western military system.[1] (Emphasis added).

In sum, far from being responsive in character or directed towards *negotiating* a settlement which would end the division of Europe and the cold war, US post-war policies of containment and of creating situations of strength were designed, basically, to translate an existing military and economic *superiority* of power into an absolute *supremacy* of power, meaning the ability to dictate terms to the Soviet Union.[2]

---

[1] Blackett, *Studies of War*, p. 157. 'Such possibilities became less and less plausible as the Soviet nuclear stockpile gradually grew; and they had finally to be abandoned after 1954 when H-bombs became available both to the East and to the West. This collapse of the "liberation" policy left unfulfilled the promise to unite Germany within the present Western military system.'

[2] This terminology is taken from Walter Lippmann, see discussion in Chapter xxv below.

CHAPTER XV

The Atomic Bomb

America can get what she wants if she insists on it. After all, we've got it – the bomb – and they haven't and won't have for a long time to come.

BERNARD BARUCH

THE early approaches to the control of atomic energy reveal a similar pattern in the strategy of US leaders in this period. Indeed just as there were two divergent views on the problem of Europe, so there was a wide split in high policy circles on how to come to grips with the Atomic question. Moreover, the basis for this split also rested squarely on an assessment of the Soviet future.

On September 11, 1945, Henry L. Stimson, retiring Secretary of War (and former Secretary of State under Hoover), sent a memorandum to President Truman on proposed action for control of the Atomic Bomb. Stimson's proposals were discussed at a crucial cabinet meeting ten days later. As the memorandum[1] is a primary document in the sources of the cold war, it deserves to be considered at length.

The introduction of the Atomic Bomb, wrote Stimson, 'has profoundly affected political considerations in all sections of the globe. In many quarters it has been interpreted as a substantial offset to the growth of Russian influence on the continent'. The Soviet Government would be certain to have sensed this tendency, and 'the temptation will be strong for the Soviet political and military leaders to acquire this weapon in the shortest possible time'.

Britain, Stimson noted, had already in effect acquired the status of a 'partner', with the United States, in the development of the weapon. 'Accordingly, unless the Soviets are voluntarily invited into the partnership upon a basis of cooperation and trust, we are going to maintain the Anglo-Saxon bloc over against the Soviet in the

[1] Henry L. Stimson and McGeorge Bundy, *On Active Service in Peace and War*, 1947, pp. 642–6.

possession of this weapon.' Such a condition, Stimson concluded, would almost certainly stimulate 'feverish' activity on the part of the Soviet Union toward the development of the bomb. This would mean 'a secret armament race of a rather desperate character'. There was evidence, he added, 'that such activity may have already commenced'.

Whether Russia got control of the bomb in four years or a maximum of twenty, Stimson argued, was not as important as to make sure that when she got it, she was a willing and cooperative partner among the peace-loving nations of the world. 'To put the matter concisely,' he wrote, '*I consider the problem of our satisfactory relations with Russia as not merely connected with but as virtually dominated by the problems of the atomic bomb.*' Except for these problems, relations with Russia, while vitally important, might not be pressing. But with the discovery of the bomb, they have become 'immediately emergent'. [Emphasis added.]

'*Those relations,*' he stressed, '*may be perhaps irretrievably embittered by the way in which we approach the solution of the bomb with Russia. For if we fail to approach them now and merely continue to negotiate with them having this weapon rather ostentatiously on our hip, their suspicions and their distrust of our purposes and motives will increase.*' [Emphasis in original.]

A failure to approach Russia in such a way as to inspire her confidence would stimulate her to greater efforts in an all-out effort to solve the problem of the bomb. If a solution were achieved in that spirit, 'it is much less likely that we will ever get the kind of covenant we may desperately need in the future'.

Stimson therefore proposed that a direct approach be made to Russia by the United States. He was careful to underline his opinion that it must not appear as an Anglo-American gesture, which the Russians would be sure to distrust, nor as an action of any international group of nations, which would not be taken seriously by the Kremlin. 'I emphasize *perhaps beyond all other considerations,*' he wrote, 'the importance of taking this action with Russia as a proposal of the United States.' [Emphasis added.]

Stimson's idea of an approach to Russia was to make a direct proposal to the effect that the United States would be prepared 'to enter an arrangement with the Russians, the general purpose of which would be to control and limit the use of the atomic bomb as an instrument of war and so far as possible to direct and encourage the development of atomic power for peaceful and humanitarian purposes'.

In the light of what actually became the American course in the early negotiations over atomic control, the concrete steps which Stimson suggested to implement his approach assume a special importance. 'Such an approach [he wrote] might more specifically lead to the proposal that we would stop work on the further improvement in, or manufacture of, the bomb as a military weapon, provided the Russians and the British would agree to do likewise. It might also provide that we would be willing to impound what bombs we now have in the United States provided the Russians and the British would agree with us that in no event will they or we use a bomb as an instrument of war unless all three governments agree to that use.'

In other words, under Stimson's plan, the United States would have agreed to yield its temporary military advantage, as a step towards proving its good faith as the more powerful of the two participants and the one that had actually used the bomb in a military operation. In return, the initial steps would have been taken to create a framework for cooperation in the development and control of atomic energy. The loss to the United States of a temporary military advantage would have been amply compensated by the great gain for humanity and ultimately for the United States as well. 'Our objective,' wrote Stimson, 'must be to get the best kind of international bargain we can – one that has some chance of being kept and saving civilization not for five or twenty years, but forever.' If the arrangement he outlined could be initiated, thought Stimson, the chances for real control would be much greater 'than . . . if the approach were made as a part of a general international scheme or if the approach were made after a succession of express or implied threats or near threats in our peace negotiations'.

Both the wisdom of these proposals and their practicality were appreciated by the majority of those present at the September 21 cabinet meeting. Seven cabinet members, including Dean Acheson, agreed with Stimson's appraisal and approach; Forrestal, Fred Vinson and Tom Clark were opposed, and two members wished to defer the decision until a later time.[1] *Yet, in every subsequent step*

---

[1] Truman *Memoirs*, I, pp. 526–7; Acheson was sitting in for Byrnes.

taken by the Truman Administration on this vital question, Stimson's major recommendations were not only disregarded but actually reversed.

Above all else, Stimson had recommended that the approach to Russia on the atomic energy question to be an initiative of the United States alone, neither an Anglo-American proposal nor an action of any international group of nations. On November 15, scarcely two months after Stimson's strong admonitions against giving Russia the impression that the Anglo-Saxon bloc was to be maintained against her, the President of the United States, the Prime Minister of the United Kingdom (Attlee) and the Prime Minister of Canada (King) issued a joint statement calling for the establishment of a United Nations Commission for the control of atomic energy. They declared: 'We desire that there should be full and effective cooperation in the field of atomic energy between the United States, the United Kingdom and Canada.'[1] And four months later, Truman sat on the platform at Fulton Missouri, while Churchill called for an Anglo-Saxon alliance against Soviet Russia.

Stimson's warning against making implied threats during the approach to the Soviet Union over the question of atomic controls, as well as his specific injunction against negotiating with the bomb 'rather ostentatiously on our hip' were also completely ignored. Indeed, as with the previous initiative, to say merely that they were ignored is something of an understatement. The United States presented its first plan for the control of atomic energy to the United Nations on June 14, 1946, while the Soviet Union submitted its own proposals four days later. *Then, on July 1, with the discussions still in progress, the United States exploded an atomic bomb at Bikini as its first post-war atomic test.* Pravda immediately charged that the United States was trying to influence the talks (i.e. by 'implied threat' exactly as Stimson had warned) and that the tests showed that the United States was not aiming at the restriction of atomic weapons, but at their perfection.[2]

Even the proposals presented at the United Nations conform to this remarkable pattern. For the Russian proposals took precisely the line advocated by Stimson and seven other US cabinet members,

[1] ibid., pp. 542–4.
[2] New York *Times*, July 4, 1946, cited in Fleming, p. 380.

while the American proposals adopted a position *diametrically opposed to what Stimson had recommended.*

The text of the Sovet Union's proposed draft for an international agreement on atomic energy reads in part:[1]

Article I: The high contracting parties solemnly declare that they will forbid the production and use of a weapon based upon the use of atomic energy, and with this in view, take upon themselves the following obligations:

(a) Not to use, in any circumstances, an atomic weapon.
(b) To forbid the production and keeping of a weapon based upon the use of atomic energy.
(c) To destroy within a period of three months from the entry into force of this agreement all stocks of atomic energy weapons whether in a finished or semi-finished condition.

With the exception of the proposal to destroy existing weapons (Stimson had said 'impound') this is the heart of what Stimson had advocated as an approach: the United States would sacrifice its initial lead in nuclear weapons, thereby providing the basis for a working agreement.

The other major Soviet articles elaborated the terms of the initial agreement and set forth the conditions for its ratification. The Soviet delegate also proposed that a Committee should be set up to prepare recommendations on various subjects including 'the elaboration and creation of methods to forbid the production of [nuclear] weapons' and 'measures, system, and organization, of control in the use of atomic energy', as well as 'the elaboration of a system of sanctions for application against the unlawful use of atomic energy'.

By contrast both the original US plan (Lilienthal) and the one presented to the UN (Baruch) had as their distinctive feature the fact that the United States would make no concessions, It would go on expanding its nuclear stockpile and developing its weapons, until such time as an effective and foolproof international control and inspection system had been set up; then, and only then, would the United States agree to turn its own nuclear stocks over to an international commission which would have authority over atomic energy

[1] Blackett, *Military and Political Consequences of Atomic Weapons*, p. 153.

development for peaceful purposes in all nations. This commission would, in the nature of things, have a majority which agreed with the United States, and there would be no power of the veto.

In other words, in a way remarkably foreshadowing the Churchill–Acheson statements, the USSR was being asked to accept *in toto* a Western arrangement[1] that entailed opening its borders, its military secrets, its target areas,[2] its lower living standards, its police methods, its slave labor camps, and to trust the United States, with its 'absolute weapon', not to take military or political advantage of the difficulties (perhaps even upheavals) that would undoubtedly ensue. In his letter to Truman of July 1946, Wallace objected to the Baruch approach:

> ... we are telling the Russians that if they are 'good boys' we may eventually turn over our knowledge of atomic energy to them ... But there is no definite standard to qualify them as being 'good' nor any specified time for sharing the knowledge.[3]

On the other hand, if Churchill and Kennan were right, the fulfillment of such pre-conditions as would entail the opening of Soviet borders, would preclude the need for such certification – it would *cause* the Soviets to become 'good boys', since it would mean the undermining of the control of the Communist Party and hence the break-up of Soviet power. It is not surprising to find, therefore, that this consideration was very much in the minds of the men who drafted the proposals:

> In the Hearings in 1954, Oppenheimer states that at the time [1946] he did not expect the Soviet Union to accept the plan, because he thought that if they did so and opened their frontiers and freely admitted Western inspection, the Soviet system as it existed would collapse. Exactly the same view was expressed to me in New York in 1946 by the late Lord Inverchapel, then the

[1] 'It was clear that the US would make no actual surrender of the military power until the Soviet Union had demonstrated its loyal acceptance of what was a Western solution of a problem now common to both great systems.' – Walter Millis, editor of the *Forrestal Diaries* in *The Nation*, February 15, 1958.

[2] cf. Blackett, op. cit., for a full discussion of this and other aspects of the Baruch Plan.

[3] Blackett, *Military and Political Consequences of Atomic Weapons* p. 167.

British Ambassador in Washington. I am surprised now, as I was then, that it was considered realistic diplomacy to ask the Soviet Union voluntarily to accept a plan which, in the views of its author and the American and British Governments, would lead to the collapse of the system.[1]

The question of controls was matched in its influence on the future course of the cold war, by that of sanctions:

When . . . the Acheson–Lilienthal Plan became metamorphosed into the Baruch Plan, . . . there was added the conception of 'instant and condign punishment' for any transgressions of the control arrangements, to be voted by a veto-less security council, on which Russia was bound to be in a minority. . . . Of all the unfortunate aftermaths of this abortive attempt to control atomic energy was the credence it gave to the practicability of waging preventive war against a great power. For this is just what is meant by the infliction of 'instant and condign punishment' by atomic bombs.[2]

The prescription of sanctions gave rise to the illusion that a great power could be cheaply and decisively defeated by Atomic Bombs, while at the same time ensuring that, priority would be placed on maintaining security and keeping tight controls on the bomb. Both of these misplaced emphases aroused great anxieties in the United States, especially fear of Soviet atomic attack, though the Russians had virtually no means of delivering the bombs even if they had had them, until the middle fifties. The quest for security also gave rise to the false hope that the 'secret' of the bomb could be kept, and conversely to the false belief that the greatest immediate danger to the United States was the internal threat of espionage and conspiracy. Herein lay a chief source of the McCarthy sickness that exercised such power over American politics in the next period.

[1] Blackett, *Atomic Weapons and East–West Relations*, p. 90; 'The story is told that a well-known General who, with Mr Baruch, had been "putting teeth" into the Lilienthal Plan [which became the Baruch Plan] said . . . "Now we have made it so stiff that even the Russians won't be fool enough to fall for it." ' – ibid., p. 91.

[2] ibid., pp. 90–92.

While the myth that the United States' bomb monopoly could be kept has been exploded by independent Russian advances in the field of technology, the misconceptions once held about the early power of Atomic Bombs are not so readily disposed of, nor are their implications well known.

The view that the Atomic Bomb was an absolute weapon, that atomic air power alone could inflict decisive defeat upon a continental power was challenged by Blackett in 1948. Blackett made quantitative studies of the effects of allied strategic bombing in World War II, including the two Atomic Bomb explosions in Japan. These studies convinced him that the then existent nuclear power of the West did not, in fact, constitute a means of inflicting swift and decisive defeat upon the Soviet Union:

> When the Anglo-American bombing offensive got into its stride, that is from 1943 to 1945, Germany took a still higher punishment from the air. In these two and a half years sixty German cities received 600,000 tons of bombs, but German civilian morale never broke, and war production rose steadily till August 1944, by which time the German Armies had been decisively defeated on two vast land fronts.
>
> The Anglo-American bombing offensive was neither decisive nor cheap. The number of air personnel lost was 160,000 – some of the best youth of the two countries; the loss in planes was 20,000 bombers and 18,000 fighters.[1]

According to the United States Strategic Bombing Survey, the effect of the Atomic Bomb on industrial production in Nagasaki and Hiroshima was not decisive either. It estimated, for example, that 74 per cent of industrial production in Hiroshima could have been resumed within thirty days.[2] As for the power of Atomic Bombs:

> Official American figures show that the early types of atomic bombs produced about the same destruction as some 2,000 tons of ordinary bombs evenly spread over the same area ... more than 1,000 atomic bombs of the Hiroshima type would have been

[1] Blackett, *Studies of War*, p. 7.
[2] Cited in Blackett, *Military and Political Consequences of Atomic Weapons*, p. 39.

required to inflict on Germany and the occupied territories the same industrial damage as was done by the 2·7 million tons of chemical bombs actually dropped on them.[1]

Blackett's views on the potential of the new atomic weapons were shared by the Russians (and by the Commander of the American Strategic Air Force in 1948,[2] though there was considerable disagreement among American military leaders on this subject throughout the period). From his knowledge of Soviet military strategy, Blackett had speculated that the Russians would incline to be sceptical about the effectiveness of the strategic use of atomic weapons. The belief in 'true air power' was strictly a Western belief, had been practiced only in the West, and had been openly criticized by Soviet military strategists.[3]

In the West, the erroneous view that atomic power could be quickly and cheaply decisive led on the one hand to the conclusion that the Western powers could formulate their demands and issue an ultimatum to the Soviet Union, and on the other, that when the USSR achieved similar or superior capabilities, it would do the same. Moreover, the fact that the Russians showed no signs of being cowed in the period of American nuclear monopoly, seemed in this view to underscore the ruthless and determined character of the Soviet rulers. In the previously quoted speech of Winston Churchill, this view is expressed in high style:

The question is asked: What will happen when they get the atomic bomb themselves and have accumulated a large store? You can judge yourselves what will happen then by what is happening now. If these things are done in the green wood, what will be done in the dry? If they can continue month after month disturbing and tormenting the world, trusting to our Christian and altruistic inhibitions against using this strange new power against them, what will they do when they themselves have large quantities of atomic bombs? What do you suppose would be the position this afternoon if it had been Communist Russia instead

[1] Blackett, *Studies of War*, p. 9, 51. The United States had neither the stockpile nor the carriers even to deliver such quantities of bombs to Russia.
[2] ibid., pp. 11–14. For evidence of Russian agreement, cf. Forrestal, op. cit., p. 497.
[3] *Military and Political Consequences of Atomic Weapons*, pp. 68–9, 146–9.

of free enterprise America which had created the atomic weapon ? Instead of being a sombre guarantee of peace and freedom it would have become an irresistible method of human enslavement. No one in his senses can believe that we have a limitless period of time before us. We ought to bring matters to a head and make a final settlement.[1]

Based as it was on an erroneous view of the military situation, Churchill's rhetorical question ('If these things are done in the green wood, what will be done in the dry') had an unexpected answer. As the Soviets approached nuclear parity with the West, their attitude became not more menacing and intractable, but on the contrary more conciliatory. The evidence indicates, moreover, that this did not stem from a different assessment of Western intentions and character, which would have been reflected in different defense policies, so much as in a new confidence in their own deterrent power:

Though clearly the internal political changes in the USSR since Stalin's death have been profound, their fundamental defence policy does not seem to have changed much. With our present knowledge there can be little doubt that for many years past an important element in Stalin's policy was to attempt to impose coexistence on the West by achieving atomic parity. This was, in fact, achieved within six months of Stalin's death – for the first Soviet H-bomb in August 1953 can be considered as signifying the success of the policy.

In so far, then as the present *détente* is a result of the present Soviet leaders confidence in their strength, it is a result not of Stalin's death but of the ruthless methods by which he drove his country to the scientific, technological and industrial efforts, without which atomic parity would have been long delayed.[2]

Nothing reveals more vividly the fact that American leaders had no vision of peace beyond the collapse or defeat of Soviet power,

[1] Churchill, op. cit., p. 414.
[2] Blackett, *Atomic Weapons and East–West Relations*, 1956, pp. 82–3.

than the United States response to this *détente*, and to the first un-mistakeable proposals for peaceful coexistence.

In January 1952, the UN General Assembly set up a new Disarmament Commission, as proposed by Dean Acheson. When this proposal was first put forward, Vyshinsky said that it had made him 'laugh all night'. World reaction to this speech caused the Kremlin to change its mind, and the vote on the proposal was unanimous. During the next two years under United States leadership, the West proposed and refined a program for general disarmament under international controls, designed 'not to regulate but to prevent war ... by making war inherently, as it is constitutionally under the Charter, impossible as a means of settling disputes between nations.'[1]

By March–April 1955, the proposals included provisions for the reduction of armed forces to very low levels, the reduction of conventional arms, the total abolition of all weapons of mass destruction, including all existing nuclear stocks, and the creation of a single organ of control, set up in advance, and given expanding powers. 'The United States delegates asked for a clear answer, Yes or No, to these proposals. "Will it [the Soviet Union] accept the drastic reductions which the United States is prepared to accept, such as a ceiling of from 1 million to 1·5 million men?"'[2]

On May 10, 1955, after nine years of resistance to all Western plans, the USSR reversed itself and accepted the Western plan for manpower ceilings, and reduction in conventional armaments, the Western timetable, the Western arrangement for the abolition of nuclear stocks and other weapons of mass-destruction, and the Western demand that Government appropriations for armed forces and conventional armaments be reduced correspondingly.[3]

As for the controls proposed by the Russians,

> ... if they meant anything at all, they would have made an immense breach in the Iron Curtain – hundreds, if not thousands, of UN Inspectors, chosen by the UN, 'on an international basis', permanently in residence in Russia, with wide powers of access

---

[1] *The Arms Race*, by Philip Noel-Baker, 1958, p. 12. This is a classic work in the field of disarmament. In recognition for a lifetime contribution to the achievement of disarmament, Noel-Baker was awarded the Nobel Peace Prize in 1958.
[2] ibid., p. 19.
[3] ibid.

to military and other installations, and with the right to full information about all aspects of Russian military finance – in itself a powerful instrument of control. But for full measure the Russians also put forward their plan for the establishment of ground 'Control Posts' at large ports, at railway junctions, on main motor highways and in aerodromes. This was to guard against the danger of surprise attack by modern weapons; it was to start before any measures of armament reduction began; it was a spontaneous Russian suggestion, which made a further great breach in the Iron Curtain.[1]

On May 12, after consultation with his Government, the American delegate speaking 'as a representative of the United States', said:

> We have been gratified to find that the concepts which we have put forward over a considerable length of time, and which we have repeated many times during this past two months, have been accepted in large measure by the Soviet Union.[2]

At this point the West insisted on a recess, although the Russians wished to go ahead and iron out the remaining differences. The first Summit meeting was held in July, and there President Eisenhower suddenly proposed his famous 'open skies' plan to permit the two powers to conduct aerial inspections of each other's territory:

> It was a bold, dramatic, radical plan that would have swept down the whole structure of secrecy on both sides of the iron curtain if it could have been agreed to . . .[3]

Eisenhower's proposal was indeed a 'bold' plan: it was a wholesale retreat from the inspection proposals already agreed to (which were much more far-reaching and significant) and most importantly from the program for general and complete disarmament which was to have accompanied the controls. Instead of agreement which would have liquidated the nuclear threat, the arms race and the cold war, the US was asking the Soviet Union to exchange one of its most important military assets (secrecy) for information which it essen-

[1] ibid., pp. 20–21.
[2] ibid., p. 22.
[3] Marquis Childs, *Eisenhower: Captive Hero*, 1958, p. 209.

tially had, and to do this without the prospect of a program of disarmament which would liquidate the S A C bases by which it was encircled.

On August 29, the Disarmament Commission met again, but did not take up its work where it had left off. The Russians tried, 'politely but persistently' to make it do so; they 'completely failed'. The U S delegate made repeated speeches about the proposal for 'open skies'. Then after a week's debate, the U S delegate said:

> ... the United States does now place a reservation upon all of its pre-Geneva substantive positions taken in this Sub-Committee or in the Disarmament Commission or in the UN on these questions in relationship to levels of armament.

'In other words,' writes Noel-Baker 'the Six Principles (Essential Principles for a Disarmament Programme) the manpower ceilings, the disarmament programme of the Anglo-French Memorandum of 1954, the 50 per cent arrangement about the "cut-off", the 75 per cent arrangement about the elimination of nuclear stocks, the detailed plan for Inspection and Control, all the other proposals urged with such vigour and persistance only three months before – all were withdrawn. . . .'[1]

Apparently the Western disarmament negotiators had worked at a genuine disarmament program with too much zeal. 'The proposals were withdrawn, and they have remained withdrawn until today [1958].' In 1956, the Russians made further efforts to meet the West; 'on every point they were rebuffed'.[2] And as late as February 8, 1960, Senator Joseph Clark (D-Pa.) declared on the floor of the Senate:

> The U S is the only nuclear power which has not accepted total and permanent disarmament under adequate international safeguards as its goal and put forward a comprehensive plan to achieve that end. I think that is a disgrace. The British have done it. The Russians have done it. We have not done it . . .[3]

[1] Noel-Baker, op. cit., pp. 22–3.
[2] ibid.
[3] Cited in Fred J. Cook, 'Juggernaut the Warfare State', *The Nation*, October 28, 1961 (published in expanded form as *The Warfare State*, 1963). The situation was finally rectified by President Kennedy in September 1961.

Just before the 1955 Summit Eisenhower had said, 'There is no alternative to peace.' But when the prospect of a peace that meant coexistence presented itself, the US Leadership was not prepared to accept it and, therefore did not seize the opportunity. After the Summit, in August, the Soviet Union announced that it would soon reduce its armed forces by 640,000 men. But two weeks later Eisenhower declared that there could be no true peace which involved 'acceptance of a *status quo* in which we find injustice to many nations, repressions of human beings on a gigantic scale . . .'

The next day (four days before the Disarmament Commission reconvened) Vice-President Nixon called on the Russians to 'prove their sincerity' by (1) agreeing to free elections and the unification of Germany and Korea;[1] (2) accepting President Eisenhower's aerial inspection plan; (3) dismantling the Iron Curtain; (4) freeing the European satellites; and (5) curtailing the activities of the Moscow controlled organizations in other countries.[2] Thus the United States leadership had retreated from the summit to the pre-*détente* position of Churchill (who no longer held it) and Acheson (who apparently did); indeed the position was never left in the first place.

For just, prior to the Summit, Dulles testified before a Congressional sub-committee that Russia's economy was 'on the point of collapse'.[3]

Thus, in their approach to the nuclear problem and in their approach to the problem of divided Europe, the American leadership pursued clearly discernible and parallel courses. In neither case, did American policy include any serious attempt to negotiate a solution to the problems or to avoid the conflict latent in them. If the American leadership had any intention of making such an attempt in regard to the nuclear problem, for example, they certainly would not have gone

---

[1] It is significant that American leaders never called for unifying elections in Viet Nam, the one divided country which has more people living in the Communist area.

[2] Cited and summarized in Fleming, p. 760.

[3] New York *Times*, July 7, 1955, cited in Fleming, p. 747. When he repeated this view the following February, saying that the Soviet system was 'bankrupt' and that the unity of the free world had caused its policies to fail, it brought the retort from George Kennan: 'I don't recognize the world Mr Dulles is talking about.'

so far in reversing the specific recommendations of the most senior statesman in the United States cabinet,[1] on an issue which he felt 'virtually dominated' US–Soviet relations. Nor would they have made the cardinal assumption of their policy in Europe, the impossibility of negotiating a settlement with the Soviet Union. That there was little factual ground at the time for such an assumption hardly needs to be stressed. 'It is idle to reason or argue with the Communists', observed Churchill in January 1948; 'it is, however, possible to deal with them on a fair, realistic basis, and, in my experience, *they will keep their bargains as long as it is in their interest to do so*, which might, in this grave matter, be a long time, once things were settled.' But even more important than Churchill's testimony, at the time, is the general fact that international agreements are not necessarily based on the good-will of the parties, nor is negotiating them necessarily dependent on the development of good-will. As President Kennedy noted in his address at the American University, June 10, 1963, 'even the most hostile nations can be relied upon to accept and keep those treaty obligations, and only those treaty obligations, which are in their own interest'.

If the strategy of the American leadership was not to negotiate a settlement to the 'Russian problem', nor merely to leave matters as they stood, what then was its purpose? In the fall of 1945 when the outlines of the policy became clear,[2] this purpose certainly was not to contain any threatened Russian aggression. Indeed, George Kennan, who until 1946 was stationed in the American Embassy in Moscow and afterward became the first Director of the State Department's Policy Planning Staff, admitted in 1958: 'I have never thought that the Soviet Government wanted a general world war at any time since 1945, or that it would have been inclined for any rational political reason, to inaugurate such a war, even had the atomic weapon never been invented. I do not believe, in other

[1] Stimson had served in four cabinets as Secretary of State or War, since 1911.

[2] On November 15, the Truman–Attlee–King declaration reversed Stimson's recommendation about avoiding the impression that the Anglo-Saxon bloc was to be maintained against Russia over the bomb. Two weeks later Truman announced that there would be no more meetings of the leaders of the wartime coalition. At the same time, as the New York *Times* later revealed, the global anti-Communist crusade, embodied in the Truman Doctrine, began to mature as a policy in Truman's mind, and he set about looking for an opportunity to proclaim it.

words, that it was our possession of the atomic bomb which prevented the Russians from overrunning Europe in 1948 or at any other time.'[1]

One is left with the conclusion that the American policy of isolating Russia politically and economically, of maintaining its own atomic monopoly, while encircling Russia with military bases and hostile military alliances, had two strategic objectives (a third, defensive objective – stabilizing and reconstructing Western Europe – could have been achieved with the policies recommended by Stimson and Lippmann, and hence is not relevant to our analysis at this point).

Of these objectives, the minimum was to deny Russia the influence she had won in Europe as a result of her wartime victories. To accomplish this, the United States embarked on a course designed to *compel* Russia to relinquish her positions in East Europe, without any compensation in the way of recognition of her security interests in the Central and East European areas.[2] Such recognition would have been expressed, for example, in the peace settlement with Germany, and it was towards this settlement that Lippmann had, in vain, urged that US policy be directed.

The maximum objective of the American leadership, in so far as it is deducible from their statements and actions looked beyond the unilateral withdrawal of Soviet forces from East Europe to the break-up of Soviet power itself, and beyond that, to the collapse of the Russian Revolution. Indeed, the two objectives were virtually interdependent, since only the near collapse of Soviet power would cause the Russians to undertake a unilateral withdrawal from their European positions.

In the eighteen years between the adoption of these goals and their tentative abandonment for a policy of coexistence and *détente* (at least in the European area) no appreciable progress was made towards their achievement. On the other hand, the consequences of embarking on a course in pursuit of these objectives, instead of a

---

[1] Kennan, *Russia, the Atom and the West*, 1958, p. 53.

[2] Certainly one of the more legitimate sources of early Russian suspicions of US policy was the United States' insistence on unilaterally organizing the Pacific area, including Japan and the Japanese bases as part of her security zone, while denying Russia the same prerogatives in East Europe. cf. Ingram, p. 25, and Fleming, p. 313.

policy directed towards a negotiated settlement, were immense. It is to the unforeseen consequences of containment, and the subsequent (and unforeseen) evolution of the containment policy that we now turn.

CHAPTER XVI

East Europe: 1949-56

The proposition that peace is the necessary precondition for the advance of freedom applies generally. . . .

JOHN F. KENNEDY

THE intensification of the cold war, especially after the outbreak of the Korean conflict, took a heavy toll on East Europe. For it was partially under the cloak of a supposedly imminent war threat from the west that the Stalinists ascended within the East European Communist parties and, directed by Moscow, drove their countries through an intense period of Stalinist construction. Between 1949 and 1953, Stalinist policies and tactics had brought the economies of these countries near ruin, strangled their internal political life, and reduced them to colonial status. Not unpredictably, these years of political purge and economic and national exploitation left in their wake the passions of nationalist revolt. Thus, just as the Soviet Union reached its first goals of reconstruction, the security of great power status and atomic parity, the satellites not only ceased to be economically necessary to Soviet power, but became a tremendous political liability as well.

When Stalin died in March 1953, one of the central problems facing the new Soviet leadership was this liability in East Europe. At the center of the problem was the division of Germany, which perpetuated the division of Europe and was used to justify the presence of large American forces on the continent, hence, the military 'threat' to the Soviet bloc. This threat expressed itself concretely in the refusal of the American leadership to recognize the *status quo* in East Europe, and in its avowed purpose to 'liberate' the satellite peoples.

The policy of liberation was proclaimed by the Republicans in the 1952 presidential campaign, when after a long conference with Eisenhower in August, Dulles declared that the policy of containment was a 'ticket for World War III'. He decried containment as depending on the hope that 'Communist dictators would become so gorged with 800 million people that they would stay where they were'. Depending on such a belief would not do, said Dulles. The United States must try to split the satellites away from Russia. 'The only way to stop a head-on collision with the Soviet Union is to break it up from within.'[1]

Four months prior to these pronouncements, the Russians had relaxed their position and proposed the resumption of serious negotiations about Germany. Their published drafts for a treaty included such unexpected Soviet concessions as Germany's admittance to the UN, the right of Germany to maintain a national army and the possibility of holding free German elections. The unification of the Germanies, according to the draft proposals, was to take place under the guidance of all-German commissions, and the one stipulation was to be that a reunited Germany would remain neutral as between East and West. These proposals did not lead to the opening of serious negotiations, however, because in view of the prospects of bringing West Germany fully into the American alliance system, the US State Department and the Pentagon 'did not really wish to explore them'.[2]

Actually the Russians at the time were very serious indeed about negotiating the reunification of Germany and preventing the entrance of West Germany into Nato. In fact, the Russians were so anxious to reach an accord which would mean German neutrality, that early in 1952 'the East German Communist leaders were told by the Kremlin that their régime would have to be liquidated in the interests of unifying Germany'.[3] The orders to the East German party were issued preliminary to Moscow's appeal in March for four power negotiations to end the occupation of Germany, unify the country and establish a peace treaty. The Soviet bid was rejected by the West and 'several months later, the East German régime was advised that it would continue to exist'.[4]

But this did not exhaust Soviet attempts to end the cold war in

[1] Fleming, p. 806.
[2] John Lukacs, *A History of the Cold War*, 1961, pp. 103–4.
[3] Harrison Salisbury in the New York *Times*, Int. Edn., March 16, 1963. The information was reported by Pietro Nenni, Italian Socialist leader.
[4] ibid.

Europe during this 'middle' period. The following spring, when Stalin died, the new Moscow leadership took dramatic steps 'to explore the lines of retreat in Germany'. In the single week which preceded the June revolts in Berlin, the whole policy of the Pieck–Ulbricht régime was scrapped. After Soviet General Chuikov was recalled, the Iron Curtain between East and West was nearly demolished; labor policy was reversed; the Government's struggle with the Evangelical Church was called off; farm collectivization was halted and those who had fled were invited to come back to take possession of their property.[1]

'From the Russian viewpoint,' commented Isaac Deutscher, 'these moves made no sense at all unless they were part and parcel of a policy calculated to bring about the unification of Germany and the withdrawal of occupation armies.' There was little doubt in Berlin that Moscow was, in fact, ready to abandon the Pieck–Ulbricht régime. 'So strongly indeed did Soviet representatives in Berlin encourage this belief and so frankly did they negotiate with non-Communist leaders about a change of régime that by this alone the Russians themselves unwittingly induced the people of Berlin to descend upon the streets, to clamour for the resignation of the Communist government, and to storm that government's offices.'[2]

The June revolt which pitted stones hurled by German rebels against Soviet tanks, did bring about an upheaval; 'but the upheaval took place in Moscow, not in Berlin'. Starting from the chaos which the new Kremlin policies had produced in Germany, the critics of the new line 'could point out that not only Germany but the West at large was receiving Russian concessions as proof of Russian weakness; and that Washington in particular was using these concessions as the starting-point for an intensified onslaught on Russia's positions in Eastern and Central Europe'.

East German events 'followed by the call to revolt addressed to Eastern Europe from the West' tipped the scales in the Kremlin and gave weight to a tougher, more cautious policy towards the

---

[1] Deutscher, *Heretics and Renegades*, 1955, pp. 173 et seq. In March 1963 Khrushchev corroborated Deutscher's main account in a speech in which he drew attention to his own exploits in thwarting attempts by Malenkov and Beria to liquidate the East German régime. Reported by Salisbury, New York *Times*, Int. Edn., op. cit.

[2] Deutscher, ibid.

West. The core of the ruling group still consisted of men prepared to seek agreements, but 'even the men "of the centre" must have been affected by the arguments against "appeasement" . . .' That the East German revolt did not cause a complete about-face in the Kremlin, however, is evidenced, among other things, by the Politburo's appointment of Imre Nagy to the premiership in Hungary in the same month.

Under Nagy, there was 'great and undeniable progress'.[1] Living standards improved; political internees were set free; private enterprise was allowed again on a small scale; forced collectivization was stopped and 250,000 members of the collectives were allowed to withdraw.[2] Nagy was prevented from carrying this 'June Road' even further by the presence of the former Premier, Mátyás Rákosi, who had been allowed to remain head of the Hungarian Communist Party by the Soviet Politburo (now Presidium), a result of the caution induced by the German events.

The next year and a half witnessed a covert struggle between these men and their supporters, a struggle which Rákosi won, with tragic consequences for the Hungarian people. For when the growing revolt against the Rákosi oppression brought Nagy to power a second time, events had swept Hungary beyond the point of peaceful evolution towards its goals of full national independence, neutrality and political freedom, and into the maelstrom of violence and brutal suppression.

In assessing the significance of this struggle and its relation to the policy of liberation, an element of key importance is the political outlook of Imre Nagy, in whose person the revolution found its leader and its expression. . . . 'The popular demands fitted exceedingly well into the conceptual framework of the Prime Minister . . ., when he listened to the *vox populi* he must have had the impression he was listening to his own voice.'[3] Nagy had been a Communist since 1917 and was firmly committed to the building of Socialism under the leadership of the Communist Party. But he believed that once in power the Communist Party must merit that leadership, not maintain it by force, that the dictatorship of the proletariat must

---

[1] George Mikes, *The Hungarian Revolution*, 1957, p. 60.

[2] The latter figure is from Ferenc Váli, *Rift and Revolt in Hungary*, 1961, p. 131.

[3] Váli, op. cit., p. 378.

mean a visible betterment of life for the people. During the period of his 'disgrace' in 1955, Nagy wrote a defense of his program for the Central Committee of the Hungarian Communist Party, which contained his analysis of the Hungarian crisis:

> The violent contrast between words and deeds, between principles and their realization, is rocking the foundations of our people's democracy, our society and our Party. . . . The people cannot understand how it is that the greater the results they achieve in the economic, political, social or cultural field, the greater their burdens become. . . .
>
> . . . Power is increasingly being torn away from the people and turned sharply against them. The People's Democracy as a type of dictatorship of the proletariat . . . is obviously being replaced by a Party dictatorship which does not rely on Party membership, but relies on a personal dictatorship and attempts to make the Party apparatus, and through it the Party membership, a mere tool of this dictatorship. . . .
>
> . . . What sort of political morality is there in a public life where contrary opinions are not only suppressed but punished with actual deprivation of livelihood; where those who express contrary opinions are expelled from society with shameful disregard for the human and civil rights set down in the Constitution . . . ?
> . . . This is not socialist morality. Rather it is modern Machiavellianism.[1]

Nagy's writings, of course, were not made public until after the revolution, since they were meant for the eyes of the Central Committee of the Communist Party. Still, much of Nagy's position was manifested in his attempt to liberalize Hungarian society, which was thwarted by the Rákosi forces who controlled the levers of power: the Party, the Secret Police and the Army. Moreover the US Central Intelligence Agency was in a position to know of developments in Hungary and East Europe. It was a CIA operative who smuggled Khrushchev's attack on Stalin out of the closed

[1] *Imre Nagy on Communism*, 1957, pp. 46, 50, 55–6.

session of the Twentieth Party Congress and made it available in the West some years before it was published in the Soviet Union. Why then did US policy not address itself to fostering these nationalist, liberalizing forces which had manifested themselves in East Europe in the years after the death of Stalin, and prior to the fateful explosions of 1956?

The question is hardly peripheral to these events, since the foreign political situation in which the Soviet bloc found itself was constantly invoked by the different factions to justify their positions. The Rákosi forces, for their part, laid heavy emphasis on the 'war danger' in attacking the Nagy program.[1] According to Nagy himself the purposes of those who 'aimed at the liquidation of democracy and the sharpening of the dictatorship of the proletariat' were strengthened by a tense international atmosphere, while the supporters of greater liberalization were given great impetus by events like the summit of 1955.

It is significant, therefore, that Dulles had 'long and bitterly opposed' Churchill's 1953 proposal for a summit conference because it would have the effect of recognizing the *status quo* in Europe. Dulles had 'always pointed out that photographs of the American and Russian leaders smiling together were sure to be taken. Then these pictures would be distributed throughout the Soviet satellite countries' signifying that 'all hope of liberation was lost and that resistance to Communist rule was henceforth hopeless'.[2]

When he spoke of resistance and liberation, Dulles obviously did not have the kind of evolutionary forces represented by men like Nagy and the imprisoned Polish leader Gomulka in mind, despite the fact that the programs of these men would entail great strides towards the development of more liberal political and economic policies in their countries. This is more than evident in the European policy that Dulles pursued in the two years following the abortive attempt by the new Soviet leadership to liquidate the régime in East Germany.

The German question was, of course, critical for the Soviets and the main thrust of Soviet policy in Europe during the years 1952–1955 was to obtain a settlement which would mean German

[1] Nagy, ibid.
[2] Stewart Alsop, reported in Fleming, p. 750.

neutrality. Such a settlement, along the lines of the Locarno Treaty, was proposed by Churchill in his call for a summit in May 1953. But Dulles, 'following the strategy of the Truman Administration . . . wished to avoid any serious negotiation with the Soviet Union until the West could confront Moscow with German rearmament within an organized European framework, as a *fait accompli*'.[1]

The prospect of a rearmed Germany entering the Nato alliance was not the only factor undermining the position of the de-Stalinizers in East Europe during these years, for 'massive retaliation' was producing crises in the Far East. Indeed, it was during the First tension over the Formosa straits, when it became clear that the US was committed to the defense of the Chinese offshore islands Quemoy and Matsu even if it meant World War III, that Malenkov was removed from power. Nagy, whose main supporter had been Malenkov, was removed shortly afterward.[2] While the removal of these two men cannot be causally related to the intense war atmosphere of the period, neither can it be separated from that atmosphere, since their policies entailed a slackening in defense output and greater tolerance of internal dissent.[3]

A German settlement would have had, of course, an immediate strengthening effect on East European nationalism, and Polish nationalism in particular. A *quid pro quo* reduction of forces as proposed on at least seven occasions by the Russians from 1947 to 1955,[4] a willingness to explore a reasonable German settlement,[5] and the promotion of cultural exchanges and economic trade likewise would have undermined the Stalinist position in East Europe and strengthened the pressures for independence. Yet, these policies were diametrically opposed to those which the US in fact adopted: resistance to all negotiation, refusal to recognize the *status quo* in

[1] W. W. Rostow, *The US in the World Arena*, pp. 344–5.
[2] Váli, op. cit., pp. 96–9, 159 et seq; Mikoyan and Khrushchev also supported Nagy in the June period.
[3] 'The economic program identified with Mr Malenkov had apparently been predicated on a fairly prolonged relaxation of international tension – . . .' – Stebbins, op. cit., p. 195.
[4] Eugene Hinterhoff, 'The Case for Disengagement', *The Correspondent*, November–December 1963.
[5] In October 1954, the Soviet Government expressed readiness to examine Eden's plan for free elections in Germany provided that the Federal German Republic did not join Nato. – Hinterhoff, ibid. On the unreasonableness of the Western position, cf. p. 306 below.

East Europe, avowed intentions to 'liberate' the satellite states and constant propaganda campaigns aimed at the East European countries inciting the peoples' sympathies against the régimes.

One is thus led to the conclusion that the expectation of eventual Soviet collapse with the attendant prospect of revolution in East Europe dissuaded the American leadership from attempting to strengthen those evolutionary forces of liberalization and independence which were present. Another factor which may have influenced this failure was the nature of the intelligence forces on which the United States depended for information.

The principal source of East European intelligence information for the United States was the Gehlen organization,[1] formed and directed by Reinhold Gehlen, and financed by the CIA.[2] Gehlen, a member of the *Reichswehr* since 1920, was appointed chief of the German Army's intelligence section on the Russian Front in 1942, where he rose to the rank of Lieutenant General at the age of forty-three.

After the war, General Gehlen was captured by the Americans and given autonomous command of his own 'army' of private agents, with a personally chosen German staff to organize cold war espionage in the Soviet Zone (of Germany) for the United States. Gehlen was given $6 million annually by the US to finance his operations. His organization included the élite of the old German Army's counter-intelligence corps, and agents of diverse nationalities scattered through Eastern Europe and the Balkans. 'On [Gehlen's] secret reports which evaluate the findings of the costly anti-Soviet espionage program operating as far beyond the Iron Curtain as Siberia, much of American defense planning admittedly depends today [1953].'[3]

The fact that an organization like Gehlen's was the major intelligence source for the CIA certainly serves to explain some of the failure of US 'liberation' policy to adjust itself to the realities of the East European situation in the period 1953–6; it also begins to

[1] New York *Times*, July 20, 1955: 'the mainstream of East European information received by the US–CIA, originates with the Gehlen organization.' – cited in *The Nation*, June 24, 1961.

[2] This account is taken from Fred J. Cook, "The CIA' in *The Nation*, June 24, 1961. Cook's article is a compilation of previously published accounts.

[3] Daniel De Luce for the Associated Press, cited in Cook. The De Luce article appeared in the fall of 1953.

explain the tragic role played by that policy during the events of October.

In October 1956, a bloodless revolution in Poland brought Wladyslaw Gomulka to power. With the Polish nation behind him, Gomulka was able to defy the Soviet Presidium which (with the exception of Molotov and Zhukov) had flown to Warsaw on October 19 and reportedly threatened armed intervention. Gomulka 'won' and was able to preserve his revolution because he had popular support and the Soviet chiefs could count on Polish fear of Germany to keep Poland loyal to the Russian alliance.

Appraising the situation with a soon to be vindicated foresight, Walter Lippmann wrote that the United States could not afford to forget that 'no Russian Government will tolerate, if it can prevent it, the existence of an unfriendly Poland which had become a part of the military system of the West'. Unless the Polish crisis could be stabilized, warned Lippmann, a far-reaching crisis would ensue for there would be 'no power and authority – be it Soviet, Western or local to organize Central Europe'. The relaxation of the fear of a World War was loosening the Soviet grip, but it was 'not in our own interest that the movement in Eastern Europe should go so far that no accommodation with Russia is possible, [for] that could lead to bloody deeds in which we would be called upon to intervene, our honor being involved, though we could not intervene knowing that the risks were incalculable'.[1]

On October 21–23, demonstrations occurred in Hungary motivated by the same nationalist and democratic desires that had rocked Poland.[2] But in Hungary the demands were met with hostility by the Stalinist leadership (in the person of Ernö Gerö) and the crowds were fired upon, thus triggering the revolution. In the emergency which ensued, Gerö appointed Nagy premier, and without consulting Moscow, called in Soviet troops to put down the people. Suslov and Mikoyan (the latter furious that Soviet troops had been called in) arrived, removed Gerö and agreed to withdraw the Soviet forces when order had been restored.

---

[1] Cited in Fleming, p. 793.

[2] From the first, however, the revolutionary fervor in Hungary was more intense because of the greater suffering of the Hungarians under the vicious Rákosi régime. For some insight into this suffering, cf. George Mikes, *A Study in Infamy*, André Deutsch, London, 1959.

It is against this background that US 'liberation' policy as manifested in broadcasts to Hungary by Western propaganda stations must be assessed. Leslie B. Bain, a Hungarian-speaking reporter who was in Budapest during the revolution and listened to the broadcasts, recorded 'that Radio Free Europe and to some extent the Voice of America greatly embarrassed the Nagy revolutionary government with their broadcasts by insisting on goals which by no stretch of the imagination that government could have reached'.[1]

Tibor Méray, in his eye-witness account, has described the effect of these broadcasts in even more damning terms. On October 24 Nagy broadcast a speech calling for 'Order, calm, discipline', but 'It was from this moment on that a vehement radio campaign was launched from abroad against Nagy – a campaign that had a fatal effect on all that followed.'[2] On October 29, the military expert of Radio Free Europe said of the cease-fire order of the Nagy Government:

> Imre Nagy and his supporters want to revise and modernize the Trojan horse episode. They need a cease-fire so that the present Government in power in Budapest can maintain its position as long as possible. Those who are fighting for liberty must not lose sight even for a minute of the plans of the government opposing them. Otherwise there will be a repetition of the Trojan horse tragedy.

On the 31st, Radio Free Europe proclaimed: 'The Ministry of Defense and the Ministry of the Interior are still in Communist hands. Do not let this continue, Freedom Fighters. Do not hang your weapons on the wall. Not a lump of coal, not a drop of gasoline for the Budapest Government, until Interior and Defense are in your control.'[3]

On October 29, it had been announced that the Soviet troops would withdraw from Budapest and appeals were made to the rebels to cease fire, because they had won. But the revolution

---

[1] Leslie B. Bain, 'Have We Failed in Hungary?', The *Reporter*, January 24, 1957, cited in Fleming.

[2] Tibor Méray, *Thirteen Days that Shook the Kremlin*, 1959, p. 98, cited in Fleming.

[3] ibid.

continued and a general strike began in Györ, its leaders declaring that it would end only when the last Russian soldier left Hungary.

> . . . It was Nagy's dilemma that to keep his position he had to have the confidence of the Russians and at the same time show hostility toward them.
>
> Moving with the tide, Nagy broadened his Cabinet to include some representatives of the old political parties, . . . He abolished the one-party system and announced that free elections would follow.[1]

This was October 30, 1:28 P.M. Three hours later, an Anglo-French ultimatum was delivered to Israel and Egypt, as a pretext for armed intervention to reoccupy the Suez Canal.[2] In the context of these events, the Soviets reversed themselves. An influx of new Russian troops began, and Mikoyan arrived in Budapest again, this time to overthrow Nagy and set up a puppet régime under János Kádár.

> Early on the morning of November 4 Russian artillery opened fire on Budapest and Soviet tanks roared into the city and filled the streets with rubble again. . . .
>
> These troops acted with a savagery that surpassed the outrages of 1945, often firing on breadlines and razing a building from which a single shot had come. Looting and raping were frequent. . . .[3]

When order was restored, 7,000 Russian soldiers and 30,000 Hungarian citizens were dead, and Hungary was an occupied country. As Isaac Deutscher has written, in despite of their own interests, and of their having given up many of Stalin's methods,

---

[1] Fleming, p. 800.

[2] There has been a great deal of speculation about the influence of this particular event on the Hungarian tragedy. It has been noted, for example, that Western and particularly US attention was diverted from Hungary at the crucial moment. But the CIA knew of the Suez invasion well in advance and specifically warned the White House twenty-four hours before-hand that Israelis would attack Egypt and that the English and Israelis would invade Suez. (Cook, p. 553.) No steps were taken, however, to stop the English or the French from taking this action.

[3] Fleming, p. 803.

the de-Stalinizers had now 'burdened themselves with a moral and political liability far worse than any bequeathed to them by Stalin.'[1]

The Soviet contention that the 'bloody events in Budapest' were 'instigated by the provocational actions of . . . Fascist–Horthyist bands' and that 'the Hungarian events had been carefully prepared by reaction for a long time'[2] is belied by the November 1 radio address of János Kádár, First Secretary of the Communist Party and Soviet appointed successor to Imre Nagy.[3]

Hungarian workers, peasants and intellectuals:

> We can safely say that the ideological and organizational leaders who prepared this uprising were recruited from among your ranks. Hungarian Communist writers, journalists, university students, the youth of the Petöfi Circle, thousands and thousands of workers and peasants, and veteran fighters who had been imprisoned on false charges fought in the front line against the Rákosiite despotism and political hooliganism. We are proud that you, permeated by true patriotism and loyalty to socialism honestly stood your ground in the armed uprising and led it.[3]

The same assessment was offered by Tito, despite his extenuation in behalf of the intervention:

> . . . It should be borne in mind that the Soviet Union, too, is now in a very difficult situation. Their eyes have now been opened and they realize that not only are the Horthyites fighting but also workers in factories and mines, that the whole nation is fighting.[5]

---

[1] Isaac Deutscher, 'October Revolution, New Style', The *Reporter*, November 15, 1956.

[2] Paul E. Zinner, *National Communism and Popular Revolt in Eastern Europe*. A selection of documents; 1956, pp. 546–6; *Pravda*, November 23.

[3] On June 16, 1958, a communiqué broadcast in Moscow announced that 'Hungarian legal authorities concluded the proceedings in the case of the leading group of those persons who on October 23, 1956, started a counter-revolutionary armed uprising.' Among those sentenced to death were Imre Nagy. The broadcast further announced that 'the death sentences have been carried out'. Thus did this extraordinary man pass from the Hungarian scene. The trial and executions were announced after the fact to minimize the political ramifications and also because there was no legal basis for the charges. cf. Váli, op. cit., pp. 443–7.

[4] Paul E. Zinner, p. 465.   [5] ibid., p. 529.

Through all this the United States stood by, failing to exercise any of the initiatives which were open to it. These ranged from a show of force to the use of diplomacy:

> . . . The astonishing Russian announcement of October 30 promising a revision of Russia's relations with her satellites and a transformation of the Warsaw Pact, was greeted by Washington with satisfaction; . . . But. . . . There were no American counterproposals. . . . Washington . . . showed some but not sufficient understanding of Russia's strategic interests and obsession about her Eastern European satellite buffer zone; and they showed no willingness at all to turn the great occasion toward mutual accommodations with Russia in Europe. Nor was this occasion limited to the twenty-four hours between the 30 October Moscow announcement and the 31 October Politburo session. As late as 17 November a significant Russian note still suggested the possible revision of the Warsaw Pact and a willingness to explore European divisions anew. The American government was obviously and sincerely affected by the specter of the brutal second Russian intervention in Hungary, but it preferred to demonstrate its sentiments in indignant rhetoric.[1]

It was only seven years later that US policy began to act effectively in behalf of the Hungarian people. A secret deal between the Kennedy Government and the Kádar régime exchanged the release of political prisoners for the abolition of the post of special UN representative on Hungary, and the gradual development of normal relations.[2] In 1963 Lajos Lederer reported:

> The development of liberalization in the past year has been uninterrupted and impressive. Mr Kádar's political line has brought about a relaxation, which can be compared in Eastern Europe only with that in Poland. The ideas that sustained the October revolt of 1956 and were at the time rejected by Mr Kádar are now being implemented by the same man.[3]

[1] Lukacs, op. cit., pp. 134–5.
[2] London *Observer*, December 19, 1962; the New York *Times*, March 29, 1963.
[3] London *Observer*, February 24, 1963.

II. Agonizing Reappraisals

... I believe ... that the strategical conception and plan which Mr X recommends is fundamentally unsound, and that it cannot be made to work, and that the attempt to make it work will cause us to squander our substance and our prestige.

WALTER LIPPMANN, 1947

For twelve years the United States, under administrations of both political parties, has followed a policy of cold war. This policy has carried us time and again to the edge of disaster ...

Communism has not been contained. Democracy has not been extended. A position of strength has not been achieved ...

We are unwilling to remain, along with the Russians and the Chinese, captives of cold war ...

Therefore, we urge that the Government and the people of the United States, through every possible means, enter into a discussion and reconsideration of our entire foreign policy.

ELEANOR ROOSEVELT and 43 others, 1958

CHAPTER XVII

Lippmann, Kennan and Sputnik

IN the fall of 1957, after ten years of open cold war climaxed by the launching of the Soviet Sputnik, George Kennan gave the BBC's annual Reith lectures, and in doing so, created a stir in the councils of Europe. The storm aroused by Kennan's lectures stemmed in part from their having been given on the eve of a crucial meeting of the Nato powers,[1] in which the future course of the Nato alliance was at issue, and in part by what he had to say about that future. For the man who had formulated the policy of containment now reassessed the cold war in Europe and proposed a new policy to deal with it. In brief, Kennan's analysis led him to the conclusion that the achievement of Western goals demanded not more Nato strength, but on the contrary military disengagement.

As Kennan saw it, the problem of the satellite countries and East Germany had been, and remained still, the only basic issue of 'genuine gravity between Russia and the West'. The ill-starred Hungarian revolution had shown that the presence of Western military strength could not advance the liberation of this area, and indeed, that increased Western strength could only be interpreted by the Soviets as a military threat, leading them in their own security interests to tighten the reins on the satellites, which they had shown a clear and discernible interest in slackening.

'I can conceive of no escape from this dilemma,' Kennan said, 'that would not involve the early departure of Soviet troops from the satellite countries. Recent events have made it perfectly clear that it is the presence of these troops, coupled with the general military and political situation in Europe, which lies at the heart of the difficulty. Only when the troops are gone will there be possibilities for

---

[1] Sputnik was launched October 4, 1957. Kennan's talks were given in the period November 14–December 19, 1957, and the Nato conference began on December 16, 1957. Kennan's lectures have been published under the title: *Russia, the Atom and the West*, 1958.

the evolution of these nations toward institutions and social systems most suited to their needs; . . . [but] it is plain that there can be no Soviet military withdrawal from Eastern Europe unless this entire area can in some way be removed as an object in the military rivalry of the Great Powers.'[1]

Since a greater show of force would fail to effect the removal of Soviet troops and would thus postpone, further, the realization of the avowed aim of Western cold war policy, Kennan concluded that the problem of Eastern Europe could only be solved by a *negotiated* settlement of the German problem. 'It involves the German problem not only because it implies the withdrawal of Soviet forces from Eastern Germany, but so long as American and other Western forces remain in Western Germany it will be impossible for the Russians to view their problem in Eastern Europe otherwise than in direct relation to the overall military equation between Russia and the West . . .'[2]

Thus, after a decade of cold war, Kennan had arrived at Walter Lippmann's position of ten years before. Lippmann's 1947 analysis was premised, it will be remembered, on the same appraisal of the general problem: 'the immediate and the decisive problem of our relations with the Soviet Union is whether, when, on what conditions the Red Army can be prevailed upon to evacuate Europe.'[3]

This evacuation could be accomplished, Lippman had argued, only if peace treaties could be signed with Germany and Austria. 'For the peace treaties about eastern Europe, which is between Germany and Russia, cannot become effective until there are German and Austrian treaties.' Lippmann had foreseen in 1947, moreover, that containment would not only not solve the problem of divided Europe, but instead would greatly complicate it:

In its approach to the German problem which is crucial in a world settlement, we come upon the most dangerous and destructive consequences of what Mr X calls a policy of firm containment and what the world knows as the Truman Doctrine . . .

For the policy of containment envisages the western zones of Germany as an essential part of the 'unassailable barriers' which Mr X tells us we should erect in the path of the Soviet Union.[4]

[1] Kennan, op. cit., p. 37.   [2] ibid.
[3] Lippmann, *The Cold War*, p. 26.   [4] Lippmann, op. cit., p. 35.

Thus, the chief problem which Kennan's 1957 policy of disengagement had to face, the problem of neutralizing a now rearmed Germany, was a problem *created* by the very policy of containment which he had formulated in 1947, when a rearmed Germany was not yet in prospect.

To have taken the course Lippmann proposed then, to have set forth the aim of American policy as the withdrawal of all foreign forces from Europe, as 'not a Germany to contain Russia but a Germany neutralized as between Russia and the West', would have been sound politically and militarily, even had a settlement, at that time, been impossible. For as Lippmann argued, it would have identified the United States with a policy which opposed the revival of German power to threaten her neighbors, instead of with a policy which placed the European nations in a 'German–Russian nutcracker', compelling them to choose sides for a Third World War, and turning 'their territory into a battlefield of that world war'.

If, nevertheless, it turned out that the Soviet Government would not negotiate such an agreement, if the price of a settlement were impossibly high, if the ransom were deliberately set in terms which would have meant that Russia did not intend to evacuate Europe, then the situation would have been 'no more dangerous than it is today'.[1]

Now, ten years later, the situation was, in fact, a great deal more dangerous because of the presence of a rearmed Germany, despite the fact that within the Soviet Union there had been serious and far-reaching internal reforms and the Soviet leaders had repeatedly expressed a willingness to consider precisely the kind of settlement that Lippmann had envisaged. Indeed, half of Lippmann's 1947 prescription had already been fulfilled in the Austrian peace treaty which exchanged the withdrawal of Soviet forces for the pledge of Austrian neutrality. One can only conclude, therefore, that responsibility for the increased danger in 1957 rested squarely on the American leadership and its strategic conceptions based on the policy of containment:

Ten years ago our government said that it would never acquiesce in German rearmament. In 1950 our government demanded

[1] Lippmann, op. cit., p. 39.

German troops for Nato but said that it would never allow
Germany to rebuild its own war industries. In 1959 our government has agreed to give Germany everything except nuclear
warheads, and has permitted our war industries to go into partnership with Krupp, Kloechner, Heinckel, and Messerschmidt
in re-creating German capacity to build almost every kind of
war equipment.

If we are serious and sincere in wishing to halt the arms race
and to reach a European settlement, the least we can do is to call
a halt in rearming Germany while we negotiate.[1]

Although in his 1957 lectures Kennan skirted this question of
United States responsibility, he did register his criticism of the
proposals, then under consideration, to strengthen the Nato forces
with atomic weapons and missiles. 'The Soviet reluctance to withdraw from Eastern Germany and to give full freedom to the Eastern
European peoples is based partly on political considerations that
would not be in any way affected by a stronger Nato, *and partly on
the existence of precisely that Anglo-American military position on the
Continent, which it is now proposed that we should reinforce.*'[2] [Empha-
sis added.]

Thus Kennan recognized that the military alliance was an obstacle
to the settlement of those political questions which divided Europe
and prevented the European nations from achieving full independence. Seeking to relieve himself of some of the onus for what he
had earlier called the 'over-militarization' of American thinking
about the cold war, he said:

I certainly had no idea at that time [1947] that the military
instrument we were creating was to be the major vehicle of
Western policy in the coming years.[3]

The Nato alliance was to have been just a shield,

And behind this shield, I supposed, we would go ahead confi-
dently to meet the Communist danger in its most threatening

---

[1] James P. Warburg in *The Liberal Papers*, 1959, James Roosevelt, Ed., p. 70.
[2] Kennan, op. cit., p. 90.
[3] ibid., p. 92.

form – as an internal problem, that is, of Western society, to be combated by reviving economic activity, by restoring the self-confidence of the European peoples, and by helping them to find positive goals for the future.[1]

Nato had a role to play, 'but I think everyone of us hoped that its purely military role would decline in importance as the curse of bipolarity fell from the Continent, as negotiations took place, as armies were withdrawn, as the contest of ideologies took other forms'.[2]

Kennan was forgetting, however, that his root premise in 1947[3] had been that a settlement of the issues was impossible, that there could be no fruitful negotiations with the Soviet Union and that the task of American foreign policy was to place 'unassailable barriers' (a military metaphor) in the path of Soviet power. How, then, was the curse of bipolarity to fall from the Continent, how were the armies to be withdrawn, and how could the contest of ideologies take other forms?

Indeed Kennan's view of the Soviet administrative apparatus had been deeply despairing in tone and outlook:

> The accumulative effect of these factors is to give to the whole subordinate apparatus of Soviet power an unshakeable stubbornness and steadfastness in its orientation. This orientation can be changed at will by the Kremlin but by no other power. Once a given party line has been laid down on a given issue of current policy, the whole Soviet governmental machine, including the mechanism of diplomacy, moves inexorably along the prescribed path, like a persistent toy automobile wound up and headed in a given direction, stopping only when it meets with some unanswerable force.[4]

Kennan in 1947 had found the Soviets prisoners of their own dogmatic practices. But, now, ten years later, the extent to which the American leadership was bound by its own dogmas associated

[1] ibid., pp. 92–3.
[2] Kennan, op. cit., p. 94.
[3] Lippmann, op. cit., p. 46.
[4] Kennan, *American Diplomacy*, p. 97.

with containment, after Kennan himself had 'repudiated' at least the evolved conception of that doctrine, was certainly a supreme irony.

Containment, i.e. the encirclement by military, political and economic bastions of the largest land mass on the face of the earth, had been premised on the assumption of the imminent decay of Soviet power. This image of an unstable Communist Russia was amenable to the new military metaphysic which had become predominant within the political directorate during the post-war years.[1] Strengthened by the conceptions of Manichean McCarthyism, this view envisioned the outcome of the developing world struggle in military terms of victory and defeat, as though the characters of the nations involved were static, and, indeed as though they were sufficiently defined by the very fact of their enmity itself. The world strategy of the American leadership geared the nation for an all-or-nothing, either/or struggle which not only encouraged the quest for quick, absolute solutions, but ironically fostered the strengthening of the very forces it sought to defeat.

In his 'X' article on the sources of Soviet conduct, Kennan had drawn attention to the 'tremendous emphasis' that the Bolshevik rulers placed on the 'original Communist thesis of a basic antagonism between the capitalist and socialist world'. It was 'clear', according to Kennan, that this emphasis was 'not found in reality'.[2] The idea of capitalist encirclement he regarded as a fiction, fostered by Soviet leaders to 'explain away the maintenance of dictatorial authority at home'. Noting that the potential opposition to the Soviet régime in 1945–6 was 'far greater and more dangerous than it could have been before [the] excesses began', Kennan concluded that, '*least of all can the rulers dispense with the fiction by which the maintenence of dictatorial power has been defended*'. [Emphasis added.]

Now it is not too difficult to reconstruct what happened in the post-war years in Russia on the basis of Kennan's analysis.[3] The declared hostility of the capitalist nations (most notably in Churchill's Fulton speech and the Truman Doctrine) combined with

[1] cf. Mills, *The Power Elite*, Chapters 9 and 12.
[2] cf. Wm. A. Williams, *American–Russian Relations*, pp. 281 et seq., for a critique of Kennan's thinking on this point.
[3] cf. Wm. A. Williams, 'The Irony of Containment', *The Nation*, May 5, 1956.

the presence of American bases around the perimeter of the Soviet Union, and the proposed resurrection of German military power, served to underwrite the intensification of Stalinist methods and plans for an exhausted but deeply nationalist population that had just defended its homeland against a foreign invasion on what was perhaps the largest scale in history. This second forced march of the Russian people from their status as a fourth or fifth[1] among the industrial powers to nuclear parity with the United States could only have been accomplished under the shadow of the constant threat of nuclear blitz and in the belief that salvation lay solely in the achievement of deterrent atomic power. Indeed, Molotov in 1956 remarked that no one in the Kremlin ever dreamed as of 1945–6 that Russia's position could be so strong as it was ten years later.[2] And it can hardly be doubted that the Soviet leadership's deliberate exacerbation of the early cold war conflict (the formation of the Cominform, the stormy exit from the Marshall Plan negotiations, etc.) stemmed in part from the exigencies of the rapid reconstruction under Stalinist modes and methods of industrial development.

'The harder the Soviet Union is pressed,' Chester Bowles said, at the end of the period, 'the more vigorously her people will rally behind their leaders.' Nothing set the stage for American 'defeat' in the Sputnik year 1957 as much as American policy decisions and pronouncements made ten years earlier. American leaders had defined the struggle, and defined it in such a way that the United States could only come face to face with frustration and defeat.

The launching of Sputnik was not only a blow to the specific analyses and expectations of containment, but it also struck at the very heart of that peculiarly American conception of history, the hegemony of the American Way in the modern world. In 1941, Henry Luce had announced in a *Life* editorial, the coming of 'The American Century'. It was time, he said, 'to accept whole-heartedly our duty and our opportunity as the most powerful and vital nation in the world and in consequence to exert upon the world the full impact of our influence, for such purposes as we see fit and by such means as we see fit'.[3]

---

[1] Isaac Deutscher, *Heretics and Renegades*, p. 115.

[2] Williams, 'The Irony of Containment', *The Nation*, May 5, 1956.

[3] Cited in Williams, 'The American Century: 1941–57' *The Nation*, November 2, 1957, pp. 297–301. *Life*, February 17, 1941.

And Secretary of State Byrnes, in similar fashion, confided to General H. H. Arnold at Potsdam in 1945, 'What we must do now is not to make the world safe for democracy, but make the world safe for the United States.'[1] As for the President:

> Soon after he took office, Truman made it clear that he intended to reform the world on American terms. He casually told one early visitor 'that the Russians would soon be put in their places; and that the United States would then take the lead in running the world in the way that the world ought to be run . . .'[2]

These expectations were frustrated by forces which found their symbolic expression in Sputnik. As Lyndon Johnson put it: 'We have got to admit frankly that the Soviets have beaten us at our own game – daring, scientific advances in the atomic age.'[3]

The main, irreducible meaning of the Sputnik, however, was the fact, from which there could no longer be any retreat, that the Soviet Union was a viable, competing social system, with an advanced technological base. Recognition of this reality caused a weakening of American confidence, and initiated the first steps of an agonizing reappraisal of the assumptions and the direction of American policies.

The 'Sputnik crisis' as William A. Williams observed, was not caused by a laxness in the American weapons program, for the crisis had developed and matured during a period when Americans enjoyed a significant weapons advantage. 'The crucial factor was the way Americans interpreted this as an *absolute* superiority, and the manner in which they sought to use their supposed supremacy.'

Thomas J. Hamilton of the *Times* provided a concise summary of the thinking that guided American policy-makers during those years: in 1946, he recalled, 'and in fact, until 1949, the United States . . . had the means of forcing the Soviet Union to its knees with a preventive war'. Secretaries of State Acheson and Dulles translated that assumption into a bipartisan program of 'total diplomacy' designed to win the victory without war. But

[1] H. H. Arnold, *Global Mission*, 1949, p. 589.
[2] Williams, *The Tragedy of American Diplomacy*, p. 168.
[3] Fleming, p. 885.

the improvement in the power position of the Soviet Union destroyed the logic of Acheson's old argument that America could not negotiate until it established 'positions of strength'. By now it is apparent that America, assuming that it enjoyed a position of strength in the absolute sense, refused to negotiate during the years when it did hold a relative advantage . . . *The assumption that the United States has the power to force the Soviet Union to capitulate to American terms is the fundamental weakness in America's conception of itself and the world.*[1] [Emphasis in original.]

The seeds of decay which Kennan had seen in the USSR in 1947 were not only sprouting, but they no longer showed evidence of existing at all. The whole basis on which the American cold war was set had been eliminated in one dramatic thrust. For the launching of the Sputniks eliminated the *possibility* of victory in the terms that victory had been understood in America: the break-up of Soviet power, the unchallenged supremacy of the American leadership, the triumph of the American Way.

It is no accident, therefore, that Kennan's 1957 Reith lectures began with an analysis of Soviet power and economic growth and found both to be formidable and healthy. That the visible growth of internal soviet power (and not, for example, the 'mellowing' attitudes of Soviet leaders) played the key role in the reappraisal of United States policies is confirmed by Sherman Adams, special assistant to President Eisenhower:

At the time that the hard line policy was fashioned and put to work, little was said against it. The evaluation of a foreign policy is essentially a pragmatic process. If it works, it is fine. If it fails, it is bankrupt, no matter how well it may have been conceived originally. If Russia and China had weakened internally under the pressure of Dulles' antagonism, there would have been no criticism of his tactics. But while he was trying to put a hammer-lock on the Communists, they continued to show economic progress.[2]

[1] Wm. A. Williams, 'The American Century: 1941–1957', *The Nation*, November 2, 1957, pp. 297–301.
[2] Sherman Adams, op. cit., pp. 88–9.

With the Soviet Union exhibiting all the signs of a stable system, the acceptance of coexistence became little more than realism in foreign affairs. But the difference between *peaceful* coexistence and mere nuclear stalemate was a real one and not to be glossed over. There were dangerous outstanding tensions, the leftovers of an outmoded epoch still to be eliminated. To live with the Soviet Union meant first to take up the diplomatic tasks which had been abandoned twelve years before.

The means by which diplomacy deals with a world in which there are rival powers, Lippman reminded Americans in 1947, is to organize a balance of power to deprive the rivals of a good prospect of successful aggression. This is what a diplomat means by the settlement of a conflict among rival powers. 'He means that whatever they think, whatever they want, whatever their ideological purposes, the balance of power is such that they cannot afford to commit aggression.'[1]

A policy of settlement in the conflict between the United States and Russia, he pointed out, 'would aim to redress the balance of power, which is abnormal and dangerous because the Red Army has met the British and American armies in the heart of Europe. . . A genuine policy would, therefore, have as its paramount objective a settlement which brought about the evacuation of Europe. That is the settlement which will settle the issue which has arisen out of the war'. The Communists would continue to be Communists. The Russians would continue to be Russians. 'But if the Red Army is in Russia, and not on the Elbe, the power of the Russian Communists and the power of the Russian imperialists to realize their ambitions will have been reduced decisively.' Therefore, American power must be exerted 'in support of a diplomatic policy which has as its concrete objective a settlement that means withdrawal'.[2]

[1] Lippmann, op. cit., p. 47.
[2] Lippmann, op. cit., pp. 47–48.

CHAPTER XVIII

Dogmas and Disengagement

DIPLOMACY had not been entirely eclipsed by cold war containment on the Continent. Its presence, however, was fitful. On May 15, 1955, Dulles, Molotov, Macmillan, Pinay (for France) and Figl (for Austria), signed a peace treaty which restored Austrian sovereignty, and provided for the withdrawal of occupation troops, in return for a guarantee that Austria 'will not join any military alliances or permit military bases on her territory'. The way to this agreement had been effectively paved by the signing of a truce in Korea and by the Geneva Agreement on Indo-China, in a word, by the growing restoration of diplomacy to its proper place and function.

A similar settlement for Germany, offered by the Soviets, however, was rejected by the Western Allies. Eisenhower had responded initially to the Austrian settlement with cautious optimism about the future, but Chancellor Adenauer, was deeply shocked by the President's acceptance of the idea of 'a series of neutralized states from north to south through Europe'.[1] Adenauer argued that the Soviets were weak and could be made to accept more stringent Western demands, and his views prevailed. On May 18, the New York *Times* reported that 'many essential points in the Allies' brief in the [preliminary] Geneva Conference were contributed by Dr Adenauer and adopted at his insistence'. And on July 19, the *Times* noted that 'The Chancellor's theory about the Soviet Union's internal weakness was accepted in Washington and explains some of the recent statements by United States officials.'[2]

On July 18, at the summit meeting, Eisenhower explained the United States position on the German question:

Ten years have passed since the German armistice, and Germany is still divided. That division does a grievous wrong to a people ...

[1] Cited in Fleming, p. 745.
[2] Cited in Fleming, p. 749.

it creates a basic source of instability in Europe. Our talk of peace has little meaning if at the same time we perpetuate conditions endangering the peace . . . . In the interest of enduring peace, our solution should take account of the legitimate security interests of all concerned. That is why we insist a united Germany is entitled at its choice, to exercise its inherent right of collective self-defense.[1]

In other words, a 'just' solution of the problem of Germany must leave a united Germany free to join Nato. But such a solution would have meant complete Soviet capitulation on the German question and would have required no negotiation at all, since the Soviets could achieve Eisenhower's 'settlement' simply by withdrawing their troops. This was recognized by Kennan in 1957:

> . . . The Western governments have insisted that such an all-German government must be entirely free to continue to adhere to the Nato Pact. . . . The Soviet Union is, of course, not a member of Nato; and while British, French, and American forces would presumably remain in Germany under the frameowrk of the Nato system, one must assume that those of the Soviet Union would be expected to depart. If this is so, then Moscow is really being asked to abandon – as part of an agreement on German unification – the military and political bastion in Central Europe which it won by its military effort from 1941 to 1945, and to do this without any compensatory withdrawal of American armed power from the heart of the continent. . . .
>
> Now this, in my opinion, is something the Soviet Government is most unlikely to accept, if only for reasons of what it will regard as its own political security at home and abroad. . . . *The Soviet leaders will therefore see in these present Western proposals a demand for something in the nature of an unconditional capitulation of the Soviet interest in the German question generally;* and it will surely occur to them that if they ever should be so weak as to have no choice but to quit Germany on these terms, it would scarcely take an agreement with the Western Powers to enable them to do so.[2] [Emphasis added.]

[1] Eisenhower, *Peace With Justice*, pp. 124–5.
[2] Kennan, *Russia, the Atom, and the West*, pp. 38–40.

A 'just' solution that is not workable, of course, is no solution at all, and, therefore, can only serve to perpetuate the very injustice it was intended to correct. But in a world in which the forces are not static, the failure to settle a problem like that of divided Germany not only tended to prolong the dangerous and unjust situation, but to deepen the division itself.

On October 23, 1954, a Soviet note to the West had proposed a November conference on Germany and European security. A note of November 13, addressed to twenty-three European governments and the United States, urged such a conference in Moscow or Paris on November 29. When these overtures were rejected, Moscow convened a conference of Premiers and Foreign Ministers of the Soviet bloc in late November to consider countermeasures against the Paris Pacts, which in October had prepared Germany's entry into Nato.[1]

On May 6, 1955, three weeks after the Austrian accord, but before its actual signing, the Nato Conference in Paris ushered West Germany into the Alliance. Eight days later, the Warsaw Pact was signed setting up a counteralliance, with Marshal Ivan S. Konev as Chief of the unified command.[2] The subsequent summit meeting in July failed to alter this situation.

Thus, the compelling logic of the containment thesis and its prescription to build barriers instead of seeking settlements caused the United States not only to reject Soviet overtures but to fail to make any genuine offers of its own. Moreover, it spurred the United States in its effort to build up German military strength, thus creating a new factor in the existing power situation, which would inevitably make eventual settlement of the European question even more difficult.

Ironically, this effort to build up German military strength came after the ostensible goal of containment had been realized, i.e. the 'mellowing' of Soviet power. For after Stalin's death a rapid (though very incomplete) process of de-Stalinization had taken place within Soviet society, and the policy of peaceful coexistence had emerged as official foreign policy. To be sure, the Soviet version of coexistence was not unreservedly peaceful, but as Senator William

---

[1] Schuman, *Russia Since 1917*, p. 436.
[2] ibid.

Fulbright reminded the Senate on June 20, 1958, Russian policy was 'not only what happened in Hungary'.

> If it were only a question of a policy of military oppression, we would have, in my opinion, a much more easily defeated adversary. But Russian policy is also the military withdrawal from Finland; it is the Soviet signature of the Austrian Peace Treaty and subsequent military withdrawal from the country; it is also Russian acquiescence in the recent modifications in Polish communism; it is political support of the non-communist nationalist movements in Asia and Africa and economic aid to the countries of these regions. It is, most of all, an almost continuous propaganda refrain calling for action to reduce the danger of nuclear warfare, coupled with proposals for a great variety of approaches to this fundamental international problem.

In view of this, Fulbright found deplorable the fact that administratively the United States was 'organized to brand Soviet proposals as propaganda within the hour', but not 'to explore the feasibility of new proposals or to analyze old proposals in light of the power orientation of recent years which may give them new meaning'. Are we destined, Fulbright asked, 'to see the gradual sinking of the prestige of this nation, the steady dimming of its message to mankind because we go round and round in the same policies, because we have not the flexibility, the imagination, or the national determination to break this inertia, move out of this orbit into new directions ?'[1]

The 'mellowing of Soviet power' did not liberate American strategy from the sterile orbit of containment, because it had not mellowed in the manner in which containment had predicted (i.e. out of weakness) and thus had not 'mellowed' at all. The United States had looked to unilateral surrender by the Soviet of its positions, not to bargaining with a vigorous, tough, often intransigent, but often flexible opponent.

Perhaps no incident suggests so vividly the extent to which the United States was trapped in its own cold war dogmas, as its response to the pressures for disengagement, at the time of Kennan's Reith lectures and the Nato meeting of December 1957. This was

[1] Fleming, pp. 941–2.

two years after the Austrian treaty and after the first suggestions for a denuclearized zone had been put forth by Sir Anthony Eden, then Prime Minister of Great Britain. It was also a year after the Polish Foreign Minister Adam Rapacki had formally proposed a plan for the denuclearization of Central Europe, and a year after the tragic events in Hungary had shown the impotence of Nato in promoting the 'liberation' of the Eastern nations. Indeed, the fact that it was the *Polish* Foreign Minister making the proposal, in the wake of the Polish revolution, was indication enough that disengagement would promote a further independence of Eastern Europe and hence the eventual realization of avowed United States cold war aims.

The Soviets, moreover, had achieved capability in the field of Intercontinental Ballistic Missiles in early 1957.[1] With the development of the ICBM, the 'deterrent' value of the Red Army ceased to be crucial or even important. Hence, there was no military obstacle to negotiated withdrawal on the Soviet side, as there might have been earlier.[2] The time seemed ripe, from all angles, for opening negotiations.

On November 2, 1957, the Russians sent their second Sputnik hurtling into the sky, and three days later, Secretary of State Dulles 'hinted' that the United States would seek to equip its system of overseas bases with intermediate-range missiles.[3] The next day Premier Khrushchev addressed the Supreme Soviet and called for a new meeting 'to reach an agreement based on the consideration of true and mutual understanding' about stopping 'the cold war and the armaments race', and settling ideological disputes by peaceful competition 'in the best satisfaction of human requirements and needs'. In Washington, the United States responded 'with chilly

[1] On August 30, US Defense Dept. officials revealed that four Soviet ICBMs had been detected, and 'probably six' – the last one in June. The Soviets announced a successful test on August 27. Fleming, p. 863.

[2] This does not mean that Lippmann's proposal for a settlement meaning withdrawal was unrealistic in the early cold war period. On the contrary. Together with the subsequent withdrawals and reductions of Soviet forces, it strengthens the view that Soviet penetration of East Europe was precipitated by defensive rather than revolutionary or expansionist considerations. Had Lippmann's prescription been followed early enough and had the US been prepared to play a major economic role in Soviet reconstruction, there is no readily apparent reason why a withdrawal could not have been negotiated.

[3] Fleming, p. 893.

disinterest, though careful not to reject the proposal openly and out of hand'.[1]

On December 11, Lester Pearson, former Minister of External Affairs of Canada received the Nobel Peace Prize in Oslo. In his acceptance speech he said that war used as an instrument of policy would lead to 'total war' and that total war would mean 'total destruction'. Therefore, 'the best defense of peace is not power, but the removal of the causes of war . . . the solution of the tangled, frightening problems that divide . . . the two power-blocs and thereby endanger the peace'. What was needed, Pearson said, was vigorous determination to use every technique of negotiation to try to solve problems 'one by one', and 'stage by stage', if not on the basis of confidence and cooperation, then 'at least on that of mutual toleration and self-interest'.

Here was an eloquent plea for consideration of the kinds of proposals that were being put forth by European leaders of both sides (most notably Gaitskell and Rapacki) in hopes of lifting the pall of cold war terror from the Continent.

On December 10, the eve of the Nato conference, Bulganin had sent notes to the various Nato powers expressing Russia's readiness to consider a ban on the stationing of nuclear weapons in Poland, East Germany, Czechoslovakia and West Germany. 'In my opinion,' wrote Denis Healey, M.P.,[2] 'it may mark a turning point in Soviet diplomacy':

. . . this is the first time Russia has been prepared to offer concessions in Poland and Czechoslovakia, as well as East Germany, in return for Western concessions which are limited to the Federal Republic. She has, in fact, accepted the territorial limits which Hugh Gaitskell, . . . put forward last spring for a program of disengagement in Central Europe.

The idea of a general military disengagement is also repeated in the Bulganin letters, and in a form which, though not corresponding precisely to the Gaitskell Plan, is substantially more negotiable than ever before. Bulganin talks about Russia's readiness to consider either a reduction or a total withdrawal of her

[1] ibid., p. 894.
[2] Subsequently Minister for Defense in the Wilson Government.

troops in East Germany and the countries of the Warsaw Pact if America, Britain, and France agree to comparable withdrawals from West Germany and the territory of their Nato partners. Such vagueness is an obvious invitation to serious negotiation.[1]

As the Nato Conference opened on December 16, Dulles offered the European allies nuclear missiles, the Bulganin note having been 'promptly dismissed by the State Department as a mischief maker, before the President had seen it'.[2] The first day's response of the Nato leaders to Dulles' proposal was 'tepid and inconclusive' (New York *Times*) and on the second day there was open revolt:

> The first shock came from Premier Gerhardsen of Norway, who bluntly declared that Norway had no plans 'to let atomic stockpiles be established . . . or launching sites' for IRBMs. He thought the right course would be to postpone the decision about missiles and negotiate.
>
> The Norwegian Premier shook his colleagues at the round table by reading his speech in 'a harsh, passionate voice'. As one of his hearers reported, 'He put into words what millions of plain people are thinking all over Europe and made the heads of government feel the breath of public opinion.'[3]

Gerhardsen's stirring speech impelled Prime Minister Macmillan to put aside his prepared manuscript and 'guardedly' support negotiations. The Canadian and Dutch Premiers gave the Norwegian still stronger backing and even Chancellor Adenauer executed a tactical retreat and urged 'very thorough study' of recent Soviet approaches. By the end of the next day, 'a general feeling of uncertainty appeared to have overcome both the United States and British delegations'. The British tried Churchill's slogan 'We aim to parley', and the Americans, variations of Acheson's 'Positions of Strength', but there was little to response to either.

The outcome was a compromise. The United States yielded to the European desire for negotiations first, in return for an agreement

---

[1] *New Leader*, December 30, 1957.

[2] Fleming, p. 897.

[3] ibid., p. 898.

in principle that missile bases would be accepted eventually. Since the missiles would not be ready for three years, there was time for negotiation.[1]

What happened to the negotiations had been foreshadowed by Lester Pearson in his Nobel Prize speech when he warned that 'our policy and diplomacy is becoming as rigid and defensive as the trench warfare of forty years ago, when the two sides dug in, deeper and deeper and lived in their ditches'. In the ensuing months, however, one side did more 'digging-in' than the other.[2]

On January 9, 1958, a new note arrived from Bulganin proposing summit talks on topics including bomb tests, a nuclear free zone in Central Europe, and negotiations between the two halves of divided Germany. On January 12 President Eisenhower replied to a previous note of Bulganin's of December 10, saying that he was ready to meet the Soviet leader if preparation at lower levels offered 'good hope' of advancing 'peace and justice'. He called for free elections in Germany, self-determination in East Europe, a limitation of the veto in the United Nations, and said, further, that the heart of the arms problem was the 'production' of nuclear weapons, thus referring to Soviet intransigence on the question of inspection.[3] Bulganin's January 9 note was similarly rebuffed in less than a fortnight.[4]

On January 26, Khrushchev declared that a top-level parley was urgent; two days later he again asked for talks. Dulles, however, who by this time was virtually in control of United States foreign policy,[5] was off on a trip to the Middle East to revitalize the ill-conceived and abortive Baghdad Pact, or, in other words, to patch up the wall of containment over which the Soviet Union had so recently vaulted. Dulles' persistence in applying old strategies to new conditions produced a hostile reaction in some circles. John S. Knight, publisher of the Knight chain of Republican newspapers, wrote at the beginning of February: 'As I see it, we have the choice of negotiating with Russia or going to war. . . . I am against the Dulles policies because they have proved sterile and unworkable. When Mr Dulles

---

[1] Fleming.

[2] For a fuller account of these events, see Fleming, pp. 898–968.

[3] The Soviet Union objected to controls that were not part of a program for general disarmament. The US refused to consider general disarmament.

[4] Fleming, op. cit., pp. 905–6.

[5] Joseph Alsop, cited in Fleming, p. 920.

thought we held all the cards, he was a "bluff and bluster" man. But nobody, including our Allies and Russia, was bluffed worth a damn. . . . Mr Dulles has become a liability to peace.'[1]

On February 20, Macmillan suggested that there be a new summit meeting, and Gaitskell demanded that the Prime Minister call for long-term negotiations independent of the United States and the unilateral suspension of tests by Britain. On March 1, the Soviets put aside their aversion to Dulles and proposed a foreign ministers' conference to arrange a summit, but not to discuss substantive issues. This disappointed the United States which said that the qualifications for the meeting barred progress.

Five days later, Khrushchev offered to come to the United States. Dulles was vigorously opposed to giving the Kremlin 'gangsters' any social recognition.[2] It was feared that granting the Soviet leaders social amenities would contribute to the 'fiction that the cold war has come to an end'.[3] On March 6, a new sixteen-page note from Bulganin arrived, several hours before the State Department formally rejected the Soviet version of the foreign ministers meeting. And so on. On April 25, 1958, the editor of the Washington *Post* found that there were 'still evidences here of the sort of thinking that does not accept negotiation on the basis of equality and virtually demands the retreat of the Soviet Union as a prior condition'. He warned, that 'Too much rigidity without conciliatory gesture could have the effect of persuading the Russians that the West does not really want negotiation . . .' On May 18, three days after the Soviets launched their third Sputnik, Dana Adams Schmidt, the New York *Times* analyst, wrote: 'It is still fundamentally U S policy to maintain pressure upon a supposedly weak Soviet Union, as though the U S maintained superiority of nuclear power.'[4] By contrast, the seriousness with which the Soviets pursued their call for negotiations to reduce world tensions was shown in their surprise announcement on March 31 that they were halting tests unilaterally.

Thus, months after the Nato Conference, while the international situation had seriously deteriorated both in the Near East and the

[1] Cited in Fleming, p. 907.
[2] Fleming, p. 911.
[3] Schmidt, the New York *Times*, March 6, 20, 1958, cited in Fleming, p. 911.
[4] Fleming, p. 917.

Far East, engaging the armed forces of the United States, there was still no prospect of negotiations on the question of European disengagement. Meanwhile, the Nato powers had been pledged to accept intermediate range missiles on their territory. The full implications of this were realized by few people at the time. To describe it, as was generally done, in terms of 'adapting the Atlantic Alliance to the Missile Age', was, in the words of one perceptive observer, 'a gross understatement'. Intermediate-range ballistic missiles with a radius of 1,500 miles, he pointed out, could not 'by any stretch of the imagination' be called 'defensive' weapons. 'Armed with 1,500 mile missiles . . . Nato automatically ceases to be a defensive and becomes an offensive alliance; this revolutionary idea of making Nato into an offensive weapon has produced a crisis of conscience in Europe.'[1]

If the employment of offensive missiles in the Nato alliance produced a 'crisis of conscience' in Europe, it combined with the deteriorating international situation and the continued failure to begin negotiations, to produce a different strategy in the Kremlin. On November 10, 1958, Khrushchev announced that the Soviet Union was ready to turn control of Berlin over to East Germany and that the United States would have to negotiate its rights of access. With this warning, the 'Berlin crisis' was under way. On November 30, Khrushchev declared that he was willing to wait on his proposition if talks started within six months. On February 21, 1959, Macmillan went to Moscow to talk with Khrushchev. Then Khrushchev announced his rejection of a previous Western proposal for a foreign ministers' conference which further cast doubt on the prospect of a summit meeting. At this point Macmillan's warning, in a Leningrad speech, of the unforeseen dangers that lay ahead was echoed in the United States by Lyndon Johnson's 'the countdown has begun'. However, on March 2, Khrushchev reversed himself and proposed a foreign ministers' conference, the Czechs and Poles to be among the participants. On April 16, Dulles resigned for reasons of health.

By the spring of 1959 it was becoming apparent to many observers that 'the main issue was the nuclear arming of West Germany. Although Khrushchev wanted to change the situation in Berlin, his

[1] Geoffrey Barraclough, *The Nation*, January 4, 1958.

primary aim was to forestall missile sites in West Germany.'[1]

It was equally plain also that he [Khrushchev] was blocked by Chancellor Adenauer. The power of one 'strong' man on Western policy [Dulles] had ended, but Adenauer was as totally devoted as Dulles had been to the building of a third armed Germany in this century. He was still committed also to the belief that he could deal with the Russians when nuclear armed.[2]

The rearming of Germany actually was already well under way. It was estimated that by 1961 the West German Army would be expanded to twelve rocket-equipped divisions of 200,000 men. The power situation in Europe was becoming more and more complicated. The solution to the only genuine situation of gravity between Russia and the West, the problem of the satellite countries and East Germany, was now further and further from realization.

In May, Kennan appeared before the Senate Foreign Relations Committee and retreated from his Reith lecture position. The time might have passed, he said, for the application of his philosophy. Plans for German armament were now far along. The same reservations were expressed by John F. Kennedy in December 1959:

Q.: To go a step beyond Berlin, do you see any possibility of some partial disengagement in Central Europe, along the lines of any of the plans suggested by George Kennan or Mr Gaitskell in England or Rapacki in Poland?

A.: [Kennedy] Well, I thought there was really more chance two or three years ago than I do today. I think it's rather difficult to extract the missile capacity now from the West Germans, and to extract Germany from Nato. They may not have the warhead, but they have the missiles.

Western insistence on putting missiles into the Nato alliance and thereby increasing the West's military posture in Europe had served

---

[1] Fleming, p. 957. The acute stage of the Berlin crisis came to an end in August, but obviously not to solution, when Khrushchev was invited to the US and it became apparent that with Eisenhower and without Dulles, a summit was in the offing.

[2] Fleming, p. 959.

to push a European settlement further into the future, as Kennan in 1957, and Lippmann in 1947 had warned it would.

The Nato decision had been made in the context of tremendous criticism of Dulles and of his ill-concealed contempt for negotiation. But there was no corresponding opposition in the United States to putting missiles in the Nato countries, and no notable support of disengagement.[1] The explanation for this paradox requires a close study of the nature of the decision itself. It was not, for example, a decision motivated by concern for the safety of the European Nato powers, who had already been within range of Soviet Union IRBM's for the past year and a half. Hence, in a military sense, the development by the Soviet Union of the ICBM did not alter the strategic situation *in Europe*.[2] From where Washington stood, however, the strategic situation had been greatly altered and it had to be 'corrected' until the balance of ICBM's could be restored. It was feared in the United States that the Soviet advantage in missile development would enable the Russians to do what the United States could not do in all the years of its atomic monopoly, namely, blackmail its opponents into acceptance of its own 'just demands'.

The emplacement of short range missiles on European territory was not required by European needs but was undertaken as a stopgap measure while the United States regained its parity position; should the balance of forces change again, Europe would be left in a worse position than before. For if the IRBM's were to play a significant role in the United States defense system for only a short while[3], that is, until the United States developed an ICBM, where would the alliance stand when the United States no longer considered these bases a necessary part of its defense system? Instead of being part of a denuclearized Europe, West Europe would still have Soviet missiles directed against it, and its only defense would be missiles controlled by the United States.

---

[1] On January 12, 1958, Acheson said 'that Mr Kennan's opinion is not shared by any responsible leader of the Democratic party in the United States' and though Stevenson and a number of other Democrats declined to endorse Acheson's statement, there was no noteworthy support for Kennan.

[2] Rostow, *The US in the World Arena*, p. 377.

[3] The fact is that they did not play any such significant role, not only because the missile gap never materialized, but also because missiles did not constitute an 'ultimate weapon' nor did they at the time change 'significantly' the effectiveness of US striking forces. cf. Blackett, *Atomic Weapons and East-West Relations*, p. 35.

Actually, the decision to place missiles in the European alliance was dictated not by military but by political considerations. This is evident from the fact that Dulles had proposed the move, and had sought confirmation of it, even before the missiles were available. The urgency could only have stemmed, therefore, from some non-military source.

At the time of the launching of Sputnik, two sweeping criticisms of the Eisenhower defense policies were in the process of being filed, known as the Gaither, and Rockefeller Reports. Support for these reports was widespread among the national élite of both political parties. Members of the Rockefeller Panel, for example, included Dean Rusk, Chester Bowles, Jacob Potofsky, Henry Kissinger, Henry R. Luce and Lucius Clay.

> Point by point, Rockefeller Panel Report II was a public rejection of the . . . specific policies which the Eisenhower administration had built . . . over the previous five years. The report rejected the notion that healthy recognizable American society required for the maintenance of its institutions a rigid limitation of budgetary expenditures. It rejected the concept that an ability to retaliate with nuclear weapons was a sufficient deterrent to Soviet strength. It rejected the continued denial to Nato of information about nuclear weapons and the weapons themselves . . . .[1]

Coming as they did at the height of the Sputnik crisis, when the public's confidence in Eisenhower had been shaken, these reports carried considerable political weight and thus constituted a serious challenge to Eisenhower's position. As it was, 'the Administration . . . on the whole, successfully resisted the pressures for expanded and accelerated military programs of attack and defense'. Where Eisenhower did yield was in the area of reorganization of the Pentagon,[2] and, of course, the emplacement of missiles in the Nato alliance.

Because the view of defense policy embodied in these reports was adopted by the Democratic Party in its 1960 platform and eventually became the practice of the Kennedy Administration, the outlook

[1] Rostow, p. 372–3.
[2] ibid., p. 374.

behind some of the recommendations is of considerable importance. A central theme was the fear that the United States had tied itself to a massive inflexible deterrent. By concentrating on strategic air power, the Eisenhower Administration had allowed conventional forces to deteriorate and, further, had failed to develop a wide range of tactical nuclear weapons for varying circumstances. Because of this, the deterrent itself was in danger of losing credibility. In the words of the Rockefeller Report:

> The world knows that we would never fight a preventive war. But we and the rest of the free world must be prepared to resist any one of three types of aggression: all-out war, limited war, and *non-overt* aggression concealed as internal takeover by *coup d'état* or by civil war.
>
> In order to deter aggression, we must be prepared to fight a nuclear war either all-out or limited.
>
> At present there are major shortcomings in our posture for both all-out war and limited war.[1]

In the event of a limited aggression, these critics argued, the threat of retaliation with H-bombs would not be a credible deterrent, since the United States would not wish to involve itself in an all-out nuclear war unless the stakes demanded it. The development of a 'graduated deterrent' was necessary, so that retaliation could be commensurate with the circumstances that provoked it.

Thus, it is clear that the brinkmanship and massive retaliation policies of John Foster Dulles played no small part in stimulating these reappraisals. It is also clear that the liberal élite was very much involved in putting forth these criticisms at the time that Kennan was advocating disengagement, and thus serves to explain in part, why they failed to support Kennan's proposals for disengagement.

Politically, the Sputnik was offered as an argument for marshalling public opinion in support of this revised and substantially increased defense program, in effect, a renewed containment strategy. In fact, it took not only Sputnik, but a whole series of diplomatic defeats to break the Eisenhower spell and elect Kennedy, who shared these

[1] Cited in Rostow, pp. 371–2. For a critique of the theory of limited nuclear war, written in 1958, see Blackett, *Studies of War*, p. 54 et seq., 'Nuclear Weapons and Defence: Comments on Kissinger, Kennan and King-Hall'.

views. But the desire to exploit a political moment cannot completely explain the failure to back a policy which, if successful, would have significantly eased the international situation and gone a long way towards eliminating the root causes of the conflict.

The only way to explain this liberal failure is first, to see the desire to exploit the Sputnik situation as also a reaction *to* Sputnik, and second, to set the thinking of these critics in its cold war context, in particular, to see its relation to the two compartments of the cold war crucible: the conceptions of containment and the psychological reaction to the Atomic Bomb.

During the formative years of the cold war and the atomic monopoly of the United States, the threat of atomic strike against Soviet cities was considered the sole deterrent to a possible Soviet land attack in Europe. This meant, as P. M. S. Blackett has pointed out, that most official, military, religious and moral leaders in the West came to accept as justifiable, a military doctrine which previously they would have denounced as wicked, immoral and inconceivable as a policy. For 'if in response to a Soviet aggression with conventional forces, the American and British atomic bombers had been set in motion to carry out the plans for which they are trained, then the six million victims of Hitler's gas chambers would be hardly remembered: the humane and civilized West would have sunk below the level of Genghis Khan.'

Therefore, to justify to the consciences of the Western people the deliberate plan, in certain military circumstances, to annihilate tens of millions of Russian men, women and children, 'it was necessary to believe the USSR to be innately aggressive and wicked. Once a nation pledges its safety to an absolute weapon, it becomes emotionally essential to believe in an absolute enemy'.

Thus, at the intellectual level, it came to be believed that the USSR might attack the West as soon as she estimated that she had a superiority in military power. The slightest falling behind in the West in military capability would, in this view, precipitate a holocaust. 'It was this set of beliefs,' Blackett suggests, 'which in 1957 led to the violent reaction to Sputnik I' and which afterward continued to lead to an 'excessive concern with the precise relative strength of the American and Soviet atomic striking power'.[1]

[1] Blackett, *Studies of War*, p. 94.

The Rockefeller Report also demanded 'accelerated research and development support . . . for such key programs as speeding up of the program of equipping both surface and underwater ships with missiles of various types' and procurement of aircraft 'to modernize existing units . . . into the 1960s while pressing for the most rapid development of Operational Intermediate Range and Inter-Continental Ballistic Missiles'. All this (including a crash program providing for an additional $3 billion *each* year 'for the next several years' to fill up 'current deficiencies') despite the fact that the Eisenhower Administration had a very adequate missile program, a program so adequate in fact that a missile gap never developed.[1]

If the 'élite consensus'[2] represented by the Rockefeller and Gaither Reports was very much conditioned in its thinking by the apocalyptic overtones of nuclear power, it was no less bound by the fundamental categories of containment. Among other recommendations, the Rockefeller Report urged that nuclear weapons be given to Nato. It further declared that,

> We must face the fact that a meaningful reduction of armaments must be preceded by a reduction of tensions and a settlement of outstanding issues that have divided the world since World War II.[3]

In other words, the build-up of strength, even in Europe, must continue *until* a settlement was reached, and only such a settlement of outstanding issues would warrant a reduction of arms. But that was to go back to the positions of 1947–9 and to throw over the lessons of the ten intervening years: that the arms themselves had become a bar to settlement and that they could not move the situation towards a solution. Thus, as though nothing had really happened, a concensus of the American élite in 1957 proposed as part of its basic policy *revision*, precisely the underpinning dogma of the whole stagnated cold war effort in Europe!

---

[1] 'The "missile gap", like the "bomber gap" before it, is now being consigned to the limbo of synthetic issues, where it always belonged. The missile gap – the prediction of an overwhelming Soviet superiority in ICBM in the early 1960s – was the product of partisan politics and service (primarily Air Force) pressures.' (New York *Times*, November 27, 1961.)

[2] Rostow's phrase.

[3] Rostow, p. 372.

Nor was this re-emphasis of old approaches in the wake of the Sputnik crisis (and the larger crisis precipitated by Soviet parity and partial superiority) limited to the liberal élite. As *The Nation* editorialized on November 30, 1957:

> For the December 16 meeting in Paris, Mr Dulles proposes merely a restatement of our 1949 position. In 1949 we wanted air bases; now we want sites for missile installations. In 1949 we would not negotiate with the Soviets because we held the trump cards; we will not negotiate now because the Soviets hold them.

Indeed, the passions over military policy which rose to fever pitch during the Sputnik crisis and led to the emplacement of missiles in the United States defense system in Europe, were already strong in 1955, in fact, were based on the same illusions held in the West in 1945 when the cold war began:

> [In 1955] Senator Jackson put it: 'America's *superiority* in advanced weapons systems is a *minimum* requirement of peace.' We all remember the talk after Hiroshima of atomic bombs as absolute weapons: the possessor would rule the world. This did not happen. Now it is the ICBM which is billed as the new absolute weapon. 'Whoever gets there first will have the world by the tail' – these are Bernard Baruch's words . . .
> So we now find the West being urged once again to stake its whole survival on winning another technological race.[1] [Emphasis added.]

For a half decade the United States thought it had an 'ultimate weapon' in the Atomic Bomb which would soon[2] allow it to contain and contract Soviet power by ultimatum instead of negotiation. When the Soviet Union exploded its first atomic bomb, the United States placed its faith in an H-bomb, a thousand times more powerful than the A-bomb and offering the same sort of absolute supremacy as a prospect. When the Soviet Union not only approached the United States in nuclear technology, but established a small lead in

---

[1] Blackett, *Atomic Weapons and East–West Relations*, pp. 65–6.

[2] i.e. when the balance of conventional power on the Continent had shifted to deprive the Soviets of their deterrent force.

ballistic missiles, it was evident that thinking in the United States had not changed. It was now the Soviet Union which was on the brink of an ultimate weapon, with which they could force the United States to contract its power without negotiation. 'Mr President,' warned Senator Jackson ('the gentleman from Boeing') in 1955, 'we and our free-world partners may soon face the threat of ballistic blackmail.'

Thus, at a crucial moment of reckoning in the cold war, to borrow Kennan's literary formulation, the United States' 'whole governmental machine, including the mechanism of diplomacy [moved] inexorably along the prescribed path, like a persistent toy automobile wound up and headed in a given direction, stopping only when it [met] with some unanswerable force'.

III. The Eisenhower Years

. . . just as the Russian élite has felt that the United States would somehow collapse in economic ruin, the United States élite has clung to the view that the Soviet system is always politically tottering. . . . In the end it has been hopefully assumed, *they* will have to seek peace; then Washington will serve on Moscow its ultimatum, the terms of which nobody knows. That has been the big dream behind it all – the containment by military encirclement, the fake promises of 'liberating the satellites of Eastern Europe', the invasion of Lebanon, the stupidity of supporting the puppet régime on Formosa, and the rest of it. . . .

In short, neither the United States nor the West generally has accepted as quite real, or legitimate, the *fact* of Soviet Communism; the possibility of 'peaceful coexistence' has been, and is, defined as mere Red propaganda. And toward the new beginnings in the Soviet bloc since the death of Stalin, US policy has been inert and monolithic.

The doctrine of violence, and the inept opportunism based upon it, are substitutes for political and economic programs. That doctrine has been and is the fundamental basis of US policy. And US policy is now bankrupt. . . .

If peace is, and can be only, a peace of coexistence, the means to peace is, and can be only, negotiation. The structure of peace has to do with the terms of national competition; the strategy of peace requires the substitution of economic and cultural terms for the military terms that now prevail.

C. WRIGHT MILLS, 1958

III. The Eisenhower Years

CHAPTER XIX

The Failure to Make Peace

IN the eighth year of cold war, three events occurred which appeared to significantly enhance the possibilities for a European settlement and the beginning of an authentic approach to the problem of disarmament. These events were the death of Stalin (followed by the beginnings of de-Stalinization), the election to the US Presidency of Dwight D. Eisenhower (not only a 'man of peace', but more importantly a man of unchallengeable patriotism and authority) and the Soviet Union's visible approach to nuclear parity with the US.

This last factor signalled the approaching bankruptcy of the policies of roll-back, liberation and containment, all premised on the expectation of Soviet collapse. By freeing the East from the threat of an atomic blitz to which it could only respond with conventional arms, Soviet nuclear power also strengthened internal forces in the Eastern bloc which sought more flexibility, freedom and genuine attempts to coexist with the West.[1]

The actual development of nuclear parity was not sudden, however, though its approach was clear, and recognition of the fact and its significance varied among different leaders on both sides of the Iron Curtain. One of the first in the West to grasp the meaning of the new situation was Churchill who called, on May 11, 1953, for a meeting at the summit. Eisenhower responded to this call in 1955 and thus acknowledged the new state of affairs after two years had passed. Dulles never acknowledged it.

Yet, no peace settlement was forthcoming, the arms race continued and the build-up of new powers (France, Germany and China) accelerated, thus complicating any future settlement.

In 1955–7, the United States was presented with not one, but three plans for general, internationally controlled and inspected

---

[1] e.g. the Malenkov faction in the USSR, proponents of the 'June Road' in Hungary, etc.

disarmament. Each plan was based on the originally developed Western plan, each 'made further efforts to meet the West',[1] each was unconditionally rebuffed. When faced with, essentially, its own proposals for complete and general disarmament, the United States responded by declaring its opposition to *any* plan for general disarmament, despite the fact that it had previously committed itself to this goal in a mutually agreed upon statement of principles with the other negotiating powers.[2]

The Russian proposals of 1955 were made, moreover, against a background of specific 'deeds' which had been demanded by Eisenhower on April 16, 1953,[3] as a test of Russian intentions, with respect to peace. These deeds included the signing of an armistice in Korea, and a settlement of issues in Southeast Asia, achieved in 1953 and 1954 respectively. In the same speech, Eisenhower said:

> *Even a few such clear and specific acts, such as the Soviet Union's signature upon an Austrian treaty* . . . would be impressive signs of sincere intent. They would carry a power of persuasion not to be matched by any amount of oratory.[4] [Emphasis added.]

On May 15, 1955, the Russians signed an Austrian treaty. But the US would not even *consider* serious negotiations on disarmament, nor on disengagement in Central Europe, nor on the Soviet proposals, urged from 1952 to 1955 for an evacuation of troops from Germany based on terms similar to that of the Austrian treaty.[5] Despite the fact that, as Lippmann had observed in 1947, 'The withdrawal of the army is . . . the acid test of Soviet conduct,' the US seemed quite unwilling to read anything very positive in the Soviets' passing of the test.

On May 14, 1956, new deeds were forthcoming from the Russians. Premier Bulganin announced that the Soviet Union was reducing its

[1] Noel-Baker, op. cit., p. 24, cf. discussion pp. 273ff. above.
[2] The so-called Six Principles – proposed by the US delegate on April 24, 1952, and accepted by the Russians on May 10, 1955. ibid., pp. 12–20.
[3] 'Toward a Golden Age of Peace', *Peace With Justice*, pp. 34–44.
[4] According to Sherman Adams, 'It was the most effective speech of Eisenhower's public career, and certainly one of the highlights of his Presidency. We heard later that people behind the Iron Curtain prayed and wept as they listened to it . . . .' Sherman Adams, op. cit., p. 97.
[5] Sebastian Haffner, 'Germany, Russia and the West', *Encounter*, October 1961.

armed forces by another 1·2 million men, in addition to the 640,000 mustered out of the service in 1955. He also announced the withdrawal of 30,000 troops from East Germany, the placing of 375 warships in reserve, and the closing of several military schools.[1]

Among the top American leaders, only Secretary of Defense Wilson expressed the belief that this was a 'step in the right direction'. But even he hastened to add that there must be no lag in defense by the US. The President's Press Secretary said that the US would be able to put more faith in the Russians if they had stopped their obstructionist tactics at the disarmament conference and accepted President Eisenhower's 'open skies' proposal.[2] When asked at his press conference if he would not prefer to have the Soviet Union keep these men in its armed forces, Secretary of State Dulles replied: 'Well, it's a fair conclusion that I would rather have these men standing around doing guard duty than making atom bombs.'[3] Other commentators and officials echoed this view, pointing out that Soviet military strength would not be reduced, since so much depended on H-bombs and missiles. No one in official circles could find any cause for optimism in the development.[4]

But this was to miss the significance of the Soviet move entirely and to ignore what the cold war conflict was originally about. Of course in overall strength, the reduction of manpower in the armed forces was not significant. Manpower released here is bound to be used there. But in terms of the critical problem of divided Europe, the reduction was a decisive step toward settlement. For the reduction in manpower was a test of whether the Soviet build-up represented preparation to overrun West Europe, or whether it was only a deterrent posture. If the posture were deterrent, as the withdrawal would seem to have indicated,[5] then the Soviets were in a position to consider the *mutual* withdrawal of armies and reduction of forces which would end the division and occupation of Europe. If the

---

[1] Cook, 'Juggernaut: The Warfare State', *The Nation*, p. 313. Between 1955 and 1960, the Armed Forces were actually cut by more than 2 million men, including 260,000 officers. – E. O. Ballance, The *Red Army*, p. 199.

[2] Cook, op. cit., pp. 313–14.

[3] Fleming, p. 789.

[4] ibid.

[5] cf. Appendix in Blackett's *Studies of War*, which contains an analysis of the Soviet build-up and reduction of land forces leading to the conclusion that they represented a deterrent posture.

Soviets had been approached with some preliminary proposals for new negotiations, and an atmosphere of *détente* had been initiated, might not the tragedy in Budapest, in the Fall of the year, have been avoided?[1]

Even after Hungary, the US response to disengagement proposals was to dismiss them, then under allied pressure to agree to negotiate, and finally, to obstruct them altogether by transforming Nato into an offensively armed alliance.

With regard to their proposals for a negotiated nuclear test ban, US policy followed a similar pattern. On August 21, 1958, a joint team of East–West scientists announced unanimously, after fifty-one days of negotiations, that a nuclear test ban could be policed effectively. The Soviets had announced earlier that they would suspend tests unilaterally for one year. By December 19, four articles of a proposed test-ban treaty had been signed on the basis of the scientists' findings. But on January 5, 1959, the US announced that new data showed that underground tests were more difficult to detect than the Geneva experts had thought. This information was released in a well coordinated effort by the Atomic Energy Commission and the military but was challenged by scientific members of the United States' own negotiating team before the Senate Sub-Committee on Disarmament.[2] As Philip J. Farley, Special Assistant to the Secretary of State for Disarmament put it: 'It is very unlikely that anyone could achieve a significant nuclear capability or a significant improvement in his existing capability without being clearly and publicly in the position of having violated or otherwise evaded the agreement.'[3] Negotiations continued and by September 1959, seventeen articles of the treaty had been signed.

Then, on November 25, 1959, the US delegation presented a theory put forward by Drs Albert Latter and Edward Teller to the effect that a very small atomic explosion (20 kilotons and less) could be 'hidden' by muffling it in a large underground hole.

But to de-couple the explosion of a 20-kiloton weapon, a spherical hole nearly 500 feet in diameter would be necessary. Moreover, the

---

[1] Nagy's 1955 proposals to the Soviet Presidium that Hungary become neutral would perhaps have been better received if there had been indications that the West was interested in a neutral belt involving some of its own allies in the Central European area.

[2] Cook, op. cit., p. 316.   [3] ibid.

hole would have to be 3,000 feet underground. The big room of Carlsbad caverns, one of the world's largest known caves, would be 'only big enough to muffle 10 kilotons'.[1]

The proponents of the so-called 'big hole' theory suggested that such a hole could be dug by flushing out a salt dome. They admitted that this would require the removal of 20 million tons of salt (the entire salt production of the US in 1959 was 5 million tons) at a cost of more than $10 million and from two to four years' labor.[2] Disposing of this salt, itself, would be a major problem. If it were emptied into a river as large as the Ohio, or the St Lawrence, it would double the salt content of the river for a year,[3] and thus would be detectable.

Supposing all these difficulties were surmounted, a nation intending to cheat on the test ban to gain a significant military advantage, would still have to carry out a series of tests. 'One violation, one nuclear test below ground, does not do much for the development of weapons. . . .'[4] But if a series of tests were carried out all at a single location, the work of the detecting agency would be greatly simplified. 'It would merely be necessary to detect the disturbances on the seismograph, not to distinguish them from earthquakes. The fact of repeated seismic disturbances originating from the same location . . . would be sufficiently suspicious to warrant dispatching an inspection team to their site.' With the accepted Geneva system of twenty stations, 'it would be necessary to find a new location for practically every test in the series' to avoid detection.[5]

Despite the enormous difficulties involved in using such a method, and the limited benefits to be gained by such small explosions, the United States decided that the possibility that a 'big hole' could be used to cheat[6] on a test ban was an effective bar to the

[1] Hans Bethe, 'The Case for Ending Nuclear Tests', *The Atlantic Monthly*, August 1960. Dr Bethe was a member of the US negotiating team.

[2] Bethe, ibid., Cook, op. cit., p. 317.

[3] Bethe, ibid.   [4] ibid.   [5] ibid.

[6] 'Having participated in the negotiations with the Russian scientists at Ceneva on three occasions, I believe that they are sincere in wanting the test cessation agreement and do not intend to cheat on it. For instance, in November 1959, although the Russians were in many ways reluctant to agree with the American delegation, they were very eager to accept any improvements in detection apparatus suggested by the Americans. If the Russians wished to violate the treaty, they would have objected to these improvements.' – Hans Bethe, op. cit.

treaty then in the process of being agreed upon. When the US delegation walked out of the negotiations, the head of the Soviet contingent declared that he felt that such action was 'aimed at undermining [the] deliberations because, just as soon as some partial agreement came into sight, just as soon as we got to that agreement, immediately the US delegation took steps to ruin it.'[1]

It would be wrong to treat this obstruction of a test ban agreement as a case of the US simply pitting its own self-interest against the self-interest of the world community, however. In fact, from the standpoint of the real military security of the United States, few things could have been more advantageous and beneficial than a negotiated test ban at a time when the US had a considerable superiority in nuclear weaponry. Continued testing by both sides inevitably would mean that the country which was behind would catch up because, as Hans Bethe pointed out, further nuclear weapons development would be limited by the laws of physics.[2]

The failure of the United States to participate in a test ban agreement or to show willingness to seriously consider Soviet initiatives on disarmament and disengagement, stemmed from factors more complex than simply the self-interested calculations of an aggressive world power.

Among the major factors was the failure of the leadership of the country to arrive at an adequate conception of coexistence with the USSR or indeed to accept the very idea of coexistence itself. The early cold war myths (the absolute evil of the enemy, the hopelessness of negotiation, the possibility of victory) were exploited by various groups (the military, the military-dependent industries, the fanatic right wing) to keep 'war' preparation at optimum pitch and to render ineffective, opposition to outmoded policies and to the dominant military metaphysic behind these policies.

The failure of leadership is best seen in Eisenhower, who viewed his role in office, as a quest for 'peace with justice', We have already seen how, in the first phase of the cold war, American leadership directed its energies towards 'justice' rather than 'peace', or what they might have called a program of 'peace *through* justice' as opposed to Lippmann's prescription: *justice through peace.*

---

[1] Cook, op. cit., p. 347.
[2] Bethe, op. cit.

Eisenhower's simple juxtaposition of the two values led to a vague and ambiguous program, which tended to revert to the earlier position (peace through justice) although with an important new emphasis – namely, the necessity and, by implication, the feasibility of peace.

This new emphasis was by no means trivial, although its effect is difficult to assess, as it depended on the peculiar quality of the national mood at the time. Symbolically it can be expressed in the contrast between Dulles' comportment at Geneva in 1954 (when he 'scrupulously avoided even looking in the direction of Communist China's Premier Chou En-Lai') and Eisenhower's bearing at the same place in the following year:

> All accounts agree that he was the outstanding leader of the conference. Coming into the conference chamber for the first time he found the Russians standing apart, somewhat awkwardly awaiting his arrival, and he cordially drew them to the conference table.[1]

It was Eisenhower's initiative at a moment when the cries of the 'war party' (both Republican and Democratic) had reached their peak, that led to an acceptance of the 'Geneva spirit' by the US public. As James Reston had written the previous November, 'perhaps the most important single fact in world politics today is that Mr Eisenhower has thrown the immense authority of the American Presidency against risking a military solution of the cold war'. The same day, the Alsops reported that Eisenhower had said publicly that he flatly ruled out preventive war and would not discuss it even in private. 'He finds the mass killing required in a knock-out blow against the Soviet Union profoundly morally abhorrent.'[2] In short, Eisenhower lent his matchless personal prestige, as well as the presige of his office to an enterprise which had been labeled appeasement and surrender for almost ten years, namely the attempt to parley with the 'atheistic despots' in the Kremlin.

But, as has been aptly said of Eisenhower, 'having had the vision of making peace he did not have the qualities of leadership to see it

---

[1] Fleming, pp. 750–1.
[2] New York *Times*, November 28, 1954: Fleming, p. 742.

through'.[1] One measure of what has been called his 'benign con-
fusion' in the area of foreign policy, was his retention of John Foster
Dulles as his Secretary of State, despite widespread pressure to have
Dulles removed.

On numerous occasions, Eisenhower was willing to negotiate on
major issues with Russia, but was dissuaded by Dulles. It was Dulles,
for example, who negated Churchill's 1953 call for a summit, and
Dulles again who in 1955 blocked the visit to Washington of Marshal
Zhukov. In October 1956, at the time of the Hungarian revolt, he
rejected the proposal to withdraw two American divisions in exchange for a Soviet withdrawal of the two Russian divisions stationed
in Hungary. In 1955, the year the US withdrew its disarmament
proposals after they had been accepted by the Russians, Dulles came
out with the thesis that 'you cannot base a security system on a
joining of forces that you do not trust'. From then on, 'do not trust'
became the keynote of American policy and it would be easy, as one
observer suggested, 'to compose a veritable doxology of instances
where Mr Dulles ... stepped in to thwart all progress toward a
détente'.[2]

The situation at the top of the American power structure was
caustically described by Kennedy in the Senate in June 1960:

> As a substitute for policy, Mr Eisenhower has tried smiling at the
> Russians; our State Department has tried frowning at the
> Russians; and Mr Nixon has tried both. None have succeeded.[3]

If Eisenhower had no defined policy to execute, the method by
which he operated from day to day compounded the existing confusion by giving free rein to conflicting forces. From his military
experience as a staff commander, he carried into the presidency a
conception of leadership by consensus and a preference for dele-
gating authority to skilled experts.[4] Thus Dulles' superior experience
and knowledge in the realm of foreign affairs qualified him, as far as
Eisenhower was concerned, to operate a foreign policy often dia-

---

[1] Fleming, p. 1020.
[2] Geoffrey Barraclough, 'More Than Dulles Must Go' – *The Nation*, January
25, 1958.
[3] *Strategy of Peace*, p. viii.
[4] cf. Adams, p. 50; Rostow, pp. 389–400.

metrically opposed to the President's own intentions. Ultimately, this preference for consensus within the staff (and by extension, within the Western alliance) played a key role in the collapse of Eisenhower's final quest for 'peace' at the 1960 Summit, and demonstrated how seriously he had failed to grasp his chosen role.

CHAPTER XX

The Summit Collapse

IN early 1958, in the wake of Sputnik and the December Nato Conference at which it was decided to place offensive missiles in the Nato countries, the Russians began calling for a new summit meeting.[1] Strong public support for such a move (a Gallup poll showed an average of 62 per cent in favor, and only 17 per cent opposed in twelve Western capitals)[2] combined with visits to the US by Mikoyan and Khrushchev, and the retirement of Dulles, to induce the United States to accept the Soviet overture.

The agreement to hold the summit in April (then May 1960) was sealed in the Eisenhower–Khrushchev talks at Camp David where the President, as in 1955, showed that he could rise above the atmosphere of tension generated by the cold war. In December 1959, Eisenhower went on a world tour, the climax of which was his triumphal visit to India where banners hailed him as 'The Prince of Peace'. In an address before a joint session of the Indian Parliament on December 10, Eisenhower declared:

In the name of humanity, can we not join in a five-year or a fifty-year plan against mistrust and misgivings and fixations on the wrongs of the past? Can we not apply ourselves to the removal or reduction of the causes of tension that exist in the world? All these are creations of governments, cherished and nourished by governments. The peoples of the world would never feel them if they were given freedom from propaganda and pressure.[3]

But while Eisenhower was putting his finger on a central source of the cold war impasse, forces were at work in his own camp seeking

---

[1] An arresting account of the drift towards the summit, and the preliminary visits of Khruschev and Mikoyan, is contained in Fleming, pp. 903–1023.

[2] Fleming, p. 904.

[3] Eisenhower, *Peace with Justice*, p. 189.

to prevent a change in the situation. On March 26 *The Economist* noted that Eisenhower had 'failed from the beginning both to work out exactly what concessions the US might have to make' at the coming summit talks, and 'to apply the energy needed to rally the country behind him'. Consequently, the opposition which had been silenced after the talks at Camp David, became active and vocal again and, since these voices were 'clearminded' where the President was 'indeterminate', they had succeeded in 'narrowing the area of manoeuvre both at the summit and in Moscow afterwards'.

The voices of this opposition included Secretary of State Herter and Under-Secretary Dillon in speeches on April 4 and 20 respectively. But even more important was the intractability of the partners of the alliance whom the United States had built up with billions of dollars in the preceding years. Chancellor Adenauer let it be known that he was opposed to having Berlin discussed at the summit, while President de Gaulle wanted everything discussed. Both joined forces to delay the meeting, first until 1960 and then until late spring.[1]

Meanwhile, Khrushchev went about preparing for the coming negotiations very differently. From Moscow he traveled to Hungary and the other satellites to make sure that no disturbances marred the prospects for the meeting; he also issued orders to the big Western Communist parties to work for coexistence. The Communists were instructed to support the visit of Eisenhower to Italy and 'they swelled the applauding Roman crowds' when he came. The Soviet Premier even went so far as to instruct the Iraqi Communist Party to support Kassem, fearing that the threatened upheaval in Iraq would wreck his policy.[2] (The Iraqi Communists complied, with disastrous results for themselves later.)

As for Eisenhower, who failed even to exert control over his own Central Intelligence Agency to prevent it from continuing the provocative U-2 flights over Soviet territory, his concept of consensus leadership stood him in poor stead. If his policy were to succeed, he would have had to see to it that real progress was made before the summit toward agreement on Berlin, nuclear testing and disarmament. Instead, he allowed endless meetings to decide that

[1] Fleming, pp. 996–9, 986.
[2] Fleming, p. 986.

nothing would be done about Berlin[1]; the disarmament negotiations drifted into deadlock and he failed to restrain his own officials from planning to resume underground atomic tests.[2]

As Eisenhower's hands became more and more tied by his own allies and officials, prospects for a successful summit became dimmer and dimmer. At least one statesman read the signs of the gathering storm correctly. On February 11, 1960, Alistair Cooke reported after a visit to Adlai Stevenson that 'He believes, in dead earnestness, that the Eisenhower Administration is committing a disastrous folly in saying that it wants nothing so much as peace, and yet spreading the notion that the only terms available to the Soviet Union are unconditional surrender.'[3]

As if to demonstrate conclusively that the cold war was the main business of the hour, and the turn towards peace only a utopian diversion, the United States announced on March 16 that it planned an underground atomic blast (which would break the moratorium) for 'peaceful purposes'[4] in 1961. At about the same time[5] the CIA authorized another U-2 flight across the heart of the Soviet Union, a clear violation of Soviet sovereignty and international law, to take place two and a half weeks before the opening of the conference. On May 7, nine days before the conference and two days after the U-2 plane was shot down, President Eisenhower announced a series of underground nuclear tests to improve the detection of subterranean explosions.[6] Then, when the heads of state had gathered in Paris, precisely on the eve of the conference opening, 'Defense Secretary Gates . . . authorized the alert of US strategic forces all over the world, with the President's consent, as a gesture of firmness and to suggest that the danger of Soviet surprise attack was real.'[7]

---

[1] 'The Russians, both at Geneva in 1959 and since, have made it clear that they are open to an arrangement [on Berlin] which would be reasonable from the point of view of the West. But the West have carried on with an old-fashioned type of diplomatic bargaining which may have seemed to hold the position but has in fact put us in an increasingly bad posture in Berlin.' – Geoffrey McDermott, *Berlin: Success of a Mission?* 1963 p. 26. McDermott was British Minister in Berlin during the Berlin crisis of 1961.

[2] Fleming, pp. 989–90.

[3] Cited in Fleming, p. 994.

[4] Fleming, p. 992.

[5] Fleming, pp. 1005–6; Hanson W. Baldwin, New York *Times*, May 30, 1960.

[6] David Wise and Thomas Ross, *The U-2 Affair*, 1962, p. 100.

[7] Fleming, p. 1012.

In the circumstances, US leaders could hardly have done more to confirm the cries of Khruschev's left wing, that the United States was firmly in the control of its military establishment.

By contrast, the Soviet Premier had announced on January 14, that the Soviet Union would reduce its armed forces from 3·6 million men to 2·4 million. This meant that 250,000 officers would be released from military life. A month later Defense Marshal Malinovsky was 'stumping the country to explain the new policy to outraged brass hats', a fact which demonstrated that the decision was being 'put through in the teeth of professional opposition'.[1]

The handling of the U-2 incident which actually broke up the conference was itself symbolic of the bizarre and confused state of American purpose and leadership in that fateful hour.

On the eve of the great gathering which would record the dissipation of his peace crusade, President Eisenhower was deep in the earth, in top-secret, top-level conference, safe presumably from Soviet bomb attacks, at the moment when the shooting down of one of his own espionage planes over Russia was announced.[2]

On May 5, Khrushchev, in a speech before the Supreme Soviet, announced that an American plane had been shot down over the Soviet Union on May 1, an 'aggressive provocation aimed at wrecking the summit conference'. He did 'not doubt President Eisenhower's sincere desire for peace', but evidently there were imperialist and militarist circles which restricted him.[3]

The National Aeronautics and Space Administration immediately put out its claim that the U-2 was merely a weather plane, whose pilot had reported that he was having oxygen trouble over Turkey. Khrushchev responded by revealing that the plane had been shot down 1,200 miles inside Soviet territory and that the pilot had admitted being on a photo-reconnaissance mission all the way over the USSR from Pakistan to Norway.

---

[1] Fleming, p. 991.
[2] Fleming, p. 1001.
[3] Harold Stassen, former disarmament advisor to Eisenhower, actually charged that the U-2 had been sent deliberately by 'some of our military officers' to blow up the summit meeting. – Wise and Ross, op. cit., p. 103.

Many newspapers expressed the opinion that Eisenhower 'should be furious with blundering subordinates who used this method of espionage so close to the summit meeting'. Perhaps the most remarkable feature of Khrushchev's speeches on the flight, as the Manchester *Guardian* noted, was 'their studied moderation, and his readiness to absolve Mr Eisenhower of any guilt or even knowledge of the actions he complains about'.[1]

But, on May 9, Secretary of State Herter in effect asserted the right and duty of the United States to violate Soviet air space and international law, because otherwise 'the Government of the United States would be derelict to its responsibility not only to the American people but to free peoples everywhere . . . it is unacceptable that the Soviet political system should be given an opportunity to make secret preparations to face the free world with the choice of abject surrender or nuclear destruction'.[2]

On May 11, President Eisenhower said that the Soviet Union had made a 'fetish of secrecy' which in turn made the United States fearful of 'another Pearl Harbor'. Therefore ever since the beginning of his Administration, he had 'issued directives to gather in every feasible way' necessary security information to protect the US against 'surprise attack'. But, as the St Louis *Post-Dispatch* was almost alone in pointing out, 'aerial mapping of bombing targets is something different from the ordinary run of espionage. It is the kind of action that is appropriate to wartime, or the brink of wartime, but is highly provocative at any other time'.[3]

'No principle of international law,' as the historian D. F. Fleming observed, 'was more firmly established than the right of a nation to control plane flights over its air space. It was fixed in multilateral treaties going back to 1919 and had never been questioned. By flying more than thirty U-2 target mapping flights over the Soviet Union, the United States had deliberately struck the principle of national sovereignty as damaging a blow as it could suffer in peace time'.[4]

On the day that Eisenhower defended the flights, Khrushchev was questioned as to whether his estimate of the President had

[1] Fleming, p. 1003.
[2] ibid., Wise and Ross, p. 117.
[3] Fleming, p. 1003; Wise and Ross, p. 131.
[4] Fleming, p. 1005.

changed. 'You know my friendly attitude toward the President,' he said. 'My hopes have not been justified. . . . I was not aware of the fact that the plan of air espionage over the Soviet Union was not the caprice of an irresponsible officer. I am responsible for the acts of my Government. I was horrified to learn that the President had endorsed those aggressive acts.'[1]

The next day, James Reston wrote that there was 'still just a chance' to save the summit, but not if the President continued his present theme. 'By demanding the *right* to intrude into the Soviet Union the President has defied Khrushchev to stop him, put Khrushchev on the spot with the Stalinists, who have always been against a *détente*, embarrassed the Allies by making their bases a target of Khrushchev's anger; and even repudiated one of Washington's own favorite principles – namely, that each nation has the right to choose its own form of government.' The President could not have it both ways; he could not 'defy Khrushchev and have his cooperation too'.[2]

Still, no assurance that the flights would be stopped was forthcoming. Up until May 12, this was all that the Russians had demanded. When Khrushchev arrived in Paris, however, he called on de Gaulle as President of the Conference and told him that he could not take part unless the U-2 incident was cleared up. The US Government must be prepared 'to condemn the action that had been taken, undertake not to repeat it, and call those responsible to account'.[3]

Actually, Eisenhower had ordered the flights cancelled on May 12, but he did not divulge this information even to Macmillan, who tried on May 15 to mollify Khrushchev and preserve the conference.[4]

---

[1] Fleming, pp. 1007–1008.

[2] Fleming, p. 1008. 'To *avow* that we intend to violate Soviet sovereignty is to put everybody on the spot. It makes it impossible for the Soviet Government to play down this particular incident because now it is challenged openly in the face of the world. It is compelled to react because no nation can remain passive when it is the avowed policy of another to intrude upon its territory.' – Walter Lippmann, cited in Wise and Ross, p. 132.

[3] Fleming, p. 1010; 'On May 13 it was announced that Khrushchev was going to Paris two days before the conference opened, as Victor Zorza (of the Manchester *Guardian*) saw it, "to give the President the opportunity to negotiate privately and provide assurance" that the flights would be stopped.' Fleming, p. 1009.

[4] Fleming, p. 1010. Macmillan was told Monday morning, May 16.

Instead, he allowed Khrushchev to read a prepared statement on the opening day of the conference (May 16) in which the Soviet Premier recalled Eisenhower's refusal to negotiate under the threat of a peace treaty with East Germany, and asked how his Government could negotiate under the threat that American aircraft would continue to fly over Soviet territory. The Soviet Union could not 'be among the participants in negotiation where one of them has made treachery the basis of his policy with regard to the Soviet Union'. If the US would declare its intention not to violate the borders of USSR in the future, that it deplored the provocative actions taken in the past, and would punish those directly guilty, the Soviet Union would be assured of equal conditions with other powers and he would be ready to participate in the conference.

Then President Eisenhower read a statement which had been prepared with knowledge of what Khrushchev would say. He denied that the US had threatened continued overflights. 'The US had made no such threat.' 'In point of fact, these flights were suspended after the recent incident and are not to be resumed. Accordingly, this cannot be the issue.'[1]

Thus Eisenhower tried nonchalantly to pass over the issue; but the issue was there, and Khrushchev had been permitted to cast the die, and he could not then simply act as if nothing had happened. De Gaulle suggested a twenty-four hour recess, which was agreed upon and a further meeting of the four was arranged for May 17. 'Khrushchev showed no desire to leave Paris immediately. He still behaved as a man who was willing to talk, provided the price was right. In the morning he left for a tour of Malinovsky's old battle-field at Sezanne.'[2] But when the Western Three met the same morning 'Mr Macmillan's aim of a decent funeral gave way to the aim of ensuring that responsibility for the failure of the conference would be seen to rest on Mr Khrushchev.'[3]

A sudden invitation to attend a summit meeting was sent after the Soviet Premier. 'According to eyewitnesses, his face lit up when he saw the document, and he at once turned back to Paris.' At the same time, Presidential Press Secretary Hagerty issued a statement asserting that Soviet participation at the three o'clock meeting

---

[1] Fleming, p. 1011; Wise and Ross, p. 154.
[2] Paul Johnson, *New Statesman*, May 28, 1960; cited in Fleming, p. 1012.
[3] Robert Stephens, the London *Observer*, May 22, 1960; cited in Fleming.

would be taken as a withdrawal of Khruschev's conditions. Khrushchev was given a copy of this statement, which had been issued without clearing it with either the British or the French, 'and at this point the conference expired'. (*New Statesman*)[1]

Khrushchev, however, was not content to let the conference expire; he had been put, as the Alsops observed on May 11, 'in a domestic political situation requiring an explosion', and explode he did. On May 18, the day after the conference had collapsed, the Soviet Premier held a press conference. He 'swaggered and bullied. He waved his arm and punched his fist in the air. He glowered ominously and then burst into sunbeams of jocular ribaldry'. (New York *Times*.) 'He seemed obsessed by the spy plane incident. The subject recurred constantly, sandwiched between scornful and hostile remarks about America and President Eisenhower.' (London *Daily Telegraph*.) The violence of Khrushchev's attack drove the entire press of Western Europe to the President's side and 'led to the practically unanimous conclusion that Khrushchev had not been justified in breaking off the conference on account of the U-2 incident'.[2] Thus, as on so many other occasions during the cold war, the Russians managed to generate an atmosphere in which their own intentions drew the very suspicions and critical judgements which they had sought to direct towards their opponents.

The two years following the summit collapse witnessed a significant reversal in Soviet policies of 'peaceful coexistence': a return to unilateral attempts to solve the Berlin question, a resumption of 'saber-rattling' and nuclear tests, a retreat on the issue of on-site inspections in regard to a test-ban treaty, and finally, the provocative and reckless emplacement of missiles in Cuba. This reversal seems to raise serious questions about the significance or perhaps even the existence of a nuclear stalemate, and also about Soviet intentions.

To assess these developments, it is necessary to analyze the power situation as it had evolved in 1960 and 1961 and also to take account of the advent of a new administration in Washington, since the more significant changes towards a 'hard' aggressive line in Soviet foreign policy occurred after this event. For the moment, we will confine outselves to an examination of those factors which were already manifest in the spring of the summit of 1960.

[1] ibid., p. 1012.   [2] ibid., p. 1014.

CHAPTER XXI

Nuclear Strategies and the Missile Gap

THE development of Soviet nuclear power during the years 1949–57, and of the capacity to deliver nuclear bombs to targets in the United States, necessitated a change in US military thinking. Two competing strategies were put forward to meet the new situation. The first, called 'counter-force', was premised on the assumption 'that thermonuclear war is possible, conceivable, acceptable and that it will be "won" or "lost" in the classical sense'. Its proponents agree that it would be preferable to prevent such a war from taking place, 'but they think the only effective prevention is the establishment of a force capable of winning such a war and accepting the surrender of the enemy'.[1]

'Counter-force', as the name suggests, is a strategic concept which envisions as targets only enemy delivery capabilities, not enemy cities. Although opponents of this theory argued that the emplacement of missile sites near cities, combined with the enormous destructive capacity of thermonuclear weapons and the hazards of fall-out, made the distinction between civilian and military targets almost meaningless, counter-force theorists maintained, that with adequate civilian defense and shelter programs, American deaths in an all-out war with the Soviet Union could be held down to thirty million, which they regarded as an 'acceptable loss'.

In opposition to counter-force, military strategists centered mainly in the Army and Navy argued for a counter-city 'limited deterrent'. Premised on the assumptions 'that "to win" or "to lose" a thermonuclear war is inconceivable; . . .' limited deterrent theory

---

[1] This account is drawn mainly from the excellent article by Arthur Waskow, 'The Theory and Practice of Deterrence' in *The Liberal Papers*. For a slightly different view of the origins of these two theories, cf. Blackett. *Studies of War*, pp. 128–46, 152–4.

holds 'that such a war must be prevented' and that prevention of such a war is possible by means of 'sharply increasing its terror'.

In contradistinction to counter-force, counter-city envisions *only* population centers as targets. Thus both sides are permitted to hold each other's cities as 'hostages'. Since neither side is militarily capable of destroying the other's delivery capacity, both sides will refrain from launching a nuclear attack – 'for any nation which under such circumstances struck first would be condemning its own population, its economy, its government, its very existence to death'.

Counter-city strategy is also known as a theory of 'limited deterrence', not only because a relatively small nuclear capability is all that is necessary to inflict heavy civilian casualties, but because to be effective, counter-city strategy demands a limitation on the build-up of nuclear arms. Otherwise, the danger arises, that one side might develop so much striking capacity as to be able to destroy its opponent's delivery capacity.[1] This would rob the deterrent of its 'deterrent' power, and strongly tempt the side that had developed the capability, to strike first.

If counter-city strategy implies a limited nuclear build-up, counter-force strategy requires a maximum nuclear effort, because from the root premise that there can be victory in thermonuclear war, it follows that the capacity must be developed to win. This capacity involves being able to destroy all of the enemy's delivery capability in a possible 'pre-emptive' first strike.

As with all military programs, these strategies have important political ramifications. If counter-city strategy were adopted, for example, a stable balance of terror would presumably come into existence. The resulting period of relative stability would be favorable to a serious attempt to negotiate a far-reaching disarmament agreement. Such an agreement would be highly desirable if for no other reason than that the balance of terror would not be stable against irrational acts or technical accidents.[2]

On the other hand, counter-force strategy is based on the view that the balance of terror is of necessity highly unstable, because an

---

[1] 'Killing' a city is easier than 'killing' a missile, especially one in a hardened base; such a missile has to be hit very accurately by a nuclear warhead. On the other hand, if a great number of warheads are available, to be used against one missile, the necessity for accuracy decreases.

[2] Blackett, op. cit., p. 153.

enemy might develop the capacity to deal a 'successful' aggressive strike, that is, with little or no fear of being hit back.[1] Counter-force depends for its effectiveness on the rapid build-up and advance of nuclear technology and therefore, a nation having adopted this strategy would tend to regard the prospects of disarmament and control with scepticism and caution. Moreover, the proliferation of weapons as a result of any counter-force build-up would complicate the problems of disarmament and control immensely.

Counter-force is by its very nature a first-strike strategy. There is no point in developing a gigantic capacity to annihilate enemy missile sites after their missiles have been fired. Even granting that missile launchers can be used for a second missile, if counter-force does not reduce the enemy's ability to inflict an unacceptable blow, it has no advantages over a minimum deterrent strategy which is far less costly and far less provocative. 'At a minimum [counter-force] leaves the opponent constantly subject to nuclear blackmail.'[2]

The provocative nature of counterforce is confirmed by Blackett:

> ... a counter-force strategy implies the necessity for a many-fold overall nuclear superiority over the enemy. Moreover, since for such a strike to have the slightest chance of success it must come as a complete surprise to the enemy, it must be a 'first-strike': that is to say, the country which makes it must be the aggressor as regards strategic nuclear war. This policy has various pseudo-nyms, a maximum deterrent posture, a first-counter-force-strike-capability, or, in plain English, providing the capability for nuclear aggression.[3]

Eisenhower failed to resolve this inter-service dispute between the Army–Navy minimum deterrent proponents and the Air Force proponents of counter-force. However as the economy began to sag the Government sought a solution in additional arms spending, which fit in well with the requirements of building a counter-force capability. In the face of the 1958 recession, and following the Rockefeller and Gaither reports, Eisenhower increased the military budget by $12 billion. Counter-force theory also fitted the psychological molds

---

[1] cf. Blackett, ibid., p. 154; cf. also p. 128 et seq. for a critique of this view.
[2] C. Bolton, 'Cuba: Pivot to the Future', *The Nation*, November 17, 1962.
[3] Blackett, op. cit., p. 154.

forged in the period of early American atomic monopoly, not only the belief in the necessity of maintaining a huge military superiority, but the strategic doctrine of creating 'situations of strength', i.e. of translating superiority into supremacy and compelling Russia to come to American terms. As a result of these and other factors, by fiscal 1960 the United States was well on the way towards the development of a counter-force-first-strike-capability, 'or in plain English, the capability for nuclear aggression'.

To measure the development of this capability, we must begin with the fact that Navy proponents of counter-city or minimum deterrent strategy maintained that 45 Polaris submarines, containing a total of 720 missiles with 360 megatons, would constitute an adequate and invulnerable minimum deterrent. Anything more than this, they argued, would turn the Polaris into a provocative counter-force weapon because with additional submarines the fleet would become capable of massing 'so many explosions in the territory of the enemy that by sheer salvo technique atomic capability would be destroyed'.[1]

Jerome B. Wiesner, Chairman of the President's Science Advisory Committee in the Kennedy Administration, has suggested a 200 missile 500 megaton minimum deterrent, designed to satisfy those those 'who contend that the Soviet leaders are prepared to sacrifice a third of their inhabitants and most of their cities if by doing so they could achieve world domination'.[2] Finally, P. M. S. Blackett has suggested that a 20 missile deterrent would be adequate on the assumption that no nation would wage an aggressive nuclear war knowing that it would lose more than 20 million citizens and its major industrial, political and population centers in the first exchange.[3]

By 1961, when the Eisenhower weapons program was superceded by the Kennedy program, the United States was estimated to possess a nuclear stockpile amounting to 30,000 megatons, or the equivalent of 10 tens of TNT for every man, woman and child on the face of the earth. The number of nuclear delivery vehicles, tactical as well as strategic, was 'in the tens of thousands' according to the Defense

[1] Waskow, op. cit., pp. 131–2.
[2] Wiesner, 'Comprehensive Arms Limitation Systems', *Daedalus*, Fall, 1960.
[3] The largest twenty cities in the US have a combined population of more than 50 million.

Department. This included over a hundred missiles of intercontinental and intermediate range, 80 Polaris missiles, 1,700 intercontinental bombers, 300 nuclear armed carrier-borne aircraft with megaton warheads and nearly 1,000 supersonic land based fighters with nuclear warheads.

Thus, in the Eisenhower years, albeit under no clear-cut strategy directive, the United States had built a nuclear capability of agressive proportions. More striking than this, however, was the fact that, under a conscious policy decision taken early in the decade, *the Soviet Union had done exactly the reverse:* it had built a small retaliatory capacity and adopted a posture of minimum deterrence.

As of January 1962, Soviet nuclear strength was estimated at only 50 ICBMs, 150 intercontinental bombers (compared with 1,700 US) and 400 intermediate range missiles trained on US overseas and Nato bases.[1]

Against this background of relative Soviet weakness and American strength, the U-2 incident takes on new meaning. Blackett points out that the only serious Soviet defense against a counter-force first strike was the secrecy surrounding the location of Soviet nuclear bases. But 'one of the main objects of the U-2 flights was to locate the Soviet nuclear bases'. It was, according to Washington sources, the failure of these flights to find any appreciable number of operational missile sites[2] that led President Eisenhower to start reducing the numbers of operational B-47 bombers.

Khrushchev, of course, was aware that the U-2 flights had been going on for some years prior to spring 1960. Presumably the Soviet Command's response was greater dispersal and camouflage. 'What must have disturbed the Soviet military staff,' Blackett conjectures, 'was President Eisenhower's justification for them as essential for American security. This implied that American security could be maintained only if the United States had sufficient information as to the locality of Russian nuclear sites to make possible a successful surprise, and therefore aggressive, nuclear attack on the Soviet

---

[1] New York *Times,* November 20, 1961, and January 6, 1962; cited in Blackett, op. cit., p. 149.

[2] '. . . at the height of the "missile gap" furore near the end of the decade, those who ran the U-2 program reported the plane was able to locate only two ICBM sites in the Soviet Union, both of them test centers.' – Wise and Ross, p. 58.

nuclear delivery system. In other words, America appeared to be planning for the capability to make a first counter-force strike.'[1]

In the face of this prospect, some time in the latter half of 1960 or early 1961, 'it seems probable that the Soviet Command began to have doubts as to the adequacy of the minimum deterrent posture in relation to America's much greater nuclear strength'.[2] These doubts would have been raised not only by the U-2 incident and the President's response, but by the current dynamic forces on the US political scene.

To Eisenhower's left, the Democratic National Committee was calling for a $7 billion increase (16 per cent) in the already enormous $43 billion Eisenhower defense outlay, which itself represented more than 50 per cent of the total budget. To the President's right, Senator Goldwater was making very clear his predilection for military solutions to cold war problems. 'We must be prepared,' he said in 1960, 'to undertake military operations against vulnerable Communist régimes.'

Even more impressive to Soviet strategists might have been institutional factors, in particular, the growth of an enormous military-industrial complex during the post-war decade in the US. In May 1957, a Government report issued under the direction of Ralph J. Cordiner, President of the General Electric Co. revealed that the Defense Department owned $160 billion worth of property, 'by any yardstick of measurement the world's largest organization'. In addition, the Defense Department employed 3·5 million persons, almost a million of them civilians. Its annual payroll was $11 billion, more than twice that of the automobile industry; the number of persons directly dependent on the military for their jobs totalled as much as one-tenth of the nation's entire labor force. The Pentagon owned more than 32 million acres of land in the US and another 2·6 million in other countries.[3] Moreover, a 1960 Congressional report showed that the top hundred corporations that split up three-quarters of the $21 billion armaments bill employed more than 1,400 retired officers from the rank of major up, including 260 generals or officers of flag rank.[4]

[1] Blackett, ibid., p. 158–9.
[2] Blackett, pp. 158–9.
[3] Cook, op. cit.
[4] Cook, op. cit.; cf. also C. Wright Mills, *The Power Elite*.

Eisenhower himself felt it necessary in his farewell address to caution the American people about the growth of this military-industrial complex whose influence was felt 'in every city, every state house, every office of the Federal Government'. 'The potential for the disastrous rise of misplaced power exists,' warned Eisenhower, 'and will persist.'

This visible growth of a military–industrial complex, the increasing power of a radical right, the gradual development of a counter-force capability, and the demand from the 'élite consensus' for a step-up in the military budget must have combined with internal Soviet political factors and fears stemming from the Soviet leaders' consciousness of their own military weakness, to change the tone and conduct of Soviet foreign policy following the 1960 summit collapse.

Even more interesting than the way Soviet policy is clarified in the light of these facts and developments, is the way in which certain patterns of American thinking are revealed. For the true situation with regard to comparative nuclear strengths was not made public in America until February 1962 and was presumably not known by many officials until after Kennedy's inauguration in January 1961. In the interim, that is from about 1957, it was generally believed that the reverse was true, namely, that the United States was about to enter a period, beginning in the early sixties, when the Soviets would have a 4:1 edge in intercontinental ballistic missiles.

The reaction of certain key sectors of the American leadership to this 'gap', despite the fact that projected American striking power for the period was formidable (1,200 intercontinental bombers,[1] 19 Polaris submarines with 304 missiles, 1,000 carrier-based and overseas-based planes capable of dropping nuclear bombs, dozens of Minuteman ICBMs, etc.) is extremely revealing.

On August 14, 1958, Senator John F. Kennedy addressed the Senate on the critical nature of the 'missile gap'. The Senator found the gap to be so critical, in fact, as to 'invalidate' ten American assumptions 'which probably are most fundamental to our thinking in the twentieth century'. 'Why can we not realize,' Senator Kennedy asked, 'that the coming years of the gap present us with a peril *more deadly than any wartime danger we have ever known*?' [Emphasis added.]

This tremendous significance attributed to superior striking

---

[1] The smaller number of bombers would be the result of the phasing out of obsolete B-47's.

power in missiles (the Senator was aware of the low numbers of Soviet heavy bombers, since that 'gap' had evaporated earlier) is reminiscent and indeed not unrelated to the early confidence in the West in the immense advantage supposedly accruing to the possessor of an atomic monopoly. Indeed, it is only by recognizing the immense importance which US leaders attributed to this new weapon that a more serious failure in their perspective can be explained.

For the most salient and striking feature of the revised estimates of Soviet nuclear strength was the way in which they provided US leaders with a basis for re-evaluating Soviet intentions. In his Senate speech on the missile gap, Senator Kennedy painted a picture of the Soviet threat in traditional, though to his mind, updated terms:

> ... nuclear destruction is not the only way in which the Soviets will be able to use their advantages in striking power. War is not so much an objective of foreign policy as an instrument – a means of securing power and influence, of advancing a nation's views and interests. In the years of the gap, the Soviets may be expected to use their superior striking ability to achieve their objectives in ways which may not require launching an actual attack. *Their missile power will be the shield behind which they will slowly but surely, advance – through Sputnik diplomacy, limited brush-fire wars, indirect non-overt aggression, intimidation and subversion, internal revolution, increased prestige or influence, and the vicious blackmail of our allies. The periphery of the Free World will slowly be nibbled away....*[1]

However, in 1961, it was not only apparent in Washington that the Soviets did not have the military power to back up these objectives, but that they had not *planned* to develop such power, and in fact, had planned to develop considerably less power than their resources would have made possible. In this case, military policy was obviously the acid test of Soviet intentions. For if they had intended to overrun Europe, for example, or to 'nibble' the Free World at its borders, they certainly could not have afforded to demobilize their armies and at the same time *plan* to develop a nuclear capability inferior to striking power in the West.

[1] Kennedy, *Strategy of Peace*, p. 65. Emphasis added.

Moreover, because these moves involved long-range planning, and because the overall strategy which they represented was adhered to over several years under varying international conditions, and maintained, in addition, in strict secrecy, it is obvious that they cannot be dismissed as part of a 'tactical maneuver' for propaganda purposes.

The only plausible explanation for this Soviet strategy that is commensurate with the messianic formulations of Marxist theory is that the policy of peaceful coexistence, meaning victory for socialism through economic competition with the West, is and has been for some years the long-term strategy of the Soviet leadership, and the only one for which they have built the requisite military capability.[1] Indeed, a 'minimum deterrent' or purely retaliatory capability is ideal for such a strategy since it exerts a minimal drain on the country's economic resources while maximizing the possibilities for disarmament (by keeping the number of arms low), which must precede a full-scale competition. And, indeed, between 1955 and 1960, the Soviet Union cut its military budget by more than half.[2]

Now it is one of the distressing facts of the whole episode of the 'missile gap', that this unique opportunity for assessing Soviet intentions went by without producing any real reappraisal in the West, and the opportunity for attempting a *détente* went unseized. The failure of the Kennedy Administration to reassess the political situation, on achieving office, and to be guided by such a reassessment is registered in the fact that the new leadership immediately undertook a substantial increase in armaments (a 2·3 billion dollar increase after two months in office, a one-quarter billion dollar increase after four months, a three and one-quarter billion dollar increase after six months, and so on) *before* attempting to test Soviet

[1] cf. Isaac Deutscher, *The Great Contest: Russia and the West*, 1960, for the setting and terms of this competition as envisioned by the Soviet leaders. The fact that Soviet foreign policy under Khrushchev did not strictly adhere to the principles of peaceful coexistence, does not contradict the view that it is the basic of long-term Soviet planning. In Deutscher's view, Soviet diplomacy seeks to freeze the demarcation lines between the two blocs, until the Soviet bloc achieves economic parity with the West. At this point, the Soviet Union will be able to adopt a policy of 'Open Doors', because open doors, 'will favor the wealthier and more efficient of the antagonists. Only then will the Soviet challenge to "peaceful competition" acquire its full force.'

[2] E. O'Ballance, *The Red Army*, p. 199.

intentions, for example, on general disarmament. Contributing to this failure was the tenacity of long-held assumptions and cold war dogmas, not only about the Soviet Union, as we shall see, but about 'absolute weapons' and 'positions of strength', as well.

IV. The Kennedy Years

. . . to those nations who would make themselves our adversary, we offer not a pledge but a request: that both sides begin anew the quest for peace, before the dark powers of destruction unleashed by science engulf all humanity in planned or accidental self-destruction. . . .

Let both sides unite to heed in all corners of the earth the command of Isaiah – to go 'undo the heavy burdens . . . [and] let the oppressed go free'.

And if a beach-head of co-operation may push back the jungle of suspicion, let both sides join in creating a new endeavor, *not a new balance of power*, but a new world of law, where the strong are just and the weak secure and the peace preserved.

> JOHN F. KENNEDY,
> Inaugural Address January 20, 1961
> [Emphasis added.]

Our problem has been that we expect the voice of terror to be frenzied, and that of madness irrational. It is quite the contrary in a world where genial, middle-aged Generals consult with precise social scientists about the parameters of the death equation, and the problem of its maximization. The most rational, orderly, disciplined minds of our time are working long hours in our most efficient laboratories, at the task of eliminating us.

> ROBERT SCHEER

CHAPTER XXII

Creating Situations of Strength

WHILE assessing somewhat sceptically the results of Nikita Khrushchev's 1959 visit to the United States, Senator John F. Kennedy expressed in characteristically pragmatic terms, a cautious optimism towards the event. 'It is far better,' he said, 'that we meet at the summit than at the brink.' Although there is a danger in overemphasizing the influence of individuals in history, it is by no means irrelevant to seek the reasons for the fact that it was Eisenhower who met Khrushchev at the summit, while Kennedy, in a relatively short time, met him at the brink.

An appropriate place to begin such a search is with Kennedy's critique of the summit failure in June 1960. The summit collapse, he said, marked the end of an era of illusion – 'the illusion that platitudes and slogans are a substitute for strength and planning' and that 'personal good will' is a substitute for 'strong creative leadership'. The conference collapse, continued Kennedy, 'was the direct result of Soviet determination to destroy the talks'. It was evident, that the effort to eliminate world tensions through a summit meeting was 'doomed to failure' because 'we have failed for the past eight years to build the positions of long-term strength essential to successful negotiation'. The Soviets knew that they had 'more to gain from the increasing deterioration of America's world position than from any concession that might be made in Paris' and for that reason, the conference was doomed.[1]

The most striking thing about this critique was its orthodoxy, its wholly traditional outlook within the context of American political debate. For this was nothing more than the old 'new realism' of Kennan and Acheson. Kennedy's commitment to Achesonian doctrine was made inescapably clear in the same speech as the Senator generalized his views on negotiations. Starting with the

[1] *Strategy of Peace*, p.v.

observation that 'as long as Mr Khrushchev is convinced that the balance of world power is shifting his way' no diplomatic approach could 'compel him to enter fruitful negotiations', Kennedy concluded: 'Our task is to rebuild our strength, and the strength of the free world – to prove to the Soviets that time and the course of history are not on their side, that the balance of world power is not shifting their way – and that therefore peaceful settlement is essential to mutual survival.'

Operating under this thesis, Kennedy was soon to encounter serious difficulties, not simply because his conception was conservative in a time demanding 'invention, innovation, imagination', but because it was not adequate. It could not, for example, explain the Soviet withdrawals from Austria and Finland, nor the unilateral reduction of Soviet forces in Europe.[1] And it did not address itself to the problem of United States' failure to test Soviet intentions on disarmament and disengagement proposals. Moreover, it did not face the problems created by those very situations of strength which had resulted from the previous application of this thesis, not only the treaty-complicating presence of new weapons, but also the emergence of a revivified and rearmed Germany and France, which had already proved to be an obstacle to settlement.

Although the problem of power lay at the center of Kennedy's approach to politics as he entered the Presidency (he has been described as a 'power-oriented pragmatist')[2] it certainly could not be said to have exhausted his approach. Kennedy's sense of the social and nationalist revolutions in the have-not areas of the world, for example, was far more sophisticated than Eisenhower's, (though probably not much more so than Acheson's in the China *White Paper*) as were the tools with which he proposed to deal with these

---

[1] Nor the conscious Soviet decision not to exploit its missile advantage, but John F. Kennedy presumably did not know this in June 1960.

[2] William V. Shannon, 'The Kennedy Administration: The Early Months', *The American Scholar*, Fall, 1961. 'Kennedy's two most central personal characteristics are his urge to power and his fear of failure. . . . His propensity to personalize substantive issues, as he did in connection with the rise in steel prices in 1962, is unusual even for a man clearly trying to telescope generations into half-decades. His candid definition of prestige, offered during the campaign in connection with foreign public opinion of the United States, is very revealing in this respect. "I define prestige as influence, as an ability to persuade people to accept your point of view." Not just esteem and respect, but power over other people.' Williams, *The US, Cuba and Castro*, p. 148.

revolutions. On the other hand, the limitations imposed by his domestic political context rendered his flexibility in these areas very small, and made the *sine qua non* for the realization of his programs, the development of a personal authority and power that Eisenhower had had by nature, and that he would have to achieve by skill.

For Kennedy had been elected by only a narrow margin (0·3 per cent of the vote) and was faced, therefore, with the post-election task of further trying to win over the electorate. The strong leadership which he felt to be most necessary for the US and the Western alliance, was impossible without a large popular mandate.

Kennedy's initial approach to this problem was to place Republicans in every key cabinet post but Secretary of State.[1] The real split in American politics at this time, however, and particularly on international issues, was not between Democrats and Republicans, but between those who maintained a rigid McCarthyist view of the world split and those who, in the main, did not. Representative Walter Judd, a member of the former group and keynote speaker at the Republican nominating convention in 1960, gave oratorical expression to the chief line of opposition that would confront Kennedy in office. Judd 'made the rafters roar and the benches shake' as he asked:

Was it the Republicans who recognized the Soviet Union in 1933 ... as if it were a respectable and dependable member thereof?

Was it the Republicans who, at Teheran, against the urgent advice of Mr Churchill, agreed to give the Russians a free hand in the Balkans? ['No,' roared the crowd.]

Was it the Republicans who secretly divided Poland and gave half of it to the Soviet Union? ['No!']

Was it a Republican Administration that divided Korea and gave North Korea to the Communists? ['No.']

And so on.[2]

[1] Lippmann, 'Kennedy at Mid-term', *Newsweek*, January 21, 1963. The Republicans were C. Douglas Dillon (Treasury), McNamara (Defense), Allen Dulles – then McCone (CIA), 'and at the center of high policy-making itself, he put McGeorge Bundy ... a lifelong Massachusetts Republican'.
[2] Cited in T. H. White, *The Making of the President, 1960*, p. 206.

With an opposition drawn along these lines, Kennedy was assured that every attempt to neutralize a torn area (such as Laos or Viet Nam), every step towards disengaging forces in Europe, every failure to intervene against left-led or Communist-dominated social revolutions, would be treated as appeasement, as would every step to normalize relations with countries such as China and Cuba, and in that way to let healthy evolutionary pressures towards democracy and industrial development take their course.

In this situation Kennedy exhibited an ambiguous attitude. On the one hand, he appreciated the danger of a number of the myths of the McCarthy legacy, and once in office made an assault upon them. In his inaugural he came out strongly against the expectation of total victory (which could only mean a military victory) and called on the nation to be ready 'to bear the burden of a long twilight struggle, year in and year out, "rejoicing in hope, patient in tribulation" – a struggle against the common enemies of man: tyranny, poverty, disease and war itself.'[1]

On the other hand, he accepted many of these mythical assumptions (the world cannot endure 'half free and half slave') and tended to recognize in others the levers to the power he needed, and to use them to that end. There is no more clear-cut example of this than his late campaign assault on the Eisenhower Administration's policies towards Cuba.

As the presidential campaign entered its final phase, the Senate Internal Security Sub-Committee, dominated by Democrats, released a report charging that Cuba 'was handed to Castro and the Communists by a combination of Americans in the same way China was handed to the Communists.' The report was largely based on the testimony of two pro-Batista ambassadors to Cuba, Earl E. T. Smith (a personal friend of Kennedy) and Arthur Gardner. Following publication of the report, Kennedy made the Cuban theme a major part of his campaign.

On October 6, he blamed the Eisenhower Administration for allowing Cuba to become 'communism's first Caribbean base'. At the same moment that he criticized the Administration for supporting the Batista dictatorship, Kennedy approvingly noted

[1] In 1962 Senator Goldwater responded with a book called *Why Not Victory?*

that Ambassadors Gardner and Smith had warned 'that communism was a moving force in the Castro leadership', but that the Administration had failed to heed their advice.

On October 18, Nixon responded, saying that 'this Communist–Cuban régime' had become an 'intolerable cancer' and that the time was now at hand 'when patience is no longer a virtue'. The next day the Administration announced a sweeping embargo on United States trade with Cuba. In New York, Kennedy hit back asserting that the embargo was 'too little and too late' and that it followed an 'incredible history of blunder, inaction, retreat and failure'. He went on to urge stiffer sanctions and that the United States should attempt 'to strengthen the non-Batista democratic forces in exile and in Cuba itself. . . .'

On October 22, Nixon accused Kennedy of advancing a 'shockingly reckless' proposal that could set off World War III. At this very moment, of course, Nixon was giving his own approval to the CIA operation in Miami. . . .[1]

One can only wonder if Kennedy assessed the difficulty he was creating at the time for the man who would assume the Presidency in January. For to speak at this late hour in terms which unmistakably pointed to a military solution was to reinforce the very McCarthyist theses which had tied the hands of diplomacy with regard to China ten years before.

Not surprisingly, therefore, when Kennedy actually came to office, and found himself faced with a deteriorating situation in Laos (where a CIA *coup* of rightist forces had toppled the neutralist régime of Souvanna Phouma and increased the power of the Communists) and in Cuba (which was on the verge of receiving Soviet MIGs), knowing that he himself soon would be charged with doing nothing against this threat, he opted for a power solution to the problem.

When the ill-conceived invasion of Cuba collapsed, Kennedy was faced with an incredibly difficult moment, for he had 'lost' Cuba, and since by his option he had legitimized a military solution, the charges that he had not gone far enough (e.g. he had failed to provide the invaders with US air cover) would be difficult to answer. Thus, Kennedy found it necessary to 'prove' himself, and to prove himself

[1] This account is taken from Szulc and Meyer, op. cit.

on grounds that could only lead him back to the sterility and peril of the worst cold war postures.

On April 20, 1961, following the débacle at the Bay of Pigs, Kennedy addressed the American Society of Newspaper Editors. Gone were his words about the complex challenges to be faced, the social, the technological, the nationalist revolutions, the manifold waves which the Communists rode to power and the manifold responses necessary to meet these challenges. Instead, he declared, in accents strange for the leader of a liberal democracy:

> The message of Cuba, of Laos, of the rising din of Communist voices in Asia and Latin America – these messages are all the same. The complacent, the self-indulgent, the soft societies are about to be swept away with the debris of history. Only the strong, only the industrious, only the determined, only the courageous, only the visionary who determine the real nature of our struggle can possibly survive.

This was, of course, a low point for Kennedy, a moment of deep stress, and it would be wrong to judge his leadership in this one episode. None the less, other indications point to the fact that a very central Kennedy nerve was laid bare here, one so central as to have important repercussions later on:

> The crisis [of October 1962] was really born at the Bay of Pigs. . . . Six months later, in October 1961, President Kennedy, still bearing his scars from the disaster, secretly ordered the Joint Chiefs of Staff to prepare an invasion plan for Cuba – to be used when and if needed. This top secret war plan took months to prepare, but when the strategists and computers had finished, with every plane, warship and assault unit tagged, it was calculated that the first troops could hit Cuban beaches eight days after a 'go' signal. . . .[1]

When Kennedy did use his political wisdom as, for example, in accepting a settlement in Laos which would make the country neutral, he found himself hedged in by his opponents (and by his

[1] Fletcher Knebel, 'Washington in Crisis', *Look* Magazine, December 18, 1962.

own conservative approach) and unable to even consider such a settlement for the failing situation in South Viet Nam. It was argued that this would initiate a pattern of 'falling dominoes' in Southeast Asia, creating one neutral state after another. Therefore, Kennedy's response to the weakening of the Diem régime in Vietnam was to step up the US military commitment there (including a ten-fold increase in US military personnel).

By the summer of 1961, Senator Fulbright was warning:

> In the long run, it is quite possible that the principal problem of leadership will be, if it is not already, to restrain the desire of the people to hit the Communists with everything we've got, particularly if there are more Cubas and Laoses. . . .[1]

Fulbright's memorandum was issued in the heat of a struggle by the Kennedy Administration to bring the military under civilian control and to prevent them from indoctrinating the public with right-wing propaganda. Kennedy's victory in this battle was significant and hard-won; but it was fought against the background of the Berlin crisis, a militant stand by the President on the defense of the *status quo* in Berlin, and a huge military build-up by the United States. There is no question that Kennedy was aided by these factors, nor conversely that his conduct on the international scene was in some measure influenced by his domestic political context.

When Kennedy assumed office, he immediately discovered that there was no 'missile gap' and that Intelligence estimates of Soviet missile strength had been revised down 70 per cent since December 1959. Moreover, in June, they were reduced to 15 per cent and, in September 1961, to 3.5 per cent of their original size.[2] (Thus, on the strength of the Eisenhower program alone, by December 1961, the US had a 3 : 1 advantage in missiles and a 10 : 1 advantage in heavy bombers over the Soviet Union.[3]) To take just the figure which Kennedy became aware of when he first took office, together

---

[1] Cited in Fred Cook, 'Juggernaut – The Warfare State', p. 322.
[2] P. M. S. Blackett, 'Steps Towards Disarmament', *Scientific American*, April, 1962. The figures are drawn from an authoritative article by Senator Stuart Symington in the Feb. 15, 1962 issue of *The Reporter*.
[3] *US News and World Report*, November 6, 1961.

with the revised heavy bomber figure (which was already known to Kennedy in 1960), even these could only have meant that the Russians had decided not to exploit their time advantage in missile development, but to accept a period of stability until some scheme of disarmament could be worked out. The Russians would have had an intrinsic interest in disarmament (since not only was such a balance not stable against accident and irrational acts, but a minimum nuclear arm could not be used as an instrument of policy against another comparable or greater nuclear arm).

With the new administration unburdened by the collapse of the previous year's summit talks, the situation was once again ripe for some progress towards an agreement reducing the risks of war. But no progress was in fact made. When U S Ambassador Thompson saw Khrushchev in March, he received the impression that the Soviets had lost interest in a separate test-ban agreement and were no longer willing to sign it ahead of a comprehensive treaty on 'general and complete disarmament'.[1]

The reversal of the Soviet position stemmed, as we saw earlier from fear of the loss of the security of their nuclear bases and fear of the rise to power in the U S of groups that might try to make use of the United States' great nuclear superiority to attack the Soviet nuclear delivery system. Given these fears, writes Blackett, the rejection by the USSR of the British–American test-ban draft treaty in the spring of 1961 finds a simple military explanation.

'For if a detailed study of this document is made, it is clear that the process of setting up and operating the proposed international inspection system might conceivably have served to reveal the location of some, at least, of the Soviet missile sites. At any rate, it would be very hard to convince a military staff officer of any nationality that this possibility was negligible. . . . The obvious Soviet fear of inspection may well have been because they had so little to inspect.'[2]

Thus, when the Kennedy Administration initially asked for a delay in the resumption of the test-ban talks until March so that the subject could be studied, the Soviets readily agreed. But when the U S indicated that it felt the necessity even more strongly to

[1] R. Lowenthal. 'The Dangerous Year', *Encounter*, June 1961.
[2] Blackett, op. cit., p. 161–2.

take time for a review of disarmament issues, 'the USSR was . . . less accommodating', In a private discussion between Stevenson and Gromyko, the latter seemed 'particularly insistent on pressing the United States to take an immediate position on disarmament'.[1] (The United States had not yet resumed its April 1955 position supporting the principle of general disarmament.) As early as November 1960, according to Blackett, 'individual Russians bluntly stated that if the West continued to stall on disarmament, the USSR would be forced into massive rearmament.'[2]

As a Senator, Kennedy had shown his acumen in singling out the balance of terror as a *source* of political tensions as well as merely a symptom of them. 'Behind many political conflicts,' he had said, 'lie problems of the military balance of power . . . problems that would not arise outside the context of the arms race.'[3] In the early spring of 1961, Kennedy was in a very secure and flexible position *vis-à-vis* the Russians, because of his power advantage, and had many initiatives open to him to demonstrate to them that he was serious about disarmament and would welcome reciprocal evidence of seriousness on their part.

Knowing that the Russians had neither planned for a surprise attack nor developed a capability for one, Kennedy was in a position to *know* that he was taking no risks, should he decide to embark upon a limited reduction of strategic nuclear forces or simply freeze existing levels, and this also increased the prospects for such a move. Instead, on March 28, 1961, he began to implement his campaign pledge to increase defense preparations, despite the fact that the pledge had been made on the basis of estimates of Soviet missile strength which he now knew to be false by a margin of 70 per cent. In a special budget message to the Congress on this date, Kennedy submitted his first requests for changes in the Eisenhower defense program amounting to a $2·3 billion net increase, and falling into two main groups.

First, there were several requests designed to improve US conventional strength, including research, development and procurement of newer and better weapons, increased ship modernization, fighter-plane increases, and increased army and marine

[1] Stebbins, *The US in World Affairs, 1961*, pp. 70–71.
[2] Blackett, p. 160.
[3] Kennedy, op. cit., p. 52.

personnel, mostly for guerrilla warfare. Second, money was requested to accelerate and improve US nuclear strategic capabilities. Ten Polaris submarines with 160 missiles were added – a better than 50 per cent increase over the previous total of 19 – to those expected to be completed by 1964. In the Minuteman program, 150 stationary ICBMs were added and 90 mobile missiles dropped for a net increase of 60 ICBMs, production capacity was doubled to prepare for possible future expansion in the program, and certain design changes were introduced. Finally, extra money was requested to accelerate the Skybolt 1,000 mile air-to-ground missile, to increase the number of SAC planes on fifteen-minute ground alert to about one-half the total force, and to develop the capability of putting one-eighth the force in the air at all times if this were found necessary.

As one student of the Kennedy Administration's nuclear strategy wrote:

This acceleration in our strategic missile program, with a total of 220 missiles added to the already sizeable Eisenhower programs, and with doubled Minuteman productive capacity, may have been one of the most tragic 'improvements' in our 'defense' we have ever attempted, as it must certainly have appeared threatening to the Soviet leadership, with their already much inferior strategic forces, and may have been instrumental in the victory of the 'tougher' group within the Soviet Union which pushed successively and successfully for a resumption of nuclear tests, a hard line at Vienna, an increase in their own military spending and a renewed push on Berlin.[1]

That Kennedy was keenly aware of the provocative appearance of this build-up is evidenced by the fact that he emphasized no less than four times that 'Our arms will never be used to strike the first blow in any attack.' Two months later, after the Cuba fiasco and the upsurge of trouble in Southeast Asia, President Kennedy again went before Congress and requested a further increase in the military

[1] Michael Brower, 'President Kennedy's Choice of Nuclear Strategy'. Brower is an Instructor at MIT. This article appeared as a special supplement to the newsletter of the Council for Correspondence in June 1962. The newsletter is edited by H. Stuart Hughes, David Riesman, A. J. Muste, and Roger Hagan.

budget of a quarter of a billion dollars. This was to finance 12,000 more Marines, better conventional weapons, army reorganization, guerrilla warfare capabilities and a big push in space projects.

In this May 25th speech, he also asked for a civil defense program three times as large as the 'muddled' but 'relatively harmless' Eisenhower program. The President took pains to emphasize that the shelter program was needed as a form of insurance against irrational attack, miscalculation or accidental war, and not 'as many others within and outside the administration were arguing for', as a basic part of his defense strategy.[1] In his message, Kennedy also spoke of the need to increase Nato's conventional strength and pledged five Polaris submarines to be committed to form a Nato nuclear deterrent force.

The ambiguous significance of the shelter program lay in the fact that counter-force strategists envisioned shelters as an important component of a counter-force capability. A massive shelter program was intended to provide means for removing the 'hostages' from the reach of a counter-city force. If a nation were contemplating a first-strike on an enemy's delivery forces, it could begin by placing its own citizenry in shelters, and thus minimizing the damage done by those enemy missiles which succeeded in getting through. Thus the development of a shelter program alongside a substantially superior nuclear force, was a potentially provocative gesture.

'The Kremlin strategists might well want to ask,' observed the political scientist J. David Singer, 'how useful a shelter program would be to the nation whose doctrine is a purely retaliatory one. More specifically, how many lives would be saved by such a program if we were the victims of a surprise attack? If the [surprise] attack were against our cities, it is evident that very few people would be able to get to their shelters in time, and those that did would not find them particularly protective.' Therefore, 'the Soviets must begin to wonder whether the shelters are for protection against a surprise attack, or whether they may not reflect a first-strike strategy.'[2]

Against this background of US military build-up, Khrushchev

[1] Brower, op. cit.
[2] *Bulletin of the Atomic Scientists*, October 1961.

and Kennedy met in early June and exchanged expressions of their determination to continue the political courses they had been following up to then.

On June 21, Premier Khrushchev donned the uniform of a Lieutenant General of the Red Army, attended the twentieth anniversary commemorations of Hitler's attack on Russia, and announced that the time had come to sign a peace treaty with East Germany. The second Berlin crisis had begun.

On July 8, the Soviet Premier announced a decision of the Soviet Government to increase its military expenditures:

Comrades, the Government of the Soviet Union is attentively following the military measures taken recently by the United States of America and its Nato allies. . . .

The United States' President, Mr Kennedy, has proclaimed in his recent messages to Congress a so-called 'new course'. It provides for stepping up the program of developing rocket-missile strategic weapons. . . . President Kennedy has proposed that military allocations be increased. . . . The military expenditures in the Federal Republic of Germany have increased by 18 per cent this year.[1] A considerable growth of military expenditures is characteristic of Britain, France and other Nato countries.

This is how the Western powers are replying to the Soviet Union's unilateral reduction of armed forces and military expenditures carried out over several past years.

Would it be correct for us, in these conditions, to continue to reduce our armed forces unilaterally?

Taking into account the existing situation, the Soviet Govern-

---

[1] 'Whereas in January 1956, the numerical strength of the *Bundeswehr* was 1,500 men, at the beginning of October 1960, it reached 276,000. In 1961, according to official data, the numerical strength of the *Bundeswehr* will be 350,000 men.

'This aggressive army, commanded by surviving Hitlerite Generals is being armed by the American Imperialists with rocket-nuclear weapons and with other most up-to-date means of mass annihilation. This army is being granted military bases on the territory of other countries. Without ceasing to voice territorial claims to other states, overtly declaring their intentions to review borders within Europe, the West German revanchists are intensifying the threat against the cause of peace and the security of nations.' – Colonel A. M. Iovlev, *Red Star*, April 5, 1961; reprinted in *Survival*, September–October 1961.

ment has been compelled to instruct the Ministry of Defense to suspend temporarily, pending special orders, the reduction of armed forces planned for 1961.

In view of the growing military budgets in the Nato countries, the Soviet Government has taken a decision to increase defense expenditures in the current year. . . .

Following Khrushchev's June announcement of the Soviets' decision to sign a separate peace treaty with East Germany, Kennedy found himself in a tight position: 'Stung by criticisms of his Cuba and Laos policies, believing that Khrushchev was testing his firmness, pressured by Adenauer (who faced elections in September) and de Gaulle, and advised by Acheson and many others that to give an inch on Berlin was to give the whole of Western Europe, Kennedy decided against serious negotiations and in favor of a big show of force to convince Khrushchev we would fight and risk all rather than accept any significant changes in the unsettled Central European area.'[1]

On July 25, the President went on TV to report to the nation on the Berlin crisis and to request a $3·25 billion increase in military spending (for a total increase of $6 billion in the six months since his inauguration); this money was slated almost wholly for the build-up of conventional forces. However, in asking for an additional $207 million for his shelter program, Kennedy spoke in markedly different terms than he had before, assigning responsibility for the program now to the Secretary of Defense.

A week earlier, the *Wall Street Journal*, in a front page article had commented:

President Kennedy now appears to be viewing civil defense with new urgency; at least twice in the past three weeks civil defense has been a major topic of discussion at White House meetings of Mr Kennedy and his advisors. The President is considering a greatly stepped up civil defense effort, one purpose of which would be to convince the Soviets the US is ready to risk war in support of its commitment to . . . West Berlin.

---

[1] Brower, op. cit.

CHAPTER XXIII

Tipping the Balance of Power

A COUNTER-FORCE capability, such as the Kennedy Administration appeared to be developing, would have had two major 'advantages' when available:[1] the one, a capability for massive nuclear aggression against another nuclear power, and hence the ability to dictate terms under the implied threat of pre-emptive[2] war; the other, a flexible capacity making it possible to use strategic nuclear power in varying circumstances (and, in theory, to limit a general nuclear war once started). A further component of Kennedy's military program was the increase in conventional forces. The relation between these components was indicated in a speech by Assistant Secretary of Defense Paul Nitze, on September 7, 1961:

> In meeting the Berlin – or other Communist challenges, general nuclear war should not be our only recourse. But let me be very clear: We must have nuclear striking power before our other capacities to meet these challenges can be effective. Thus, one of the first tasks to which this Administration addressed itself was the strengthening of our nuclear deterrent capabilities both for the immediate future and the longer range future. . . .
>
> The increases in conventional capacity will strengthen, and not weaken, our policy of deterring war. For the ability to commit forces in the intermediate range makes more credible to the USSR the certain prospect that *we will back our non-nuclear forces by the use of our strategic capabilities should that be necessary.*[3] [Emphasis added.]

[1] Actually, whether there are *any* advantages to a counter-force capability is a moot question. The feasibility of a successful first strike has been challenged by Blackett in his 'Critique of Some Contemporary Defense Thinking', *Encounter*, April 1961, also in *Studies of War*. The doctrine of flexibility and controlled nuclear responses has been challenged by Arthur Waskow in *The Limits of Defense*, New York, Doubleday, 1962.

[2] As Blackett has observed, the distinction between 'pre-emptive' and 'preventive' war tends to dissolve in practice.

[3] Cited in Brower, p. 7.

Two weeks later, Senator Margaret Chase Smith attacked President Kennedy on the floor of the Senate for allegedly being unwilling to use nuclear weapons to defend Berlin. A week later, Attorney General Robert Kennedy declared that there was no question but that the President would order the use of nuclear weapons if necessary to save West Berlin.[1]

In September, previous Intelligence estimates of Soviet strength were again revised down this time to only 3·5 per cent of their December 1959 level. The actual number of Soviet ICBMs at this time is classified, but the December, 1961 issue of *Astronautics* put it at 35–50. The confidence which this produced in American defense circles can be gauged by Deputy Secretary of Defense Roswell Gilpatric's remarks on October 21, 1961.

> The fact is that this nation has a nuclear retaliatory force of such lethal power that an enemy move which brought it into play would be an act of self-destruction on his part. . . . The total number of our nuclear delivery vehicles, tactical as well as strategic, is in the tens of thousands; and of course we have more than one warhead for each vehicle.
>
> . . . In short, *we have a second strike capability which is at least as extensive as what the Soviets can deliver by striking first.*[2] [Emphasis added.]

In this same speech, Gilpatric used terminology which was only appropriate to counter-force doctrine with its expectation of 'prevailing' in a nuclear war:

> Although we are confident that we would ultimately prevail in a test of strength no matter at what level conflict might be initiated by the Soviet Union, this does not alter our determination to seek a peaceful solution to the world's problems. . . . But if forceful interference with our rights and obligations should lead to violent conflict – as it well might – the United States does not intend to be defeated.

By this time the Soviet Union had not only begun a 're-armament'

[1] Brower, p. 7.
[2] Cited in Brower, p. 8.

program but had broken the moratorium on nuclear tests.[1] Both of these steps apparently were responsive in character and adhered to the basic Soviet strategy and doctrine of minimum deterrence:

It is to be noted that even now, in early 1962, when the Soviet rearmament program must be well under way, their nuclear planning appears still to be for a purely retaliatory role – at least if Malinovsky's statements are correct. For he has said that the USSR does not need to increase considerably her missile force and that it was not now a question of stockpiling but of natural renewal and perfection of weapons: their present stocks were sufficient to defeat any enemy. These statements can be true only of a purely retaliatory counter-city strategy. A counter-force strategy, in contrast, would demand a continuous build-up of nuclear strength in order to compete with the expected gradual decrease of vulnerability of the enemy's delivery system as a result of progress in missile technology.[2] . . .

The Soviet resumption of testing in September 1961 falls into the same pattern of motivation. Though its timing may have been influenced by the Berlin crisis which Khrushchev himself brought to a head, the testing of up to 50-megaton warheads and the simultaneous and publicized success in putting 7 ICBMs on their target in the Pacific at a range of some 7,000 miles, was a very effective way of re-establishing Russian confidence in the deterrent value of the few deployed ICBMs which formed their main retaliatory force, by emphasizing to the United States their accuracy and the possible power of their warheads.[3]

President Kennedy was aware of the defensive nature[4] of the

---

[1] The Soviet decision to resume tests was taken in late 1960 or in the first few months of 1961, and was thus influenced by the factors discussed in the last chapter, but not these recent Kennedy decisions. cf. Blackett, *Studies of War*, pp. 159 et seq.

[2] Blackett, *Studies of War*, pp. 156–7.

[3] ibid., p. 161.

[4] This description is no attempt to gloss over the provocative statements which accompanied the tests, nor the damage that was done to many unborn generations through their fall-out. In assessing the effect of these tests on Kennedy's subsequent budget and policy decisions, the important factor is how the tests were interpreted by him, that is to say, by those scientists (in this case

Soviet tests. Dr Hans Bethe who was assigned by the President to study the tests concluded that they were designed to develop 'solid fuel missiles similar to our Minutemen which could be put in hardened sites' as a defense against a counter-force strike. 'The major part of their test series, therefore,' said Dr Bethe, 'may well have reduced rather than increased the danger of war.'[1]

At this point, that is, in the fall of 1961 as the budget for fiscal year 1963 was being prepared, Kennedy was faced with a major decision. He had had time to see the effects of his partial rearmament on Soviet policy. He had become aware of the even greater superiority in missiles possessed by the US, a superiority which would have been maintained even under the Eisenhower program for missile development. He had solid grounds for believing that Soviet military policy had not changed in its attitude toward maintaining a minimum deterrent, and that as a result of the Soviet nuclear tests, greater stability of the nuclear balance had been achieved. (The international situation also improved for on October 16, the Russians announced that they would not press for a conclusion of the Berlin question in 1961.)[2]

On September 25, the President addressed the UN General Assembly and outlined a US-sponsored program for general disarmament, thus readopting the goal of general disarmament that had been abandoned by the US in August, 1955. He said:

> Today, every inhabitant of this planet must contemplate the day when this planet may no longer be habitable. Every man, woman and child lives under a nuclear sword of Damocles, hanging by the slenderest of threads, capable of being cut at any

[1] From a speech by Bethe at Cornell, January 5, 1962; cf. *The Congressional Record*, February 26–7, pp. A1397 and A1450. Cited in *I. F. Stone's Weekly*, March 12, 1962; cf. also Brower, p. 23; also *Astronautics*, December 1961.

[2] In the interim, the Berlin situation had been stabilized as a result of the erection of a wall by the Communists, sealing off the Eastern from the Western sectors and thereby stopping the flow of refugees from East Germany, – G. McDermott, op. cit., pp. 28 et seq., especially p. 42.

Dr Bethe) he appointed to assess them. Khrushchev's threats could only have been 'credible' to Kennedy if the Soviets had had the nuclear advantage to back them up. They did not have this advantage, and Kennedy knew that they did not.

moment by accident or miscalculation or madness. The weapons
of war must be abolished before they abolish us.

Men no longer debate whether armaments are a symptom or
a cause of tension. The mere existence of modern weapons – ten
million times more powerful than anything the world has ever
seen, and only minutes away from any target on earth – is a source
of horror, and discord and distrust . . . in a spiralling arms race, a
nation's security may well be shrinking even as its arms increase.

Despite the eloquent wisdom of these words, and the fact that
the Soviet Union had already set an example of nuclear restraint,
President Kennedy chose *not* to adopt the minimum deterrent
strategy that would reduce the number of weapons around the globe
and lead to a period of relative stability during which disarmament
agreements could more easily be worked out. Instead he decided
upon counter-force strategy which *would require for its very maintenance a spiralling arms race* and shrink the nation's security even
as its arms increased.[1]

Thus under the President's new budget submitted to Congress in
January 1962, 13 Atlas squadrons totalling 129 ICBMs were to be
operational by June 1963, as were 12 Titan squadrons totalling 108
ICBMs. Funds for 200 additional Minuteman ICBMs were provided, bringing the total planned to 800. The program called for a
total of 1037 ICBMs in the United States to become operational
within a few years.[2] In January 1963, Kennedy's budget continued
this program. 'Funds [in the new budget] are provided to add
about 100 to 150 Minuteman intercontinental ballistic missiles to
the present program of Atlas, Titan, and Minuteman ICBMs now
programmed to about 1,300 to 1,400 all to be ready by 1965–6.'[3]

In addition to these ICBMs capable of reaching the Soviet
Union, 12 Polaris submarines carrying 16 missiles each would be
available by June 1963 (and under the next year's budget, 24 by

---

[1] The election of Nixon to the Presidency would not have affected US adoption of counter-force policy. During the campaign, Nixon stated: 'Our deterrent
force must be invulnerable to destruction, and it must have the power to destroy
the war-making ability of an enemy.' New York *Times*, October 20, 1960.

[2] Brower, pp. 9–10.

[3] Hanson Baldwin, New York *Times*, Int. Edn., January 19, 1963. The additional Minuteman missiles were projected in the previous budget, but no funds
were allotted.

June 30, 1964) with an eventual fleet of 41 in the near future. Thus to the 1,300 ICBMs would be added 656 Polaris missiles, not to mention the Strategic Air Command's fleet of 1,200 bombers (1,000 in 1963, due to the continuing phase out of the old B-47 medium bombers) or the 1,300 planes able to deliver nuclear bombs from overseas carriers and bases. In other words, the US was planning to build up a delivery force involving more than 4,000 major vehicles (nearly 3,000 already operative) capable of attacking the Soviet Union. And all this in the face of a known Soviet delivery force of only some 300 vehicles capable of reaching the US.[1]

In assessing the destructive power of this striking force it should be borne in mind that the Hiroshima A-bomb was 20 kilotons, equivalent to 20,000 tons of TNT. A Minuteman missile has been estimated to carry a warhead of one megaton or the equivalent of one million tons of TNT, or 50 Hiroshima A-bombs. The Atlas-Titan ICBMs carry from twice to five times this size warhead, i.e. from two million to five million tons of TNT equivalent, or 100 to 250 Hiroshima A-bombs. The bombs carried by the B-52's are even larger, up to 24 megatons each, or the equivalent of 1,200 Hiroshima A-bombs. 'The nuclear load in only one of our B-52's, Kennedy noted in 1959, 'is said to be greater in terms of destructive power than all of the explosives used in all of the previous wars in human history. . . .' It has been estimated that if the planes carried capacity loads, a 30,000 megaton payload could be committed to attack by the US. This would represent an equivalent force of 1,500,000 Hiroshima A-bombs.[2] In his book, *Kill and Overkill: The Strategy of Annihilation,* Dr Ralph Lapp quotes Secretary of State Dean Rusk as saying that the US stockpile might be doubled by 1966.

On May 2, 1962, Deputy Secretary Gilpatric made it clear that the US intended to maintain the margin of superiority it then enjoyed, through 1965, and to do this by doubling the present strike capability in the next three years:

. . . As a result of our Strategic Force Study we now have in our

[1] As of January 1963.
[2] Estimates taken from Dr Ralph E. Lapp, 'Nuclear Weapons Systems', *Bulletin of the Atomic Scientists*, March 1961. cf. also, Ralph Lapp, *Kill and Overkill: The Strategy of Annihilation*, 1962.

planning, at least as far as 1965, a pretty definite force structure. We will have nearly 950 bombers carrying we hope, 800 air-to-surface missiles including Skybolts as well as Hound Dogs. We will have some 1500 ICBMs operational, including Atlases, Titans, Minutemen and Polarises. We will have *more than double* the number of alert weapons than we have today by the end of 1965. By alert weapons, I mean warheads in manned bombers that are in the alert force as well as the warheads in the Polaris submarines and in other ICBMs. Those warheads will be carrying a yield, a megatonnage, of *more than twice* what our present alert force can carry. In other words, we will have *twice the striking power* by 1965 that we have at the end of FY 1962. That is why we feel that *no matter what the Soviets can do*, based on the intelligence we have today, that *we will maintain the margin of superiority that we possess today*. [Emphasis added.][1]

The seriousness with which the prospect of a counter-force thermonuclear war (in which a nation could 'prevail') was approached by US policy-makers in the spring of 1962, was indicated in a New York *Times* article on May 12. Stewart L. Pittman, Assistant Secretary of Defense in charge of Civil Defense was quoted as saying that both the President and Secretary of Defense McNamara were convinced that 'this job [of civil defense] has to be done' to insure the nation's survival in case of attack:

Under the most severe type of nuclear attack foreseeable in the late Sixties or early Seventies, Mr Pittman indicated, 110,000,000 Americans would probably die from heat, blast or immediate radiation close to the explosions.

In addition, 40,000,000 to 55,000,000 probably would die if they lacked protection, but would survive if they were in fall-out shelters. Perhaps as many as 35,000,000 would survive without protection because they were out of range of the explosions or fall-out patterns.

'Thus,' Mr Pittman said, 'enough persons could live to insure the survival of the United States as a nation.'[2]

[1] Cited in Brower, p. 12.
[2] ibid., p. 21, 'It would be illuminating to question Mr Pittman and others of his views on just what they think a "nation" is, and whether or not they have

In this spring also, the United States resumed atmospheric nuclear tests. On March 3, President Kennedy explained that the tests would be of three types. The first would be proof tests of existing weapons, the second, 'effects tests', designed to determine 'what effect an enemy nuclear explosion would have' on hardened missile sites, radar systems and 'the communications which enable . . . command and control centers to direct a response. . . .' Said the President: 'We are spending great sums of money on radar to alert our defenses and develop possible anti-missile systems . . . we cannot be certain how much of this preparation will turn out to be useless, blacked out, paralyzed or destroyed by the complex effects of nuclear explosion.' The third type of tests were designed to improve the yield/weight ratio, presumably so that more powerful warheads could be put on Minuteman and Polaris missiles.

The announced nature of these tests makes it evident that the decision to resume testing was 'based squarely on our choice of "a counter-force strategy"'.[1] Increasing the size of the Polaris warhead, for example, would convert it from a counter-city to a counterforce weapon. On the other hand, the quest for an anti-missile missile could not have been a decisive reason for resuming testing, because in the eyes of most authorities it was a hopeless one: the enemy could always penetrate such a defense by saturating it with decoys.[2]

In fact, it was reported that the 'primary technical reason that convinced the President to authorize atmospheric tests' was 'the necessity of exploring the "effects" of high altitude explosions'.[3] In other words, the tests were motivated by the fear that a high altitude Soviet explosion might blank out the complicated communications system with which the Defense Department intended to

[1] Brower, p. 24.

[2] Interview with Air Force Chief of Staff, General Curtis LeMay, *US News and World Report*, November 27, 1961; cf. also Kennedy's statements in his TV interview, December 17, 1962. A discussion of the factors involved is contained in Wiesner and York, 'National Security and the Nuclear-Test Ban', *Scientific American*, October 1964.

[3] John Finney in the New York *Times*, March 3, 1962.

ever asked themselves just what part of our heritage of respect for the individual, for law, for democratic and representative government and for orderly processes of social change they think it is that is going to "survive" a nuclear war in which 110 million people died. . . .' – Brower.

practice a policy of rational, calculated choice over which targets to hit first, and which to reserve for a second strike and as blackmail power. 'But a minimum invulnerable deterrent made up largely of Polaris subs and Minutemen missiles would be able to carry out its retaliatory mission even *without* elaborate communications networks.'[1]

The counter-force doctrine of controlling responses, even after the advent of a nuclear clash, has been assailed by critics because it depends on maintaining perfect communications between the President, Defense Department leadership and each and every bomber, missile and submarine commander before, during and after nuclear bombs are exploding on or near many missile sites, airbases, and major communications centers. In such circumstances critics maintain, 'national controls and national decisions' would be likely to disappear.

Some field commanders would decide to aim their missiles at enemy cities. Others might believe from the local situation that the United States had been defeated, and that there was no option but surrender. Still others, without orders and surrounded by chaos, might succumb to irrational fear and hatred and end up firing H-bombs at everything in sight.[2] . . .

The history of twentieth-century war suggests that as one side uses its armed might more effectively, the other's reaction is to strike back with greater strength. We know this process well enough to have called it 'total war'; there is every reason to believe that the final step in the process would result from applying counter-force theory.[3]

None the less, the Kennedy Administration believed in the feasibility of a counter-force war to the extent that it had already undertaken elaborate and extensive preparations in order to be able to wage one.

The rationale behind the strategy of control and flexibility in choice of targets, even in the midst of a thermonuclear holocaust,

[1] Brower, p. 24.
[2] Waskow, *The Limits of Defense*; cited in Brower, p. 18.
[3] Waskow in *The Liberal Papers*, op. cit., p. 128.

was officially explained by Defense Secretary McNamara on February 17, 1963. The Secretary's statement also revealed why the United States was building not only a *counter-force* capability, but a *counter-city* capability as well:

> . . . US nuclear power . . . is able to survive a nuclear surprise attack and strike back with sufficient power to destroy the enemy target system. . . .
>
> . . . our forces can be used in several different ways. We may have to retaliate with a single massive attack. Or, we may be able to use our retaliatory forces to limit damage done to ourselves, and our allies, by knocking out the enemy's bases before he has had time to launch his second salvos. We may seek to terminate a war on favorable terms by using our forces as a bargaining weapon – by threatening further attack.[1]

To Soviet eyes, which might be more concerned with what the United States was developing the capability to do *first* and not merely what it could achieve in terms of flexible responses after a Soviet strike, McNamara's strategy may have carried with it some ominous implications. For the Soviet military strategists might have reasoned that at some point the High Command in Washington would be tempted to initiate its own first strike on Soviet *forces* and then when the *forces* had been destroyed, hold the Soviet cities as hostages and dictate terms under the kind of nuclear blackmail which had been spoken of in the early days of US atomic monopoly. The Soviet Union had demobilized a large part of its conventional land forces and no longer possessed this deterrent. Moreover, the US continued through 1962 and the spring of 1963 to press the Europeans to raise larger conventional armies.[2] Could US planners expect the Soviet High Command to view these developments with equanimity?

To explain the Kennedy Administration's endorsement of a huge missile program (the Institute for Strategic Studies estimated

[1] Cited in Brower, pp. 12–13.
[2] For actual force sizes see pp. 406–7 below.

in 1962 that by 1965 the United States lead over the Soviet Union in ICBMs would increase to nearly 10: 1)[1] it is necessary to see this build-up in terms of the overall policy conceptions of the New Frontier. For a glimpse into these conceptions we need only recall President Kennedy's speech (as a Senator) on the prospect of Soviet missile superiority in the early sixties:

> . . . Their missile power will be the shield from behind which they will slowly, but surely, advance— . . . The periphery of the Free World will slowly be nibbled away. *The balance of power will gradually shift against us.* The key areas vital to our security will gradually undergo Soviet infiltration and domination. Each such Soviet move will weaken the West; but none will seem sufficiently significant by itself to justify our initiating a nuclear war which might destroy us.[2] [Emphasis added.]

P. M. S. Blackett has used the term 'looking-glass strategists' for certain military writers who have projected upon an opponent capabilities which their own side possessed, or intentions which they themselves may have unconsciously harbored. Kennedy's speech, on the 'missile gap' provides revealing insight into certain looking-glass aspects of his own strategy. Clearly, the Senator's belief that missile superiority could shift the balance of power would have been a keen argument in support of the President's expansion of the missile superiority with which he was presented on taking office.[3] This was particularly so, since Kennedy had placed decisive importance on shifting the balance of power – it was, in the Senator's formulation, the key to any negotiated settlement with the Russians, who would not enter fruitful negotiations as long as they were convinced that the balance of world power was shifting their way.

---

[1] *The Nation,* December 8, 1962.

[2] Kennedy, *Strategy of Peace,* p. 65.

[3] Even the 'nibbling' strategy may have looking-glass aspects. For the Cuban invasion was carried out under an explicit threat of Russian rockets, and it is by no means insignificant that Kennedy said as the invasion collapsed, that should the time for American intervention come, 'we do not intend to be *lectured*' by the Russians. He did not say that we do not intend to be *deterred* by them. His *own* missile superiority, then, allowed him not to regard the Russian threat as 'credible'.

[4] Blackett, *Studies of War,* p. 57.

But the very conviction that missile power could be translated, at this stage, into such decisive political power was a questionable one and had, moreover, deep roots in previously misplaced American confidence in the power of the A-bomb, and then the H-bomb, to compel the Russians to enter 'fruitful negotiations'. One key example of such thinking among Kennedy strategists, is cited by P. M. S. Blackett in his critique of views once held by Henry A. Kissinger, a Presidential advisor and highly influential in the new administration:

> Of the period of atomic monopoly, when Kissinger implicitly assumes that the United States could have destroyed the USSR easily and cheaply, he writes: 'We never succeeded in translating our military superiority into a political advantage.' This passage shows a *naïveté* of thought unexpected in so sophisticated a thinker. It is indicative of the almost mystical American belief in what technology can achieve: its implication is that it was reasonable to expect that the United States should have been able to use its monopoly of the bomb to gain permanent political advantage, without having to wage war or even threaten it.[1]

If the supposition that Kennedy hoped to translate missile superiority into political advantage along the lines of traditional power politics is a correct one, and if he believed that should a nuclear missile war break out, the destruction caused by it could be controlled, then this is a clear line of distinction between his thinking on defense matters, and Eisenhower's. For in a press conference on February 9, 1956, Eisenhower had stated, in no uncertain terms, his misgivings about whole-heartedly entering a missile race:

> Can you picture a war that would be waged with atomic missiles, well knowing that atomic missiles can be of little more value unless they have a tremendously powerful warhead on them? They cannot be as accurate as shooting a gun or dropping a bomb from a plane, consequently you must visualize these things in such numbers and using a kind of ammunition and that means just complete destruction. . . . To suddenly stop everything else

[1] Blackett, *Studies of War*, p. 57.

and just to do this [i.e. concentrate on missiles], you are working toward a theory that, to my mind, leaves no longer war, because war is a contest, and you finally get to the point where you are talking merely about race suicide, and nothing else.[1]

Not only did the Kennedy Administration disregard Eisenhower's reservations when it stepped up its missile program in the spring of 1961, but it failed to consider seriously the effects of this challenge on the policies of the Soviet Union:

The most discouraging thing about studying the development of the Kennedy Administration nuclear strategy is that not once have I found any published attempt to estimate, or take account of, or even speculate about, any changes in the rate of Soviet missile building which would be induced by our own policy. There is no way of knowing what may have been said in the censored part of the hearings, but in all of the many speeches and hundreds of pages of the public records which I have read recently, I have found not one single reference, not the slightest hint, that anyone in the Defense Department has asked: 'What will be the impact on the Soviet Union's plans for testing, for developing, procuring and installing more missiles, if we follow this strategy, or that one?' Even more incredible, more discouraging, is the fact that not one Senator, not one Congressman, has been found asking such questions of Defense Department witnesses. The assumption apparently is that we are locked in an arms race from which it is not safe to attempt to extricate ourselves, but that in this race their side is acting almost totally independently of what our side does![2]

American planners, of course, were in an excellent position to assess the responses which their Soviet counterparts might be induced to take as a result of the stepped up US arms program. For having ostensibly been on the short end of a 'missile gap' themselves previously, they could not have found it too difficult to see things as they then looked 'from the other side of the hill'.

[1] Cited in *Kennedy in Power*, Crown and Penty, 1961, pp. 139–40.
[2] Brower, p. 25.

Thus in 1957, in response to the prospect of a Soviet superiority in ICBMs, the United States moved to place intermediate range missiles in the European countries of its Nato allies. In 1962, in response to the prospect of a similar imbalance in ICBM strength, the Soviet Union moved to place intermediate range missiles in the country of its ally in the Western Hemisphere, Cuba.[1] In the context of the existing political situation, this was a reckless and provocative act.

[1] cf. Bolton, op. cit., also Lippmann: 'Very probably the madcap Soviet gamble with missiles in Cuba also originated in a desperate attempt to close the nuclear gap.' *Newsweek*, January 21, 1963. While this appears to have been the overriding motive for the Soviet move, it was not necessarily the only significant factor involved. For while in one post-crisis statement Castro seemed to corroborate the view that the emplacement of missiles was a Soviet initiative, in another, he seemed to affirm the official version to the effect that the emplacement of missiles was designed to deter an imminent US invasion of Cuba. While this does not seem plausible as a single determining factor, it cannot be dismissed out of hand. According to Miró Cardona, leader of the exiles, on May 4, 1961, after the defeat at the Bay of Pigs, President Kennedy had pledged full US support for a new invasion of Cuba. On April 10, 1962, the President assured Cardona that ' "the problem is essentially military and requiring six divisions", that the [rebel] Council should contribute the major contingent of soldiers and that we should not adopt a unilateral position because this would cause grave criticism on the continent.' Three months later, the first shipment of Soviet arms arrived in Cuba. The text of Cardona's statement appeared in the New York *Times*, April 19, 1963, and is cited in Scheer and Zeitlin, op. cit., pp. 219–22.

CHAPTER XXIV

Showdown: The Cuban Crisis

THE United States' response to the Soviet emplacement of missiles in Cuba was clear, vigorous and decisive. On October 22, President Kennedy went on TV to inform the nation, the Russians and the world, that he had ordered a blockade[1] of Cuba to prevent additional missile equipment from arriving on the island, and that if the preparation of the missile sites did not cease, and the missiles were not withdrawn, 'further action' would be taken. This action could either have meant expansion of the embargo to include petroleum shipments or an air strike. By the end of the crisis week, this latter alternative had become a real possibility.[2]

In his address, President Kennedy charged:

. . . this secret,[3] swift,[4] extraordinary build-up of Communist

---

[1] The President's word was 'quarantine', but throughout the planning stages, the action was termed 'blockade' by those involved, and this is clearly what it was. For this account, I have drawn on the detailed, day-by-day story of the crisis compiled by the Washington Bureau of the New York *Times*, and printed in the International Edition, November 6, 1962.

[2] ibid. This air strike would probably have been against the Cuban anti-aircraft batteries which had shot down one U-2 plane and fired on others.

[3] But cf. the *Wall Street Journal*, October 24: '. . . the authorities here almost all accept one key assumption: That Mr Khrushchev must have assumed his Cuban missile sites would soon be discovered. "The Russians seem almost to have gone out of their way to call attention to them," said one authority who has studied the photographic evidence.' cf. also, K. S. Karol, *New Statesman*, November 2, 1962. 'Many military men have been astonished by the openness of Soviet preparations in Cuba, under the constant surveillance of U S aircraft. It is possible, then, that the dispatch of Soviet missiles should be compared with the reinforcement of the U S Berlin garrison at the time of the last crisis there. In Berlin, Kennedy wished to emphasize that American lives would be involved, so making world war certain in the event of a Soviet thrust.'

[4] But cf. Hanson Baldwin, New York *Times*, Int. Edn., November 1, 1962: 'Considerable mystery, in the opinion of Congress and military men, still surrounds *the Administration's sudden decision* to impose a blockade of Cuba after a missile build-up that must have started weeks or months ago . . . The question that arises . . . is whether the Intelligence data that must have been collected throughout the summer and early fall was accurately evaluated, or whether policy dictated the intelligence estimated or turned them aside.' [Emphasis added.]

missiles – in an area well-known to have a special and historical relationship to the United States and the nations of the Western Hemisphere, in violation of Soviet assurances,[1] and in defiance of American and Hemispheric policy – this sudden, clandestine decision to station strategic weapons for the first time outside of Soviet soil – is a deliberately provocative and unjustified change in the *status quo* which cannot be accepted by this country, if our courage and our commitments are ever to be trusted again by either friend or foe.[2]

Thus did President Kennedy justify the extreme US action in response to the Soviet maneuver, namely, a naval blockade, which was, in fact, an act of war and hence violated the UN charter and the very OAS treaties which the President invoked as bases for United States' concern.[3] The action taken by the United States was even more momentous in that by engaging a test of will with the Soviet Union, it was risking a test of strength, and this test of strength would have involved not only the lives and destinies of the Soviet and American peoples, but hundreds of millions of people in other countries whose governments had no role in the decisions which had led up to, or, afterward, which shaped the crisis.

Therefore, it is of more than passing importance that the nature of the Soviet provocation be understood. For the Cuban crisis provides the first real basis for estimating what the nuclear future may be like without some sort of general disengagement. It is interesting to note in this regard, that the substantive issue involved in the Cuban crisis was not understood at the time and that a general misimpression has persisted in the aftermath. This mistaken view

[1] i.e. Gromyko's assurances on October 18, that the missiles were for defensive purposes. This is by no means a clear issue, however, a fact emphasized by the following passage from the above cited Baldwin article: 'Military men point out that many Administration officials, including a high State Department official, were emphatically denying the existence of any offensive Soviet missiles in Cuba until just before the President's speech.'

[2] New York *Times*, Int. Edn., October 23, 1962.

[3] It has been argued by Arthur Larson and others that because the US move was an act of self-defense, it was in keeping with the principles of the UN Charter. But this assumes that the emplacement of missiles in Cuba altered the nuclear balance of power. Such an assumption is not warranted by the facts. See below.

holds that the United States was alarmed because the presence of missiles in Cuba upset or significantly altered the military balance of power, i.e. the nuclear *status quo.*

It would seem that in this case the wish has been father to the thought, that people would like to think that thermonuclear war will be precipitated (barring accident) only when the security of one of the great powers is threatened, or when some similarly clear-cut issue involving self-defense is at stake. In addition to the confusion caused by wishful thinking, Ambassador Stevenson's remarks (October 23) before the UN, may have unintentionally served to mislead many people:

> When the Soviet Union sends thousands of military technicians to its satellite in the Western Hemisphere – when it sends jet bombers capable of delivering nuclear weapons – when it installs in Cuba missiles capable of carrying atomic warheads and of obliterating the Panama Canal, Mexico City and Washington – . . . this clearly is a threat to the hemisphere. And when it thus *upsets the precarious balance in the world,* it is a threat to the whole world.

Stevenson avoided saying 'upsets the precarious *balance of terror* in the world' or even balance of *power,* just as President Kennedy avoided any reference to a *balance* of nuclear forces in his statement, and with good reason. For if the nuclear background developed to this point in the manner in which we have described it, then the 42 Soviet missiles in Cuba[1] would have had no effect at all on the overall nuclear balance (except, possibly, to make it more stable).

That this was in fact the case was made clear by Deputy Defense Secretary Gilpatric on a television program November 11. According to the *New York Times* of November 12:

> . . . Mr Gilpatric made two observations on the over-all missile capability of the United States compared with that of the Soviet Union.
>
> First, he said, defense officials believe that the United States

---

[1] Deputy Defense Secretary Gilpatric, quoted in the New York *Times*, Int. Edn., November 12, 1962.

has a measurable margin of superiority in strategic weapons.

Second, in alluding to the Soviet missile build-up in Cuba, he said: '*I don't believe that we were under any greater threat from the Soviet Union's power, taken in its totality, after this than before.*'[1] [Emphasis added.]

What, then, was at stake in the Soviet emplacement of missiles in Cuba? What challenge or threat necessitated a US action which not only violated fundamental international law, but risked a general nuclear holocaust as well?[2] It could not have been the mere fact of the Soviet build-up, because that had been going on since July.[3] It was evidently not the material presence of 'offensive' missiles, since if we are able to believe Deputy Defense Secretary Gilpatric and the evidence of the Institute of Strategic Studies, as well as the previous statements of Gilpatric and McNamara of the relative missiles strengths of the two nuclear giants, the US was under no greater threat from the Soviet's power, taken in its totality, after the emplacement of missiles than before. What then was the nature of the Soviet provocation?

The answer to these questions was revealed by President Kennedy himself during a television interview on December 17, 1962:

[The Russians] were planning in November to open to the world the fact that they had these missiles so close to the United States. Not that they were intending to fire them, because if they were going to get into a nuclear struggle they have their own missiles in the Soviet Union. But it would have *politically* changed the

---

[1] The Institute for Strategic Studies made the following estimates of long-range missile strengths of the two powers for the end of October 1962: Soviet Union 75 ICBMs; US 450–500 missiles capable of being fired more than 2,000 miles. New York *Times*, Int. Edn., November 9, 1962

[2] The main risk was not simply that of a decision by the USSR to engage in such a war, but in the crisis generally getting out of hand. Thus the New York *Times'* account of the crisis reports that on Saturday, October 27, 'the possibility of having to knock out hostile anti-aircraft batteries on the island was very real, and *there was doubt about how much longer the crisis could be carefully controlled* . . . They sat with an over-all confidence in the nation's nuclear superiority over the Soviet Union [*sic*], but this was little comfort if the Russians chose to go to a war that neither side could win. The President gravely remarked that evening that it seemed to him to be touch and go, that it could now go "either way".' [Emphasis added.]

[3] New York *Times*, Int. Edn., November 6, 1962.

balance of power, *it would have appeared to – and appearances contribute to reality.*

Thus, it seems it was a *political* balance of power that was actually in danger of being upset, and this political balance was a question of appearances – prestige, presumably – the political consequences of what would appear in the eyes of the world and domestic critics of the Kennedy Administration[1] to be a Soviet act of defiance, perpetrated with impunity. Not to have forced the Russians into retreat would have been appeasement, a sign that the US would not stand up to Soviet power when challenged, and it would therefore have opened the door to further challenges, perhaps over Berlin. This explains why Khrushchev's offer on Saturday, October 27, to exchange the missile bases in Turkey for the bases in Cuba was turned down. And indeed, the New York *Times'* account of the rejection indicates the political-prestige nature of the decision:

Such a proposal had already been rejected as unacceptable; though the Turkey missile base had *no great military* value, it was of *great symbolic* importance to a stout ally. To bargain Turkey's safety [i.e. to *apparently* bargain Turkey's safety—D.H.] would have meant shocking and perhaps shaking the Western alliance. [Emphasis added.]

The military insignificance of the Turkish missile base and the symbolic importance of not bargaining with the Soviets was

---

[1] On October 15, Eisenhower delivered a speech in which he charged that the Kennedy Administration's foreign policy had not been 'firm'. In the eight years of his own Administration, Eisenhower declared, 'We witnessed no abdication of responsibility. We accepted no compromise of pledged word or withdrawal from principle. No [Berlin] walls were built. No foreign bases [i.e. in Cuba] were established. One was ended [i.e. in Guatemala] and incipient wars were blocked.' New York *Times*, Int. Edn., October 16, 1962. On the other hand, domestic pressure on Kennedy to do something about Cuba should not be over-emphasized. Three separate polls, including a Gallup poll, taken a week before the crisis, indicated that there had been no increase in public support for an invasion of Cuba since April 1961 (or 15 months before the Soviet build-up began). According to the Gallup poll, 24 per cent favored invasion, 63 per cent were opposed, while 13 per cent had no opinion.

emphasized in a front page story in the New York *Times*, less than three months later, on January 21, 1963:

> The Turkish Government has responded favorably to proposals that the United States remove its Jupiter missile bases. . . .
>
> The removal of these Jupiter missiles was under consideration here *some time before* the crisis last fall over the emplacement of Soviet missiles in Cuba. [Emphasis added.]

The fact that the removal of the Turkish missile bases had been considered *before* the Cuban crisis raises the question as to why there was a crisis at all. Why, for example, was not the Soviet Ambassador given an ultimatum *in private*, before the presence of the missiles was disclosed to the world and the prestige of the United States had been put on the line?[1] Such a move would have been *normal* diplomatic procedure (and was actually proposed by Stevenson)[2]. As James Reston wrote on October 27:[3]

> The new Kennedy style of diplomacy is now operating in the Cuban crisis. It is highly personal and national. It is power diplomacy in the old classic European sense that prevailed before the great men worried much about consulting with allies or parliaments or international organizations. . . .
>
> [The President] did not follow the normal diplomatic practice of giving his antagonist a quiet escape from fighting or withdrawing, but let the Soviet Foreign Minister leave the White House without a hint of what was coming and then announced the blockade on the television.

While generally approving Kennedy's 'power play', Reston expressed certain reservations about its wisdom:

> This brisk and sudden diplomacy, however, cannot be pursued without cost. The political reaction within the nation and the

[1] Since both Cuba and the ships coming to Cuba were under constant surveillance, it would have been simple for the Kennedy Administration to be very precise in framing an ultimatum or deal, and very secure about verifying Soviet compliance.

[2] Henry M. Pachter, *Collision Course*, 1963, p. 30.

[3] New York *Times*, Int. Edn., October 26, 1962.

alliance has been gratifying to the Administration, but it is misleading because it is not the same as private reaction.

Privately, there are several misgivings. First, many people find it hard to believe that the offensive Soviet missile sites in Cuba suddenly mushroomed over the weekend, and accordingly, there is considerable suspicion either that the official intelligence was not so good as maintained, or the Administration withheld the facts.

Second, many diplomats within the alliance still think it was wrong to confront Khrushchev publicly with the choice of fighting or withdrawing, especially since the security of many other unconsulted nations was involved. . . .

The mysteries attending the discovery of the build-up, the unusual nature of the crisis diplomacy, and the lack of any immediate overwhelming, military threat, all point to the existence of an important dynamic element in the planning of US policy. Further evidence that motives behind the US action in the Cuban crisis were dynamic and not only responsive in character, was offered at the time in a remarkable series of articles by the informed New York *Times* analyst, C. L. Sulzberger (appearing on October 20, 22, and 24).[1] In a retrospective glance, four months later,[2] Sulzberger summarized his previous conclusions in the following way:

Some weeks before the Cuban confrontation, Washington decided that Khrushchev's cold war offensive, begun in 1957, was petering out. It therefore resolved on a showdown with Russia at a time and place of its own choosing. Khrushchev, with his Caribbean missile game, surprisingly[3] also seemed to seek a test. He chose a time, October, that seems to have suited us. History will judge for whom Cuba was the right place.

In his October 21 article, written from Paris *before* the announce-

---

[1] International Edition, datelines: Paris, October 19, 21 and 23.

[2] International Edition, February 25, 1963, dateline: February 24.

[3] 'Surprisingly' because his power situation was so weak. This suggests that Khrushchev's move was a miscalculation. cf. James Reston, New York *Times*, Int. Edn., October 24, 'Khrushchev's Mistake on Cuba'.

ment of the blockade, Sulzberger traced the history of the cold war as seen by the Kennedy Administration and indicated the calculated reasons why a showdown was considered important by the leadership (Sulzberger felt that this showdown would be in Berlin, further indicating the unlikeliness that he knew about the imminent Cuban clash). 'Washington,' he wrote, 'is convinced a moment of truth is approaching over Berlin, and that the West cannot afford to dodge this confrontation; that if we now face and surmount the crisis, the international balance will begin to swing our way.' Because of this conviction, Sulzberger observed, Washington 'is . . . emphasizing a paramountcy of leadership' that causes some 'ripples of disquiet' among the Allies, who wish to avoid a confrontation over Berlin. 'Nevertheless, we see this as a chance to turn Russia's second cold war offensive.'

Russia's first 'offensive' according to Sulzberger, was launched by Stalin in Greece fifteen years earlier, 'halted there, blocked in Berlin and finally checked by 1951 battlefield victories in Korea'.[1] Russia's second, or 'Khrushchev offensive' dated from the launching of Sputnik, 'when Moscow hoped to trade missile prestige [*sic, not* superiority or power] against new real estate'. In this offensive, Communism 'failed to win the Arab world, Guinea, or the Congo'. While these failures were being registered, moreover, 'pressures built up inside the Communist world'. Khrushchev tried to deal with these pressures – satellite unrest, the split with China, Russia's food crisis – but, as of October 1962, had found 'no panacea'. 'The United States is consequently convinced that Khrushchev is up against vast difficulties and seeking some kind of triumph to advertise . . . we believe it is necessary to take risks in warning Khrushchev, letting him see clearly what he is up against.'

On October 23,[2] Sulzberger concluded his series with an analysis of the Cuban crisis which had begun the day before. 'The new trend in United States policy described in previous columns,' he began, 'has now culminated in a showdown with Russia. That is the real meaning of the Cuban crisis. President Kennedy decided

---

[1] Sulzberger's reference to 1951 victories indicates that he believes that the Chinese entered the Korean War as part of Stalin's offensive rather than as a result of MacArthur's provocation. As with his statement about Greece, this is untenable before the facts.

[2] New York *Times*, Int. Edn., October 24.

to move against Khrushchev's cold war offensive at a time and place of his own choosing. . . . This calculated risk has presumably been taken for the calculated reasons previously analyzed. Washington seems to feel this is the time to check and reverse Khrushchev's cold war offensive. We have opted to force the issue ourselves without prior approval of our allies and there are going to be uneasy diplomatic moments. . . .

'. . . *Some of our leaders have been hinting this for weeks.*[1] *They knew what they were talking about. One must assume it was they who planned the showdown that has started,*' [Emphasis added.]

In other words, having built a sizeable missile superiority of its own, and having laid the plans for a rapid increase in this superiority in the next few years, the Kennedy Administration had waited for an opportune moment to demonstrate its nuclear superiority to the world, and with the prestige thus gained, tip the scales of the world power balance. The test was expected to come in Berlin, when Cuba presented itself.

Even if Sulzberger weren't as close to the inner circles in Washington as he is, the handling of the crisis by the United States leadership would point to the same conclusion, namely, that once the information about the Soviet build-up was received, the only response considered was one that would precipitate a showdown.[2]

According to official accounts, the key aerial photographs were developed on October 15. On October 16, the President called a meeting of the Executive Committee of the National Security Council.[3] The results of this meeting were summarized in the New York *Times*' account as follows:

---

[1] On September 24, Kennedy obtained authorization to call up 150,000 reservists. 'General Curtis Le May ordered supplies to be flown to Florida, that mission was to be completed by October 10, and the tactical Air Command was to be combat-ready by October 20. . . . Do these dates indicate that the Chief of Staff of the Air Force expected the crisis at the end of October?' – Pachter, p. 7n.

[2] 'Most significant [of proposals to avoid a crisis] was Stevenson's proposal to present Khrushchev with a secret ultimatum. . . . The difference between his way of thinking and Kennedy's . . . [is that]: Kennedy and the majority of the Executive Committee felt it necessary to have a public showdown with Khrushchev'. – Pachter, pp. 91–92.

[3] It was actually an *ad hoc* committee which became known as the Executive Committee. Its members included Vice-President Johnson, Secretary Rusk, Secretary of Defense, McNamara, Secretary of Treasury, Dillon, Attorney General, Kennedy, Under Secretary, Ball, Deputy Secretary of Defense,

At this first meeting the President and his advisors were not yet clear on what was to be their objective to get the offensive weapons out of Cuba. Some talked, rather, about getting Premier Castro out.

The meeting produced two immediate decisions. One was to intensify air surveillance of Cuba. The second was that action should await further knowledge, *but should come as close as possible to disclosure of the Russian bases* – which could not be long delayed. [Emphasis added.]

In other words, the one point on which all were agreed was that the Russians should be caught red-handed, faced with a pre-determined show of strength and compelled to retreat. The only question was the nature of the action to be taken, air strike or blockade.[1] On Friday, October 19, an air strike was ruled out, and it was decided to use a blockade:

Attorney General Kennedy argued against a strike on moral grounds. . . . For the United States to attack a small country like Cuba without warning, he said, would irreparably hurt our reputation in the world – and our own conscience.

The moral argument won general assent. . . .

The blockade proposal was recognized as one raising most serious dangers. As recently as October 6, Vice-President Johnson had warned that 'stopping a Russian ship is an act of war'.

By the end of the afternoon meeting the blockade was clearly the indicated answer.

[1] 'Invasion was not considered as a possible first action. It would take too long to mount. Surprise would be impossible. The effect on world opinion was certain to be unfavourable. The Soviet response might rapidly "escalate" the affair.' 'But the air strike did win significant support. So did a blockade.' New York *Times'* account of events of Wednesday, October 17.

Gilpatric, General Carter, Assistant Secretary of State, Martin, General Taylor, McGeorge Bundy and Theodore Sorenson. These were joined by Alexis Johnson, John McCone, Dean Acheson and Llewellyn Thompson.

Fortunately, the immediate danger of precipitating a thermo-nuclear war was avoided, and on October 28, the crisis ended, as the Soviet Union agreed to withdraw its missiles in return for a United States guarantee not to invade Cuba. In this curious way, the United States won a prestige victory over its Soviet opponent.

By agreeing to withdraw the missiles, Khrushchev lifted the threat of nuclear annihilation from millions whose nations were not involved in the dispute, and hence who tended to view the Cuba base as comparable to U S bases in Turkey, as well as from those nations who were. And though his action of putting the missiles there in the first place in general drew harsh criticism, his withdrawal of the missiles in the face of U S intransigence[1] gave him an opportunity to demonstrate moderation and rationality which he would not otherwise have had. Moreover, the 'price' that the U S paid to have the Soviets withdraw their missiles, namely, an agreement not to invade Cuba, was surely one of the strangest facets of the whole affair. For it meant nothing less than that the United States officially recognized that it would, in fact, contemplate aggression against a sovereign state, and therefore that the Soviet build-up in Cuba had legitimate defensive purposes from the *Cuban* point of view.[2] In retrospect, it would seem that the Soviet Union also gained a 'prestige victory'.

But Kennedy's triumph, particularly within the Western Alliance and at home, was evident and impressive. From Washington's point of view, the central gain was in dispelling the illusion that the United States would not fight for its vital interests. This was considered to be important not only from the standpoint of the Allies' morale, but from the standpoint of making it clear to Khrushchev,

---

[1] The mediating proposals of U N Secretary General U Thant to stop both missile preparations and blockade, had been rejected by the U S and accepted by the Soviet Union.

[2] cf. the Washington *Star* and Washington *Daily News* of October 29 and 30. The former stated: 'Authoritative sources warned today against any feeling that the agreement with the Soviet Union will lead to "peaceful coexistence" with Fidel Castro's Cuba. . . . Once the first phase of actually dismantling and removing the Soviet weapons is completed, they said that the hemisphere and Cubans can get on with the more "limited" phase of actually getting rid of the Castro régime. . . . At a forty-five minute briefing in the State Department yesterday, Secretary of State Rusk told the nineteen Latin American Ambassadors . . . not to exaggerate the extent of the U S guarantee against invading Cuba.' Both articles cited in *I. F. Stone's Weekly*, November 5, 1962.

that the United States could not be faced down in areas such as Berlin.

It should further be noted that Kennedy immediately acted to restrain those who might want to see the advantage in the Cuban crisis pressed by further displays of power. After an interview with the President on October 28, the day the crisis ended, James Reston reported:

> President Kennedy is looking at the Cuban crisis not as a great victory but merely as an honorable accommodation in a single isolated area of the cold war. . . .
>
> The President is not even drawing general conclusions from this special case about the tactics of dealing with the Soviet Union in the future. To be specific, while he may be equally bold again in risking conflict in support of vital national interests, he is rejecting the conclusion of the traditional 'hard-liners' that the way to deal with Moscow everywhere in the world is to be 'tough', as in Cuba. . . .[1]

But if Kennedy was now eager to emphasize the limits of US power in dealing with the Communists, and thus forestall the pressures of his right wing, the months following the Cuban crisis saw him take an increasingly assertive attitude towards the Western Alliance. In December, the US abruptly announced cancellation of the program to build Skybolt missiles on which Britain had based its long-range plans for maintaining an independent nuclear deterrent. In February, an undiplomatic note accused the Canadian Government of failing to produce a 'practical' plan for joint defense. Partly as a result of this note, and the ensuing reaction, the Canadian Government fell.

If there was little question about the vigor of the new post-Cuba diplomacy, however, there were many uncertainties about its direction. As one European observer wrote:

> The series of successes in the last quarter of 1962 has confirmed the Kennedy Administration in its good opinion of its foreign policy. . . .

[1] New York *Times*, Int. Edn., October 29, 1962.

An intoxicating certainty of power is the prevailing mood. It is only when specific questions of how this power will be used in relations with enemies and allies that there is uncertainty. . . .

In East–West relations there is a new self-assurance, but hardly a sign of new ideas. The Administration which was going out of its way to warn of an impending Berlin crisis, now appears to think Cuba has made a Berlin crisis unlikely, or at least milder when it comes.

But as Mr Dean Acheson pointed out in the meat of the speech which caused such indignation in Britain, there is now no American policy in central Europe beyond an exhortation to stand firm on Berlin . . . .[1]

As we have seen, however, firmness and the development of power was itself a policy for Kennedy, who believed that strengthening the forces of freedom (to use Acheson's phrase) would induce the Soviets to become reasonable and accept a settlement on 'reasonable' terms.

Kennedy's policy after Cuba was, in fact, very consistent with the assumption that only two power centers (East and West) existed in Europe, and that so long as the balance was not tipped heavily against the East, it would not settle for a *status quo* meaning less than domination. For after Cuba, Kennedy moved to give the Nato powers a nuclear force of Polaris submarines under terms that would weld them into unity while integrating them as an arm of U S striking power. The net effect would be a stronger 'Atlantic' front against the Communist bloc.

Significantly, as the new year began, Kennedy was rebuffed in his design for European economic and military (and eventual political) unity interdependent with the United States, by de Gaulle, who reaffirmed his intention to build an independent nuclear force for France, and on January 14, vetoed Britain's entry into the Common Market.

Kennedy's reaction to de Gaulle's rebuff was significant, in that he did not emphasize the danger of independent nuclear forces and the spread of nuclear weapons, but rather stressed the threat to the

[1] Godfrey Hodgson in the London *Observer*, December 30, 1962; cf. also James Reston in the New York *Times*, Int. Edn., December 27, 1962.

Western Alliance and to the world in any weakening of the power bloc of the West:

> It would be well to remind all concerned of the hard and fast realities of this nation's relationship with Europe—
>
> The reality of danger is that all free men and nations live under the constant threat of Communist advance. Although presently in some disarray, the Communist apparatus controls more than one billion people, and it daily confronts Europe and the United States with hundreds of missiles, scores of divisions, and the purposes of domination.
>
> The reality of power is that the resources essential to defense against this danger are concentrated overwhelmingly in the nations of the Atlantic Alliance. In unity this Alliance has ample strength to hold back the expansion of Communism until such time as it loses its force and momentum. Acting alone, neither the United States nor Europe could be certain of success and survival. The reality of purposes, therefore, is that that which serves to unite us is right, and what tends to divide us is wrong....[1]

Since de Gaulle had not indicated any intention to withdraw from the Nato Alliance, or to make a separate accommodation with the Soviets, Kennedy's picture of the world situation represented a strange estimate both of the balance of forces and the present dangers. For it is inconceivable that Kennedy considered real, or immediate, the danger of a Soviet advance in Europe in any military sense. As of January, the conventional strength of the Western bloc was larger than that of the Soviet bloc by 8·1 million to 7·3 million men.[2] Politically, the Communist bloc was being rent by the Sino–Soviet schism; economically, the East was beset by significant problems. When Kennedy spoke, the general estimate in the West was that Khrushchev's recent statement had indicated the Berlin question would not be pressed. The Russians had been cooperative in tying up the loose ends of the Cuban crisis. Khrushchev had waged a

[1] New York *Times*, Int. Edn., January 25, 1963.
[2] P. M. S. Blackett, 'The First Real Chance for Disarmament', *Harper's*, January 1963. 'The total forces of the Warsaw Pact, including the Soviet Union, number about 4½ million, against 5 million men in the active armed forces of Nato.' London *Observer*, December 15, 1963.

vigorous post-Cuba campaign against the militancy of the Chinese and for the policy of peaceful coexistence. Clearly, Kennedy's concern could not have been the weakness of the Western Alliance, but rather the fact that it would not have *enough* strength to force the Soviets into 'fruitful negotiations'.[1]

On the other hand, all indications pointed to the conclusion that US missile superiority would no more induce a relinquishing of Soviet positions in 1963, than had atomic monopoly or H-bomb superiority before. As in previous stages of the cold war, it would induce, rather, a Soviet move to offset the superiority. Thus, in January it was reported that observers in Washington believed 'that the Russians may be attempting to compensate with [a] "big bang" for their inferiority in missile numbers'. A 'very few' 50 to 100 megaton bombs 'delivered in a promiscuous pattern of nationwide bombing could paralyze any nation, and could destroy or damage all except the most heavily protected military installations. Damage and casualties caused would probably be so great as to be crippling'. '*Any President*,' the report continued, '*would hesitate to invoke the threat of nuclear weapons, as we did in the Cuban crisis or even to take extremely strong action if he felt that several giant megaton weapons could be delivered on the United States*.' Thus, even a small number of these weapons 'mated to the powerful but few Russian ICBMs', though not sufficient to 'save' the Soviet Union in a nuclear war, 'might well serve, as apparently they are intended to serve, as a means of neutralizing the present superiority of the United States in numbers of ICBMs and in over-all nuclear delivery capacity'.[2] And, on February 22, the New York *Times* (International Edition) reported:

[1] For Kennedy's far-ranging optimism about the world power balance at this time, cf. the President's State of the Union Message, January 14, 1963.

[2] Hanson Baldwin, New York *Times*, Int. Edn., January 10, 1963: 'I will tell you a secret: Our scientists have worked out a 100 megaton bomb . . . we can use such a weapon only outside the confines of Europe. I am saying this in order that there should be a more realistic appreciation of what horrifying means of destruction there exist . . . Comrades, to put it in a nutshell, as I have already said during the session of the Supreme Soviet of the USSR, it is not advisable to be in a hurry for the other world. Nobody ever returned from there to report that one lives better there than here. We do not want a kingdom in heaven but a kingdom on earth, a kingdom of labor. This is the kind of kingdom we are fighting for and without stinting our efforts we shall go on fighting for it.' – Nikita S. Khrushchev, to the Communist Party Congress in East Berlin, January 16, 1963; New York *Times*, Int. Edn., January 17, 1963.

The commander-in-chief of the Soviet strategic rocket forces said today [February 21] the Soviet could launch rockets from satellites at a command from the earth.[1]

Henry Kissinger, for one, had warned the previous summer[2] that the time when all of the Soviet Union's missiles could be destroyed by a counter-force blow was limited. Dispersal, hardening of bases, and the development of missile firing submarines would make it impossible in the future to know where all of an enemy's missiles were, and hence to be free from a devastating retaliatory blow.

In the end of January, Secretary of Defense McNamara appeared before the House Armed Services Committee, and made acceptance of the impending stalemate official, declaring that 'regardless of what kind of strategic forces we build . . . we could not preclude casualties counted in the tens of millions'.[3]

Thus, Kennedy's two-year attempt to gain a decisive lead in the arms race (requiring a 20 per cent increase in the military budget) produced the same results as previous attempts: a new stage of the arms race, a further increase in the number of nuclear weapons, and consequently, a more difficult world to disarm. But the Cuban crisis added to the lessons of previous years, by presenting mankind with an unforgettable glimpse into the perils of a nuclear future,[4] a future dominated by the immense gap between man's revolutionary technological means, and his traditional, limited, political and ethical outlook. It was a lesson which underscored the President's own warning to the UN General Assembly, in September 1961, when he said:

The weapons of war must be abolished before they abolish us. . . . The risks inherent in disarmament pale in comparison to the risks inherent in an unlimited arms race.

[1] For a corroborating account and discussion of the implications of the new weapon, cf. Tom Margerison in the London *Sunday Times*, February 24, 1963.

[2] Henry A. Kissinger, 'The Unsolved Problems of European Defense', *Foreign Affairs*, July 1962.

[3] *Time*, February 15, 1963. The Air Force promptly attacked this 'no win' policy of accepting nuclear stalemate as a dangerous one. cf. New York *Times*, Int. Edn., February 1, 1963.

[4] Consider, for example, what might have happened if the 'showdown' had occurred over Berlin.

V. Détente and After

. . . In Asia, Africa and Latin America, living standards have largely remained stationary, or have even declined. Throughout the last decade, the fall in the price of raw materials, while priming the affluent societies of the West, has not only cancelled out the sum total of Western aid, but in many cases has led to an absolute drop in national income. One great lesson of this phenomenon is that the world will not live in harmony so long as two-thirds of its inhabitants find difficulty in living at all.

U THANT

For the first time since the dawn of civilization about 5,000 years ago, the masses have now become alive to the possibility that their traditional way of life might be changed for the better and that this change might be brought about by their own action. This awakening of hope and purpose in the hearts and minds of the hitherto depressed three-fourths of the world's population will, I feel certain, stand out in retrospect as the epoch-making event of our age. The tapping of atomic energy and its application to the forging of weapons and the exploration of outer space will be seen to have been trifles by comparison. As for the present-day conflict between competing ideologies, this will, I should guess, be as meaningless to our descendants, three hundred years from now, as our sixteenth-century and seventeenth-century Western ancestors' wars of religion already are to us. On the other hand. the emancipation of the world's women and industrial workers and peasants will, I believe, loom larger and larger; and, so far as this stands to the Western civilization's credit, this Western civilization will receive, and deserve, the blessing of posterity.

ARNOLD TOYNBEE

CHAPTER XXV

Nuclear Armistice

'I speak of peace, therefore, as the necessary rational end of rational men. I realize the pursuit of peace is not as dramatic as the pursuit of war – and frequently the words of the pursuer fall on deaf ears. But we have no more urgent task.'

JOHN F. KENNEDY,
June 10, 1963

IN his address before the United Nations in 1961, President Kennedy touched upon the central paradox of defense in the Nuclear Age when he said: 'in a spiraling arms race, a nation's security may well be shrinking even as its arms increase'. For evidence confirming this postulate, the President could have had no better example than the security of the United States in the two decades following World War II.

As late as May 1955, when the Soviet Union essentially accepted the Western plan for general and complete disarmament, the United States was relatively safe from Russian attack, because the Russians had only limited means of reaching the United States with their nuclear warheads.[1] In March 1957, the Soviets presented a new version of these 1955 proposals, including a provision for the abolition of all missiles: intercontinental, intermediate and short-range. The West was still interested only in partial disarmament ('The measures suggested were very "partial" indeed. . . .')[2] and no agreement was reached. The result of failing to chance the risks inherent in disarmament at this point was made apparent soon afterward when the Soviet Union launched its first ICBMs and the United States became suddenly vulnerable to a weapon against which there was no defense.

[1] Blackett, *Studies of War*, p. 141, cf. also Wiesner and York, 'National Security and the Nuclear Test Ban', *Scientific American*, October 1964.
[2] Noel-Baker, op. cit., p. 24.

In the same way, the failure of the United States to agree to stop nuclear testing in the years 1956–8, ostensibly because underground tests of small yield for tactical atomic weapons could not be completely monitored, resulted in the Russian development of an H-bomb warhead for their ICBMs, thus vastly increasing their destructive potential against the United States.[1]

Each advance in weaponry not only significanctly increased the danger to the United States, it made the risks inherent in disarmament greater and the problems more complex. For the concealment of ICBMs tipped with H-bomb warheads, by a power evading a disarmament agreement would pose a far more significant danger than the possible concealment of any weapon or delivery system available in 1955.

Moreover, the actual deployment of the new weapons posed a threat even to the powers which possessed them. Some of the dangers involved in this threat were spelled out in 1962 by John J. McCloy, the President's Advisor on Disarmament:

> The revolution in weapons development has resulted in the creation of delivery systems with fantastic rates of speed. Certain missiles that might be used in case of war have a speed of around 16,000 miles per hour, which would mean a delivery time of only about one-half hour between the Soviet Union and the United States; and missile launching submarines will provide almost no warning time at all. As a counter, defensive systems are being developed with such quick reaction times as to give real meaning to the term 'war by accident, miscalculation or failure of communication'. Indeed, *it is questionable whether the human mind can encompass all the problems involved in controlling these devices even without war. It is not inconceivable that we could blow ourselves up without help from the Russians; and vice versa.*[2] [Emphasis added.]

[1] Hans Bethe, 'The Case for Ending Nuclear Tests', *The Atlantic Monthly*, August 1960. According to Wiesner and York, the probable deaths resulting from a Soviet nuclear attack on the US have increased a hundred-fold since 1950.

[2] John J. McCloy, 'Balance Sheet on Disarmament', *Foreign Affairs*, April 1962. McCloy, a Republican, had been Assistant Secretary of War (1941–5), High Commissioner for Germany (1949–52) and Chairman of the Board of the Chase Manhattan Bank (1953–61) before his appointment in the Kennedy Administration.

These perils of the prevailing nuclear situation, the dire prospect of the possible appearance of new nuclear powers, the impossibility of waging a successful counter-force first strike (publicly acknowledged by Secretary of Defense McNamara in early 1963)[1] and the belated recognition that the balance of power could never be so tipped against a continental power as to bring it to Western terms, combined with other factors (including Gaullism and the Sino-Soviet split) to produce an important shift in United States thinking.

On June 10, 1963, President Kennedy made a major foreign policy speech at the American University. He spoke of peace as 'the most important topic on earth' – not a peace imposed by strength, or by a conversion of the Soviet opponent, or by a relinquishing of Soviet positions ('We must deal with the world as it is, and not as it might have been had the history of the last eighteen years been different.'), but a peace realized on the basis of an already existing community of interest between the two super powers:

> Today, should total war ever break out again – no matter how – our two countries would become primary targets. It is an ironical but accurate fact that the two strongest powers are the two in most danger of devastation. . . .
>
> In short, both the United States and its allies, and the Soviet Union and its allies have a mutually deep interest in a just and genuine peace and in halting the arms race. Agreements to this end are in the Soviet's interest as well as ours – and even the most hostile nations can be relied upon to accept and keep those treaty obligations, and only those treaty obligations, which are in their own interest.

The speech was climaxed by the announcement that high level discussions with the Russians (and the British) were to take place in in Moscow 'looking toward early agreement on a comprehensive test-ban treaty'. To make clear its 'good faith and solemn convictions in the matter', the United States pledged itself 'not to conduct

---

[1] 'According to Mr McNamara's report, the US will not attempt to build up forces capable of destroying all of the Soviet Union's possible ballistic missile bases. He said this would not be feasible.' New York *Times*, Int. Edn., February 1, 1963.

nuclear tests in the atmosphere so long as other states do not do so'.

On August 5, 1963, just one day short of eighteen years since the United States dropped an atomic bomb on Hiroshima, the Foreign Ministers of Great Britain, the United States and the Soviet Union fixed their signatures to a treaty banning nuclear tests in the atmosphere, under the sea and in outer space.[1]

Dean Rusk, signing for the United States said: 'Our three governments have today taken what all mankind must hope will be a first step on the road to a secure and peaceful world.' For the first time in eighteen years, sober analysts began to speak of a 'truce', a partial but significant 'thaw' in the cold war.

To draw an adequate picture of the nature of this 'truce', it is necessary to review the bare outlines of the diplomatic and military policies of the two powers in the decade prior to the test-ban. For it was in this post-Stalin, post-Korea decade, when the reconstruction and stabilization of Western Europe was an accomplished fact, that certain fundamental aspects of American policy first became inescapably clear.

From the year 1953, or approximately the time when the Soviet Union approached nuclear parity with the United States, the Soviet rulers pressed on the diplomatic front for a *rapprochement* with the West, which would include cultural and economic exchanges, and high level negotiations to resolve the points of major conflict. In accord with this approach, the Russians proposed, on several occasions, steps for the reduction and disengagement of military forces in Europe. Both these diplomatic initiatives were initially rebuffed by the United States, although under the leadership of Eisenhower and Kennedy a partial change in the American opposition to coexistence was effected.

[1] The partial treaty was substantially the same as one proposed by Eisenhower in 1958. In the intervening years the Soviets had opposed such a ban either on the grounds that it was only partial, or that it was not tied to general and complete disarmament. The change in the Soviet attitude was partly the result of complex economic and political factors. An important military factor was that the 1961 tests had given the Soviets the large warheads which they needed to counter the superior United States missile numbers. The test-ban did not involve on-site inspections and hence did not jeopardize the locations of Soviet missiles. Furthermore, reports at the time indicated that the Russians were taking steps to increase the number of their ICBMs to 1,200 by 1967.

In considering the attitudes of the two powers to the more critical questions of disengagement and the reduction of forces in Europe, it is important to recall, once again, Lippmann's conception of what would be a genuine policy of settlement in the cold war conflict. 'In our conflict with Russia,' he wrote in 1947, 'a policy of settlement ... would aim to redress the balance of power, which is abnormal and dangerous, because the Red Army has met the British and American armies in the heart of Europe. ... *A genuine policy would, therefore, have as its paramount objective a settlement which brought about the evacuation of Europe.* ... American power must be available ... to exert a mounting pressure in support of a diplomatic policy which has as its concrete objective a settlement that means withdrawal.'

It is a fact of prime significance for an assessment of Soviet policy in the cold war, that once the Soviet Union had achieved nuclear parity and thus eliminated the necessity for its land deterrent, the Soviet rulers exhibited a readiness to reduce the size of that force and to withdraw the Red Army (as in the Austrian settlement) from its strategic positions in Europe. It is supremely ironic that the United States, which had been urged by Lippmann to mount a pressure on Russia in support of a diplomatic policy whose aim would be to achieve a withdrawal of Russian forces, should *resist* disengagement, and with it, this very development. The extent of the resistance, even after the nuclear test-ban and *détente*, was summarized in January 1964 by George Kennan:

When it comes to the military factor and the question of its emphasis or de-emphasis, the bald fact is that the Western powers, over a period that now runs back for several years, have committed themselves more and more deeply against anything in the nature of a military disengagement in Europe. Not only do they reject the possibility of any extensive withdrawal of foreign troops from the Western part of the Continent, even if this were to be by way of reciprocation for a similar withdrawal of Soviet forces, but they appear to have set their face, in present circumstances, against anything in the nature of a European pact or a nonaggression pact between the Nato and Warsaw Pact members. They are also averse to any sort of arrangement for the denuclearization of the European area, even, again if this were to be on a reciprocal basis.[1]

Both Soviet willingness to consider disengagement and the US commitment against disengagement were reflected in their military policies during the second cold war decade. In 1955, the Russians began a reduction of their land forces, which by 1963, had been cut to less than half.[2] At the same time, however, the United States initiated West Germany into Nato and promoted a German military build-up in the heart of Europe (from 1,000 in 1956 to more than 300,000 in 1963) which had the effect of doubling Nato divisions in the central area. The irony of this build-up was that while Nato plans since 1952 had provided for forces to cope with 175 Soviet divisions, and while Nato planners had stressed the presence in Europe of 175 Soviet divisions, the Pentagon released studies in 1963 which showed that the Soviets had only 60 'active' divisions and that Nato was superior in the vital center.[3] A partial explanation offered for this 'miscalculation' was the belated discovery that a Nato division was twice the size of a Warsaw division. But, as two members of the Royal Institute of International Affairs asked 'Must it take fifteen years to establish the true size of a Soviet division? Is the distinction between paper strength and combat readiness so difficult to draw? *Either the Nato Command and its satellite strategists have been singularly incompetent, or they have deliberately suppressed for political reasons the true state of affairs.*'

[1] Kennan, 'Polycentrism and Western Policy', *Foreign Affairs*, January 1964.
[2] In 1955, the Soviet armed forces had 5·75 million men. In 1963, they had between 2 and 2·3 million. – London *Observer*, December 15, 1963. New York *Herald Tribune*, Int. Edn., December 16, 1963. These figures were based on a US Government report released in August: 'The latest American appraisals of the Russian military threat to Europe suggest that previous intelligence assessments have consistently overestimated the strength of the Soviet armed forces. ... Experts in the Pentagon now believe that there may be only 2 million in the Soviet Army allowing for even a rudimentary system of support and a small number of lines of communication troops; this is unlikely to support more than about 60 fully-manned active line divisions [i.e. less than 900,000 men – D.H.]' – London *Times*, August 12, 1963.
[3] New York *Times*, Int. Edn., December 2, 1963; the figures for the Central Area are Nato 975,000 to 665,000; these revised studies were released as part of a campaign to cushion the domestic political repercussions of the test ban.

[Emphasis in original.]¹ On November 18, 1963, McNamara publicly put the competing military strengths into figures, revealing that Nato forces totalled 5 million while those of the Warsaw Pact only 4·5 million men.²

The conflict between US–Nato policy and the objective of a European settlement was not confined to the military aspect. For, as Kennan observed, 'when it comes to economic policy a similar situation prevails. There are Nato arrangements for economic controls [on trade with the East]. There are the various legislative restrictions prevailing in this country. There is, finally the Common Market, established and being developed on principles that appear to leave no room for anything like the eventual economic reunification of Europe'.

Finally, US–Nato policy on the all-important German question seemed calculated to preserve rather than end the bloc division of the European Continent. For in Kennan's words, 'the Western powers have exhibited no very convincing evidence of any disposition to place effective limits on the rearmament of Western Germany where one restriction after the other, established in earlier years, has quietly gone by the board, and where the Germans are now, in the view of everybody in Eastern Germany, well on the way to becoming in all essential respects a full-fledged nuclear power. Yet at the same time the Western powers, with the exception of the French, have been unwilling to recognize the finality of Germany's eastern frontiers; and the West German Government, with the blessing of the others, still pursues a policy of total irreconcilability toward the East German State'.

. . . the spectre of the violent liberation of Eastern Germany . . . unites both governments and peoples in Eastern Europe in a common reaction of horror and apprehension; . . . the peoples of Eastern Europe . . . see in this eventuality only the beginning of a re-establishment of the German military ascendancy of unhappy memory throughout Eastern Europe, and eighteen years have

¹ Richard Gott and John Gittings, 'Nato's Final Decade', *Views* (London), Summer, 1964.
² The New York *Herald Tribune* reported a month later that authoritative western sources put the figures at Nato: 5,818,500, and Warsaw: 4,354,000. Soviet armed forces: 2–2·3 million, and US: 2·7 million – December 16, 1963.

not been sufficient to allow the horror of this prospect to fade in their minds.

Behind all this and connected with all of it, is the heavy extent of the Western commitment and particularly the American and German commitment, to the eventual destruction of communism generally. We have our Captive Nations Resolution; and the satellite régimes of Eastern Europe and Asia are specifically listed there as ones we have committed ourselves in effect to destroy.[1]

It is this commitment 'to the eventual destruction of communism generally' and the policy decisions taken to further it, which explains, as nothing else could, the fundamental conflict between the whole structure of the American cold war program and the strategic objective of a European settlement and withdrawal.[2] It explains this conflict not only in the second decade of the cold war, but as we have seen, from the very beginning.

Once the Soviet Union had demonstrated its viability, the permanence of its power, and with that the bankruptcy of containment, an adjustment of American policy became inevitable. The limited nature of this adjustment, which the foregoing review makes clear, returns us to the question of the significance of the truce itself. For if the truce was not the expression of a strategic decision to reshape American policy towards the goal of a negotiated European settlement, what then was its source?

If the preceding analysis of American cold war policy in Europe has been correct, the answer must lie (as we have already tentatively suggested) in the recognition by American leaders of the limit of American power, and in particular, of its incapacity to support a policy designed to dictate a settlement to the Soviet Union. This recognition would most certainly have been hastened and even, in a sense, compelled by the mounting dangers inherent in a continuation of the arms race.

A year after the test-ban, Walter Lippmann, who had acted in unofficial capacity as an advisor to both Kennedy and Johnson,

[1] Kennan, 'Polycentrism and Western Policy', op. cit.
[2] It also explains the conflict American nuclear policy and the objective of disarmament – cf. the discussion of a counterforce strategy (which became 'damage-limiting' strategy in January 1964) on pp. 343ff. above, cf. also P. M. S. Blackett's critique of the Russian and American disarmament programs, 'First Real Chance for Disarmament', in *Harper's*, January 1963.

offered an analysis of the *détente*[1] which confirmed, in its essentials, the picture of American policy which has been presented in the preceding pages.

Analyzing the current American policy towards Russia, Lippmann wrote that the Johnson Administration had continued from the point that the Kennedy Administration had achieved – 'from the fact that the nuclear showdown has already taken place'. 'As a test of will,' wrote Lippmann, 'the showdown took place in the Cuban missile confrontation; as a test of nuclear capability, the showdown took place in the parallel Soviet and American nuclear tests which preceded the test-ban treaty. In those tests both sides failed to win the radical breakthrough which would have changed the existing balance of nuclear power. American superiority was not challenged by the tests. *Nor was the fact changed that American superiority is very far short of American supremacy, that is to say, of American capacity to dictate a settlement to the Soviet Union.*

'The net result is a balance of nuclear power in which both sides are mutually deterred.[2] Neither side can impose its will upon the other', (nor, as Secretary of Defense McNamara admitted in January 1963,[3] has either side a real possibility of ever achieving the nuclear capacity – in the form of a threatened counter-force-first-strike – to do this – D.H.). 'As a result, there is a pause, a lull, an unratified truce, which cannot be altered drastically in our favor by brinkmanship, that is by threatening nuclear war.' American policy after the showdown, according to Lippmann was 'based on the pause the lull, the unratified truce – not on eternal peace, not on general disarmament, *but on the achievement of a balance of nuclear power which establishes and compels an armistice in the cold war.*'

Astute as it was, Lippmann's judgement that the armistice was established and compelled by the achievement of a balance of nuclear power involved a striking and perhaps unconscious admission for one so close to the inner circles in Washington. For since American nuclear power was vastly superior to Russian power throughout the post-war period prior to the truce (and still greatly superior afterward), the unavoidable implication of Lippmann's analysis is that

---

[1] Walter Lippmann, 'Goldwater *vs.* Johnson', New York *Herald Tribune*, Int. Edn., July 29, 1964.

[2] cf. above p. 396.

[3] cf. also his annual report to Congress in January 1964.

it was the development of a Soviet nuclear deterrent capable of neutralizing the superior American force and frustrating the American quest for supremacy,[1] that compelled the truce in the cold war.

As for the truce itself, its tentative and limited nature reflected the fact that the basic cold war conflicts had not been resolved, nor had the ground yet been prepared for any dramatic advance towards their resolution. In short, the truce meant not that the cold war had ended, or was about to end, but that it had entered a new, and possibly less dangerous phase.

[1] cf. above pp. 396–397 cf. also Wiesner and York, op. cit., for rising curve of unavoidable American casualties in the event of a nuclear attack.

CHAPTER XXVI

The Unity of America's Cold War Program

... there can be no doubt that, if all nations could refrain from interfering in the self-determination of others, the peace would be much more assured.

JOHN F. KENNEDY

ONE important consequence of the preceding account of military policies in the second cold war decade is to undermine the view that America's cold war program can be adequately explained as an attempt to contain a Soviet expansionary threat. The evidence for the existence of this threat has never been impressive, and has rested principally, on selective or merely superficial accounts of events in Iran, Greece and Korea in the early cold war years. A careful consideration of Greek events, to take one example, shows that the decisive foreign intervention was British, and then American. Stalin, for his part, was most eager to end the civil war (which the Yugoslavians and Bulgarians were supporting) lest he provoke American military power.[1] Yet this was *before* Nato, *before* the Marshall Plan, and at a time when the American military budget was less than one quarter of its average level during the fifties and sixties.

After 1955, it became impossible to give sober credence to the existence of any immediate Russian military threat to Western Europe, as the Red Army abandoned its forward position in Austria, and reduced its forces, while at the same time Nato continued its military build-up. In August 1963, when the revised figures for Russian forces were released, it was finally reported that '[Official] American experts on Soviet foreign policy underline [the] latest assessments with their own view that Soviet aims in Europe tend toward containment rather than expansion, and that they are

[1] cf. p. 84n. above.

411

in fact pre-occupied with the dangers of an attack from the West than with any aggressive intent of their own.'[1] Yet, this assessment by Washington's experts did not result in any immediate abatement of the Nato build-up in Europe. Indeed, eighteen months later, Secretary of Defense McNamara actually pressed the Nato allies to increase their troop numbers to the originally projected Nato force levels, which would mean adding a full six Nato divisions to the already superior Nato armies.[2]

A capsule summary of the contradiction between the official description of American cold war policy as defensive containment against the threat of Soviet expansion, and the actual military situation, is contained in the figures for the military expenditures of the two power blocs. According to reliable report 'Nato countries disburse on armaments *nearly double* the amount of the Warsaw Pact. In 1963 Nato's members spent more than $71 billion for defense; the Soviet bloc spent less than $37 billion. *This proportion has remained approximately steady during the decade since the Warsaw Pact was signed in May 1955.*'[3] [Emphasis added.]

It is the decade-long build-up of Nato power in the face of Soviet restraint in nuclear production and the reduction and withdrawal of Soviet forces in Europe, that is impossible to reconcile with a policy of containment, if containment is understood to mean defense against threatened military expansion.

In fact, George Kennan, who was at the center of American policy planning in the 1947 period, admitted ten years later that military expansion by the Soviet Union was never considered a real prospect by him. He went even further to declare that at the time of the formation of Nato, the State Department's policy planners considered 'the Communist danger in its most threatening form – as an *internal* problem, that is of Western society'. (In 1948, in accord

---

[1] London *Times*, August 12, 1963.

[2] London *Times*, December 16, 1964. 'In the last three years abroad we have doubled the number of nuclear weapons in our strategic alert forces; in the last three years we've increased by 45 per cent the number of combat-ready army divisions.' – Kennedy, Speech before the AFL–CIO Convention, November 1963. In 1963–4, the US *tripled* its missile forces, and Wm. C. Foster, director of the US Arms Control and Disarmament Agency, warned that unless the concept of 'enough' became clearer, the US would have more than eight times as many missiles by 1965 as it had in 1962. – London *Observer*, December 13, 1964.

[3] C. L. Sulzberger, New York *Times*, Int. Edn., December 16, 1964.

with this view, Secretary of State Marshall threatened to stop the flow of 'humanitarian' Marshall funds to any country which voted Communists into power.) Thus from the viewpoint of the planning staff of the State Department, containment was containment of Communist revolution (or election) rather than Russian expansion. (An enormous amount of Nato funds, moreover, went through the recipient countries to contain *non-Communist* revolutions in Algeria, Indo-China and the Portuguese enclaves in Africa.)

Once the unique and confusing early post-war period was over, it became increasingly evident that American cold war policy had, in fact, a counter-*revolutionary* rather than a counter-*expansionary* character, and that the rhetoric of opposition to aggression was a mere cover for containing internal change. In 1958, for example, when nationalist revolutions threatened the oil kingdoms of the Middle East, the Eisenhower Doctrine extruded American power into the area, under the guise of protecting the integrity of these countries from an external threat. Similar actions, under similar pretences, were undertaken in the 1950s in Iran and Guatemala, as they had been earlier in Greece.

In the early cold war years, however, the distinction between containing expansion and containing revolution was not so easily made. Among the reasons for difficulty was the fact that the mono-lithic structure of the international Communist movement, sub-ordinate as it was to the Soviet Politburo, lent substance to Western propaganda and made it seem as though potential Communist revolutions would, if victorious, mean Soviet control, and *ipso facto* made the containment of Communist revolution seem to be equivalent to the containment of Soviet expansion.

This tendency was intensified because of the extraordinary situation behind the Yalta military line in the period 1945–9. Here a series of Communist seizures of power, made possible only by the presence of the Red Army, inevitably served to make the spread of Communism seem synonymous with the spread of Soviet national power. For in this period in East Europe, there was literal truth in the proposition. Confusion was further compounded by the failure in the West to distinguish between an extension of political control *behind* existing military lines and an expansion across them. How-ever indefensible the former, it was different from aggression and did not show the same intent as aggression, particularly since

Russian 'expansion' in East Europe, an area of great strategic importance for Russian security, was closely connected with American policy towards a German settlement, with America's 1945 decisions to maintain the Atom-Bomb, the Anglo-Saxon Alliance and the former Japanese air bases off the coast of Siberia, with American resistance to Russian attempts to organize its own security zone, and finally with American failure to offer aid to the Russian reconstruction program.

This basis for blurring distinctions did not last long, however, for the emergence in Yugoslavia and China of two authentic Communist revolutions (as distinct from minority *coups* in the shadow of the Red Army) soon made it apparent that Soviet dominance of the Comintern had been very much a function of the fact that the Soviet Communist Party was the only Party representing a national state. (Subsequent Soviet dominance of the East European parties except for Yugoslavia was obviously a result of the parties having been put in power mainly by the Soviet rulers.) As soon as truly national Communist states began to emerge, the hegemony of the Soviet Party was challenged and the monolithic unity of the Communist movement was shattered. (Only American hostility to China, and the outbreak of the Korean War, delayed the Sino-Soviet split for as long as it did.) With the appearance of 'polycentrist' tendencies in the world Communist movement, any basis for identifying Communist revolution with the expansion of Soviet national power disintegrated. The consequences of this disintegration for an assessment of containment are far-reaching and profound.

In regard to countries like revolutionary Cuba, for example, these internal changes in the Communist movement served to expose the tortured logic of American cold war policy, and the way in which intervention in the internal affairs of sovereign states was carried out under the cloak of containing an external threat.

Five years after the Cuban revolution, US policy towards Cuba was accurately summed up as a 'cold war whose aim is to force the unconditional surrender of the Castro régime'.[1] In a speech to the Inter-American Press Association four days before his tragic assassination, President Kennedy justified this policy in the following terms:

---

[1] New York *Times*, Int. Edn., editorial, August 14, 1964.

It is important to restate what now divides Cuba from my country and from the other countries of this hemisphere. It is the fact that a small band of conspirators [*sic*] has stripped the Cuban people of their freedom and handed over the independence and sovereignty of the Cuban nation to forces beyond the hemisphere. They have made Cuba a victim of foreign imperialism, an instrument of the policy of others, a weapon in an effort dictated by external powers to subvert the other American republics.

The similarity between this view in its basic outlook (replete with the confusion of conspiracy and revolution), and Dean Acheson's implausible appraisal of the Chinese Revolution more than a decade earlier is too striking to be overlooked. One additional difficulty confronting Kennedy's analysis, moreover, was the task of specifying the foreign imperialism of which Cuba had been made an agent. Of whose policy was Cuba a mere instrument?

President Kennedy's answer to this question was revealed in a confidential interview which he gave to Jean Daniel on October 24, 1963, and which the latter chose to print after the President's death:

> . . . Castro betrayed his earlier promises and agreed to become a Soviet agent in Latin America. . . .
>
> You suggest you are not sure of the political effectiveness of blockade. You will see. We cannot allow Communist subversion to win a hold in Latin-American countries. We need two dams to hold back Soviet expansion [*sic*]: on the one side the blockade; on the other an effort towards economic progress.[1]

But only two weeks earlier, United States delegate Adlai Stevenson had decried in the United Nations the fact that Cuba had 'just joined Communist China' in rejecting the test-ban treaty.[2] Only two weeks before that it was reported from Washington that splits had developed between the Latin American Communist parties and the Cuban leaders because Havana was opposed to Moscow's strategy of

[1] London *Observer*, December 8, 1963.
[2] '[Stevenson's] denunciation appeared to place Cuban policy closer to Communist China's hostility toward the West than to the Soviet Union's current efforts to ease international tension.' – New York *Times*, Int. Edn., October 8, 1963.

'popular fronts' with 'bourgeois parties' in Latin America. 'Cuba favors armed insurrection' the report continued; 'it is believed significant that not a single outstanding Latin American Communist leader visited Havana for the July 26 celebrations of the revolution's anniversary.' The report added that it was known in Washington that 'the Soviet Union has repeatedly urged the United States this year to seek a settlement with Cuba on terms Dr Castro does not approve.'[1]

If on the one hand, Cuba showed independence from Moscow,[2] it would hardly be sensible to go to the other extreme and suggest that Cuba's sovereignty had been handed over to China, to become a weapon in an effort dictated by the Chinese to subvert, etc. The Soviet Union was financing the Cuban régime with approximately $1 million per day in aid, and Soviet-Chinese relations were under severe strain; it is difficult to imagine the Soviet Union or indeed any country financing a régime that was acting as a mere instrument for some third power's foreign policy.

The point hardly needs stressing. Given the tightness of Castro's position, his dependence on the USSR for economic and for military protection against possible United States aggression, it was obvious, and had been from the beginning, that he was more 'Titoist' than Tito himself. Never really a Communist like Tito, nor Stalinist as Tito had been, Castro had shown on innumerable occasions the independence of his thinking and policies.[3] His intense nationalism is attributed by many of his severest critics to have been a major factor in his break with the United States. He would thus seem to have been one of the last national leaders that could reasonably be expected to willingly play the role of anybody's tool, as indeed his actions in the midst of the Cuban Crisis had shown. To the extent that Castro submitted to Soviet pressures, he did so because of the economic and military squeeze in which he found

[1] New York *Times*, Int. Edn., September 24, 1963.

[2] Documentation for this in the year or two preceding the President's remarks is legion. The most important account of Havana–Moscow strains from the point of view of Administration conceptions is Theodore Draper's long article in *The Reporter*, January 17, 1963, 'Castro and Communism'. Draper's earlier articles on Castro's revolution provided the basic thesis for the State Department's *White Paper*.

[3] Most spectacularly in his speeches of March 13 and 26, 1962, attacking the Stalinists.

himself, and which the United States could easily have eased. The State Department was obviously aware of this, and yet policy towards Castro continued to be one of sabotage and covert aggression[1] under the painfully transparent banner of anti-imperialism.

The contrast between United States policy toward Castro's Cuba and Tito's Yugoslavia is both striking and instructive. For in the 1947–8 period, Tito was not an unambitious revolutionary leader in terms of the Balkan countries within his reach, and unlike Castro, he was not surrounded by water. Indeed, it was Tito who provided the main foreign support for the Greek rebels. Yet, in 1948, to secure the United States aid necessary to survive outside the Soviet orbit, he withdrew his support from the Greeks and refused them the use of Yugoslav territory, thus effectively ending their revolt. For its part, the United States financed Yugoslav development and independence with more than $1 billion in loans. This aid was given despite Tito's failure to relinquish his Communist ideals or practices.

Although the geopolitical situation of the United States gave it an enormously powerful bargaining position with regard to Cuba (all of whose natural markets are in the Western Hemisphere),[2] although Castro on many occasions made overtures of reconciliation, including offers to settle the claims of confiscated companies, and although the Soviet Union on repeated occasions urged such a reconciliation, the United States refused even to discuss coexistence with Cuba. Its position was unambiguously put by Adlai Stevenson at the United Nations on October 8, 1962:

> The President of Cuba professes that Cuba has always been willing to hold discussions with the United States to improve relations and to reduce tensions. But what he really wishes to do is place the seal of approval on the existence of a Communist régime in the Western Hemisphere. The maintenance of Communism in the Americas is not negotiable. . . .[3]

[1] 'Despite the Administration's public statements that it will not tolerate any armed expeditions from the United States by Cuban exiles, it is widely believed that a continuous flow of weapons is going to underground and guerrilla groups inside Cuba, . . .' – New York *Times*, Int. Edn., December 23, 1963.

[2] Before the revolution, imports amounted to 30 per cent of Cuba's GNP. Seventy-five per cent of her imports were from the US. In addition, sixty per cent of her exports were to the US

[3] New York *Times*, October 9, 1962. Also in Pachter, op. cit.

Stevenson's statement could hardly have been more inappropriate to the chambers of the United Nations General Assembly, since the primary principle of the United Nations Charter commits its members to solve all disputes through negotiation. (In similar fashion, US attempts to pursue its policy of eliminating the Castro régime, through the Organization of American States, began by violating a cardinal principle of *its* Charter.[1]) Moreover, Stevenson's position was hardly compatible with the Kennedy Administration's conception of its own foreign policy as a program to make the world safe for diversity, based on respect for the principle of non-intervention in the internal affairs of other countries.

The Kennedy Administration's justification for its Cuba policy was that Castro had made Cuba 'a weapon in an effort dictated by external powers to subvert the other American republics'. But this line of reasoning could hardly justify the policy which was undertaken.

In the first place, the experience with Tito had shown that given the right arrangements, certain revolutionary ideals were likely to be sacrificed for others, and in particular, that the survival and wellbeing of the revolution at home would take precedence over the success of the revolution abroad, in the strategy of a 'revolutionary' state. (China's friendly relations with the reactionary régime of Ayub Khan in Pakistan would be a case in point.) When Castro actually made an offer to suspend aid to revolutionary movements abroad in return for a normalization of relations with the United States, he was totally rebuffed by Washington (subversion, Washington held, was not negotiable!) an infallible indication that such subversion was not the central or even a major issue between the two countries.[2]

Indeed, this was evident prior to the rebuff, for the failure of the

[1] '... no State or group of States has the right to intervene, directly or indirectly, for any reason whatever, in the internal or external affairs of any other State. The foregoing principle prohibits not only armed force, but also any other form of interference or attempted threat against the personality of the State or against its political, economic and cultural elements.' (Article 15) cited in Lieuwen, p. 285 n.

[2] New York *Times*, Int. Edn., July 6 and 7, 1964. On July 27, after the rebuff, Castro qualified his offer saying 'aid to [revolutionary] movements is not negotiable'. But he added that he understood 'the need of countries to live in conformity with international norms'. 'Cuba would feel free, [Castro] said [according to the *Times*] 'to help any revolutionary movement *in any country that did not respect Cuba.*' [Emphasis added.] – New York *Times*, Int. Edn., July 28, 1964.

United States' own program of subversion in tiny Cuba, undertaken on a vaster scale than anything Cuba herself could hope to attempt in Latin America, was eloquent testimony that subversive and conspiratorial activities did *not* make revolutions. Revolutions were made, if Cuba were any example, by the misery of the masses, by the existence of a tremendous gap between the potential wealth of the natural environment[1] and the actual poverty produced by existing social relations, by the vision of an alternative social structure which would bring about greater social justice and, by a revolutionary movement capable of leading or mobilizing the impoverished masses towards this goal.

Once it is recognized that revolution and not conspiracy changes social orders (the partial exception being East Europe in the unique post-1945 period when the Red Army decisively altered the balance of social forces) then the nature of Cuba's 'threat' becomes apparent. It was not, even as the establishment press had to admit, a threat of active subversion: 'The real issue in the much-feared subversion by Marxist–Leninist Cuba of Latin America is not a physical one. Premier Castro is not in a position to arm any Latin-American opposition effectively even if he wanted to, . . .'[2] Cuba's threat lay in her role as an *example* to a continent trapped in poverty and misery by the existing socio-economic power structure, in which an immensely powerful United States played the central role. (It should be noted in passing, moreover, that Cuba's threat was not, and in the nature of things could not have been a threat to 'Latin America', as was suggested, but to this power structure and the social classes which benefited from it.) As was frankly admitted by the New York *Times*, it was the very presence of the Cuban régime, its mere survival, having challenged the power structure, and thus having given hope to forces seeking to change the *status quo* (for the sense of hopelessness is always the greatest prop of existing injustice) that made Cuba so formidable a threat:

'The 26th of July celebrations underline Dr Castro's effectiveness

[1] 'Latin America . . . has more cultivable high yield tropical soil than any other continent. . . . Buried in it are uncalculated but vast reserves of oil, iron, copper, tin, gold, silver, zinc, lead: the list is endless. . . . Yet Latin America contains some of the poorest and most exploited people on the planet. . . . It has remained a rich and plundered flotsam, drifting on the rival tides of European and North American avarice.' – Paul Johnson, op. cit.

[2] New York *Times*, Int. Edn., editorial, July 28, 1964.

as a subversive agent. It is the fact that he and his régime survive after more than five and a half years of turmoil, economic collapse, the exodus of a great number of middle-class and professional elements, and after everything that the United States could do to him short of military invasion, which gives him his greatest impact on Latin America. So long as he remains a towering figure on the hemispheric scene – hated, feared and despised by many, loved and admired by some – he will be a grave danger to Latin America, and because of his connections with Russia, to the United States.'[1]

It was not really plausible, however, to argue in this fashion that Cuba's danger to the United States was her connection with Russia, since the United States had never attempted to use its positive influence to wean Cuba from these connections. In fact, Washington held that 'Castro's ties of dependency with the Soviet Union' were 'not negotiable'.[2] In other words, the official US position was that Castro would have to sever his ties with Russia (including more than $1 million per day in economic aid), thereby putting himself at the mercy of the United States, as a *precondition* for opening negotiations with this same government that had sworn the destruction of his régime!

Just as it was implausible to suggest that Castro's connections with Russia were the cause of his conflict with the United States (they were, rather, the result of this conflict), so it was absurd to imply that Cuba's challenge to the Latin American power structure was separable from its challenge to the United States. For by far the largest single economic stake in the hemispheric *status quo* belonged to private US interests. As long as Washington insisted, as it did, on identifying these private interests with the US national interest, the revolutionary challenge in Latin America would be a challenge to the United States as well.

In Venezuela, for example, which provides an instructive case in point, the US-owned oil industry produced 90 per cent of the country's exports and its tax payments accounted for 60 per cent of the national budget. The crucial decisions affecting Venezuela's economic development were taken in New York, therefore, not

---

[1] New York *Times*, editorial, ibid.
[2] New York *Times*, Int. Edn., July 7, 1964.

Caracas, and they were taken with regard to the benefit of companies with interests elsewhere. From a strictly national point of view, this was an intolerable situation, and one would have expected a reform movement, like Romulo Betancourt's left-wing *Accion Democratica*, which acceded to power in 1959, to assert national control over the resource. Betancourt, however, took no steps in this direction.

At the same time, the Betancourt régime (1959–64) was hailed by the Kennedy Administration as an acceptable 'revolutionary' alternative to Castroism. According to U S spokesmen, this acceptability lay in Betancourt's commitment to democracy. Since other extremely anti-democratic Latin American régimes like Somoza's in Nicaragua, were also acceptable, however, commitment to democracy could hardly have been the decisive criterion of acceptability. In fact, Betancourt's commitment was not as firm as Alliance spokesmen often seemed to suggest. As President, he 'imposed a "suspension of constitutional guarantees" for periods totalling half his term in office. During such times there [was] press censorship, political parties [were] prohibited from meeting without government approval, the offices of Communists – and frequently other oppositionists – [were] closed, and hundreds [were] arrested without the right of *habeas corpus*.'[1]

A far more plausible explanation of Betancourt's acceptability, was that unlike Castro he chose not to challenge the existing power structure, and in particular did not seriously seek to regulate the oil interests, or to check the annual flow of between $500 million and $1,000 million in oil revenues to the United States – a figure exceeding annual U S aid to the *whole* of Latin America under the Alliance for Progress.

During Betancourt's tenure in office, the petroleum interests reduced new investment in Venezuela from approximately $579

---

[1] Sidney Lens, 'Roadblocks to Reform in Latin America', in *The Anatomy of Foreign Aid* (pamphlet), 1964. John Gerassi, former correspondent for *Time* and *Newsweek* describes the terror under Betancourt, in his book on Latin America, *The Great Fear*, Macmillan 1963. He quotes a 'non-political colonial History professor' as saying: 'The government wants the students to react, to fight back. Then it can have a pretext to invade the university grounds to shoot or arrest all suspected leftists. Since 1960 more then 300 students have been killed. It has become impossible for an honest man to support the government even if he is conservative.'

million to approximately $178 million, with the result that unemployment tripled, even though Betancourt's main election plank had been to provide jobs. Not only did Betancourt leave the oil interests intact, but he failed to carry out an effective land reform.[1] The two programs in which he did achieve impressive results were those which coincided with the less ambiguous aspects of the Alliance for Progress program, health and education, but which were also less crucial for over-all social and economic development. The failure to change the existing power structure meant increasing poverty and instability for the country, and thus an increasing 'Cuban' threat.

Just as this Cuban threat lay primarily in the fact that Cuba had challenged US interests and survived, so Betancourt's acceptability lay in his willingness to observe limits to reform, and in particular, to stop short of offending those same US interests. But these limits also restricted Betancourt's ability to alter the fundamental *status quo* in Venezuela, and by ameliorating the situation to provide a viable alternative to Castroist revolution. In this way, his predicament reflected the inner contradiction of the Alliance for Progress, its commitment to a 'revolution from the top', to transforming the continent and eliminating its poverty, while preserving the essential structures and vested interests which had produced and maintained that misery in the past.[2]

The Alliance concept had been an attempt to break out of the sterilities of pure containment that had characterized American policy in the underdeveloped world until then. Instead of waiting for revolution or civil war to develop and then pouring in military and economic 'aid', the Alliance program was designed to head off the revolution by replacing it. When two years of Alliance failures proved this to be a more formidable task than had been expected, there was a re-emphasis of the containment thesis (although the

---

[1] Lens, ibid. 'Land holdings in units of 1,000 hectares or larger, which totalled 22 million hectares before the "reform" still account for more than 21 million hectares – three-quarters of the acreage under cultivation.'

[2] The foreign aid bill passed after Kennedy's death included many new provisions which clarified the aims of the Alliance. To be approved an Alliance loan would have to meet thirty-three major tests including whether the project financed might have adverse effects on the US economy, whether it encouraged free enterprise, and whether small US business would have an opportunity to participate in it. Further provision was made that, by December 31, 1965, no aid would go to any country that had not signed an investment-guarantee with the United States.

policy towards Cuba had never really departed from this pattern). In his speech before the Inter-American Press Association, November 18, 1963, Kennedy declared:

> If the Alliance is to succeed, we must continue to support measures to halt Communist infiltration and subversion and to assist governments menaced from abroad. *The American states must be ready to come to the aid of any government requesting aid to prevent a take-over linked to the policies of foreign Communism rather than to an internal desire for change. My own country is prepared to do this.* [Emphasis added.]

In its purposeful vagueness this offer was obviously nothing less than a *carte blanche* for counter-revolutionary intervention in Latin America by the United States. For obviously any Latin American government faced with its overthrow would be willing to characterize the threatened takeover, at the very least, as '*linked* to the *policies* of foreign Communism rather than to an internal desire for change'.

As is evident from the foregoing analysis, the pattern of US cold war policy in Latin America, during the two cold war decades, was that of a program ostensibly to contain expansion by Communist powers, but in fact to contain social revolution, where social revolution meant radical change outside the lines laid down by Washington.

In the Far East, a similar pattern was evident in US cold war policy, which was oriented towards the 'containment of China'. Moreover, since, unlike Cuba, China was a great world power, US containment of the Chinese Revolution had very real links with early US containment of Russia. Consequently, a consideration of US China policy can also throw considerable light on the way in which a vast mobilization was undertaken in the post-war period against a threat of Soviet expansion that, as George Kennan later admitted, 'was largely a creation of the Western imagination', and (he might have added) of official Western propaganda.

Washington's post-war attitude toward Chinese Communism, like its attitude towards Russia, was one of intense hostility (though in the case of China the hostility was immediately open). For despite the fact that Chiang Kai-shek's despotic and deeply corrupt régime had been only a desultory ally in World War II, while Mao's Communists had virtually forced the formation of a united national front against Japan, and despite the fact that the China service of the US State Department had given its opinion that China's future belonged to the Communists as defenders of the nation and leaders of the agrarian revolution, Washington poured $2 billion into China after the war in an effort to defeat the Communist bid for power.

After the success of the Communist Revolution, the United States pursued a policy calculated to provoke maximum hostility from the new Chinese leaders. Washington began its campaign by interposing the 7th Fleet between the mainland and the defeated dictator Chiang, thereby violating its pledge not to intervene in China's civil war. Following this, the US refused recognition to the new Chinese Government, characterizing it as 'illegal' (on what grounds was Chiang's dictatorship 'legal'?) barred China from international trade and from international institutions like the UN, branded her a 'willful aggressor' in Korea – after first provoking her entry into the war – refurbished Chiang's defeated and discredited army, lent support to his bid to regain power, thereby encouraging internal opponents of the new Chinese régime to look for such a development, and guided the Kuomintang (through the CIA) in conducting espionage overflights of China with U-2s and making sabotage raids on the mainland. In addition, the United States occupied the strategic Pacific bases of China's historic enemy Japan, having displaced Japan as a power in the area. From these bases nuclear bombers of the Strategic Air Command were targeted on mainland objectives long before China herself became a nuclear power. A Polaris submarine fleet was built in the China Sea and US Secretary of Defense McNamara announced on several occasions prior to the Chinese nuclear test that in the event of nuclear war with the Soviet Union, the US had the nuclear capacity to destroy *both* Russia and China as national societies.

This catalogue of US hostility indicates some of the background against which the attitudes of the Chinese leaders towards the United States (and hence towards the Russian policy of peaceful coexistence) were formed. Penetrating insight into these Chinese attitudes, was provided by Yugoslavia's Vice-President Edvard Kardelj, in his early polemic against the Chinese position in the Sino-Soviet dispute.[1]

[1] *Socialism and War*, 1961, pp. 187–8.

China's economic backwardness, which had 'made the revolution indispensable,' wrote Kardelj, had 'become the main obstacle to any speed in internal development, and the principal source of the danger of internal reactionary forces rising again and undermining the unity of the country. The settlement of this question [of economic development] now brings into question the sheer existence of the revolution as such. . . .' As a result of US policies of intervention, active support to counter-revolutionary forces, and economic and military blockade, 'not only is it impossible for China to find a place in world trade which would contribute to a more normal internal development, and not only does China receive no support whatsoever from world industry, but pressure is additionally exerted to increase the country's material burdens.'

'All these facts,' continued Kardelj, 'have greatly increased the strains to which the peoples of China are subjected in their efforts to overcome backwardness. . . . It is perfectly natural under such conditions that there should have arisen a tendency to the view that the encircling ring imposed on China by the capitalist states by pressure and force must be broken by counter-pressure and – if necessary – by force. Under such circumstances, to many Chinese, unable to take an integral view of social developments in the whole world, a policy based on coexistence not only does not look like practical politics, but is even felt to be likely to contribute to the maintenance of this state in which the peoples of China are now situated, that is, they see it as a brake on Chinese progress.'

Kardelj's observations are but the obverse of the lesson we have already drawn in our analysis of containment, namely, that industrialization, economic well-being and a place in the international community 'mellow' régimes, while containment increases their militancy. This lesson, so painfully apparent after nineteen years of cold war in Europe, was already evident before Kennan's 'X' article had 'announced' the policy. For the isolation and containment of Russia from 1917 to 1941 had not perceptibly mellowed the Bolshevik régime. Conversely, and as an indication that the strategy of containment was a strategy designed only for intractable *revolutionary* régimes and not other 'expansionist' states, it was obvious that American post-war policy towards defeated Germany (after both wars) was premised on the belief that economic prosperity and a normal place in the international community were essential and indispensable elements in the attempt to create a 'mellowed', less ambitious and less arrogant national mentality.

An even more striking indication of the counter-revolutionary nature of the logic of containment as applied to China was offered by Kennan in a favorable review of America's China policy written in 1964.[1] Discounting the existence of any legitimate causes of Chinese antipathy towards the United States, even as in his earlier 'X' article he had dismissed as mere fictions Russian fears of capitalist antagonism[2] Kennan argued that Chinese hostility was principally attributable to the fact that China had 'fallen into the hands of a group of embittered fanatics'. These fanatics were 'absolutely per- meated with hatred toward ourselves, not only because the ideology pictures us all as villains,[3] but also *because we, more than any other people, have had the temerity to stand in their path and to obstruct the expansion of their power.* . . . . . . as part of [our] effort at containment (for that is really what it is), we have tried to see to it that China was denied recognition, denied admission to the UN, denied the advant- ages of normal participation in the life of the international com- munity until such time as its leaders would moderate their ambitions, desist from their *expansionist efforts* and accommodate themselves to the continued existence of truly independent govern- ments elsewhere on the Asiatic continent.' (Emphasis added.)

Thus, in Kennan's retrospective view American containment of China was compelled by Chinese ambition and Chinese expansionist efforts. It would be interesting to know what specifically *Chinese* efforts, according to Kennan, dictated the American policies of non-recognition and the blockade of China in early 1950, since the statements of Dean Acheson and Dean Rusk at the time make clear

[1] 'A Fresh Look at Our China Policy', New York *Times Magazine*, November 22, 1964.

[2] Despite Western intervention in Russia's civil war (1917–21), and the avowed interest of Western leaders in seeing the destruction of the Bolshevik régime, and despite the military threat during the thirties from the anti- Comintern axis, especially Germany and Japan.

[3] But Chinese propaganda is generally acknowledged to make careful distinc- tion between the villainous American Government and the 'exploited' American people. Moreover, despite their absurd doctrinalism in the Sino–Soviet dispute, the Chinese Communists exhibited a far more pragmatic outlook than the Russians (cf. W. W. Rostow, *The Prospects for Communist China*, 1958). An excellent brief account of the Chinese viewpoint can be found in Joan Robinson, *Notes on China*, 1964.

that these American policies were supposed to be directed not at a *Chinese* régime ('The Peiping régime may be a colonial Russian Government – a Slavic Manchukuo on a larger scale. It is not the Government of China. . . . It is not Chinese.') but at the *Russians* who had 'taken over' China 'at a ridiculously small cost'.[1] In his 1964 analysis Kennan had overlooked the fact that it was Russian expansionary ambitions, and not Chinese, that had served in 1950 as a pretext for hostility to the revolution.

While this historical oversight was itself revealing about the fragile foundations of the justifying logic of containment, the main argument of Kennan's 1964 approach to China was even more illuminating. Writing in unofficial capacity, Kennan could afford to be more candid than in his 'X' article, particularly about the long-range goals within whose framework a particular policy was preferred. Thus, Kennan expressed sympathy for whose who would make it an 'immediate objective' of US policy 'to ecompass the overthrow and destruction' of the Chinese régime. 'If any political régime in history [wrote Kennan] has ever asked for its own violent destruction, it is this group of men in Peking. . . .' Such a policy, however, was not feasible for the present, according to Kennan, and the best alternative, in the circumstances, was a policy of containment to frustrate Chinese 'ambition' – but this did 'not mean that we need to lose all hope for the future'.

Just as Kennan was more candid about what the long-term objectives of American policy should be, so he allowed himself greater frankness in describing the Chinese 'expansionist' effort. Kennan did not have in mind military expansion, for already existing American military power (including its nuclear arm) made such an attempt unlikely. The Chinese problem, according to Kennan, was thus 'not purely, or even primarily a military problem'. 'Military force has a part in it and there is at least one area, the island of Taiwan where the Chinese Communists would probably set about to achieve their objectives at once by purely military means if our armed forces did not stand in the way.[2] But in most instances,

[1] cf. above, pp. 111–112.

[2] However, the United States could hardly, in good conscience, take the view that a Chinese invasion of Taiwan to complete the revolution would constitute 'expansion', since in several agreements during World War II, the United States had recognized Taiwan to be a part of China (the *justice* of such a position, from the point of view of the native Taiwanese, is of course another question entirely).

Chinese forces are not involved; and *even direct military aid from the Chinese side is probably less of a factor than we commonly think.*'[1] [Emphasis added.]

In fact, continued Kennan, '*The weapons with which the Chinese are operating here are primarily the political reactions of the people of the threatened areas themselves:* their inherited resentments, their fears, their weariness, and such error and prejudice against ourselves and their own régimes as can be artificially pumped into their minds.' [Emphasis added.] In other words, the Chinese expansionary threat was, in essence, *Chinese support for indigenous nationalist and revolutionary movements,* which were, for one reason or another, hostile to the United States and to the political régimes (like that of Ngo Dinh Diem) which the United States had foisted on them.[2]

While considerably more candid with regard to its operative assumptions, Kennan's view of America's China policy as a program of containment was not different in essentials from Washington's:

> Behind the American determination to preserve South Viet Nam's independence is the long-range plan for developing a 'containment' policy of Communist China. Some leading experts in the Johnson Administration strongly believe that the situation in the Far East resembles that in Europe after the second world war when the Soviet Union embarked on an expansionist policy which led to the West building a protective dam in the form of the Nato alliance.
>
> (London *Sunday Times,* November 29, 1964)

One immediate difference between the situation in Southeast Asia and the early cold war situation in Europe, however, was the fact that in fighting 'to preserve South Viet Nam's independence' (accurate as a description of explicit American policy and also in the sense that Washington consistently opposed unification and neu-

---

[1] Reports on China's military strength indicate that she has a very small (2,600 planes) obsolete air force, a navy with 'virtually no amphibious capability', and is generally beset by shortages in mechanized equipment. Chalmers Johnson, 'How Sharp Are the Chinese Dragon's Claws?' – New York *Times,* Int. Edn., March 31, 1965.

[2] On the nationalism of the revolutionary movements supported by China and the limits of Chinese control over them because of this and other factors, cf. Richard Lowenthal, 'Has the Revolution a Future?', *Encounter,* January 1965.

tralization of the country[1]) the United States was acting in direct violation of the Geneva Agreement of 1954. This agreement stipulated that the 17th Parallel dividing North from South Viet Nam was a mere provisional military demarcation line and 'should not in any way be interpretated as constituting a political or territorial boundary'. Moreover, the US military presence itself in South Viet Nam, which long preceded the Vietcong rebellion, was also illegal since the agreements stipulated that 'the introduction into Viet Nam of foreign troops and military personnel as well as of all kinds of arms and munitions is prohibited'.

Legal considerations aside, the official American contention that the US was containing 'aggression' in Viet Nam[2] was difficult to reconcile with the fact that as late as March 1964, reliable sources reported that 'no capture of North Vietnamese in the South has come to light',[3] whereas it was also reliably reported that raids *into North Viet Nam* by South Vietnamese forces under US guidance had been going on since 1961.[4]

Similarly, the main ostensible justification for the American effort in Viet Nam, namely, the containment of Chinese expansion, did not conform to the known facts of the situation,[5] in particular

[1] In May 1964, for example, James Reston reported from Washington: '. . . it may be useful to define what the immediate danger [in South Viet Nam] is. It is not that South Viet Nam is about to be overrun by the Communists. It is not that the US is preparing to attack North Viet Nam or even order its own troops into the South Viet Nam units. *It is that the South Vietnamese Government will be overthrown by a neutralist coup and that the US will then be invited to leave.*' [Emphasis added.] New York *Times*, Int. Edn., May 23–24.

[2] In his State of the Union message for 1963, for example, President Kennedy spoke of the 'spearpoint of aggression' as having been 'blunted' in South Viet Nam.

[3] New York *Times*, March 6, 1964.

[4] New York *Times*, Int Edn., December 5–6, 1964.

[5] Some of the more cynical aspects of strategic thinking in Washington were revealed by C. L. Sulzberger in the New York *Times*, Int. Edn., of December 5–6, 1964: 'Important factions in Washington would prefer to step up *riposte* against Hanoi by open assaults and mass bombardments. An influential Pentagon group even welcomes the risk that this could involve Communist China; that might give UN bombers a chance to destroy the Sinkiang plant which produced China's first nuclear device. . . .

'Ho Chi Minh's Communist supporters are doing alarmingly well in the South; nevertheless, Ho worries about Washington's ultimate trump – the threat of wholesale escalation. Destructive air raids could upset Ho's wobbly economy and invite intervention by Peking's infantry. The last thing Ho wants is Chinese occupation.'

that the continued war strengthened the Communists' minority faction in the Vietcong, and forced the pro-Moscow Communist Party of North Viet Nam to shift its allegiance, reluctantly, towards China, which was under no diplomatic pressure (as Russia was) to reduce its aid. Even without taking these elements into consideration, the plain and inescapable fact was that a victory for the Communists (let alone for the Vietcong) in South Viet Nam, would no more necessarily mean an expansion of Chinese power than the victory of the Communists in Yugoslavia, or in China for that matter, had meant the expansion of Soviet power. Accordingly, US policy in South Viet Nam and in Southeast Asia generally must have been oriented by other considerations than the necessity of containing Chinese expansion.

At the time of the nuclear test-ban, it was reported that the Kennedy Administration was convinced that the isolation of China 'takes second place only to the prevention of nuclear war . . . senior officials have said that the United States has an intrinsic interest in the isolation of China'.[1] The foregoing analysis makes it evident that this 'intrinsic interest' in China's isolation had nothing to do with the threat of Chinese expansion and, therefore, that this containment policy could only have been an attempt to prevent China from emerging as a great Asian power. The United States' intrinsic interest in preventing or at least in retarding this development was obvious, since revolutionary China's survival had already served to challenge the vast American presence in Asia. China's further emergence would inevitably entail an even more formidable 'threat' to the over-extended United States, whose vulnerability as a white non-Asian power, committed to the support and maintenance of reactionary political and social forces extending in a wide arc through Asia and the Pacific regions was painfully obvious.[2]

It is only in this light that the theory of 'falling dominoes' invoked

[1] London *Times*, August 5, 1963.

[2] Of course there was no intrinsic reason why the tactics of preserving the American stake in Asia should have been as rigid and inflexible as they were, nor was there any intrinsic reason why the very definition of that stake by Washington should itself not be subject to change. The pattern which American policy did take towards Bolshevik Russia, revolutionary Cuba and Communist China, was certainly indicative of US motives and interests, but given these interests, there was still no 'inevitability' about the particular strategies employed.

so often by American officials to explain the strategy of containment in Southeast Asia made any sense. For in terms of military expansion, there was no obvious reason why even Chinese occupation of South Viet Nam, for example, would have meant the 'fall' of Malaysia or Indonesia, any more than a Communist presence on the mainland had meant the fall of Taiwan. However, in terms of indigenous nationalist, peasant or Communist revolutions, it was clear that an increase in China's international prestige, or a Vietcong victory *would* threaten corrupt and potentially unstable dictatorships like those in Thailand and South Korea, or the semi-stable governments of the poverty-stricken but mineral rich Southeast Asian Archipaelego, and, because American power and prestige had been staked in the preservation of such régimes and the social forces they represented, it would undermine the pro-American *status quo*. This was the 'Chinese threat', as Kennan had accurately indicated, and in preventing these developments lay the significance of containment.

In line with these observations it is instructive to recall the way both sides in the conflict in South Viet Nam, viewed its real significance. In a report from Washington (New York *Times*, Int. Edn., March 29, 1965) James Reston cited the following statement by North Vietnamese General Giap:

> South Viet Nam is the model of the national liberation movement of our time. . . . If the special warfare that the United States imperialists are testing in South Viet Nam is overcome, this means that it can be defeated everywhere in the world.

'On this point . . .' commented Reston, 'the Johnson Administration tends to agree. They see the war in Viet Nam as a critical test of the Communist technique of military subversion, which must be defeated now or faced in many other places in the world, including the Western Hemisphere.' The issue could not be made much more explicit. (Indeed, cf. C. L. Sulzberger, New York *Times*, March 3, 1965: 'The heart of the crisis is not truly in Viet Nam. The quintessential problem is how to defeat revolutionary warfare.')

The overall consistency of the containment pattern of America's cold war policy from Latin America to Asia was reflected in the foreign aid program and in President Kennedy's failure even to begin its transformation from a weapon of 'security' to an instrument of economic growth and development. So immutable was the fundamental shape of American policy in this area, that in the end President Kennedy himself came to defend the program, as a program of containment. Defending foreign aid in a speech on November 8, 1963, the President said it was a way of maintaining 3·5 million allied troops in foreign countries. (In addition there were, in 1963, one million American soldiers deployed overseas on more than 200 major US bases and over a thousand additional 'installations' in foreign countries.) The foreign aid program, declared Kennedy, 'helps to stave off the kind of chaos or Communist takeover or Communist attack that would surely demand our critical and costly attention'. In view of the fact that the vast majority of foreign aid funds were used to support military forces maintained by dictatorial régimes in poverty-stricken countries, the President's meaning was unmistakably clear. For if the Turkish Army, to mention but one example, were reduced to a size commensurate with the poverty that successive dictatorships had sustained in the country, there would most certainly ensue a 'chaos' that would demand the 'critical and costly attention' of the United States. But there would hardly be a Communist 'attack'. For under the Nato Pact (and the United States had similar agreements with more than thirty countries on the periphery of the Soviet Union) an attack on Turkey would be equivalent to an attack on the United States. If the Soviet rulers wanted to go to war with the United States, they would hardly choose such an indirect method as an invasion of Turkey. The inevitable conclusion is that the 400,000 Turkish Nato troops, financed by the US foreign aid program, served only one purpose: to contain any internal revolution, which the social injustice perpetuated during sixteen years of United States tutelage there might engender.

The 'anti-revolutionary' nature of America's policy of global containment, to which Toynbee had drawn attention in 1961, was also reflected in new developments in American military policy, and in particular in the growth of a new 'counter-insurgency' arm.[1] This development was dictated in part by the growing military stalemate with the Soviet Union (and the increasing independence of Europe) which limited American maneuverability in pursuing its interven-

---

[1] The Rockefeller Report had anticipated this development, recommending that the US prepare to meet 'non-overt aggression concealed as internal takeover by *coup d'etat* or by civil war'.

tionist policies, and by the burgeoning of revolutionary movements in the underdeveloped world. In November 1963, President Kennedy announced that in the preceding three years his Administration had 'increased by 600 per cent the number of our *counter-insurgency* forces . . .'

By 1964, a new Counter-Insurgency Program (of which the military was but one part) was already costing $500 million annually 'and with Viet Nam, perhaps a full billion dollars'.[1] The directors of the Counter-Insurgency Program in the Kennedy Administration included the Attorney-General, the Chairman of the Joint Chiefs of Staff, the Assistant Secretary of Defense, the Foreign Aid Administrator, the Director of the CIA, the Director of the US Information Agency and a member of the White House Staff.

Counter-insurgent activity was 'of two main types: military and civic action. In Thailand, 60 per cent of US aid comes under the counter-insurgency program, and most of this is military: the remaining 40 per cent is under the separate Military Assistance Program.'

The military aspect of the program included teaching counter-insurgent military tactics 'on the spot' in countries like Viet Nam and Bolivia, or in the United States, where 24,000 foreign military men were trained, or in special training schools in Panama and Okinawa, or in Germany, where Europeans and Americans were trained 'for possible future activity in Africa'.

'The civic action side of counter-insurgency' was directed by 'the Agency for International Development'. Under the program, a country's military was trained for public works 'to gain the sympathies of its people'. In Thailand under this program, however, the military was enabled to build a road in an inaccessible area 'so that they could subdue tribesmen of questionable loyalty'.

Another program in the category of counter-insurgency was called 'Public Safety' and trained police forces 'in a couple dozen countries'. There was also a counter-insurgency project of 'aid in producing government propaganda, provided by the United States Information Service'.

[1] This, and the following, are taken from Roger Hagan, 'Counter-Insurgency and the New Foreign Relations', *The Correspondent*, Autumn 1964. The material for this article is to be found in Arthur Herzog, *The War–Peace Establishment*, 1965.

Covert operations which included the infiltration of 'insurgent groups which might threaten established governments' were conducted by the CIA as part of the program. Other covert operations were run by the Defense Department. Finally, the State Department conducted its own course for foreign service officers and ambassadors called 'Overseas Internal Defense'.

Considered to be the 'new wave' in the American 'defense effort', the counter-insurgency program was already acknowledged as having 'altered in large ways – and yet secretly – the course of events in Iran, Guatemala, Southeast Asia and Central Africa'. Viewed in the overall context of America's policy of global containment, however, and set against the background of American actions in the cold war, there was nothing new about the 'counter-insurgency' effort: it merely made explicit the underlying pattern of the strategic goals of the American cold war program.

In 1964, as in 1947, America was (in Toynbee's formulation) the 'leader of a world-wide anti-revolutionary movement in defence of vested interests'. As of Rome, it could be said of her that she 'consistently supported the rich against the poor in all foreign countries that fell under her sway; and, since the poor, so far, [had] always and everywhere been far more numerous than the rich, [her] policy made for inequality, for injustice, and for the least happiness of the greatest number.'

In these dark times, when the nation's historic and revered role as a light and hope to oppressed peoples was being tragically reversed and the new world colossus was taking its place as one of the great and hated oppressor nations, the American people could ponder with rue the prophetic words uttered by John Quincy Adams in his Independence Day Oration of 1821. Observing with pride that 'America goes not abroad in search of monsters to destroy,' he warned that if she did, though 'she might become dictatress of the world, she would no longer be the ruler of her own spirit.' And indeed, when America set out on her post-war path to contain revolution throughout the world, and threw her immense power and influence into the balance against the rising movement for social justice among the poverty stricken two-thirds of the world's population, the first victims of her deeds were the very ideals for a better world – liberty, equality and self-determination – which she herself, in her infancy, had done so much to foster.

Bibliography

Acheson, Dean. *Strengthening the Forces of Freedom.* Washington D.C.: Government Printing Office, 1950

Adams, Sherman. *Firsthand Report.* New York: Harper, 1961

Aguilar, Alonso. *Latin America and the Alliance for Progress* (pamphlet). New York: Monthly Review Press, 1963

Alexander, Robert J. 'Latin American Communism,' *Soviet Survey,* August 1962

Alexander, Robert J. and Charles O. Porter. *The Struggle for Democracy in Latin America.* New York: Macmillan, 1961

Altman, George. 'New Doubts on the Hiss Case,' *The Nation,* October 1, 1960

Arnold, H. H. *Global Mission.* New York: Harper, 1949

Bain, Leslie B. 'Have We Failed in Hungary?', *The Reporter,* January 24, 1957

Barraclough, Geoffrey. 'More Than Dulles Must Go,' *The Nation.* January 4, 1958

Barth, Alan. *The Loyalty of Free Men.* New York: Viking, 1952

Bell, Coral. *Negotiation from Strength.* London: Chatto & Windus, 1962

Berle Jr., A. A. 'The Cuban Crisis,' *Foreign Affairs,* October 1960

Bethe, Hans. 'The Case for Ending Nuclear Tests,' *The Atlantic Monthly,* August 1960

Blackett, P. M. S. *Military and Political Consequences of Atomic Weapons.* London: Turnstile Press, 1948 *Fear, War and the Bomb.* New York: McGraw-Hill, 1949

Blackett, P. M. S. *Atomic Weapons and East-West Relations.* Cambridge University Press, 1956

Blackett, P. M. S. *Studies of War.* New York: Hill and Wang, 1962

Blackett, P. M. S. 'The First Real Chance for Disarmament,' *Harpers,* January 1963

Bolton, Charles. 'Cuba: Pivot to the Future,' *The Nation,* November 17, 1962

Brower, Michael. 'President Kennedy's Choice of Nuclear Strategy,' *Council for Correspondence Newsletter* (Cambridge, Massachusetts), June 1962

Buck, Pearl. 'What Asians Want,' *The Christian Century,* June 27, 1951

Bundy, McGeorge. 'Appeasement, Provocation and Policy,' *The Reporter,* January 9, 1951

Bundy, McGeorge and Henry L. Stimson. *On Active Service in Peace and War.* New York: Harper, 1947

Byrnes, James F. *Speaking Frankly.* New York: Harper, 1947

Castro, Fidel. *Plan for the Advancement of Latin America* (pamphlet). Havana, 1959

Childs, Marquis. *Eisenhower: Captive Hero.* New York: Harcourt and Brace, 1958

Churchill, Winston. *Europe Unite.* London: Cassell, 1950

Churchill, Winston. *The Second World War.* Vol. VI. London: Cassell, 1953

Cook, Fred J. *The Unfinished Case of Alger Hiss.* New York: Morrow, 1957

Cook, Fred J. 'C.I.A.', *The Nation*, June 24, 1961
Cook, Fred J. 'Juggernaut—The Warfare State,' *The Nation*, October 28, 1961
Crofts, Alfred. 'Our Falling Ramparts—The Case of Korea,' *The Nation*, June 25, 1960
Crown, James Tracy and James Penty, *Kennedy in Power*. New York: Ballantine, 1961

Deutscher, Isaac. *Stalin: A Political Biography*. Oxford University Press, 1949
Deutscher, Isaac. *Russia After Stalin*. London: Hamilton, 1953
Deutscher, Isaac. *Heretics and Renegades*. London: Hamilton, 1955
Deutscher, Isaac. *The Great Contest*. Oxford University Press, 1960
Deutscher, Isaac. 'October Revolution, New Style,' *The Reporter*, November 15, 1956
Djilas, Milovan. *Conversations With Stalin*. London: Hart-Davis, 1962
Dozer, Donald M. *Are We Good Neighbors?* Univ. of Florida Press, 1959
Draper, Theodore. *Castro's Revolution: Myths and Realities*. New York: Praeger, 1962
Draper, Theodore. 'Castro and Communism,' *The Reporter*, January 17, 1963

Eden, Anthony. *Full Circle* (Memoirs). London: Cassell, 1960
Edwardes, Michael. *Asia in the Balance*. Harmondsworth: Penguin, 1962
Eisenhower, Dwight D. *Mandate for Change*. London: Heinemann, 1963
Eisenhower, Dwight D. *Peace with Justice*. Columbia Univ. Press, 1953

Fall, Bernard B. 'Anti-Americanism: Will South Vietnam Be Next?' *The Nation*, May 31, 1958
Feis, Herbert. *Churchill, Roosevelt, and Stalin*. Princeton, 1957
Fishel, W. (ed). *Problems of Freedom*. Michigan State Univ. Press, 1961
Fleming, D. F. *The Cold War and Its Origins*. 2 vols. New York: Doubleday, and London: Allen and Unwin, 1961
Forrestal, James V. *The Forrestal Diaries*. (Walter Millis, ed.). New York: Viking, 1951
Frank, Andrew Gunder. 'Varieties of Land Reform,' *Monthly Review*, April 1963.

Gayn, Mark. *Japan Diary*. New York: Sloane, 1948
Gerassi, John. *The Great Fear*. Macmillan, 1963
Gervasi, Frank. 'Watchdog in the White House,' *Colliers*, October 9, 1955
Goldman, Eric F. *The Crucial Decade and After*. New York: Vintage, 1961
Gott, Richard and John Gittings, 'Nato's Final Decade,' *Views* (London), Summer 1964
Graham, David. 'Liberated Guatemala,' *The Nation*,. July 14, 1956
Gunther, John. *The Riddle of MacArthur*. London: Hamilton, 1951

Haffner, Sebastian. 'Germany, Russia and the West,' *Encounter*, October 1961
Hagan, Roger. 'Counter-Insurgency and the New Foreign Relations,' *The Correspondent*, Autumn 1964
Halle, Louis J. *American Foreign Policy*. London: Allen & Unwin, 1960
Hammer, Ellen J. *The Struggle for Indo-China*. Stanford University Press, 1954
Herzog, Arthur. *The War-Peace Establishment*. New York: Harper, 1965
Hinterhoff, Eugene. 'The Case for Disengagement,' *The Correspondent*, November–December 1963

Hitchcock, Wilbur. 'North Korea Jumps the Gun,' *Current History*, March 1951
Huberman, Leo and Paul Sweezy, *Cuba: Anatomy of a Revolution*. New York: Monthly Review Press, 1960
Hull, Cordell. *Memoirs*. 2 vols. New York: Macmillan, 1948

Ingram, Kenneth. *History of the Cold War*. London: Darwen Finlayson, 1955

Johnson, Paul. 'The Plundered Continent,' *New Statesman*, September 17, 1960
Jones, Joseph M. *The Fifteen Weeks*. New York: Viking, 1955

Kardelj, Edvard. *Socialism and War*. London: Methuen, 1961
Kennan, George. *American Diplomacy, 1900–1950*. Univ. of Chicago, 1951
Kennan, George. *Russia, the Atom and the West*. Oxford University Press, 1958
Kennan, George. *Russia and the West Under Lenin and Stalin*. London: Hutchinson, 1961
Kennan, George. 'Polycentrism and Western Policy,' *Foreign Affairs*, January 1964
Kennan, George. 'A Fresh Look at Our China Policy,' *New York Times Magazine*, November 22, 1964
Kennedy, John F. *The Strategy of Peace*. London: Hamilton, 1960
Kirk, Betty. 'U.S. in Latin America—Policy of the Suction Pump,' *The Nation*, October 5, 1957
Kissinger, Henry. 'The Unsolved Problems of European Defense,' *Foreign Affairs*, July 1962
Knebel, Fletcher. 'Washington in Crisis,' *Look*, December 18, 1962
Korakas, Manolis. 'Greek Communists Stage a Comeback,' *New Leader*, May 26, 1958

Lancaster, Donald. *The Emancipation of French Indo-China*. Oxford University Press, 1961
Lapp, Ralph E. 'Nuclear Weapons Systems,' *Bulletin of the Atomic Scientists*, March 1961
Lapp, Ralph E. *Kill and Overkill: The Strategy of Annihilation*. New York: Basic Books, 1962
Leahy, William F. *I Was There*. London: Gollancz, 1950
Leckie, Robert. *The Korean War*. London: Pall Mall, 1963
Lederer, William J. *A Nation of Sheep*. London: Cassell, 1961
Lens, Sidney. 'Building on Quicksand,' *The Commonweal*. November 1, 1963
Lens, Sidney. 'Roadblocks to Reform in Latin America,' *The Anatomy of Foreign Aid* (pamphlet). London: Housmans, 1964
Levin, N. Gordon. 'Our Men in Honduras,' *Dissent*, Autumn 1963
Lieuwin, Edwin. *Arms and Politics in Latin America*. New York: Praeger, 1961
Lippmann, Walter. *The Cold War*. New York: Harper, and London: Hamilton, 1947
Lippmann, Walter. *The Communist World and Ours*. London: Hamilton, 1959
Lippmann, Walter. 'Kennedy At Mid-Term,' *Newsweek*, January 21, 1963
Lippmann, Walter. 'Goldwater vs. Johnson,' New York *Herald Tribune*, July 29, 1964
Lowenthal, Richard. 'The Dangerous Year,' *Encounter*, June 1961
Lowenthal, Richard. 'Has the Revolution a Future?' *Encounter*, January 1965
Lukacs, John. *A History of the Cold War*. New York: Doubleday, 1961

Manger, Wm. (ed). *The Alliance for Progress: A Critical Appraisal.* Washington: 1963

Marzani, Carl. *We Can Be Friends: Origins of the Cold War.* New York: Topical Books, 1951

MacLaurin, John. *United Nations and Power Politics.* New York: Harper, 1951

McCloy, John J. 'Balance Sheet on Disarmament,' *Foreign Affairs,* April 1962

McCune, George M. *Korea Today.* Harvard University Press, 1950

McDermott, Geoffrey, *Berlin: Success of a Mission?* London: Deutsch, 1963

McNeil, Wm. H. *The Greek Dilemma.* Phila: J. B. Lippincott, 1947

Meade, E. Grant. *American Military Government in Korea.* Oxford University Press, 1951

Méray, Tibor. *Thirteen Days that Shook the Kremlin.* London: Thames and Hudson, 1959

Meyer, Karl E. and Tad Szulc. *The Cuban Invasion.* New York: Ballantine and Praeger, 1962

Mikes, George. *The Hungarian Revolution.* London: Deutsch, 1957

Mikes, George. *A Study in Infamy.* London: Deutsch, 1959

Millis, Walter (ed). *The Forrestal Diaries.* New York: Viking, 1951

Mills, C. Wright. *The Power Elite.* Oxford University Press, 1956

Mills, C. Wright. *The Causes of World War III.* New York: Ballantine, 1958

Mills, C. Wright. *Listen Yankee.* New York: Ballantine and McGraw-Hill, 1960

Nagy, Imre. *Imre Nagy On Communism.* London: Thames & Hudson, 1957

Noel-Baker, Philip. *The Arms Race.* London: Atlantic, 1958

O'Balance, Edgar. *The Red Army.* London: Faber, 1964

O'Brien, Conor Cruise. *To Katanga and Back.* London: Hutchinson, 1962

Pachter, Henry. *Collision Course.* New York: Praeger, 1963

Porter, Charles O. and Robt. J. Alexander. *The Struggle for Democracy in Latin America.* New York: Macmillan, 1961

Reischauer, Edwin O. *Wanted: An Asian Policy.* New York: Knopf, 1955

Riggs, E. *Politics in the U.N.* Illinois University Press, 1958

Roberts, Chalmers. 'The Pious Truculence of John Foster Dulles,' *The Reporter,* January 23, 1958

Robinson, Joan. Notes on China. Oxford: Blackwell's and New York: Monthly Review Press, 1964.

Robinson, Joan, 'The Korean Miracle,' *Monthly Review,* January 1965

Roosevelt, James (ed). *The Liberal Papers.* New York: Doubleday, 1959

Rosen, Bernard. 'Counter-Revolution: Guatemala's Tragedy,' *The Nation,* July 31, 1954

Ross, Thomas and David Wise. *The U-2 Affair.* New York: Random House, 1962

Ross, Thomas and David Wise. *The Invisible Government.* New York: Knopf, 1964

Rostow, W. W. *The Prospects for Communist China.* New York: Wiley, 1954

Rostow, W. W. *The U.S. in the World Arena.* New York: Harper 1960

Scheer, Robert and Maurice Zeitlin. *Cuba: Tragedy in Our Hemisphere.* New York: Grove, 1963. Published in England by Penguin as *Cuba: An American Tragedy.* Harmondsworth: 1964

Scheer, Robert. 'Hang Down Your Head Tom Dooley,' *Ramparts* (California), January–February 1965

Schneider, Ronald. *Communism in Guatemala.* New York: Praeger, 1959

Schuman, Frederick L. 'The Devil and Jimmy Byrnes,' New York: *Soviet Russia Today*, 1948

Schuman, Frederick L. *Russia Since 1917.* New York: Knopf, 1957

Seton-Watson, Hugh. *The East European Revolution.* London: Methuen, 1950

Seton-Watson, Hugh. *The Pattern of Communist Revolution.* London: Methuen, 1961

Shannon, Wm. V. 'The Kennedy Administration: The Early Months,' *The American Scholar*, Fall, 1961

Shapiro, Samuel. 'Peru and the Alianza' *Studies on the Left* III. No. 2, 1962

Sherwood, Robert E. *Roosevelt and Hopkins.* New York: Harper, 1948

Smith, Howard K. *The State of Europe.* New York: Knopf, 1949

Snell, John. *The Meaning of Yalta.* Louisiana State Univ. Press, 1956

Spanier, John. *The Truman–MacArthur Controversy and the Korean War.* Harvard University Press, 1959

Stark, H. *Modern Latin America.* Florida: 1957

Stebbins, Richard. *The U.S. in World Affairs, 1954.* New York: Harper, 1956

Stebbins, Richard. *The U.S. in World Affairs, 1961.* New York: Harper, 1962

Stettinius, Edward. *Roosevelt and the Russians.* New York: Doubleday, 1949

Stimson, Henry L. and McGeorge Bundy. *On Active Service in Peace and War.* New York: Harper, 1947

Stone, I. F. *The Hidden History of the Korean War.* Monthly Review Press, 1952

Stone, I. F. 'A Reply to the White Paper,' *I. F. Stone's Weekly*, March 16, 1965

Sweezy, Paul and Leo Huberman. *Cuba: Anatomy of a Revolution.* New York: Monthly Review Press, 1960

Szulc, Tad and Karl E. Meyer. *The Cuban Invasion.* New York: Ballantine and Praeger, 1962

Taylor Jr., Philip B. 'The Guatemalan Affair: A Critique of U.S. Foreign Policy,' *The American Political Science Review*, September 1956

Toynbee, Arnold J. *America and the World Revolution.* Oxford University Press, 1961

Toynbee, Arnold J. *The Economy of the Western Hemisphere.* Oxford University Press, 1962

Truman, Harry S. *Memoirs.* 2 vols. New York: Doubleday, 1955 & 1956

Váli, Ferenc. *Rift and Revolt in Hungary.* Harvard University Press, 1961

Vandenberg Jr., Arthur H. and J. A. Morris (eds.). *The Private Papers of Senator Vandenberg.* Boston: 1953

Wagner, E. W. 'Failure in Korea,' *Foreign Affairs*, October 1961

Ward, Barbara. *The West at Bay.* London: Allen Unwin, 1948

Waskow, Arthur. *The Limits of Defense.* New York: Doubleday, 1962

Welles, Sumner. *Where Are We Heading?* New York: Harper, 1946

White, Theodore. *Fire in the Ashes.* New York: Sloane, 1953

White, Theodore. *The Making of the President 1960.* New York: Atheneum, 1962

Whitney, Courtney. *MacArthur: His Rendezvous with History.* New York: Knopf, 1956

Wiesner, Jerome B. 'Comprehensive Arms Limitation Systems,' *Daedalus*, Fall, 1960

Wiesner, Jerome B. and William York, 'National Security and the Nuclear Test Ban,' *Scientific American,* October 1964

Williams, Wm. A. *American–Russian Relations.* New York: Rinehart, 1952

Williams, Wm. A. 'The Irony of Containment,' *The Nation,* May 5, 1956

Williams, Wm. A. 'American Century: 1941–1957,' *The Nation,* Nov. 2, 1957

Williams, Wm. A. *The Tragedy of American Diplomacy.* Cleveland: World, 1959

Williams, Wm. A. *The U.S., Cuba and Castro.* New York: Monthly Review Press, 1962

Wise, David and Thomas Ross. *The U-2 Affair.* New York: Random House, 1962

Wise, David and Thomas Ross. *The Invisible Government.* New York: Knopf, 1964

Ydigoras Fuentes, Miguel. *My War With Communism.* New Jersey: Prentice Hall, 1963

York, William and Jerome B. Wienner. 'National Security and the Nuclear Test Ban,' *Scientific American,* October 1964

Zeitlin, Maurice and Robert Scheer. *Cuba: Tragedy in Our Hemisphere.* New York: Grove Press, 1963

Zinner, Paul E. *National Communism and Popular Revolt in East Europe.* Columbia University Press, 1956

Index

Acheson, Dean, vetoes meeting of Truman and Stalin (1950), 13–14; on the objects of the Marshall Plan, 76n; attitude to Truman Doctrine, 102; associated with Hiss, 106; contradictory assessments of the Chinese revolution, 109–11, 112–13; on the 38th parallel in Korea, 114n; on Chinese intervention in Korea, 129; on conditions for co-existence with Russia, 255–6; proposes disarmament Commission (1952), 273

Adams, John Quincy, 434

Adams, Sherman, on American aid to France in Viet Nam, 147–8; on Dulles' policy, 303

Adenauer, Chancellor, influence before the 1955 Summit, 305; and the 1960 Summit, 335

Aiken, George D., 217

Alexander, Field-Marshal, 27

Alexander, Holmes, 120

Alexander, Robert J., 185n, 233n

Alliance for Progress, announced (1961), 217; a result of the Cuban revolution, 217–18; social and economic conditions of Latin America, 218–19; proposals in the charter, 219–20; slow progress in land reform, 220–22; and tax reform, 222–3; decline in economic growth, 223; effect of world commodity prices, 223–4; the Alliance contrasted with the Marshall Plan, 224–5; attitude of the Latin American business élite, 225–6; protection of American corporations, 226–8, 422n; insistence on monetary stability to stimulate private investment, 229–33; US supply of arms and support of military régimes, 233–6; maintenance of the status quo, 236–7, 422–3

Alsop, Joseph, 122

Anglo-Iranian Oil Company, 188

Arana, Javier, 168

Arbenz, Guzmán Jacobo, 163–7, 171, 179–82

Arévalo, José, 169–70, 186

Argentina, admission to the UN, 38–40

Armas, Col. Carlos Castillo, 163, 171, 176, 178, 184–5

Arneson, Gordon, 60

Artime, Captain, 211

Attlee, C. R., on the Guatemalan putsch, 163; on the UN and regional bodies, 181n

Austria, the peace treaty, 305, 326

Azerbaijan, 187

Baghdad Pact, 312

Bain, Leslie B., on the Hungarian revolt, 289

Baldwin, Hanson, 382n, 396n

Bao Dai, 145, 146

Baruch Bernard, on economic advantages over Russia, 248

Batista, General, 198–9, 200

Beals, Carleton, on Batista, 200

Bedell Smith, Gen. Walter, 64

Bell, Coral, 257

Benes, President, 81

Berle, A. A., Jr., 209

Berlin, the blockade, 104, 258; the 1958 crisis, 314; negotiations, 336n; the 1961 crisis, 366, 368–9, 371

Bern Incident, the, 27

Betancourt, Romulo, 421–2

Bethe, Dr Hans, 329–330; 371

Bevin, Ernest, 72; at the Moscow (1947) Conference, 77

Bissell, Richard, 209

Blackett, P. M. S., 18; on US and USSR post-war disarmament, 29; on the policy of massive retaliation, 144; on the 'year of decision', 262; on the atomic bomb as an absolute weapon, 270–71, 319, 379; on Soviet atomic parity, 272; on US reaction to the Sputnik, 319; on counter-force strategy, 344; on the U-2 incident, 346–7; on Soviet rejection of the test-ban draft (1961), 362, 363; on Soviet nuclear power (1962), 370; on 'looking-glass strategists', 378

Bohlen, Charles, on Truman and Molotov, 31–2; suggests Hopkins for Moscow, 42

Bonsal, Philip, 199

Boothby, Robert, 70n

Bosch, Juan, 235–6
Bowles, Chester, on Batista, 197; serves on the Rockefeller Panel, 317
Bradley, General, on MacArthur, 142
Brazil, private capital in the telephone system, 232; military *coup* (1964), 237–8n
Briceno, Col. Gonzalo, 235n
Britain, intervention in Greece, 54, 65–8; financial position in 1947 – leaves Greece, 72; in the Iranian oil crisis, 188–9
Brower, Michael, 364n
Brownell, Herbert, Jr., 101
Buck, Pearl, 135
Bulganin, offers to ban nuclear weapons in E. Europe, 310; and suggests Summit talks (1958), 312, 313; announces reduction in Soviet armed forces (1956), 326
Bulgaria, post-war Communist régime, 28; discussed at Potsdam, 54; US protests to Russia over elections, 58–9
Bundy, McGeorge, 133n, 209
Burma, achieves independence, 72
Butler, Senator Hugh, 106
Byrnes, James F., appointed Secretary of State, 54; protests over Bulgarian elections, 58–9, 246; on finishing Japan before Russia got in, 56–8, 60; in the Council of Foreign Ministers, 60–61; reaches agreement in Moscow – admonished by Truman, 61–2; on American world leadership, 302

Cardona, Dr Miró, 210; reveals new invasion plan, 381n
Castro, Fidel, hopes for US co-operation (1959), 199; on the mean between capitalism and communism, 201; his commitment to the Cuban constitution, 201–3; his initial reforms, 203–4; fails to obtain US financial aid, 204–5; the Agrarian Reform Law and US reaction, 205–8; approaches to Russia, 207; his independence of thought and policies, 416
Ceylon, nationalization of oil and end of aid, 227
Chambers, Whittaker, 99, 104
Chamoun, President, 190
Chang, John M., 138
Chiang Kai-shek, 109, 120, 196, 423–4
Childs, Marquis, on the Republican party's communist scare, 99; attitude to Truman Doctrine, 102

China, impact of revolution on America, 105, 106–13; State Department White Paper on, 108–9; reasons for intervention in Korea, 129–33; position after Korea, 137; splits the communist world by her independence, 414; provocative US postwar policies and actions, 423–4; Chinese reaction, 424–5; Kennan's justification of US policy, 426–8
China Service, reduction by Democrats and forecasts of Chinese revolution, 107–9, 424
Chronology of Cold War, 25
Chuikov, General, 282
Churchill, Sir Winston, on Russian good faith at Yalta, 35–6; agreement with Stalin on Bulgaria, Rumania and Greece, 28, 58–9; on the bomb, 60; the Fulton speech, 64, 266; 'jaw-jaw or war-war', 150–51; on the withdrawal of Russia from E. Europe, 252–4; on Russia and the atomic bomb, 271–2; on Soviet good faith (1948), 277; proposal for German neutrality, 286; calls for Summit (1953), 325
Clark, Senator Joseph, 275
Clark, Tom, 53
Clark Kerr, Sir A., 49n
Clay, Lucius D., 216–17, 317
Clifford, Clark, 74
Collins, General, 131(n)
Cominform, statement countering the Marshall Plan, 80
Connally, Senator Tom, 119
Cook, Fred, 189–90, 275n
Cordiner, Ralph J., 347
Council of Foreign Ministers, established at Potsdam, 54; meetings in London and Moscow, 60–61; effect of the Truman Doctrine on the Moscow (1947) meeting, 74–7, 246; division of Korea, 114
Counter-Insurgency Progam, 432–4
Coups, Czechoslovakia, 81–3, 95; Korea, 138; Viet Nam, 161; Guatemala, 163, 178–182, 186; Iran, 188–9; Iraq, 190, 193n, Cuban exile camp, 211; Latin America, 235n; Dominican Republic, 235–6; and US policy, 235–7; Laos, 359
Crofts, Alfred, 115n, 116n
Cuba, Adlai Stevenson's UN speech on, 12–14; US embargo on (1960–62), 15; US antipathy to Castro before and after the revolution, 198–200; little communism in the

early revolutionary régime, 200–201; US economic interests, 201; implications of the Cuban constitution, 201–3; Castro's reforms and financial difficulties, 203–7; the swing away from the US and towards the USSR, 207–8; American invasion plans, 209–12; the revolution results in the Alliance for Progress, 217; Kennedy's pre-election views, 358–9; his position after the Bay of Pigs failure, 359–60; motives behind the Soviet missile emplacement, 381; Kennedy announces the blockade, 382–3; Soviet emplacements alter the political and not the nuclear balance of power, 383–6; refusal to exchange Turkish bases, 386–7; the crisis viewed as dynamic rather than responsive US action, 388–91; the settlement and its implications, 392; US aim of bringing down the régime, 414–15; differences between Castro's régime and other communist parties, 415–16; contrasted with Yugoslavia, 416–17; US fears of its example rather than its power, 418–20

Cutforth, René, on napalm, 136

Czechoslovakia, the communist *coup* (1948), 81–2; European reactions to, 82–4; strategic importance to Russia, 95

Dairen, 57–8

Daniel, Jean, 415

Denmark, reaction to the *coup* in Czechoslovakia (1948), 82–3

De Gaulle, President, before the 1960 Summit, 335; announces the French independent nuclear force, 394

Deutscher, Isaac, 91–94; 282; 350n

Díaz, Col. Carlos Enrique, 168, 180, 182

Dienbienphu, 146, 147

Dillon, C. Douglas, 209

Dominican Republic, the military *coup* against Bosch, 235–6

Dozer, Donald M, on America in Guatemala, 171–2

Draper, Theodore, 202n

Dulles, Allen, 164, 209

Dulles, John Foster, 14; at the London meeting of the Council of Foreign Ministers, 60; at the Moscow (1947) meeting, 77; on Russia's unwillingness for war, (1949), 85; inaugurates the policy of Massive Retaliation

and brinkmanship, 143–5; on the Communist threat in SE Asia, 147; plans to use US troops in Viet Nam, 148; indifference to the Geneva Conference on Viet Nam, 148–51; attitude to the Guatemala *putsch*, 163–4, 184; on the United Fruit Company's claim, 172; his resolution on Communism in the OAS, 172–4; on the Guatemalan shipment of arms, 174, 177; financial interests in Iran, 188–9; on the Russian economy, (1955), 276; on breaking the satellites from Russia, 280–81; opposition to Summits, 285; blocks negotiations (1957–59), 309–16, 332; first suggests missile bases, 309, 311; on Soviet reduction of armed forces, 327; retirement, 334

Duong Van Minh, 161

EAM, 59, 65

Eden, Sir Anthony, on freedom and 'liberation', 114; policy on Viet Nam, 148–50; on American policy in Iran, 188; on Lebanon landings, 192; on American policy in Guatemala, 175, 177; suggests European denuclearized zone, 309

Eisenhower, President Dwight, defines the Cold War, 143; on the strategic importance of Viet Nam, 147; plans to use US forces in Viet Nam, 148; on the Guatemala *putsch*, 164; announces the Eisenhower Doctrine, 190; proposes the 'open skies' plan, 274; on the German situation (1955), 305–6; reaction to the Rockefeller report, 317; failure to agree on disarmament (1955–57), 325–8; demands 'deeds' from Russia (1953), 326; the 'benign confusion' of his foreign policy, 330–32; the influence of Dulles, 332–3; to the Indian Parliament on world tension, 334; with Khrushchev at Camp David, 334; fails to restrain military activity before the 1960 Summit, 335–6; during the Summit failure, 337–41; increases the military budget (1958), 344–6

Eisenhower Doctrine, as applied to Lebanon, 190

ELAS, 65

Erlander, 82

Europe, Lippmann's analysis suggesting the withdrawal of armies from Europe, 243–7; Forrestal and Baruch exemplify the exponents of 'toughness' to Russia, 247–8; the influence of Kennan's assumption of Soviet weakness, 248–50; the policy of containment rather than of aid, 250–52; Churchill and Acheson on terms for Russia, 252–6; the policy of no negotiation adopted before the invasion of Korea, 256–9; the NSC paper on the communist and non-communist worlds, 259–61; strategic values of Nato, 261–2; suggestions for denuclearized zone, 309, 310; failure to reach negotiation (1957–59) and spread of missile sites, 309–16; communism as an internal rather than an external threat, 412–13; Soviet occupation of E. Europe defensive, not expansionist, 413–14

Farley, Philip J., 328
Figueres, José, on the world market system, 223–4
Fleming, D. F., 21, 124, 137
Foreign Aid Program, Kennedy announces a 'decade of development', 215; statistics of aid since the Marshall Plan, 215–16; Clay Committee reductions, 216–17; Kennedy launches the Alliance for Progress, (q.v.), 217; aid as a weapon of security, 431–2
Formosa, American decision to defend, 118–19; present military strength, 196; effect of the defence of Quemoy and Matsu on Soviet policy, 286
Forrestal, James, advocates a tough line with Russia, 35, 62, 247–8; on Russia's unwillingness for war (1949), 85n
France, post-war policy in Viet Nam, 145; Dienbienphu and American aid, 146–8; conflict with US on Viet Nam, 152
Fuentes, Gen. Miguel Ydigoras, 171, 176, 185–6
Fulbright, Senator William J., on US military aid, 196; opposes the Cuban invasion plan, 209; on constructive Soviet policy, 307–8; on restraint in foreign policy, 361

Gaither Report, 317–20, 344
Gaitskell, Hugh, suggests denuclearized zone, 310; and unilateral action by Britain, 313

Gardner, Arthur, 358
Gehlen Organization, 287–8
Geneva Conference on Viet Nam, 146, 148–51, 305, 429
George II of Greece, 66
Gerassi, John, 421n
Gerhardsen, Premier, 82; on the offer of IRBM's, 311
Germany, Soviet attempts to negotiate reunification, 280–83; Nato proposals and 'massive retaliation' harden Russian policy, 285–6; the Gehlen Organization, 287–8; rearmament and negotiation, 296–8; US attitude in 1955, 305–6; further Soviet overtures rejected, 307; W. Germany entering Nato leads to the Warsaw Pact, 307; impact of the nuclear arming of the W. German army, 314–15; western and eastern European attitudes to a divided Germany, 407–8
Gerö, Ernö, 288
Gilpatric, Roswell, 369, 373, 384–5
Gittings, John, 407n
Goldman, Eric, on the New Deal, Communism and McCarthyism, 105
Gomulka, Wladyslaw, 288
Gott, Richard, 407n
Grafton, Samuel, 102
Greece, discussed at Potsdam, 54; British post-war operations in, 65–8; social conditions, 66–8, Britain, replaced by America, 73, 74; effects of US economic aid, 193–4
Gross, E., 71n
Guatemala, an example of US influence in Latin America, 17; overthrow of the Arbenz régime (1954), 163–4, 178; US responsibility, 164; extent of communist influence in country and government, 164–8; overthrow of Gen. Ubico, (1944), 168; Arévalo's social reforms, 169–70; Arbenz in conflict with the United Fruit Co., 171; US claims compensation, 171–2; the anti-communist vote in the OAS, 172–4; the shipment of arms from Czechoslovakia, 174–7; US build-up in Nicaragua and Honduras, 177–8; appeal to the UN on the Armas invasion, 178–81; Arbenz resigns – formation of the *junta*, 182; achievements of the Arévalo-Arbenz program, 182–3; measures of the Castillo Armas régime, 184–5; and

Cuba, 208; progress of land reform, 221; private capital in electrification, 231–2
Guevara, Ché, 206
Gunther, John, 120, 121

Hagan, Roger, 364n, 433n
Haiti, US military mission to, 200n
Harkins, Gen. Paul D., 157
Harriman, W. A., urges Stalin to send Molotov to US, 32; advocates tough line with Russia, 35, 44n, 51–2; during Hopkins' mission to Moscow, 42–52; asserts Russia's failure to keep military commitments, 44–6; on Russian power politics in Poland, 48–50; advocates discriminatory aid, 69n; advises US aid to Russia (1945) but recants, 250–51
Healey, Denis, on Soviet offers of disengagement (1957), 310–11
Herrera, Felipe, on the Alliance for Progress contrasted with the Marshall Plan, 224–5
Herter, C., during the U-2 incident, 338
Hiroshima, 55–8
Hiss, Alger, 104–6
Ho Chi Minh, 145
Hodge, Gen. John R., 115
Hodgson, Godfrey, on Kennedy's foreign policy, 393–4
Honduras, aggression against Guatemala, 179; agrarian reform and the United Fruit Co., 227–8
Hoover, J. Edgar, on communism in the US, 99
Hopkins, Harry, sent to parley with Stalin, 42; to Stalin on the end of Lend-Lease, 43; on American public opinion, 46–7; on the veto, 50; on policy toward Russia, 52; to Truman on the imminent collapse of Japan, 55–6
Hotham, David, 16–17, 153, 160–61
Hughes, H. Stuart, 364n
Hull, Cordell, on the US attitude to Russia at San Francisco (1945), 39–40; on Russia's attitude to the veto, 41
Humphrey, Senator Hubert, 190
Hungary, the election of 1945, 28; Nagy's liberalizing policies in opposition to Rákosi, 283–5; lack of support from the US, 285; opening of the 1956 revolt, 288; effect of US propaganda, 289; action by the Red Army, 290–91; quality of the revolt, 291; no action by US, 292

ICBMs, Soviet ability in (1957), 309; strategic purposes of, 316; effect of the Gaither and Rockefeller Reports, 317–20; Soviet numbers (1961), 369, 370; American strength in the 1962 budget, 372–4
India, achieves independence, 72
Ingram, Kenneth, on the UN invasion of N. Korea, 126–7
Inverchapel, Lord, 68
Iran, Russia withdraws from Azerbaijan, 89, 187; Mossadegh nationalizes oil, 188; Anglo-US differences, 188; Mossadegh overthrown, 188; US aid and its effects, 189–90
Iraq, deposition of Nuri es-Said, 190; Kassem takes power, 191; Anglo-US attitude, 192; the *coup* of 1963, 192n
Italy, American influence in the 1948 election, 87–8

Jackson, Senator, on the 'absolute weapon', 321, 322
Japan, sues for peace before Hiroshima, 55–6; the ultimatum before the bomb, 56–7
Johnson, Chalmers, 428n
Johnson, President L. B., support of military *coups*, 235, 237n; on Soviet scientific advances, 302
Johnson, Paul, 204n, 419n
Jones, Joseph M., 102
Judd, Walter, 357

Kádar, János, appointed Premier, 290; address to the nation, 291; liberalizing policies, 292
Kardelj, Edvard, on China and US policy, 424–5
Karol, K. S., 382n
Kassem, Col. Karim, 191
Kennan, George Frost, on the West's image of Russia, 23; dispatch from Moscow (1946), 62; on Stalin and foreign communism, 93; attitude to Truman Doctrine, 102; on American militarization, 145; his assumption of Soviet weakness, 248–50; Reith Lectures (1957) on a negotiated settlement, 295–6, 298; contrasted with his (1947) view of containment, 299–300; on the health of the Soviet power, 303; on the proposal of Soviet withdrawal from

Germany, 306; on rearming W. Germany, 315; on the rigidity of US policy, 322; on disengagement in Europe, 405; on the West's attitude to Germany, 407; on communism as an internal problem for European nations, 412; on Chinese 'expansion', 426–8

Kennedy, John F., on America's world rôle, 15; on Viet Nam, (1951) 146, (1954), 151, 162, (1956), 154; increases forces in Viet Nam, 156; on aid to Turkey and Greece, 194n; decision on the Cuban invasion, 209; on the 'rule of courage and freedom', 210; on the Foreign Aid Program, 215; action on the Foreign Aid Program, 215–17; launches the Alliance for Progress, 217, 218, 220; on economic development and democratic rule, 234–5, 237; on the value of treaty obligations, 277; on rearming W. Germany, 315; on the Republican party's foreign policy, 332; on the missile gap, 348–9; on the 1960 Summit failure, 355; on negotiating from strength, 355–6; influence of the opposition on his attitude to the Presidency, 356–61; on Cuba in his election campaign, 358–9; increases arms expenditure (1961), 362–4; increases conventional forces, 368; to the UN on nuclear disarmament, 371–2; rearmament figures of the 1962 budget, 372–4; his thinking on nuclear force and the balance of power, 378–80; announces the blockade of Cuba, 382–3; on the significance of Soviet missiles in Cuba, 385–6; his 'power diplomacy' over Cuba, 387–8; attitude to the Western Alliance after Cuba, 392–6; on the unity of the Western Alliance, 395; on the 'spiralling arms race', 401, 403; on Russian control of Cuba, 415; on the Alliance for Progress and counter-insurgency, 423; on the Foreign Aid Program, 431–2

Kennedy, Robert, 369, 391

Kesselring, General, 27

Khruschchev, Nikita, calls for negotiation (1957 and 1958), 309, 312, 313; with Eisenhower at Camp David, 334; before the 1960 Summit, 335, 337; during the Summit failure, 337–40; proposes peace treaty with E. Germany, 366; announces increased military expenditure, 366–7; withdraws from Cuba, 392; attacks Chinese militancy, 395–6; on the 100 megaton bomb, 396n

Kim Il-Sung, 116, 122

Kimm Kiu Sic, 123

Kim Loo, 123n

Kirk, Admiral Alan G., 85n

Kissinger, Henry, 317, 379, 397

Knight, John S., 312

Konev, Marshal Ivan S., 307

Korea, divided at the 38th parallel (1945), 114; dissolution of the People's Republic and setting up of Syngman Rhee's Council, 115–16; Soviet and American policies in North and South, 116–17; failure of UN to achieve unification, 117–18; the North Korean attack, 120; responsibility for the outbreak – unlikely to have been Russian, 120–22; elements of civil conflict, 122–3; Security Council condemns N. Korea, 123–5; MacArthur invades the North – approved by UN, 125–9; reasons for Chinese intervention, 129–33; Chinese advance, 133–4; China declared aggressor, 134–5; 'Operation Killer' and its cost, 135–7; subsequent political struggles for power, 137–9; economic contrast between N. and S. Korea, 139–40; the national army and the US army, 196

Krock, Arthur, on Russia at the San Franscisco Conference, 40; on the Truman Doctrine, 73–4

Ladejinsky, Wolf, 155n

La Guardia, Fiorello, 69–70

Lalouette, M., 160

Land reform in Korea, 116–17; in Viet Nam, 154–5; in Guatemala, 171–2, 184, 208, 221; in Cuba, 205–8; in Venezuela, 221–2, 422; Toynbee on, 220, 222; and the Alliance for Progress, 220–2, 226–8; in Honduras, 227–8;

Lange, Oskar, Professor, 49

Lapp, Dr. Ralph, 373

Latifundia system, 218–19, 220, 222

Latin America, social and economic conditions, 218–19, 223–4, 419; influence of US private interests, 420–23

Latter, Dr. Albert, 328

Lawrence, David, 259n

Leahy, Fleet Admiral, on Truman and Molotov, 31; on Yalta, 34
Lebanon, the US landing (1958), 190–92
Lederer, W. J., 137n
Lemnitzer, General, 209
Lend-Lease, stoppage of, 43
Lieuwin, Edwin, 167n, 200
Lens, Sidney, 222, 225, 421n
Lippmann, Walter, on US cold war policy (1947), 14; on the US attitude at the San Francisco Conference, 39; attitude to the Truman Doctrine, 102; on the policy of containment, 103, 143–4; on the UN declaring China the aggressor, 135; on the frustrations of containment, 143; on the example of Communist progress, 194–5; on the post-war withdrawal of alien armies from Europe, 243–7, 296–7, 405; on Kennan's assumption of Soviet weakness, 248–9; on US atomic capabilities (1946), 255; on the Polish 1956 revolution, 288; on the restoration of the balance of power and a military withdrawal, 304; on the 1963 test ban treaty, 408–9
Litvinov, demands second front, 45
Lleo, Manuel Urrutia, 199
Lodge, Henry Cabot, 160, 179–80
Lowenthal, Richard, 428n
Loyalty Oath in the US, 100
Luce, Henry, 301, 317
Lukacs, John, 281n, 292
Lynh Woon Hyeung, 123n

MacArthur, Gen. Douglas, on Europe and the East, 106; praises Chiang Kai-shek, 125; crosses the 38th parallel, 125–6; on the unification of Korea, 131; relieved of his post, 131, 141; final attack on the Yalu River, 132–3; on appeasement, 142
Maclaurin, John, 71
Macmillan, Harold, calls for a Summit (1958 and 1959) 313, 314; during the 1960 Summit, 339
Malenkov, 286
Malinovsky, Marshal, 337
Manchuria, looted by Russia, 112
Mann, Thomas C., on US policy in Latin America, 237n
Mansfield, Mike, 152
Mao Tse-tung, relations with Stalin, 111
Marshall, Gen. George C., on Russia in Poland (1945), 35; attacked by McCarthy, 106–7

Marshall Plan, as a counter offensive to Russia in E. Europe, 75–9, 90; rejected by Russia, 78–9; political effects in W. Europe, 80; and in E. Europe, 80–81; denied to nations voting communist, 88; contrasted with the Alliance for Progress, 224–5
Martin, Gen. H. G., on Iraq, 191n
Martinez, Major Alfonso, 176
Masyryk, Jan, 81
Mateos, López, 207n
Matos, Major Huber, 206n
Matsu, 286
Matthews, Francis P., on the doctrine of preventive war, 94n
McCarthyism, its Manichean rigidity, 101; the theory of the Red conspiracy, 105–6, 113; attacks on Acheson and Marshall, 106–7; exploiting the 'loss' of China, 107–10
McCloy, John J., 402
McCune, George M., 116n, 117n
McNamara, R. S., 109; on the flexibility of US nuclear power, 377
Mejia, Señor, on Colombia's economy, 224
Méray, Tibor, 289
Mexico, aid under Alliance for Progress, 230–31
Meyer, Karl E., 200
Michener, James, 135n
Mikolajczyk, Stanislaw, 48, 49
Mills, C. Wright, 201, 226n
'Missile gap', the, 348–51, 361–2
Molotov, V. M., first meeting with Truman, 31–2, 36–7, 246; on the admission of Argentina to the UN, 39; rejects the Marshall Plan, 78–9
Monzon, Gen. Elfego, 168, 182
Morgenthau, Henry, Jr., 53–4, 54n
Morse, Senator Wayne, 141, 197, 227–8
Morton, Thurston B., 164
Moscoso, Teodoro, on private investment under the Alliance for Progress, 230, 231; resignation, 238n
Mossadegh, Dr Mohammed, 187–8
Muste, A. J., 364n
Mutual Security Program, statistics of economic and military aid, 195–6

Nagasaki, 55–8
Nagy, Imre, conflict with Rákosi, 283, 285; his liberalizing policies, 283–4; removed by Russia, 286; premier again during the revolt, 288–90; removal, 290; execution, 291n

Napalm bombs, 136, 156
National Security Council, 'Paper 68', 259–61; meeting on Cuba, 390–91
Nato, changing strategic purposes (1949 and 1952), 261–2; admission of W. Germany, 307; with IRBMs becomes aggressive, 314; forces compared with Soviets (1963), 406–7; build-up of power during Soviet reductions, 411–12
Navarre, General, 146
Nehru, Pandit, on the socialist order, 214
Nelson, Donald, 250n
New Deal, associated with communism, 104–5
Ngo Dinh Diem, 16–17, 152–61
Ngo Dinh Nhu, 157, 159–60, 161
Nguyen Ngoc Tho, 162
Nicaragua, aggression against Guatemala, 176n; social conditions, 229n
Nitze, Paul, 209, 368
Nixon, Richard, on Dienbienphu, 147; on invading Cuba, 208–9; his terms for the Russians to 'prove their sincerity', 276; on Cuba in his election campaign, 358–9; and counter-force, 372
Noel-Baker, Philip, 273n, 275
Norway, reaction to the *coup* in Czechoslovakia (1948), 82–3
Nuclear Power, Hiroshima and Nagasaki, 55–8; first Russian explosion, 144, 255; Stimson's suggestions (1945) for control by direct approach to Russia, 263–5; US, UK and Canada call for a UN commission, 266; effect of the Bikini test, 266; Soviet propose international agreement, 267; US insistence on international inspection, 267–9; and sanctions, 269; A-bomb not necessarily decisive, 270–72; the Disarmament Commission (1952) and the Soviet acceptance of Western proposals, 273; Eisenhower's 'open skies' plan, 274; breakdown of subsequent negotiations, 274–6; US policy based on the break-up of Soviet power, 276–9; effect of Russian parity with US, 325; failure to agree on test ban (1958), 328–32; counter-force and counter-city strategies, 342–4; US build-up and Soviet reaction (1958–62), 344–8, 362–71; US thinking on the 'missile gap', 348–51; significance of the US shelter program, 365,

367; Soviet resumption of tests, 370–71; American increased striking power in the 1962 budget, and resumption of tests, 372–7; US thinking on missile power in relation to political power, 377–80; the balance of nuclear power after the Cuban crisis, 396–7; 'a nation's security may shrink as its arms increase', 401–2; implications of the 1963 test ban treaty, 403–10
Nuri es-Said, deposition of, 190

O'Donnell, Gen. Emmet, on destruction in Korea, 135
'Operation Forty', 211–12
Organization of American States, resolution on communism (1954), 172–4; its charter violated by US subversion in Cuba, 418

Pacific war, Russian entry into, 44–6
Papandreou, 66
Pawley, William D., 198–9
Pazos, Felipe, 206
Pearson, Drew, on Truman and Molotov, 31; attitude to Truman Doctrine, 102
Pearson, Lester, on the need for negotiation, 310, 312
Peru, oil nationalization and the Alliance for Progress, 227n; military *coup* in, 235n
Pittman, Stewart L., 374
Poland, problem of the Lublin government, 32–5, 42, 47–50; the 1956 revolution, 288
Port Arthur, 57–8
Potofsky, Jacob, 317
Potsdam Conference, 54–5
Puerifoy, John, 168, 176, 182
Punta del Este, 219

Quemoy, 286

Radek, Karl, 99
Radford, Admiral, on the use of H-bombs, 146
Rákosi, Mátyás, 283, 285
Ramadier, Paul, 80
Rapacki, Adam, 309, 310
Rau, Sir Benegal, 134
Ray, Manuel, 206, 210
Reeve, W. D., 114n, 120n
Reischauer, Edwin O., 145
Reston, James, on Russian concessions at San Francisco, 40; on Eisenhower's peace policy, 331; on

Kennedy's 'power diplomacy', 387–8; on the US in Viet Nam, 429n, 431

Rhee, Syngman, 116, 120, 137–8

Riesman, David, 364n

Robinson, Professor Joan, on Korean economics, 139, 140n

Rockefeller Report, 317–20, 344

Roosevelt, President F. D., on the 'Bern Incident', 27; last words on the Soviet problem, 31

Rosenthal, A. M., 138

Rostow, W. W., 29n, 74–5, 77, 79n, 156, 261

Rumania, post-war communist régime, 28; discussed at Potsdam, 54

Rusk, Dean, on the Chinese revolution, 112; serves on the NSC, 209; and the Rockefeller panel, 317

San Francisco Conference (1945), 37–41

San Román, Capt. José P., 211

Santos, Eduardo, on US arms in Latin America, 233–4

Scheer and Zeitlin, 199n

Schlesinger, Arthur, Jr., 209 and n

Schmidt, D. A., on rigidity in US policy, 313

Schneider, Ronald M., 165n; on communism in Guatemala, 166–7; on Arbenz and agrarian reform, 167; on Ubico and Arévalo, 169; on the Guatemalan arms shipment, 176; on Arbenz and the army, 180–81; on Guatemala under Arbenz, 182–3

Second front, the delay, 45

Service, John Stewart, 108n

Seton-Watson, Hugh, on the British in Greece, 65

Shelter program, US, 365, 367

Shirer, William L., 102

Singer, J. David 365

Skybolt missiles, 393

Smith, Earl T., 199, 358

Smith, Howard K., on Truman's cabinet, 53n; on the British in Greece, 65–8; on the effect of the Truman Doctrine on the Moscow (1947) conference, 76–7; on US and Soviet security zones, 90–91

Smith, Senator Margaret Chase, 369

Somoza family of Nicaragua, 229n

Sophoulis, T., 66

Sorensen, Reg, 194n

Soviet Union, conduct in East Europe (1945) 28; demobilization after war, 29; and Yalta agreements on Poland, 32–6, 48–9, on Far Eastern War, 44–6; wartime devastation, 51n; reparations claims, 54; and U.S. decision to use Atom Bomb, 57–60; Truman's policy towards (1945), 61–4; aid requests, 69n, 78, 250–1; and UNRRA, 70n; veto in UN, 71; and Moscow Conference, 75–9; and Marshall Plan, 78–80; and Western fears, 81–2; self-containment and 'expansion', 84–5, 90–6; and Iran, 89–90; and division of Korea, 114, 116–7; and outbreak of war, 121–2; Guatemala veto, 180; and Cuba, 207, 415–420; and division of Europe, 244–6; U.S. leaders' attitude towards (1945), 247–60; Nato policy towards, 261–2; nuclear control proposals (1945) 266–7; and U.S. nuclear monopoly, 255, 271–2; acceptance of Western disarmament proposals, 273–5; unilateral reduction of arms, 276, 326–7, 337, 406; subjection of East Europe (1949–53) 280; concessions on German question, 281; repression of East German revolt, 282; and Polish revolt, 288; intervention in Hungary, 288–291; progress under containment, 300–1; and disengagement, 286, 310; withdrawal from Austria, 326–8; and test-ban (1958) 328–30; minimum deterrent and policy of coexistence, 346, 349–50; 404, 406; reversal on test-ban (1962) 362–3; 'rearmament', 366, 370; and U.S. 'threat', 346–8, 377–81; provocation in Cuba (1962) 383–6; response to U.S. superiority (1962) 395–7; and *détente* (1952) 272, (1963) 409–10; and myth of expansion, 85n, 411–12, 423; and international Communist movement, 413–4

Spain, effects of American aid, 214n; amount of aid 195; compared to Latin America, 217

Spellman, Cardinal, 152

Sputnik I, launching of, 301; effect on US policy of containment and assumption of supremacy, 301–4; Sputnik II, 309; Sputnik III, 313

Stalin, Josef, agreement with Churchill on Bulgaria, Rumania and Greece, 28, 58–9; sends Molotov to founding UN conference, 32; on the end of Lend-lease, 43; talks with

Harry Hopkins, 42–52; makes concessions on the Lublin government, 47–50; and on the veto, 50; attitude at Moscow (1947) Conference, 75–7; extent of his power in Europe, 81; the schism with Tito and subsequent purges, 83–4; but does not use military force, 84–5; caution in Greece, 84n; his policy of self-containment, 91–2; his attitude to foreign communist parties, 92–3; decides to integrate Eastern Europe, 94–5; attitude to Chinese revolution, 111–12

Stebbins, Richard P., 173

Stettinius, Edward, on the Lublin government, 32; on Yalta, 35; at San Francisco Conference, 39; on Russia and the veto, 50; replaced by Byrnes, 54

Stevenson, Adlai, speech to the UN on Cuba, 12–13, 28–9, 384; on Eisenhower before the 1960 Summit, 336; proposes secret ultimatum to Khrushchev on Cuba, 390n; on no negotiation with Cuba, 417–18

Stilwell, Gen. Joseph, 109n

Stimson, Henry L., on Russia in Poland (1945), 33, 48; Memorandum on control of atomic bomb (1945), 263–5

Stokes, Thomas L., 102

Stone, I. F., 119n

Suez, in relation to Hungary, 290

Summit (1960) collapse, 334–41

Sulzberger, C. L., on the US in Viet Nam, 152, 153, 429n, 431; on Cuba as a deliberate showdown, 388–90

Sweden, reaction to the *coup* in Czechoslovakia (1948), 82–3

Szulc, Tad, 200

Taft, Senator, on US Korean strategy, 141

Taylor, Gen. Maxwell D., 156

Taylor, Philip B., on Arbenz and communism, 166; on the OAS conference (1954), 173; on the Guatemalan arms shipment, 176

Teller, Edward, 328

Test ban, Russia rejects British-US draft treaty (1961), 362; Soviet resumption of tests (1961), 370–71; American resumption of tests (1962), 375; announcement and signing of the 1963 ban, 403–4; policies and counter-policies preceding the ban, 404–8; the ban as a temporary truce due to stalemate, 408–10

Thailand, under the counter-insurgency program, 433

Thich Quang Duc, 159

Tito, President, the schism with Stalin, 83, 93–4, 96n; on the Hungarian revolt, 291

Ton That Dinh, General, 160, 161

Toriello, Guillermo, 168, 173–4, 182

Toynbee, Arnold, on America's anti-revolutionary rôle, 15; on the social revolution, 213–14; on aid to Latin America, 220, 221, 222

Tran Van Don, 161

Truman, President H. S., terminates the Big Three meetings (1945), 13; confrontation with Molotov, 31–2, 36–7, 246; sends Hopkins to Moscow, 42; cabinet changes before Potsdam, 53–4; justifies the dropping of the bomb, 55; memorandum to Byrnes on no compromise with Russia, 61–2; reaction to Wallace's moderation, 62–4; and to Churchill's Iron Curtain speech, 64; on Greece and Turkey (1947), 67–8; disclaims responsibility for cold war, 71n; announces the Truman Doctrine, 72–4, 90; institutes security checks and the loyalty oath, 100; on McCarthyism, 101–2; orders military action in Korea, Formosa and Viet Nam, 124; on weapons in Korea, 133; recalls MacArthur but fails to settle Korea, 141–2; on American world leadership, 302

Truman Doctrine, in relation to McCarthyism, 101–3; moderate American and British critics of, 102

Tsaldaris, 67

Turkey, effects of US economic aid, 194, 432; value of missile bases in, 386–7

U-2 incident, 335–41, 346

Ubico, Gen. Jorge, 168

UNICEF, 70n

United Fruit Company, in Guatemala, 169–70, 171–2; in Honduras, 227–8

United Nations Organization, the San Francisco conference, 37–41; admission of Argentine, 38–40; Russian attitude to the veto, 41, 71; US dominance in voting power, 71–2; Commission for Korean independence, 117–18; condemns N. Korea,

123–5; approves American invasion of the North, 126–9; declares China the aggressor in Korea, 134–5; refuses action for Guatemala, 178–81; proposals on the atom bomb, 266–7; sets up disarmament commission (1952), 273

UN Special Fund (SUNFED), 19n

UNRRA, 69–90

Urrutia, Manuel, 206

Vandenberg, Senator Arthur H., on the Truman-Molotov meeting, 36–7; part in the Marshall Plan, 37n; on the settlement of the veto crisis, 50–51

Venezuela, problem of land reform, 221–2; influence of the US power structure (1959–64), 420–22

Viet Nam, American responsibility for Ngo Dinh Diem, 16–17; French post-war policy, 145; Ho Chi Minh rebels, 146; Dienbienphu and increasing US involvement, 146–8; Dulles and the Geneva Conference, 148–51; conflicting views of France and US, 152; Ngo Dinh Diem and the failure of the election plan, 152–3; efforts at land reform, 154–5; the National Liberation Front (Vietcong) rebels, 155–6; US steps up military action, 156; character of the war and the Diem régime, 156–9; the Buddhist 'revolt', 159–60; De Gaulle suggests reunification under neutral government, 160–61; deposition of Diem, 161–2; US intervention in relation to the containment of China, 428–31; as a test of defeating revolutionary war, 431

Villafaña, Capt. Miguel, 211

Vinson, Fred, 53

Wagner E. W., on military rule in S. Korea, 138n; comparing N. and S. Korea, 139, 140

Wallace, Henry A., urges moderation and trade with Russia (1946), 62–4; letter to Truman, 68, 255

Warburg, James P., 297–8

Ward, Barbara, on American aid, 79

Warsaw Pact, 307

Waskow, Arthur, 368n

Welles, Summer, on changed US policy after Roosevelt's death, 55; on the Council of Foreign Ministers, 60; on US retention of Pacific bases, 86

Wherry, Senator, 106

White, Harry Dexter, 101n

White, Theodore H., 107–8

Wiesner, Jerome B., 345

Wigforss, Dr Ernst, 82

Williams, William A., on Cuba, 199n, 202, 204n, 206n, 207, 209n; on containment, 257–8, 302–3

Willoughby, Maj.-Gen. Charles A., 121

Wilson, Charles E., 164

Yalta Agreement, Russia's interpretation on Poland, 32–5; Russian concessions at, 35; Russian commitment to enter Pacific war, 44–6

Yugoslavia, contrasted with Cuba, 416–17